JAPAN'S CRITICAL YEARS

JAPAN'S CRITICAL YEARS

As Witnessed by an English Diplomat

ERNEST MASON SATOW

EDITED BY WILLIAM DE LANGE

TOYO REFERENCE SERIES

First edition, 2017

Originally published as *A Diplomat in Japan*

Published by TOYO PRess
Visit us at: **www.toyopress.com**

ISBN 978-94-92722-06-5

Contents

1	Appointment
6	Yokohama Society
17	Political Conditions
26	Treaties
34	Richardson's Murder
45	Visits to Edo
56	Demands for Reparation
68	Bombardment of Kagoshima
76	Shimonoseki
83	Naval Operations
95	Peace with Chōshū
112	The Murder of Bird and Baldwin
119	Ratification of the Treaties
134	Fire at Yokohama
145	Kagoshima and Uwajima
163	First Visit to Osaka
172	Audience with the Shōgun
182	From Osaka to Edo
205	Sado Gold Mines
216	From Nanao to Osaka

229	Osaka to Tokushima
243	Tosa and Nagasaki
259	Downfall of the Bakufu
273	Outbreak of Civil War (1868)
288	Hostilities at Fushimi
297	The Kōbe Incident
310	First Visit to Kyoto
321	Harakiri
329	Massacre of French Sailors at Sakai
334	Audience with the Emperor at Kyoto
342	New Credentials at Osaka
351	Mito Politics
364	Capture of Wakamatsu
373	Enomoto Seizes Ezo
378	Audience with the Emperor at Edo
387	Last Days in Edo
391	Glossary
397	Index

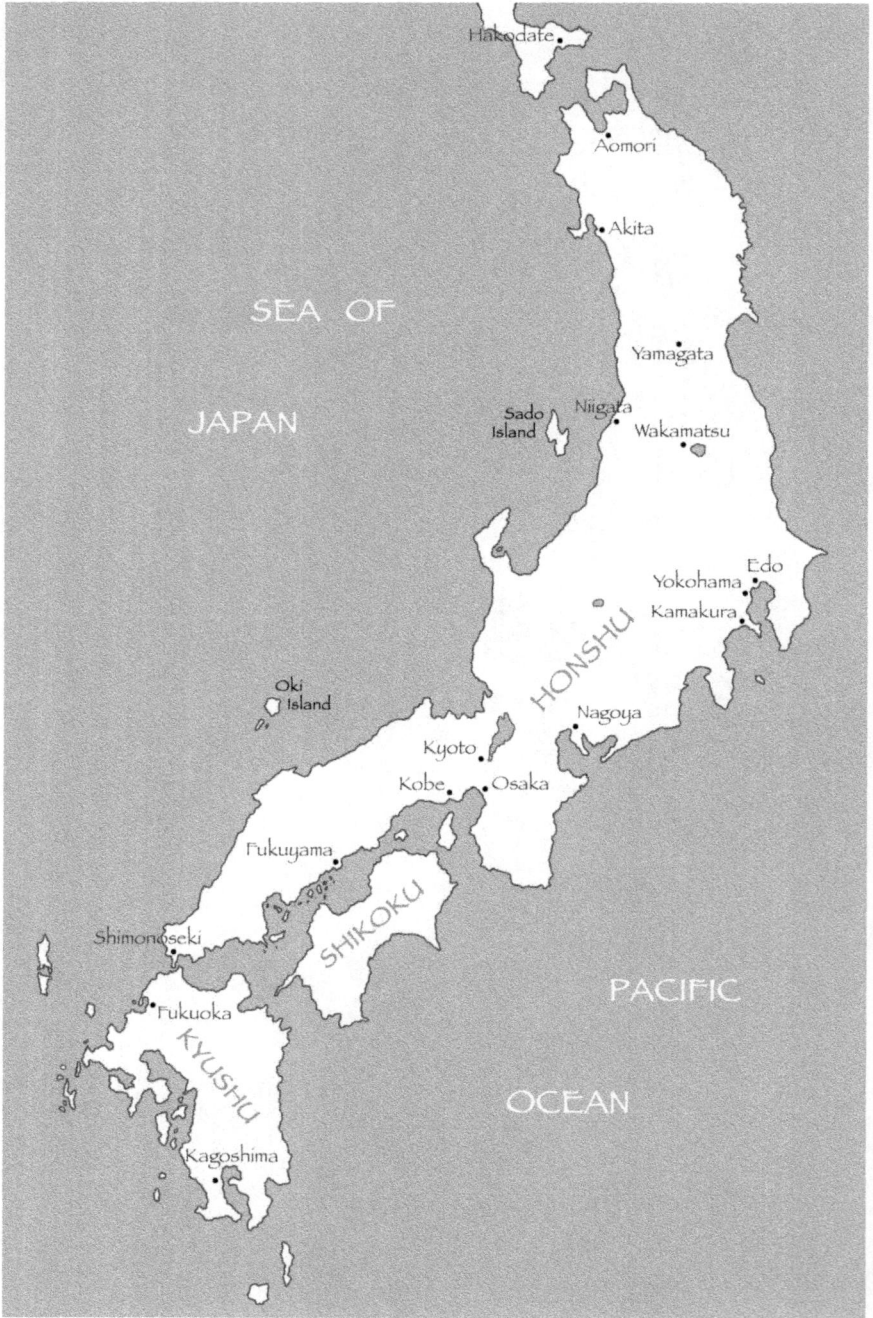

SEA OF

JAPAN

Hakodate

Aomori

Akita

Yamagata

Sado
Island

Niigata

Wakamatsu

Yokohama

Edo

Kamakura

HONSHU

Oki
Island

Nagoya

Kyoto

Kobe

Osaka

Fukuyama

SHIKOKU

Shimonoseki

PACIFIC

Fukuoka

KYUSHU

OCEAN

Kagoshima

Appointment

My thoughts were first drawn to Japan by a mere accident. In my eighteenth year an elder brother brought home from Mudie's Library the interesting account of Lord Elgin's Mission to China and Japan by Lawrence Oliphant. The book having fallen to me in turn, inflamed my imagination with pictures verbal and coloured of a country where the sky was always blue, where the sun shone perpetually, and where the whole duty of man seemed to consist in lying on a matted floor with the windows open to the ground towards a miniature rockwork garden, in the company of rosy-lipped black-eyed and attentive damsels—in short, a realised fairyland. But that I should ever have a chance of seeing these Isles of the Blest was beyond my wildest dreams. An account of Commodore Perry's expedition, which had preceded Lord Elgin's Mission, came in my way shortly afterwards, and though much more sober in its outward appearance and literary style, only served to confirm the previous impression. I thought of nothing else from that time onwards. One day, on entering the library of University College, London, where I was then studying, I found lying on the table a notice that three nominations to student-interpreterships in China and Japan had been placed at the disposition of the dean. Here was the chance for which I had been longing. Permission to enter myself for the competition was obtained (not without difficulty) from my parents, and having gained the first place in the public examination, I chose Japan. To China I never wished or intended to go. My age was sufficient by a few hours to enable me to compete. I was formally appointed in August 1861, and quitted England full of joyful antic-ipation in November of that year.

Owing to the prevalence of a belief among those who then had the direction of our affairs in Japan that a knowledge of Chinese was a necessary preliminary to the study of Japanese, my fellow-student, R. A. Jamieson, and myself were at first stationed for a few months at Beijing, where we were joined early in 1862 by Russell Robertson, who also belonged to the Japanese establishment. I pass over our sojourn there, which, though not without its own interest, was not long enough for me to gain any useful knowledge of China. But I learned a few hundred Chinese characters which were of great help to me afterwards, and I even began the study of Manchu.

Our stay at the Chinese capital was suddenly cut short by the arrival of a despatch from Edo, containing the original text of a note from the Japanese ministers, which it was found no Chinaman could decipher, much less understand. This was decisive of the question whether the shortcut to Japanese lay through the Chinese language. I thought then, and still think, that though an acquaintance with Chinese characters may be found useful by the student of Japanese, it is no more indispensable than that of Latin is to a person who wishes to acquire Italian or Spanish. We were consequently bundled off to Japan with the least possible delay.

Of the eight students belonging to the China establishment then at Beijing, three only are still (1885) in H.M. service—H. J. Allen, C. T. Gardner, and W. G. Stronach, each of whom attained the rank of consul in 1877. They had all passed the examination at the same time as myself. The man who came out second was "allowed to resign" in 1867, three are dead, and one, the best man of the whole set, and who oddly enough was last or last but one in the examination list, passed in 1872 into the Chinese customs service, in which he now holds one of the highest appointments. So unequal are the results obtained by even limited competitive examination. When the competition was afterwards thrown open to the public, the results became even more uncertain, as later experience has shown, at least in Japan, and perhaps elsewhere.

The great fault of the system is that it takes no account of moral qualities. Whether a candidate has the manners or feelings of a gentleman cannot be ascertained from the way in which he will reproduce a proposition of Euclid or translate a passage from a Greek author. It does not test the intellectual powers, for a stupid young man who has been properly coached will almost always beat the real student who has not got the right "tips." Nowadays, every candidate for a public examination goes to a crammer, who trains him in a few months for the contest, and enables him to bring forth forced fruit for a moment. Show me a successful examinee, and I will show you a well-coached candidate. In the majority of cases the process disgusts the man who has undergone it, and takes away any inclination he may previously have had for study. And without serious study it is not possible to acquire such languages as Chinese, Siamese or Japanese. The scheme of examination is no test of the linguistic capabilities of the men, and sometimes sends into the service those who can no more learn to speak a foreign language than they can fly. My own success in the examination was due to my having left school more recently than any of the other competitors.

While I was at Beijing the whole body of students was invited to dine one evening with the bishop of Victoria, who was stopping at the legation in the absence of Frederick Bruce, the minister. The conversation fell upon the effects of Chinese studies on the intellectual powers, and the bishop inquired of us whether we did not find that the mind was weakened by close application to such a dry, unproductive form of learning. At least, his own experience had been to that effect. This was a curious admission to make, but the matter of his conversation certainly corroborated it. I do not think any of us was candid enough to confess to a similar result in his own case.

I should like to dwell longer on our life in Beijing—the rides in the early morning over the plain on the north of the city, excursions to the ruins of the Summer Palace, beautiful still in its desolation, the monasteries among the blue mountains west of the city, the magnificent temples inside and outside the walls, the dirt and dust of the streets in wet or fine weather, the pink lotus blossoms on the lake of the marble bridge, the beggars with their cry of *K'olien, k'olien, shang i-ko ta*, the bazaar outside the Ch'ien-men gate, with its attractive shops, the Temple of Heaven, the view of yellow, brown and green-tiled roofs embosomed in trees as one saw them from the city wall, the carts bumping over the stone pavements worn into deep ruts, the strange Eastern life that surrounded a band of boys fresh from school or college or their mothers' apron-strings, and the splendour of the newly restored buildings of the Liang Kung Fu, occupied by the British legation—which will never be effaced from my memory. But there is no time.

Our minister then was Mr, afterwards Sir Frederick, Bruce, a tall man of about fifty, with a noble forehead and brown eyes, grey beard, whiskers and moustache; altogether a beautiful appearance. The Chinese secretary was Mr, afterwards Sir Thomas, Wade, a great Chinese scholar, to whom we looked up with awe, and who was said to be of an irascible temper. A story was told of his visiting the Chinese ministers with the chief, and waxing very warm in argument. The president of the Ts'ung-li Ya-mên remarked: "But, Mr. Wade, I do not observe that Mr. Bruce is so angry." "D'ye hear that, Mr. Bruce, they say you're not angry." Whereupon Bruce, with a benevolent smile and with the most good-tempered expression in the world, replied: "Oh, tell them I'm in a deuce of a rage."

We, that is to say Jamieson, Robertson and myself, got away early on the morning of August 6, arriving that evening at Ho-si-wu, a town on the way, and reached Tientsin next day. From there we took boat to Taku, where we passed some days under the hospitable roof of the Vice-consul Gibson. He was later on transferred to a post in Formosa, where he got into difficulties with the Chinese officials and called on the commander of a gunboat to bombard the custom house, for which he was smartly reprimanded by the Foreign Office. Shortly afterwards he died, it was said, of a broken heart. This happened in the days when the so-called "gunboat" policy was no longer in favour, and poor Gibson fell a victim to his excess of zeal.

At Shanghai Jamieson left us, to start a newspaper on terms which promised him a better future than the consular service could offer. Robertson and I embarked in the steamer *Lancefield*, and started for Japan on September 2. The first land we sighted after leaving the coast of China was Iwōjima, a volcanic island to the south of Kyushu, and on the 7th we found ourselves close to Cape Izu in a fog. Luckily it lifted for a moment, and the captain, who was new to the coast, ordered the ship to be put about, and we ran down among the islands. Early next morning we were steaming over the blue waves east of Ō Island, passed the serrated wooded range of Mount Nokogiri on our right and the tiny inlet of Uraga to our left, and stood across the broad bay towards Yokohama. It was one of those brilliant days that are so characteristic of Japan, and as we made our way up the bay of Edo, I thought no scenery in the world could surpass it. Irregular-shaped hills, covered with dark-green trees, lined the whole southern coast, and above them rose into the air for twelve thousand feet and more the magnificent cone of Mount Fuji, with scarcely a patch of snow visible. The noble ranges of Ōyama and others bounded the plain on its western side, while by way of contrast, a low-lying sandy coast trended rapidly away on our right, and speedily sank below the horizon in the direction of the capital.

Curious duck-shaped boats of pure unpainted wood, carrying a large four-square sail formed of narrow strips of canvas loosely tacked together, crowded the surface of the sparkling waters. Now and then we passed near enough to note the sunburnt, copper-coloured skins of the fishermen, naked, with the exception of a white cloth round the loins, and sometimes a blue rag tied across the nose, so that you could just see his eyes and chin. At last the white cliffs of Mississippi Bay[1] became closer and more distinct: we rounded treaty Point and dropped anchor on the outer edge of the shipping. After the lapse of more than a year I had at last attained my cherished object.

1 Missisippi Bay has been largely reclaimed and Traty Point is now the western landing point of the Tokyo Bay Aqua Line. Indeed, it is questionable wether the Japanese ever used these names.

Yokohama Society

Three years had now elapsed since the opening of the country to foreign trade in consequence of the treaties of 1858, and a considerable number of merchants had settled at the ports of Nagasaki and Yokohama. Hakodate, however, offered then, as now, few attractions to mercantile enterprise, and being far removed from the political centre, shared very slightly in the uneasy feeling which prevailed elsewhere. At Nagasaki most of the territorial nobles of western Japan had establishments whither they sent for sale the rice and other produce received in payment of tribute from the peasants. Their retainers came into frequent contact with foreigners, whose houses they visited for the purchase of arms, gunpowder and steamers. Some sort of friendly feeling thus sprang up, which was increased by the American missionaries who gave instruction in English to younger members of this class, and imparted to them liberal ideas which had no small influence on the subsequent course of events.

At Yokohama the foreign merchants had chiefly to do with a class of adventurers, destitute of capital and ignorant of commerce. Broken contracts and fraud were by no means uncommon. Foreigners made large advances to men of straw for the purchase of merchandise which was never delivered, or ordered manufactures from home on the account of men who, if the market fell, refused to accept the goods that would now bring them only loss. Raw silk was adulterated with sand or fastened with heavy paper ties, and every separate skein had to be carefully inspected before payment, while the tea could not be trusted to be as good as the sample. Now and then a Japanese dealer would get paid out in kind, but the balance of wrongdoing was greatly against the native, and the conviction that Japanese was a synonym for dishonest trader became so firmly seated in the minds of foreigners that it was impossible for any friendly feeling to exist.

The Custom House officials were in the highest degree corrupt, and demanded ever-increasing bribes from the foreigners who sought to elude the import duties. One of the worst abuses was the importation of large quantities of wines, beer, spirits and stores, for which exemption from the payment of duty was claimed as goods intended for "personal use."

The local administration was carried on by a large staff of officials established at the Custom House. There were two *bugyō*, or commisioners; two *kumi-gashira*, or vice-governors; two *metsuke*, whose function was that of keeping an eye on the doings of the others; a number of *shirabeyaku*, or directors; and *jōyaku*, or chief clerks, besides a host of scribes, interpreters, tidewaiters and policemen, in black or green robes. Dutch was the common medium of communication both orally and in writing, for English was as yet scarcely studied by the natives, and the foreigners who could speak Japanese might be counted on the fingers of one hand. Yet all knew a little. A sort of bastard language had been invented for the uses of trade, in which the Malay words *peggi* and *sarampan* played a great part, and with the addition of *anata* (you) and *arimasu* (there is) everyone fancied himself competent to settle the terms of a complicated transaction. In this new tongue all the rich variety of Japanese speech, by which the relative social position of the speakers is indicated, and the intricate inflexion of the verbs, were conspicuous by their absence. Outside the settlements it was of course not understood, and its use by Europeans must have contributed not a little to the contempt for the "barbarian" which was characteristic of the native attitude towards foreigners.

By virtue of the treaties Kanagawa had been at first fixed upon for the residence of Europeans, but, lying on the Tōkaidō, or principal highway between Edo and Kyoto, it was only too well calculated to afford occasion for collision between the armed followers of the Japanese nobles and the foreign settlers. Early in the day the *shōgun*'s government sought to avoid this difficulty by erecting a Custom House and rows of wooden bungalows at the fishing village of Yokohama, across the shallow bay to the south. Some of the foreign representatives, more intent upon enforcing treaty provisions than desirous of meeting the convenience of the native officials and the European merchants, strongly opposed this arrangement. But the practical advantages of proximity to the anchorage and personal security won the favour of the merchants, and Yokohama became recognised as the port. Long after, and perhaps to this day, the foreign consuls continued to date their official reports from Kanagawa, though they were safely ensconced at the rival site, where a town of 100,000 inhabitants now exists, and curious stories are told of the difference in freight that used to be earned on goods shipped from Europe to Yokohama or Kanagawa as the case might be.

The foreign settlement, for greater security, was surrounded on the land side by wide canals, across which bridges were thrown, while entries and exits were controlled by strong guards of soldiers placed there with the double object of excluding dangerous characters and levying a tax on the supplies introduced from the surrounding country. At first land was given away freely to all applicants, some of whom were employees of the different consulates. These latter afterwards sold their lots to new arrivals bent upon commercial pursuits, and thus pocketed gains to which they had no shadow of a right. When further additions were afterwards made to the "settlement," precautions were taken which effectually prevented anyone, whether merchant or official, from obtaining land without paying an adequate price. Later on, title deeds were made out, by which the ground was conveyed to the holders, their heirs, administrators, executors and assigns, thus creating a form of property new to English experience, which purported to be at once real and personal. Streets were laid out with but little thought of the general convenience, and slight provision for the future. The day of wheeled carriages had not dawned upon Japan. It was sufficient if space were left for handcarts, and the most important Japanese commercial town of the future was thus condemned in perpetuity to inconveniences of traffic, the like of which can be best appreciated by those who knew the central parts of business London fifty years ago, or the successive capitals of the Italian kingdom when they were raised to that rank. Architectural ambition at first was contented with simple wooden bungalows, and in the latter part of 1862 there were not more than half a dozen two-storied buildings in the foreign portion of the town.

Behind the settlement lay a newly filled-in tract of ground known as the "swamp," still unoccupied except by a racecourse track, and in the rear of this again, across a foul marsh, were conspicuous the flimsy buildings of the Yoshiwara, euphemistically described by a noble duke from his place in parliament as an "establishment for the education of young ladies," and where a colonial bishop, to the intense amusement of the younger and more irreverent of the foreign community, had innocently left his visiting-card upon the elderly female who presided over the pleasures of the place. But in those days all the residents were young.

Two churches, however, had already been erected, by Catholics and Protestants respectively, and a foreign cemetery had been set apart on the outside of the settlement. The health enjoyed by the European and American inhabitants was such that the only occupants of the burial ground were some Russian officers and two Dutch merchant captains, who had fallen victims to the deadly and mistaken patriotism of Japanese samurai (two-sworded men). No one had yet succumbed to disease in that beautiful sunny climate.

The foreign community of Yokohama of that day was somewhat extravagantly described by an English diplomat as "the scum of Europe." No doubt there was a fair sprinkling of men who, suddenly relieved from the restraints which social opinion places upon their class at home, and exposed to the temptations of Eastern life, did not conduct themselves with the strict propriety of students at a theological college. That they were really worse than their co-equals elsewhere is unlikely. But in a small community, where the actions of everyone are semi-public and concealment is not regarded as an object of first-rate importance, the vices that elsewhere pass unnoticed become prominent to the eyes of those who are not exposed to the same temptations.

There were also not a few who came there without much capital to make a livelihood, or, if possible, something more, and hastened to the attainment of their object without being troubled with much scruple. And the difficulty which soon presented itself of obtaining a sufficiency of native coin in exchange for the silver dollar of Eastern commerce was the cause of extravagant demands being presented to the Japanese treasury. But the compromise eventually arrived at, by which the merchant had to buy his *ichibu* in the open market, while the official obtained the equivalent of his salary, and often much more, in native coin nearly weight for weight of his

Mexicans dollars, was to the minds of all unprejudiced persons a far greater scandal. Detractors said that the advantages thus given to ministers, consuls, sailors and soldiers was a bribe to induce their compliance with violation of treaty stipulations to the prejudice of their non-official countrymen; but this is unfair. It was the result of false theories as to the nature and function of money, and personal interest worked against a conversion to views more in accordance with the principles of political economy.

The fact remains, that in September 1862 the current rate of exchange was 214 *ichibu* for 100 dollars, though the latter were really exchangeable for 311 *ichibu* according to the treaty. Each diplomatic or consular establishment was allowed to exchange monthly a certain number of dollars, supposed to represent the total salaries of the staff, and other government charges, thirteen *ichibu* per $100 being deducted for coinage. An official whose salary was $100 received 298 *ichibu*, the surplus of which over his bazaar expenses he proceeded to change back into dollars; but practically he received $139.25, or a profit of nearly 40 percent.

The gains of a minister whose salary was £3000 a year it may easily be seen were very large. This was not all. The balance of the monthly quota of *ichibu* was then reconverted into dollars, the amount due to the official chest was deducted, and the profit then divided among the staff in proportion to their salaries. On a nominally small income it was consequently possible to live well, keep a pony and drink champagne. As time went on, the number of *ichibu* thus put into circulation increased, and the rate of exchange eventually declined to par. Then and only then the system was abandoned. Where the money came from that was thus transferred to the pockets of officials can be best explained by those who are versed in economical questions. For my own part, I cannot look back on that period without shame, and my only excuse, which is perhaps of little worth in the court of history, is that I was at the bottom of the ladder, and received the proportion paid to me by those who were in charge of the business.

A few words may be devoted to describing the Yokohama society of those days. There were few ladies in the settlement. Japan was a long way from Europe, with no regular steam communication, and the lives of foreigners were supposed to be not very safe at the hands of the arm-bearing classes. The two great China firms of Jardine, Matheson & Co. and Dent & Co.

were of course represented. The latter came down with a crash a year or two after my arrival. Fletcher & Co., another important Shanghai firm, had a branch, and so had Barnet & Co., both now long forgotten. Most of the remainder were Japanese firms, amongst whom Aspinall, Cornes & Co., Macpherson, Marshall & Co., were the foremost English, and Walsh, Hall & Co., the leading American firms. Germans, French and Dutch were considered of "no account." Money was abundant, or seemed to be, everyone kept a pony or two, and champagne flowed freely at frequent convivial entertainments.

Races were held in the spring and autumn, and real horses competed in some of the events. A favourite Sunday's excursion was the ride along the Tōkaidō to Kawasaki for tiffin, and back again toward evening. Longer outings were to Kanazawa, Kamakura and Enoshima; but anyone who had ventured as far as Hachiōji or Hakone, which were beyond the treaty limits, was regarded as a bold, adventurous spirit. The privilege of travelling beyond a distance of twenty-five miles from Yokohama was reserved to the diplomatic representatives of foreign powers, and Edo could be visited only in the disguise of a member of one of the legations, with the permission of its head. Such favours were regarded with extreme jealousy by those who were debarred by circumstances from obtaining them, and loud murmurs were heard that it was the minister's duty to invite his countrymen to the capital, and give them board and lodging, irrespective of the shape which their private relations with him might have assumed. Then, and perhaps even yet, there existed a theory that public servants were practically the servants of the extremely small section of the public that inhabited Yokohama, and when the servants failed to comply with the wishes of their employers they were naturally and rightly abused—behind their backs.

So strong was the hostility excited in the breasts of the English-Scotch-Irish portion of the community by the unlucky phrase, "scum of Europe," that no member of either legation or consulate of their country was allowed admittance into the Yokohama Club, composed chiefly of British merchants. This feeling lasted until the year 1865 brought about a permanent change in the representation of Great Britain. The excuse for such relations between the British residents and one who ought to have been the leader of the small society, is to be found in the comparative youthfulness and ignorance of the world which characterised the former. The experience of men and manners which saves the dwellers in Little Peddlington from believing that others are deliberately plotting to inflict insults on them is seldom attained before middle life, especially when Little Peddlington happens to be located in an Eastern land where the mind's growth comes to a standstill, and a man's age is virtually to be reckoned by the years actually spent in the mother country. For all purposes of mental and moral development the time passed on the opposite side of the world must be left out of the calculation.

It was agreed in the treaties that Edo should be the residence of the foreign diplomatic representatives, and four Buddhist monasteries had, in accordance with Japanese custom, been assigned to the representatives of the four chief powers—Great Britain, France, Holland and the United States. Sir Rutherford Alcock occupied Tōzen-ji, in the suburb of Takanawa; Dirk de Graeff van Polsbrock lived in Chōō-ji, a little nearer the city; then came Saikai-ji, the residence of Duchesne de Bellecourt; and Townsend Harris had settled down at Zenpuku-ji in Azabu.

A series of alarming occurrences, however, had caused the European portion of the diplomatic body to transfer their quarters to Yokohama, and the American minister alone held out, declaring his confidence in the good faith of the Japanese government and their ability to protect him. In September of 1862 he had already been replaced by General Pruyn, who followed the example of his predecessor, until eventually driven out of the capital by a fire which destroyed his house, whether purely accidental or maliciously contrived. The English legation in 1861 had been the object of a murderous attack in which the secretary, Laurence Oliphant, and George Staunton Morrison were wounded. The assailants were principally retainers of the *daimyō* of Mito, but others belonging to various clans were concerned in the affair, and some of these are still living. Sir Rutherford Alcock had consequently moved to Yokohama, where the strong guard placed by the Japanese government at the entrances to the town and the foreign men-of-war in the harbour offered sufficient guarantees for safety. On his quitting Japan for a term of leave early in 1862, his locum-tenens, Colonel Edward Neale, not believing in a danger of which he had no experience, brought the legation back to Tōzen-ji. But he had no sooner installed himself there than an event occurred which led him to change his opinion. This was nothing less than the murder of the sentry who stood at his bedroom door and of a corporal on his rounds, at the hands of one of the Japanese guard, in revenge for an insult offered to him, it is said, by the youngest member of the staff, a heedless boy of fifteen or sixteen.

So the British legation packed up their archives and hastened back to Yokohama, where they installed themselves in a house that stood on the site of the present Grand Hotel. This building belonged to an Englishman named Hoey, who was murdered in his bed in 1870, apparently from motives of private revenge. The foreign consuls were all stationed at Yokohama with the exception of the American consul, Colonel Fisher, who remained at Kanagawa. Harris, it is said, would never admit that Yokohama could be rightfully substituted for Kanagawa, the town mentioned in the treaty, and would not permit his consul to reside there. He even carried his opposition so far as to declare that he never would countenance the change of settlement, and carried out his vow by leaving Japan without having set foot in Yokohama.

At the time of my arrival there, Colonel Edward Neale, an old warrior who had seen service with the Spanish Legion commanded by Sir de Lacy Evans, and who, gossip said, regarded Sir Rutherford Alcock, formerly attached to the Marine Brigade of Portugal in the quality of surgeon, with no friendly feelings, was secretary of legation, and consequently chargé d'affaires in the absence of his chief. He had great command of his pen, and composed most drastic notes to the Japanese government, some of which have been printed by my friend, Francis Otiwell Adams in his *History of Japan*. He had previously been consul at Varna and Belgrade, and consequently had a sufficient experience of the system known as "extra-territoriality," which in most non-Christian countries of the East exempts Europeans from the operations of the local law. In stature considerably less than the average Englishman, he wore a heavy grey moustache, and thin wisps of grizzled hair wandered about his forehead. His temper was sour and suspicious. Of his political capacity there is not much to be said, except that he did not understand the circumstances amongst which he was thrown, as his despatches sufficiently indicate, well-written and incisive as they are. But this is only an example of the fact that power of speech with tongue or pen is not a measure of a man's fitness for the conduct of affairs. In his jovial moments he easily unbent, and would entertain his companions with snatches of operas of which he carried a large assortment in his memory. At this period he was about fifty-five, and probably already affected with the beginnings of the disease which carried him off a few years later at Quito.

The second in rank was the so-called Japanese secretary. He was neither a native of Japan nor had he any knowledge of the language, so that the title must be understood as signifying "secretary in charge of correspondence with the Japanese government." At our mission in China there is always an official who bears the corresponding title of Chinese secretary, but there the post has always been held by a scholar. Dutch was the only European language of which the Japanese knew anything, and therefore when the Foreign Office came to provide a staff of officials for the consular establishment, they sought high and low for Englishmen acquainted with that recondite tongue. Four were at last discovered, one of whom was first appointed interpreter to the legation and afterwards accorded the higher title. Part of his salary was expressly granted by way of remuneration for instructing the student-interpreters in the language of the country, and consequently could not be said to be earned. He retained his office for eight years, when a consulate became vacant, and the opportunity was at once seized of "kicking him up the ladder." All the domestic virtues were his, and of actively bad qualities he showed no trace.

Next to this gentleman came a First Assistant, sociable and accomplished, musical, artistic and speaking many languages beside his own, but no lover of hard work. In his hands the accounts fell eighteen months in arrear, and the registers of correspondence were a couple of years behind hand. It was his function to preside over the chancery, and he left it to his successor in a condition which the latter aptly compared to that of an "Aegean stable." He was the sort of man who is always known among his friends by his Christian name, and no higher tribute to personal qualities is possible. In the course of time he became a consul, and retired from the service at an early age, carrying with him the regrets and good wishes of everybody who knew him.

In the legation staff there were also included two doctors, who at the same time discharged the functions of assistants in the chancery. One of them shortly quitted the service, and set up in Yokohama as a general practitioner, to retire with a competent fortune after but a few years. The other merits more extended notice, on account both of his character and public services of every kind. I mean my life-long friend, William Willis. Perhaps no other man ever exhibited in a greater measure the quality which we are wont to call conscientiousness, whether in his private relations or in the discharge of his duties. Those who have had the fortune to profit by his medical or surgical aid, feel that no man could be more tender or sympathetic towards a patient. He was devoted to his profession, and lost no opportunity of extending his experience. In those days a doctor had frequently to encounter personal risks such as fall to the lot of few civilians; he exposed himself freely, in order to succour the wounded. In the chancery his services were indispensable. He it was who swept the Aegean stable, arranged the archives in order, and brought the register up to date. Always on the spot when he was wanted, an indefatigable worker, and unswervingly loyal to his chief. After nine years service he was promoted to be a vice-consul, but by this time the Japanese had become so impressed with his value as a surgeon and physician that they begged him to accept a salary more than four times what he received from the Foreign Office, and he went where his great qualities were likely to be of more use than in trying petty police cases and drawing up trade reports of a city which never had any foreign commerce. His gigantic stature made him conspicuous among all the Europeans who have resided in Japan since the ports were opened, and when I first knew him he was hardly five and twenty years of age. A man endowed with an untiring power of application, accurate memory for words and things, and brimful of good stories from the three kingdoms. Big men are big-hearted, and he was no exception. We shall come across him again repeatedly in the course of these reminiscences, and for the present these few words must suffice.

Besides these, the legation staff included Russell Brooke Robertson and myself, as student-interpreters.

Last, but not least, were the officers of the mounted escort and infantry guard. The latter was commanded by Lieut. Price of the 67th Regiment, and was soon replaced by fifty marines under the command of a man widely known in the service to which he belonged as "Public-spirited" Smith. I shall say more of him later on. The cavalry escort consisted of a dozen men from the Military Train, a corps which went by the honorary title of "Pig-drivers," and at their head was a lieutenant, a good, harmless sort of fellow, whose only weakness was for fine uniforms and showy horses. Not being learned in the extremely complicated subject of military costume, full dress, half dress, and undress, I cannot say what it was that he had adopted for himself, but it was whispered about that he had been audacious enough to assume the insignia of a field-officer, which is undoubtedly a serious offence against discipline. However that may be, the blaze of gold which decorated his person was wonderful to behold, and on at least one occasion, when we were going in solemn procession to an audience of the *shōgun*, caused him to be mistaken for the envoy by the Japanese officials, who gave him the salutes that rightfully belonged to his less conspicuously adorned diplomatic chief. To determine whether the pleasure derived from this confusion of persons by the one outweighed the mortification which might not unnaturally have been felt by the other would have required a delicate moral balance, which was not available at the moment. But judging from the relative scale of the two men in other points of character, I am inclined to infer that the good preponderated largely over the evil, and that applying consequently the criterion so unfairly attributed to the utilitarians by their opponents, we must arrive at the provisional conclusion that the lieutenant's uniform was highly virtuous and worthy of the applause of mankind.

But it is time to quit this gossiping tone and speak of more serious matters.

Political Conditions

At this period (1862) the movement had already commenced that finally culminated in what may fitly be called the Revolution of 1868, by which the feudal system was destroyed and the old imperial government revived. The tendency of the times was as yet scarcely perceived by foreigners, with but one or two exceptions. They generally supposed that political strife had broken out between the sovereign and a few unruly vassals dissatisfied with the treaties that permitted the sacred soil of Japan to be defiled by the footsteps of "barbarians," and secured all the profits of trade to the head of the state, the vassals being enabled to defy their suzerain owing to his own feebleness and the incapacity of his ministers. It was still believed that the potentate in whose name the treaties had been concluded was the temporal sovereign, and that the emperor was little more than the head of the priesthood, or spiritual emperor.

This theory of the Japanese constitution was almost as old as the earliest knowledge of the country possessed by Europeans. Marco Polo, indeed, says nothing of its system of government in the two short chapters which he devotes to Zipangu, but the Jesuit missionaries who laboured in Japan during the 16th and 17th centuries uniformly held the emperor to be a spiritual dignitary, and spoke of the *shōgun* as the real ruler of the country, the temporal king, and even emperor. Kaempfer, the best known and most often quoted of the authorities on Japan, writing at the beginning of the 18th century, calls the two potentates ecclesiastical and secular emperors, and his example had, up to the time I am writing of, been followed by all his successors without exception. The truth is that the polity of the Japanese state had assumed already in the 12th century the form which it was still displaying at the beginning of the latter half of the 19th, and institutions which could boast of such a highly respectable antiquity might well be supposed to have taken a deep enough hold to be part and parcel of the national life.

The history of Japan has still to be written. Native chronicles of the emperors and annals of leading families exist in abundance, but the Japanese mind is only just now beginning to emancipate itself from the thraldom of Chinese literary forms, while no European has yet attempted a task which requires a training different from that of most men who pursue an Eastern career. Until within the last two decades, the literature of Japan was almost entirely unknown to Europeans, and the existing keys to the language were ridiculously inadequate. The only historical works accessible to foreigners were the scanty *Annales des Dairi*, translated by Titsingh with the aid of native Dutch interpreters and edited by Klaproth with a degree of bold confidence that nothing but the position of a one-eyed man amongst the blind can give; and a set of chronological tables, translated by Hoffman for Siebold's *Nippon*. It is no wonder, therefore, if at the outset of treaty relations, the foreign representatives were at a loss to appreciate the exact nature of the political questions that confronted them, and were unable to diagnose the condition of the patient whose previous history was unknown to them.

To trace in detail the development of the Japanese imperial house, from its beginnings as a pure theocracy of foreign invaders, attracting to itself the allegiance of a number of small tribal chieftains, the fusion of these tribes with their conquerors into one seemingly homogeneous race, the remodelling of the administration which followed upon the introduction of Chinese laws and philosophy, the supplanting of the native hero and native worship by the creed of Gautama, the rise of a military caste brought about by the constant warfare with the barbarous tribes in the east and north of the country, the rivalry of the Taira and Minamoto clans, both sprung from base-born younger sons of the emperors, and the final suppression of the civil administration in the provinces by the distribution of the country amongst the followers of the Minamoto and their allies, would require a profound study of documents which no one has yet undertaken.

With the appointment of Yoritomo to be commander-in-chief, the feudal system was fully established. The ancient official hierarchy still existed at Kyoto, but in name only, exercising no influence whatever over the conduct of affairs, and in the 14th century its functions were already so far forgotten as to become the subject of antiquarian research. The civil and penal codes borrowed from the great empire of Eastern Asia fell into disuse, and in part even the very traces of them perished. Martial law reigned throughout the land, half the people were converted into a huge garrison, which the other half toiled to feed and clothe. Reading and writing were the exclusive accomplishments of the Buddhist priesthood and of the impoverished nobles who formed the court of a emperor shorn of all the usual attributes of a sovereign, and a deep sleep fell upon the literary genius of the nation. The absence of danger from foreign invasion rendered the necessity of a strong central administration unfelt, and Japan under the *shōguns* assumed the aspect of Germany in the middle ages, the soil being divided between a multitude of petty potentates, independent in all but name, while their nominal head was little better than a puppet.

This state of things lasted till the second quarter of the 14th century, when an attempt was made under the emperor Go-Daigo to re-establish the pristine rule of the legitimate sovereigns. A civil war ensued that lasted for over fifty years, until the Ashikaga family finally established themselves in the office of hereditary *shōguns*. Before long they split up into two branches which quarrelled among themselves and gave opportunity for local chiefs to re-establish their independence. In the middle of the 16th century a soldier of fortune, Oda Nobunaga by name, profited by the central position of the provinces he had acquired with his sword to arrogate to himself the right of arbitrating between the warlike leaders who had risen in every direction. After his assassination a still greater warrior, Toyotomi Hideyoshi, carried on the work of pacification: every domain who opposed his authority was in turn subdued, and he might have become the founder of a new line of "*maires du palais.*" He died, however, before time had sufficiently consolidated his position, leaving an inexperienced youth heir to his power, under the tutelage of guardians who speedily quarrelled. The most distinguished of these was Tokugawa Ieyasu, who, besides the vast domains which he had acquired in the neighbourhood of Edo, modern Tokyo, possessed all the qualities which fit a man to lead armies and rule kingdoms. He had been Hideyoshi's sole remaining competitor for power, and at the death of the latter naturally assumed the most prominent position in the country. A couple of years sufficed for the transference to him of all, and more than all, the authority wielded by his two predecessors. No combination against him had any chance of success. The decisive Battle of Sekigahara in 1600 brought the whole nation to his feet, and he made full use of this opportunity to create checks upon the *daimyō* of whose fidelity he was not sufficiently assured, by grants of territories to his own friends and followers, a few of the older families alone being allowed to retain their ancient fiefs. Among these were Shimazu in the south of Kyushu, Mōri in the extreme west, and Date, Nanbu and Tsugaru in the northern provinces of the main island. His own sons received portions in Owari, Kishū, Mito and elsewhere.

In 1616, at Ieyasu's death 19-20ths of the whole country was held by his adherents. Thus there arose five or six classes of barons, as they may best be called, to render their position intelligible to the English reader. Firstly, there were the Three Families descended from his most favoured sons, from whom according to the constitution established by him in case of a default of direct heirs, the successor to the Bakufu was to be chosen (as a matter of fact resort was had only to Kishū when a break in the line occurred). Next came the related families (*kamon*) sprung from his younger sons, and in the third place were ranked the lords of provinces (*Kokushi*). The members of these three classes enjoyed the revenue of fiefs comprising one or more provinces, or lands of equivalent extent. Below them in importance were the hereditary lords (*fudai*) and Banner-men (*hatamoto*) composed as has been said before of the immediate retainers of the Tokugawa family, and the outside lords (*tozama*), relics of the former barons, who had submitted to his supremacy and followed his banner in his last wars. The qualification of a *daimyō* was the possession of lands assessed at a production of 10,000 *koku* (about 5 bushels) of rice and upwards. The *hatamoto* were retainers of the Tokugawa family whose assessment was below 10,000 *koku* and above 1000. Below them came the ordinary vassals (*go-kenin*).

The fiefs of all classes of the *daimyō* were in their turn at first partitioned out among their retainers, and called *kerai* in their relation to their immediate lords, and *baishin* (under vassals) as being vassals of those who acknowledged the suzerainty of the *shōgun*. samurai and *ashigaru* denoted the two ranks of sword-bearing gentlemen and common soldiers among the retainers of the *daimyō*. In the end every retainer, except the samurai of Satsuma, received an annual allowance of so much rice, in return for which he was bound to perform military service and appear in the field or discharge the ordinary military duties required in time of peace, accompanied by followers proportioned in number to his income. In Satsuma the feudal sub-division of the land was carried out to the fullest extent, so that the vassal of lowest rank held the sword in one hand and the hoe in the other. No taxes were paid by any feudal proprietor. The *kokushi* and other barons of equal rank ruled their provinces absolutely, levying land-tax on the farmers and imposts on internal trade as they chose. They had further the power of life and death, subject only to the nominal condition of reporting once a year the capital sentences inflicted by their officers. The other nobles were less independent. Every *daimyō* had to maintain an establishment at the capital, where his wife and children resided permanently, while the lord passed alternate years in Edo and in his territories.

On his journeys to and fro he was accompanied by a little army of retainers, for whose accommodation inns were built at every town on the main roads throughout the country, and the expense involved was a heavy tax on his resources. A strict system of etiquette regulated the audiences with which the *daimyō* were favoured on their arrival and departure, and prescribed the presents they were to offer as a symbol of their inferiority. There was little social intercourse among them, and they lived for the most part a life of extreme seclusion surrounded by vast numbers of women and servants. A fixed number of hereditary councillors (*karō* and *yōnin*) checked all initiative in the administration of their fiefs. They were brought up in complete ignorance of the outer world, and the strings of government were pulled by the unseen hands of obscure functionaries who obtained their appointments by force of their personal qualities. After a few generations had passed the descendants of the active warriors and statesmen of Ieyasu's time were reduced to the state of imbecile puppets, while the hereditary principle produced a similar effect on their councillors. Thus arose in each fiefdom a condition of things which may be compared to that of a Highland clan, where the ultimate power was based upon the feelings and opinions of a poor but aristocratic oligarchy. This led to the surprising results of the revolution of 1868, when the power nominally exercised by the chief *daimyō* came to be wielded by the more energetic and intelligent of their retainers, most of whom were samurai of no rank or position. These men it was who really ruled the clan, determined the policy of its head and dictated to him the language he should use on public occasions. The *daimyō*, it cannot be too often repeated, was a nobody; he possessed not even as much power as a constitutional sovereign of the modern type, and his intellect, owing to his education, was nearly always far below par. This strange political system was enabled to hold together solely by the isolation of the country from the outer world. As soon as the fresh air of European thought impinged upon this framework it crumbled to ashes like an Egyptian mummy brought out of its sarcophagus.

The decline of the emperor's power dates from the middle of the 9th century, when for the first time a boy of nine years ascended the throne of his ancestors. During his minority the country was governed by his father-in-law, the chief of the ancient Fujiwara family, who contrived for a long period to secure to themselves the power of setting up and removing their own nominees just as suited their convenience. A similar fate befel the institution of the Bakufu. After the murder of Yoritomo's last surviving son, the country was nominally ruled by a succession of young lords, none of whom had emerged from the stage of boyhood when appointed, and who were deposed in turn after a few years of complete nullity, while the real heads of the government were the descendants of Hōjō Tokimasa, Yoritomo's father-in-law. The vices of the hereditary principle in their case had again full sway, and the later Hōjō were mere puppets in the hands of their principal advisers. A revolution in favour of the emperor overthrew this system for a short interval, until the Bakufu was restored for a time to reality by the founder of the Ashikaga family. But after the lapse of a few years its power was divided between Kyoto and Kamakura, and the two heads of the family fell under the dominating influence of their agents the *kanrei* Uesugi and Hosokawa.

Towards the end of the Ashikaga period the *shōgun* had become as much an empty name as the emperor himself, and the country was split up among the local chieftains. The bad condition of the internal communications between the provinces and the capital probably contributed to this state of things. Ieyasu was the first to render consolidation possible by the construction of good military roads. The governmental system erected by him seemed calculated to ensure the lasting tranquillity of the country. But the hereditary principle again reasserted its influence. The third *shōgun*, Iemitsu, was a real man. Born four years after the battle of Sekigahara and already twelve years of age when his grandfather died in the year succeeding his final appearance in the battlefield, he had the education of a soldier, and to his energy was owing the final establishment of the Tokugawa supremacy on a solid basis. Ieyasu and his successor had always been in the habit of meeting the *daimyō* on their visits to Edo outside the city. Iemitsu received them in his palace. He gave those who would not submit to their changed position the option of returning home, and offered them three years for preparation to try the ordeal of war. Not a single one ventured to resist. But he was succeeded by his son Ietsuna, a boy of ten. During Ietsuna's minority the government was carried on in his name by his Council of State, composed of hereditary lords *fudai daimyō*, and the personal authority of the head of the Tokugawa family thus received its first serious blow. But worse than that, the office of chief councillor was from the first confined to four baronial families, Ii, Honda, Sakakibara and Sakai, and the *rōjū* or ordinary councillors were likewise *daimyō*.

On them the hereditary principle had, in the interval between the close of the civil wars and the accession of the fourth *shōgun*, produced its usual result. Nominally the heads of the administration they were without any will of their own, and were guided by their own hereditary councillors, whose strings were pulled by someone else. The real power then fell into the hands of ministers or *bugyō*, chosen from the *hatamoto* or lesser vassals, and many of these were men of influence and real weight. The habit of delegating authority into the hands of anyone of sufficient industry and energy to prefer work to idleness was invincible, and in the end the dominions of the Tokugawa family came to be ruled by the *oku go-yūhitsu* or private secretaries. The machine in fact had been so skilfully constructed that a child could keep it turning. Political stagnation was mistaken for stability.

Apart from one or two unsuccessful conspiracies against the government, Japan experienced during 238 years the profoundest tranquillity. She resembled the sleeping beauty in the wood, and the guardians of the public safety had a task not more onerous than that of waving a fan to keep the flies from disturbing the lordss's slumbers. When her dreams were interrupted by the eager and vigorous West the ancient, decrepit and wrinkled watchers were found unfit for their posts, and had to give way to men more fit to cope with the altered circumstances which surrounded them.

Socially the nation was divided by a wide gulf which it was impossible to pass. On the one hand the sword-bearing families or gentry, whose frequent poverty was compensated for by their privileges of rank; on the other the agricultural, labouring and commercial classes. Intermarriage was forbidden between the orders. The former were ruled by the code of honour, offences against which were permitted to be expiated by self-destruction, the famous *harakiri* or disembowelment, while the latter were subject to a severe unwritten law enforced by cruel and frequent capital punishment. They were the obedient humble servants of the two-sworded class.

Japan had already made the experiment of free intercourse with European states in the middle of the 16th century, when the merchants and missionaries of Portugal were welcomed in the chief ports of Kyushu, and Christianity bade fair to replace the ancient native religions. They were succeeded by the Spanish, Dutch and English, the two latter nations confining themselves to commerce. The gigantic missionary undertakings of the two great English-speaking communities of the far West were the creation of a much later time. It will be recollected that in 1580 Spain for a time absorbed Portugal. The Roman Catholics began before long to excite the enmity of the Buddhist and Shintō priesthood, whose temples they had caused to be pulled down and whose revenues they seemed on the point of usurping. Nobunaga had favoured them, but in the civil wars that raged at that period the principal patrons of the Jesuits were overthrown, and the new ruler Hideyoshi soon proclaimed his hostility to the strangers. Their worst offence was the refusal of a Christian girl to become his concubine. Ieyasu, a devout Buddhist, pursued the same religious policy as his predecessor in possession of the ruling power. His dislike of Christianity was stimulated by the fact that some of Hideyori's adherents were Christians, and the young lord Hideyori was himself known to be on friendly terms with the missionaries. The flame was fanned by the Dutch and English, now become the hereditary political foes of Spain, and the persecution was renewed with greater vigour than ever. Missionaries were sought out with keenness, and in the company of their disciples subjected to cruel tortures and the most horrible deaths. The fury of persecution did not relax with Ieyasu's disappearance from the scene, and the final act of the drama was played out in the time of his grandson.

An insurrection provoked by the oppression of the local *daimyō* broke out in the island of Amakusa, where thousands of Christians joined the rebel flag. After a furious struggle the revolt was put to an end on the 24th February, 1638, by the assault and capture of Shimabara castle, when 37,000 people, two-thirds of whom women and children, were put to the sword. It is hardly possible to read the native accounts of this business without a feeling of choking indignation at the ruthless sacrifice of so many unfortunate creatures who were incapable of defence, and whose only crime was their wish to serve the religion which they had chosen for their rule of life.

The Portuguese were forbidden ever to set foot again in Japan. The English had previously retired from a commercial contest in which they found their rivals too fortunate and too skilful, and the edict went forth that the Dutch, who now alone remained, should thenceforth be confined to the small artificial island of Deshima, off the town of Nagasaki, where for the nextwo and a quarter centuries they and the Chinese were permitted to carry on a restricted and constantly diminishing trade. Attempts were made once or twice by the English, and early in the present century by the Russians, to induce the government of Japan to relax their rule, but in vain. The only profit the world has derived from these abortive essays is the entrancing narrative of Golownin, who was taken prisoner in Ezo in connection with a descent made by Russian naval officers in revenge for the rejection of the overtures made by the Russian envoy Resanoff, perhaps the most lifelike picture of Japanese official manners that is anywhere to be met with. No further approaches were made by any Western government until the United States took the matter in hand in 1852.

Treaties

The expedition of Commodore Perry to the Ryukyu Islands and Japan was not the first enterprise of its kind that had been undertaken by the Americans. Having accomplished their own independence as the result of a contest in which a few millions of half-united colonists had successfully withstood the well-trained legions of Great Britain and her German mercenaries (though not, it may be fairly said, without in a great measure owing their success to the very efficient assistance of French armies and fleets), they added to this memory of ancient wrongs a natural fellow-feeling for other nations who were less able to resist the might of the greatest commercial and maritime power the world has yet seen. While sympathising with Eastern peoples in the defence of their independent rights, they believed that a conciliatory mode of treating them was at least equally well fitted to ensure the concession of those trading privileges to which the Americans are not less indifferent than the English.

In 1836 they had dispatched an envoy to Siam and Cochin-China, who was successful in negotiating by peaceful methods a treaty of commerce with the former state. In China, like the other western states, they had profited by the negotiations which were the outcome of the Opium War, without having to incur the odium of using force or the humiliation of finding their softer methods prove a failure in dealing with the obstinate conservatism of Chinese mandarins. For many years their eyes had been bent upon Japan, which lay on the opposite side of the Pacific fronting their own state of California, then rising into fame as one of the great gold-producing regions of the globe. Warned by the fate of all previous attempts to break down the wall of seclusion that hemmed in the 'country of the gods,' they resolved to make such a show of force that with reasonable people, unfamiliar with modern artillery, might prove as powerful an argument as theories of universal brotherhood and the obligations imposed by the comity of nations. They appointed to the chief command a naval officer possessed of both tact and determination, whose judicious use of the former qualification rendered the employ of the second unnecessary. Probably no one was more agreeably surprised than Commodore Perry at the comparative ease with which, on his second visit to the Bay of Edo, he obtained a treaty, satisfactory enough as a beginning. No doubt the counsels of the Dutch agent at Nagasaki were not without their effect, and we may also conjecture that the desire which had already begun to manifest itself among some of the lower samurai for a wider acquaintance with the mysterious outer world was secretly shared by men in high positions. Fear alone would not have induced a haughty government like that of the *shōgun*s to acquiesce in breaking through a law of restriction that had such a highly creditable antiquity to boast of.

Most men's motives are mixed, and there was on the Japanese side no very decided unwillingness to yield to a show of force, which the pretext of prudence would enable them to justify. England and Russia, then or shortly afterwards at war, followed in the wake of the United States. Next an American consul-general took up his residence at Shimoda, to look after the interests of whaling vessels, and skilfully made use of the recent events in China to induce the *shōgun*'s government to extend the concessions already granted. In 1858 the China War having been apparently brought to a successful conclusion, Lord Elgin and the French minister, Baron Gros, ran across to Japan and concluded treaties on the same basis as Harris, and before long similar privileges were accorded to Holland and Russia. In 1859 the ports of Nagasaki, Hakodate and Yokohama were thrown open to the trade of the Five Powers, and a new age was inaugurated in Japan.

It was not without opposition that the *shōgun*'s government had entered into its first engagements with the United States, Great Britain and Russia. An agitation arose when the first American ships anchored in the Bay of Edo, and there were not wanting bold and rash men ready to undertake any desperate enterprise against the foreign invaders of the sacred soil of

Japan. But at this time there was no leader to whom the malcontents could turn for guidance. The emperor was closely watched by the *shōgun*'s resident at Kyoto, and the *daimyō* were divided among themselves. The principal opponent was the former lord of Mito, whose constitutional duty was to support the *shōgun* and aid him with his counsels in all great national crises.

During the presence of Commodore Perry the reigning *shōgun* Ieyoshi had fallen ill, and he died not long after the squadron had sailed. He was succeeded by his son Iesada, a man of 28, who does not seem to have been endowed with either force of character or knowledge of the world. Such qualities are not to be expected from the kind of education which fell to the lot of Japanese lords in those days.

In view of the expected return of the American ships in the following year, forts were constructed to guard the sea-front of the capital, and the former lord of Mito was summoned from his retirement to take the lead in preparing to resist the encroachments of foreign powers. By a curious coincidence, this nobleman, then forty-nine years of age, was the representative of a family which for years had maintained the theoretical right of the emperor to exercise the supreme government, and was at the same time strongly opposed to any extension of the limited intercourse with foreign countries then permitted. Nor can it be wondered that Japan, who had so successfully protected herself from foreign aggression by a policy of rigid exclusion, should have believed that the best means of maintaining peace at home and avoiding an unequal contest with Europe, was to adhere strictly to the traditions of the past two centuries. After all, they had seen the humiliation of China consequent upon disputes with a Western Power arising out of trade questions at the very moment when she was being torn by a civil war which owed its origin to the introduction of new religious beliefs from the West. But when the intrusive foreigners returned in the beginning of the following year, Japan found herself still unprepared to repel them by force. The treaty was therefore signed, interdicting trade, but permitting whalers to obtain supplies in the three harbours of Nagasaki, Hakodate and Shimoda, and promising friendly treatment to shipwrecked sailors.

While making these unavoidable concessions, the Japanese buoyed themselves up with the belief that their innate superiority could enable them easily to overcome the better equipped forces of foreign countries, when once they had acquired the modern arts of warfare and provided themselves with a sufficient proportion of the ships and weapons of the nineteenth century. From that time onwards this was the central idea of Japan's foreign policy for many years, as the sequel will show. Even at this period there were a few who would have willingly started off on this new quest, and two Japanese actually asked Commodore Perry to give them a passage in his flagship. They were refused, and their zeal was punished by their own government with imprisonment. The residence of Harris at Shimoda and the visit which he insisted on paying to the capital created fresh difficulties for the advisers of the *shōgun*. Written protests were delivered by non-official members of his Council, and he was obliged at last to ask the emperor's sanction to the treaties, in order to strengthen his own position. This invocation of the emperor's authority may fairly be called an innovation upon ancient custom. Neither Nobunaga, Hideyoshi nor Ieyasu had thought it necessary to get their acts approved by him, and Ieyasu granted trade privileges entirely on his own responsibility, without his right to do so ever being questioned. This reference to Kyoto is the first sign of the decadence of the *shōgun*'s power.

The supremacy of the emperor having been once admitted, his right to a voice in the affairs of the country could no longer be disputed. His nobles seized the opportunity, and assumed the attitude of obstruction, which has always been a powerful weapon in the hands of individuals and parties. One man out of a dozen, of sufficient determination, can always force the others to yield, when his position is legal, and cannot be disturbed by the use of force. On the one hand, Harris pressed for a revision of the treaty and the concession of open ports at Kanagawa and Osaka; on the other was the court, turning an obstinately deaf ear to all proposals. In its desperation the *shōgun*'s government appointed to be prime minister, or regent as he was called by foreigners, the descendant of Ieyasu's most trusted retainer, the *daimyō* Ii Kamon no Kami of Hikone. And thus Harris, as has already been said, skilfully turning to account the recent exploits of the combined English and French squadrons in the Chinese seas, obtained his treaty, achieving a diplomatic triumph of the greatest value purely by the use of "moral" pressure. English, French, Russian and Dutch treaties followed. The *shōgun* stood committed to a policy from which his new allies were not likely to allow of his receding, while to the anti-foreign party was imparted a consistency that there had previously been little chance of its acquiring.

Scarcely was the ink of these engagements dry, when the *shōgun*, who had been indisposed for some weeks past, was gathered to his fathers, leaving no heir. According to the custom which had been observed on two previous occasions when there had been a break in the direct line, a lord was chosen from the house of Kishū to be his successor. The ex-lord of Mito, and several of his sympathisers among the leading nobles, namely, Hizen, Owari, Tosa, Satsuma and the Date of Uwajima, a man of abilities superior to the size of his tiny fief in Shikoku, had desired to choose a younger son of Mito, who had been adopted into the family of Hitotsubashi. But the prime minister was too strong for them. He insisted on the election of his own nominee, and forced his opponents to retire into private life. Thus to their disapproval of the political course adopted by the Bakufu, was added a personal resentment against its chief minister, and this feeling was shared in a remarkable degree by the retainers of the disgraced nobles. A bloody revenge was taken two years later on the individual, but the hostility to the system only increased with time, and in the end brought about its ruin.

Mito was the ringleader of the opposition, and began actively to intrigue with the emperor's party against the head of his own family. The foreigners arrived in numbers at Kanagawa and Yokohama, and affronted the feelings of the haughty samurai by their independent demeanour, so different from the cringing subservience to which the rules of Japanese etiquette condemned the native merchant. It was not long before blood was shed. On the evening of the 26th August, six weeks after the establishment at Edo of the British and American representatives, an officer and a seaman belonging to a Russian man-of-war were cut to pieces in the streets of Yokohama, where they had landed to buy provisions. In November, a Chinese servant belonging to the French vice-consul was attacked and killed in the foreign settlement at Yokohama. Two months later, Sir Rutherford Alcock's native linguist of the British legation was stabbed from behind as he was standing at the gateway of the British legation in Edo, and within a month more two Dutch merchant captains were slaughtered in the high street at Yokohama. Then there was a lull for eight or nine months, till the

French minister's servant was cut at and badly wounded as he was standing at the gate of the legation in Edo. On the 14th January, 1861, Heusken, the secretary of the American Mission, was attacked and murdered as he was riding home after a dinner-party at the Prussian legation. And on the night of July 5 occurred the boldest attempt yet made on the life of foreigners, when the British legation was attacked by a band of armed men and as stoutly defended by the native guard.

This was a considerable catalogue for a period of no more than two years since the opening of the ports to commerce. In every case the attack was premeditated and unprovoked, and the perpetrators on every occasion belonged to the swordbearing class. No offence had been given by the victims to those who had thus ruthlessly cut them down; they were assassinated from motives of a political character, and their murderers went unpunished in every instance. Japan became to be known as a country where the foreigner carried his life in his hand, and the dread of incurring the fate of which so many examples had already occurred became general among the residents. Even in England before I left to take up my appointment, we felt that apart from the chances of climate, the risk of coming to an untimely end at the hands of an expert swordsman must be taken into account. Consequently, I bought a revolver, with a due supply of powder, bullets and caps. The trade to Japan in these weapons must have been very great in those days, as everyone wore a pistol whenever he ventured beyond the limits of the foreign settlement, and constantly slept with one under his pillow. It was a busy time for Colt and Adams. But in all the years of my experience in Japan I never heard of more than one life being taken by a revolver, and that was when a Frenchman shot a carpenter who demanded payment for his labour in a somewhat too demonstrative manner. In Edo I think we finally gave up wearing revolvers in 1869, chiefly because the few of us who resided there had come to the conclusion that the weight of the weapon was inconvenient, and also that if any bloodthirsty two-sworded gentleman intended to take our lives, he would choose his time and opportunity so as to leave us no chance of anticipating his purpose with a bullet.

In the spring of 1862 Sir Rutherford Alcock returned to England on leave of absence, and Edward Neale was left in charge. As I have said before, disbelieving in the validity of the reasons which had led the minister to remove his official residence to Yokohama, the chargé d'affaires reestablished himself at the temple formerly occupied as the British legation. On the anniversary, according to the Japanese calendar, of the attack referred to on a previous page, some commissioners for foreign affairs in calling upon Neale, congratulated him and themselves on the fact that a whole year had elapsed since any fresh attempt had been made on the life of a foreigner. It was not unnatural, therefore, that in the first impulse of indignation at the savage and bloody slaughter of the sentry and corporal almost at his bedroom door, he should have conceived the suspicion that the visit of the commissioners and their language in the morning, had been intended to put him off his guard, and that consequently the Japanese government, or rather the *shōgun*'s ministers, were implicated in what looked like a barbarous act of treachery that deprived the Japanese nation of all right to be regarded as a civilized community; more especially as the native watch had been recently changed, and fresh men substituted for those who had fought so well in defence of Sir Rutherford Alcock the year before.

On reflection it will easily be seen that there was no real justification for such a belief. The assassin was one of the guard. After the murder of the two Englishmen he returned to his quarters and there committed suicide by ripping himself up in the approved Japanese fashion. We may be sure that if his act had been the result of a conspiracy, he would not have been alone. Ignorant as the *shōgun*'s ministers may have been, and probably were, of the sacred character of an envoy, it was not their interest to bring upon themselves the armed vengeance of foreign powers at a moment when they were confronted with the active enmity of the principal clans of the west. I think they may be entirely absolved from all share in this attempt to massacre the inmates of the English legation. But on the other hand it seems highly probable that the man's comrades were aware of his intention, and that after his partial success they connived at his escape. But he had been wounded by a bullet discharged from the pistol of the second man whom he attacked, and drops of blood on the ground showed the route by which he had made his way out of the garden. As his identity could not be concealed, he had to commit suicide in order to anticipate the penalty of death which the *shōgun*'s government could not have avoided inflicting on him. The apparent cognisance of the other men on guard (who were what our law would call accessories before the fact), and the fact that nevertheless they took no share in his act, is consonant with the statement that he was merely accomplishing an act of private revenge. His selection of the darkness of night seems to indicate that he hoped to escape the consequences. Willis said that when he arose and looked out, the night was pitch dark. It was the night before full moon, and in the very middle of what is called in Japan the rainy season. He informed me that there was a high wind and that heavy black clouds were drifting over the sky. The stormy weather and the lateness of the hour (11 to 12 o'clock) might perhaps account for the native lanterns which were hung about the grounds having ceased to give any light, but even under those circumstances it is a little suspicious that the guard should have neglected to replace the burnt out candles.

It was at Taku on our way down from Beijing that Robertson, Jamieson and I heard of this new attack on the legation. I believe our feeling was rather one of regret that we had lost the opportunity of experiencing one of the stirring events which we had already learned to regard as characteristic of life in Japan. It certainly did not take us by surprise, and in no way rendered the service less attractive. But Jamieson had found a better opening in Shanghai, and the remaining two went on to Yokohama as soon as they could get a passage.

Richardson's Murder

The day after my arrival at Yokohama I was taken over to Kanagawa and introduced to Samual Robbins Brown, an American Missionary, who was then engaged in printing a work on colloquial Japanese, and to James Curtis Hepburn, who was employed on a dictionary of the language. The former died some years ago, but the latter is at this moment (1886) still in Japan, bringing out the third edition of his invaluable lexicon and completing the translation of the Bible on which he has been occupied for many years.

In those days we had either to take a native sculling boat for an *ichibu* across the bay to Kanagawa or ride round by the causeway, the land along which the railway now runs not having been filled in at that time. Natives used to cross by a public ferry, paying a *tempō* (16-1/2 to the *ichibu*) a-piece, but no foreigner was ever allowed to make use of the cheaper conveyance. If he was quick enough to catch the ferry before it had pushed off, and so seize a place for himself, the boatmen simply refused to stir. They remained immovable, until the intruder was tired of waiting, and abandoned the game. It was only after a residence of some years, when I had become pretty fluent in the language and could argue the point with the certainty of having the public on my side, that I at last succeeded in overcoming the obstinacy of the people at the boathouse who had the monopoly of carrying foreigners.

There was in those days a fixed price for the foreigner wherever he went, arbitrarily determined without reference to the native tariff. At the theatre a foreigner had to pay an *ichibu* for admittance, and was then thrust into the "deaf-box," as the gallery seats are called, which are so far from the stage that the actors' speeches are quite indistinguishable. The best place for both seeing and hearing is the *doma*, on the area of the theatre, close in front of the stage. On one occasion I walked into the theatre, and took my place in one of the divisions of the *doma*, offering to pay the regular price. No, they would not take it. I must pay my *ichibu* and go to the foreigner's box. I held out, insisting on my right as one of the public. Did I not squat on the floor with my boots off, just like themselves? Well then, if I would not come out of that, the curtain would not rise. I rejoined that they might please themselves about that. In order to annoy a single foreigner, they would deprive the rest of the spectators of the pleasure they had paid to enjoy. So I obstinately kept my place, and in the end the manager gave way. The "house" was amused at the foreigner speaking their language and getting the best of the argument, and for the rest of my time in Yokohama I had no more difficulty in obtaining accommodation in any part of the theatre that I preferred.

In those days the Yokohama theatre used to begin about eleven o'clock in the morning and keep open for twelve hours. A favourite play was the *Chūshingura*, or *treasury of Faithful Retainers*, and the *Sarayashiki*, or the *Broken Plate Mansion*. The arrangement of the interior, the fashion of dress and acting, the primitive character of the scenery and lights, the literary style of the plays have not undergone any changes, and are very unlikely to be modified in any marked degree by contact with European ideas. There is some talk now and then of elevating the character of the stage and making the theatre a school of morals and manners for the young, but the good people who advocate these theories in the press have not, as far as I know, ventured to put them to practical proof, and the *shibai* will, I hope, always continue to be what it always has been in Japan, a place of amusement and distraction, where people of all ages and sizes go to enjoy themselves without caring one atom whether the incidents are probable or proper, so long as there is enough of the tragic to call forth the tears which every natural man sheds with satisfaction on proper occasions, and of the comic by-turns to give the facial muscles a stretch in the other direction.

On September 14, (1862) a most barbarous murder was committed on a Shanghai merchant named Charles Lennox Richardson. He, in company with a Mrs Borradaile of Hongkong, and Woodthorpe Charles Clarke and William

Marshall both of Yokohama, were riding along the high road between Kanagawa and Kawasaki, when they met with a train of *daimyō's* retainers, who bid them stand aside. They passed on at the edge of the road, until they came in sight of a palanquin, occupied by Shimazu Hisamitsu, father of the lord of Satsuma. They were now ordered to turn back, and as they were wheeling their horses in obedience, were suddenly set upon by several armed men belonging to the train, who hacked at them with their sharp-edged heavy swords. Richardson fell from his horse in a dying state, and the other two men were so severely wounded that they called out to the lady: "Ride on, we can do nothing for you." She got safely back to Yokohama and gave the alarm. Everybody in the settlement who possessed a pony and a revolver at once armed himself and galloped off towards the scene of slaughter.

Howard Vyse, the British consul, led off the legation mounted escort in spite of Neale's order that they should not move until he or their own commander gave the word. Gustave du Chesne de Bellecourt, the French minister, sent out his escort, consisting of a half-dozen French troopers. And Lieut. Price of the 67th Regiment marched off part of the legation guard, accompanied by some French infantry. But amongst the first, perhaps the very first of all, was doctor William Willis, whose high sense of the duty cast on him by his profession rendered him absolutely fearless. Passing for a mile along the ranks of the men whose swords were reeking with the blood of Englishmen, he rode along the high road through Kanagawa, where he was joined by some three or four more Englishmen. He proceeded onwards to Namamugi, where poor Richardson's corpse was found under the shade of a tree by the roadside. His throat had been cut as he was lying there wounded and helpless. The body was covered with sword cuts, any one of which was sufficient to cause death. It was carried from there to the American consulate in Kanagawa, where Clarke and Marshall had found refuge and surgical aid at the hands of doctor Hepburn and later on of Jenkins, our other doctor.

There was only one British man-of-war lying in the harbour, but in the course of the evening Admiral Küper arrived in his flagship, the *Euryalus*, with the gun-vessel *Ringdove*. The excitement among the foreign mercantile community was intense, for this was the first occasion on which one of their own number had been struck down. The Japanese sword is as sharp as a razor, and inflicts fearful gashes. The Japanese had a way of cutting a man to pieces rather than leave any life in him. This had a most powerful effect on the minds of Europeans, who came to look on every two-sworded man as a probable assassin, and if they met one in the street thanked God as soon as they had passed him and found themselves in safety.

It was known that Shimazu Hisamitsu was to lie that night at Hodogaya, a post town scarcely two miles from Yokohama. To surround and seize him with the united forces of all the foreign vessels in port would, in their opinion, have been both easy and justifiable, and viewed by the light of our later knowledge, not only of Japanese politics but also of Japanese ideas with regard to the right of taking redress, they were not far wrong. In the absence of any organised police or military force able to keep order among the turbulent two-sworded class it cannot be doubted that this course would have been adopted by any Japanese clan against whom such an offence had been committed, and the foreign nationalities in Japan were in the same position as a native clan. They were subject to the authorities of their own country, who had jurisdiction over them both in criminal and civil matters, and were responsible for keeping them within the bounds of law and for their protection against attack.

A meeting was called at Hooper's (W. C. Clarke's partner) house under the presidency of Colonel Howard Vyse, the British consul, when, after an earnest discussion and the rejection of a motion to request the foreign naval authorities to land a thousand men in order to arrest the guilty parties, a deputation consisting of some of the leading residents was appointed to wait on the commanding officers of the Dutch, French and English naval forces and lay before them the conclusions of the meeting. The British admiral, however, declined to act upon their suggestion, but consented to attend another meeting which was to be held at the residence of the French minister at 6 a.m. on the following morning. The deputation then went to Neale, who with great magnanimity waived all personal considerations and promised to be present also. The idea had got abroad amongst the foreign community that Neale could not be trusted to take the energetic measures which they considered necessary under the circumstances. In fact, they found fault with him for preserving the cool bearing which might be expected from a man who had seen actual service in the field and which especially became a man in his responsible situation. They thought that pressure could be put upon him through his colleagues and the general opinion of the other foreign representatives. But in this expectation they were disappointed. At the meeting Neale altogether declined to authorise the adoption of measures, which, if the *shōgun's* government were to be regarded as the government of the country, would have amounted virtually to making war upon Japan, and the French minister expressed an opinion entirely coinciding with that of his colleague. Calmer counsels prevailed, and diplomacy was left to its own resources, arrangements, however, being made by the naval commanders-in-chief to patrol the settlement during the night and to station guard-boats along the sea-front to communicate with the ships in case of an alarm.

Looking back now after the lapse of nearly a quarter of a century, I am strongly disposed to the belief that Neale took the best course. The plan of the mercantile community was bold, attractive and almost romantic. It would probably have been successful for the moment, in spite of the well-known bravery of the Satsuma samurai. But such an event as the capture of a leading Japanese nobleman by foreign sailors in the dominions of the *shōgun* would have been a patent demonstration of his incapacity to defend the nation against the "outer barbarian," and would have precipitated his downfall long before it actually took place, and before there was anything in the shape of a league among the clans ready to establish a new government. In all probability the country would have become a prey to ruinous anarchy, and collisions with foreign powers would have been frequent and serious. Probably the slaughter of the foreign community at Nagasaki would have been the immediate answer to a blow struck at Hodogaya, a joint expedition would have been sent out by England, France and Holland to fight many a bloody battle and perhaps dismember the realm of the emperors. In the meantime the commerce for whose sake we had come to Japan would have been killed. And how many lives of Europeans and Japanese would have been sacrificed in return for that of Shimazu Hisamitsu?

I was standing outside the hotel that afternoon, and on seeing the bustle of men riding past, inquired what was the cause. The reply, "A couple of Englishmen have been cut down in Kanagawa," did not shock me in the least. The accounts of such occurrences that had appeared in the English press and the recent attack on the legation of which I had heard on my way from Beijing had prepared me to look on the murder of a foreigner as an ordinary, every-day affair, and the horror of bleeding wounds was not sufficiently familiar to me to excite the feelings of indignation that seemed to animate everyone else. I was secretly ashamed of my want of sympathy. And yet, if it had been otherwise, such a sudden introduction to the danger of a horrid death might have rendered me quite unfit for the career I had adopted. This habit of looking upon assassination as part of the day's work enabled me later on to face with equanimity what most men whose sensations had not been deadened by a moral anæsthetic would perhaps have considered serious dangers. And while everyone in my immediate surroundings was in a state of excitement, defending Vyse or abusing Neale, I quietly settled down to my studies.

In those days the helps to the acquisition of the Japanese language were very few. A thin pamphlet by the Rev. John Liggins, containing a few phrases in the Nagasaki dialect, a vocabulary compiled by William Medhurst, senior, and published at Batavia many years before; João Rodriguez' *Japanese Grammar*, by Landresse; a grammar by MM. Donker Curtius and Johann Joseph Hoffmann in Dutch, and a French translation of it by Léon Pagès; a translation by the latter of part of the Japanese-Portuguese Dictionary of 1603; Hoffmann's dialogues in Japanese, Dutch and English; Leon de Rosny's *Introduction à la langue Japonaise*, were about all. And but few of these were procurable in Japan. I had left London without any books on the language. Luckily for me, Dr S. R. Brown was just then printing his *Colloquial Japanese*, and generously allowed me to have the first few sheets as they came over at intervals from the printing office in Shanghai. A Japanese reprint of Medhurst's vocabulary, which could be bought in a Japanese bookshop that stood at the corner of Benten Dōri and Honchō Itchōme, speedily proved useless. But I had a slight acquaintance with the Chinese written characters and was the fortunate possessor of Medhurst's Chinese-English Dictionary, by whose help I could manage to come at the meaning of a Japanese word if I got it written down. It was very uphill work at first, for I had no teacher, and living in a single room at the hotel, abutting too on the bowling alley, could not secure quiet. The colonel ordered us, Robertson and myself, to attend every day at the "office" (we did not call it the chancery then) to ask if our services were required, and what work we had consisted chiefly of copying despatches and interminable accounts. My handwriting was, unfortunately for me, considered to be rather better than the average, and I began to foresee that a larger share of clerical work would be given to me than I liked. My theory of the duty of a student-interpreter was then, and still is, to learn the language first of all. I considered that this order would be a great interruption to serious work if he insisted upon it, and would take away all chances of our learning the language thoroughly. At last I summoned up courage to protest, and I rather think my friend Willis encouraged me to do this; but I did not gain anything by remonstrating. The colonel evidently thought I was frightfully lazy, for when I said that the office work would interfere with my studies, he replied that it would be much worse for both to be neglected than for one to be hindered.

At first there was some idea of renting a house for Robertson and myself, but finally the Colonel decided to give us rooms at one end of the rambling two-storied building that was then occupied as a legation. It stood at the corner of the bund and the creek, where the Grand Hotel now is, and belonged to a man named Hoey, who took advantage of my inexperience and the love of books he had discovered to be one of my weaknesses to sell me an imperfect copy of the *Penny Cyclopædia* for more than a complete one would have cost at home. I used to play bowls sometimes with Albert Markham (of Arctic fame), who was then a lieutenant on board HMS *Centaur*, and Charles Wirgman, the artist-correspondent of the *Illustrated London News*. Towards the end of October we induced the colonel to consent to our getting two lessons a week from the Rev. S. R. Brown, and to allow us to engage a native "teacher," at the public expense. So we had to get a second, and pay for him out of our own pockets. He also agreed to leave us the mornings free for study up to one o'clock.

A "teacher," it must be understood, does not mean a man who can "teach." In those days, at Beijing and in Japan also, we worked with natives who did not understand a word of English, and the process by which one made out the meaning of a sentence was closely akin to that which Poe describes in the *Gold Beetle* for the deciphering of a cryptograph. Through my "boy," who was equally ignorant of English, I got hold of a man who explained that he had once been a doctor, and having nothing to do at the moment would teach me Japanese without any pay. We used to communicate at first by writing down Chinese characters. One of his first sentences was literally "Lord loves men, I also venerate the lord as a master"; lord, as I afterwards divined, being merely a polite way of saying *you*. He said he had lots of dollars and *ichibu* and would take nothing for his services, so I agreed with him that he should come to my room every day from ten to one. However, he never presented himself again after the first interview.

My "boy" turned out to be what I considered a great villain. I had at an early date wanted one of the native dictionaries of Chinese characters with the Japanese equivalents in *katakana*. I sent him out to buy one, but he shortly returned and said that there were none in the place, and he must go over to Kanagawa, where he would be sure to find what I wanted. After being out the whole day, he brought me a copy which he said was the only one to be found and for which he charged me four *ichibu*, or nearly two dollars. This was just after my arrival, when I was new to the place and ignorant of prices. Six weeks afterwards, being in the bookseller's shop, I asked him what was the price of the book, when he replied that he had asked only one and a half *ichibu*. My boy had taken it away and returned next day to say that I had refused to give more than one, which he consequently accepted. Unconscionable rascal this, not content with less than 300 percent. of a squeeze! I found out also that he had kept back a large slice out of money I had paid to a carpenter for some chairs and a table. He had to refund his illicit gains, or else to find another place.

After a time I got my rooms at the legation and was able to study to my heart's content. The lessons which Samual Robbins Brown gave me were of the greatest value. Besides hearing us repeat the sentences out of his book of *Colloquial Japanese* and explaining the grammar, he also read with us part of the first sermon in the collection entitled *Kyu-ō dōwa*, so that I began to get some insight into the construction of the written language. Our two teachers were Takaoka Kaname, a physician from Wakayama in Kishū, and another man, whose name I forget. He was stupid and of little assistance. Early in 1863 Robertson went home on sick leave, and I had Takaoka Kaname to myself. In those days the correspondence with the

Japanese government was carried on by means of Dutch, the only European tongue of which anything was known. An absurd idea existed at one time that Dutch was the court language of Japan. Nothing was farther from the truth. It was studied solely by a corps of interpreters attached to the Dutch settlement at Nagasaki, and when Kanagawa and Hakodate were opened to foreign trade, some of these interpreters were transferred to those ports. On our side we had collected with some difficulty a body of Dutch interpreters. They included three Englishmen, one Cape Dutchman, one Swiss, and one Dutchman from Holland, and they received very good pay. Of course it was my ambition to learn to read, write, and speak Japanese, and so to displace these middlemen.

So Takaoka began to give me lessons in the epistolary style. He used to write a short letter in the running-hand, and after copying it out in square character, explain to me its meaning. Then I made a translation and put it away for a few days. Meanwhile I exercised myself in reading, now one and now the other copy of the original. Afterwards I took out my translation and tried to put it back into Japanese from memory. The plan is one recommended by Roger Ascham and by the late George Long in a preface to his edition of *Cato Maior de Senectute*, etc., which had been one of my school books. Before long I had got a thorough hold of a certain number of phrases, which I could piece together in the form of a letter, and this was all the easier, as the epistolary style of that time demanded the employment of a vast collection of merely complimentary phrases. I also took writing lessons from an old writing-master, whom I engaged to come to me at fixed hours. He was afflicted with a watery eye, and nothing but a firm resolve to learn would ever have enabled me to endure the constant drip from the diseased orbit, which fell now on the copy-book, now on the paper I was writing on, as he leant over it to correct a bad stroke, now on the table.

There are innumerable styles of caligraphy in Japan, and at that date the *one-ryū* was in fashion. I had unluckily taken up with the mercantile form of this. Several years afterwards I changed to a teacher who wrote a very beautiful hand, but still it was *one-ryū*. After the revolution of 1868 the *kara-yō*, which is more picturesque and self-willed, became the mode, and I put myself under the tuition of Takasai Tanzan, who was the teacher of several nobles, and one of the half dozen best in Edo. But owing to this triple change of style, and also perhaps for want of real perseverance, I never came to have a good handwriting, nor to be able to write like a Japanese. Nor did I ever acquire the power of composing in Japanese without making mistakes, though I had almost daily practice for seven or eight years in the translation of official documents. Perhaps that kind of work is of itself not calculated to ensure correctness, as the translator's attention is more bent on giving a faithful rendering of the original than on writing good Japanese. I shall have more to say at a later period as to the change which the Japanese written language has undergone in consequence of the imitation of European modes of expression.

The first occasion on which my knowledge of the epistolary style was put into requisition was in June 1863, when there came a note from one of the *shōgun*'s ministers, the exact wording of which was a matter of importance. It was therefore translated three times, once from the Dutch by Richard Eusden, once by Siebold with the aid of his teacher from the original Japanese, and once by myself. I shall never forget the sympathetic joy of my dear Willis when I produced mine. There was no one who could say which of the three was the most faithful rendering, but in his mind and my own there was, of course, no doubt. I think I had sometime previously translated a private letter from a Japanese to one of our colleagues who had left Yokohama. It must have been done with great literalness, for I recollect that *sessha* was rendered "I, the shabby one." But it could not be made use of officially to testify to my progress in the language.

After the Richardson affair the *shōgun*'s government erected guardhouses all along the Tōkaidō within treaty limits, and even proposed to divert the trains of the *daimyō* to another route which ran through the town of Atsugi, but this project fell through. Foreigners were in the habit of using it for their excursions, but Robertson and I had to pass along it twice a week on our way to and from our Japanese lesson at Brown's, and though determined not to show the white feather, I always felt in passing one of these trains that my life was in peril. On one occasion as I was riding on the Tōkaidō for my pleasure, I met a tall fellow armed with the usual two swords, who made a step towards me in what I thought was a threatening manner, and having no pistol with me, I was rather alarmed, but he passed on, content probably with having frightened a foreigner. That is the only instance I can recollect of even seeming intention on the part of a samurai to do me harm on a chance meeting in the street, and the general belief in the bloodthirsty character of that class, in my opinion, was to a very great extent without foundation. But it must be admitted that whenever a Japanese made up his mind to shed the blood of a foreigner, he took care to do his business pretty effectually.

My first experience of an earthquake was on November 2 of this year. It was said by the foreign residents to have been a rather severe one. The house shook considerably, as if some very heavy person were walking in list slippers along the verandah and passages. It lasted several seconds, dying away gradually, and gave me a slight sensation of sickness, insomuch that I was beginning to fancy that a shaking which lasted so long must arise from within myself. I believe the sensations of most persons on experiencing a slight shock of earthquake for the first time are very similar. It is usually held that familiarity with these phenomena does not breed contempt for them, but on the contrary persons who have resided longest in Japan are the most nervous about the danger. And there is a reason for this. We know that in not very recent times extremely violent shocks have occurred, throwing down houses, splitting the earth, and causing death to thousands of people in a few moments. The longer the interval that has elapsed since the last, the sooner may its re-occurrence be looked for. We have escaped many times, but the next will be perhaps our last. So we feel on each occasion, and the anticipation of harm becomes stronger and stronger. Where we at first used to sit calmly through a somewhat prolonged vibration, the wooden joints of the house harshly creaking and the crockery rattling merrily on the shelves, we now spring from our chairs and rush for the door at the slightest movement.

My experiences in Japan of an exciting kind were pretty numerous, but, I regret to say, never included a really serious earthquake, and those who care to read more about the insignificant specimens that the country produces now-a-days must be referred to the pages of the Seismological Society's journal and other publications of the distinguished geologist, my friend Professor John Milne, who has not only recorded observations on a large number of natural earthquakes, but has even succeeded in producing artificial ones so closely resembling the real thing as almost to defy detection.

Visits to Edo

During the later months of 1862 a good deal of correspondence went forward about the Itō Gumpei (murderer of the sentry and of the corporal) affair and the Richardson murder, and Neale held various conferences with the *shōgun*'s ministers. The diplomatic history of these proceedings has been already recounted by Sir Francis Adams, and as for the most part I knew little of what was going on, it need not be repeated here. The meeting-place for the more important discussions was Edo, whither the colonel used to proceed with his escort and the larger portion of the legation staff. Some went by a gunboat, others rode up to the capital along the Tōkaidō.

At that period and for several years after, the privilege of visiting Edo was by treaty restricted to the foreign diplomatic representatives, and non-official foreigners could not cross the Rokugō ferry, halfway between Kanagawa and Edo, except as the invited guest of one of the legations. And now all the foreign ministers had transferred their residences to Yokohama in consequence of the danger which menaced them at Edo. We younger members, therefore, appreciated highly our opportunities, and it was with intense delight that I found myself ordered to accompany the chief early in December on one of his periodical expeditions thither.

We started on horseback about one o'clock in the afternoon in solemn procession, the party consisting of Neale, A von Siebold, Russell Robertson, and myself, with Lieutenant Applin commanding the mounted escort. It was a miserably cold day, but Robertson and I combated the temperature by dropping behind to visit Brown on our way through Kanagawa, and then galloping on after the others. They had evidently been going at a foot's pace during the interval. At Kawasaki we encountered an obstruction in the shape of an obstinate head ferryman, who did not recognize the British chargé d'affaires, and refused to pass us over. The men on guard at the watch-house commanding the ferry, on seeing some of us approach to demand their assistance, ran away. The colonel fumed with wrath, but fortunately at this moment there arrived in breathless haste a mounted officer from Kanagawa, who had followed us of his own accord on hearing that the English chargé d'affaires had passed without a Japanese escort. So the ferryman collected his men, and we got over without further trouble.

A couple of miles beyond the river we came to the well-known gardens called Ume-*yashiki*, the plum-orchard, where we were waited on by some very pretty girls. Everybody who travelled along the Tōkaidō in those days, who had any respect for himself, used to stop here, in season or out of season, to drink a cup of straw-coloured tea, smoke a pipe and chaff the waiting-maids. Fish cooked in various ways and warm *sake* (rice beer) were also procurable, and red-faced native gentlemen might often be seen folding themselves up into their palanquins after a mild daylight debauch. Europeans usually brought picnic baskets and lunched there, but even if they started late were glad of any excuse for turning in to this charmingly picturesque tea-garden. Everyone now-a-days is familiar with the Japanese plum-tree as it is represented in the myriad works of art of these ingenious people, but you must see the thing itself to understand what a joyful surprise it is to enter the black-paled enclosure crowded with the oddly angular trees, utterly leafless but covered with delicate pink or white blossoms which emit a faint fragrance, and cover the ground with the snow of their fallen petals. It is early in February that they are in their glory, on a calm day when the sun shines with its usual brilliance at that season, while in every shady corner you may find the ground frozen as hard as a stone. But to my taste the plum-blossom looks better on a cloudy day against a dull background of cryptomeria when you sit by a warm fire and gaze on it out of window. In December, however, only the swelling buds are to be seen stretching along the slender shoots of last spring.

We proceeded on our way without any special incident until we reached the notorious suburb of Shinagawa, half consisting of houses, or rather palaces, of ill-fame, where a drunken fellow who stood in the middle of the road and shouted at us got a fall from one of the troopers, and so we reached the legation about sunset. The rest of the staff and the infantry guard, who had come by sea, landed about an hour later.

The building occupied as the legation was part of a Buddhist temple, Tōzen-ji, behind which lay a large cemetery. But our part of it had never been devoted to purposes of worship. Every large temple in Japan has attached to it a suite of what we might call state apartments, which are used only on ceremonial occasions once or twice in the year, but from time immemorial it has been the custom to accommodate foreign embassies in these buildings. A suitable residence for a foreign representative could not otherwise have been found in Edo. As a general rule every Japanese, with the exception of the working classes, lives in his own house, instead of renting it as do most residents in an European capital. The only purely secular buildings large enough to lodge the British minister and his staff were the *yashiki* or manors of *daimyō*, but the idea of expropriating one of these nobles in order to accommodate a foreign official was probably never mooted.

There remained, therefore, only the state apartments of some large monastery as a temporary residence until a site could be obtained and the necessary buildings constructed. Consequently there was no ground for the reproach which one writer at least has leveled against the foreign ministers, that by turning sacred edifices into dwelling-houses they had insulted the religious feelings of the Japanese people. In the early years of our intercourse with Japan it is true that we were regarded as unwelcome intruders, but in native opinion we polluted the temples by our presence no more than we should have polluted any other residence that might have been assigned to us.

The Tōzen-*ji* lay in the suburb of Takanawa fronting the seashore, and was therefore conveniently situated for communication with our ships, the smallest of which could anchor just inside the forts, at a distance of perhaps a mile and a half. Owing to the shallowness of the bay, boats were unable to get up to the landing place at low tide, and the assistance which could have been rendered by a gunboat in the event of a sudden attack, such as had been experienced in 1861, was *nil*. There remained the comfort derived

47

from knowing that a refuge lay at no great distance, and no doubt the appearance of a gunboat within the line of forts that had been built to keep out foreign fleets produced a considerable moral effect upon the general population, though desperadoes of the sort that assaulted the guard in July 1861 would certainly have been no whit deterred by any number of threatening men-of-war which could not reach them. Behind the house there was a small ornamental garden with an artificial pond for gold fish, on the opposite side of which rose a hill covered with pine-trees.

A good way off from the quarters of the minister, and at the back of the cemetery belonging to the temple, there was a small house named Jōtōan, which was occupied by the senior chancery assistant. A tall bamboo fence cut us off entirely from this part of the grounds, and joined the house at either end. The rooms were not spacious, and very little attempt had been made to convert them into comfortable apartments. I think there was an iron stove or two in the principal rooms, but elsewhere the only means of warming was a Japanese brasier piled up with red hot charcoal, the exhalations from which were very disagreeable to a novice. The native who wraps himself up in thick wadded clothes and squats on the floor has no difficulty in keeping himself warm with the aid of this arrangement, over which he holds the tips of his fingers. His legs being crumpled up under him, the superficies he presents to the cold air is much less than it would be if he sat in a chair with outstretched limbs in European fashion. To protect himself against draughts he has a screen standing behind him, and squats on a warm cushion stuffed with silk wool. These arrangements enable him even in winter to sit with the window open, so long as it has a southern aspect, and foreigners who adopt the same system have made shift to get on. But if you are going to live in Japan in European style, you must, in order to be moderately warm during the winter months, replace the paper of the outer wooden slides with glass, stop up the openwork above the grooves in which the slides work that divide the rooms, and either build a fireplace or put up an American stove. But even all this will not make you altogether comfortable. Underneath you there are thick straw mats laid upon thin and badly jointed boarding, through which the cutting north-west wind rises all over the floor, while the keen draughts pierce through between the uprights and the shrunken lath-and-plaster walls. The unsuitability of such a building as a residence for the minister and his staff had been perceived from the outset, and long negotiations, having for their object the erection of a permanent legation, had by this time resulted in the assignment of an excellent site, on which a complete series of buildings was being constructed from English designs, but at the expense of the *shōgun*'s government. Other sites in the immediate vicinity had been given to the French, Dutch and Americans for the same purpose. All these were carved out of what had been once a favourite pleasure resort of the people of Edo, whither in the spring all classes flocked to picnic under the blossoms of the cherry-trees in sight of the blue waters of the bay.

Gotenyama was indeed a famous spot in the history of the Bakufu. In its early days the head of the state was wont to go forth thither to meet the great *daimyō* on their annual entry into Edo, until Iemitsu, the third of the line, to mark still more strongly the supremacy to which he felt he could safely lay claim, resolved that henceforward he would receive them in his castle, just like the rest of his vassals. From that time the gardens had been dedicated to the public use. But already before the foreign diplomats took up their abode in Edo, Gotenyama had been partially diverted from its original purpose, and vast masses of earth had been carried off to form part of the line of forts from Shinagawa to the other side of the junk channel that leads into the river.

The British minister's residence, a large two-storied house, which from a distance seemed to be two, stood on an eminence fronting the sea. Magnificent timbers had been employed in its construction, and the rooms were of palatial dimensions. The floors were lacquered, and the walls covered with a tastefully designed Japanese paper. Behind and below it a bungalow had been erected for the Japanese secretary, and a site had been chosen for a second, destined for the assistants and students. On the southern side of the compound was an immense range of stables containing stalls for forty horses, and on the second storey quarters for a portion of the European guard. Some slight progress had been made with the buildings for the French and Dutch legations. But we knew that the people disliked our presence there. The official and military class objected to the foreigner being permitted to occupy such a commanding position overlooking the rear of the forts, and the populace resented the conversion of their former pleasure-ground into a home for the "outer barbarians." To press on the completion of the houses and to take possession was rightly considered an important matter of policy. A deep trench was being dug round the enclosure, and a lofty wooden palisade was built on the inner margin, which, it was expected, would afford sufficient protection against a repetition of such attacks as that of the 5th July 1861, and the British ensign was to be hoisted again in Edo as soon as the buildings should be ready for occupation. We all looked forward to that event with the liveliest feelings of anticipation, and for myself I anxiously expected its arrival because Yokohama was a hybrid sort of town, that by no means fulfilled my expectations, and I hoped before long to become a resident of the famous city to which I had looked with longing eyes from the other side of Europe.

We rode daily in the environs of Edo, to the pretty teahouse at Oji, which is depicted with such bright colours in Laurence Oliphant's book, to the pond of Jiū-ni-sō on the road to Kōshū, to the other pond called Senzoku halfway to Mariko, and to the Ryūsen temple at Meguro, where the pretty damsels at the teahouses formed more than half the attraction. Within the city we made excursions to the Sensō temple at Asakusa, then and for long afterwards the principal sight of interest to the foreign visitor, to Atagoyama, where other pretty damsels served a decoction of salted cherry-blossoms, and to the Kanda Shrine for the view over the city. But the gorgeous mausoleums of the *shōgun*s at Shiba and Ueno were closed to the foreigner, and remained so up to the revolution of 1868. We were allowed in riding back from Asakusa to catch a passing glimpse of the lotus pond Shinobazu no Ike, which is now surrounded by a racecourse after the European manner, but the Fukiage Park, since known as the emperor's garden, and the shortcut through the castle from the Sakurada Gate to the Wadagura Gate of the inner circle were shut to us in common with the Japanese public.

A large portion of the city in the immediate neighbourhood of the castle, and large areas in every quarter were occupied by the *yashiki* of *daimyō* and *hatamoto*, of which little could be seen but long two-storied rows of stern barrack-buildings surrounding the residence of the owner. From the top of Atagoyama alone was it possible to get a view of the interior of such enclosures, and it must be admitted that the knowledge thus gained completely upset the idea that the nobles lived in palaces. Irregular masses of low brown roofs and black weather-boarded walls alone were visible. The use of telescopes was strictly forbidden on Atagoyama, lest the people should pry into the domestic doings of their masters.

Wherever we went a band of mounted guards surrounded us, ostensibly for our protection, but also for the purpose of preventing free communication with the people. These men belonged to a force raised by the *shōgun*'s ministers from the younger sons of the *hatamoto*, and numbered a thousand or twelve hundred. They wore the customary pair of swords (*i.e.* a long and short sabre thrust through the belt on the left side), a round flat hat woven from the tendrils of the wistaria, for the rank and file, and a mound-shaped lacquered wooden hat for the officers, a mantle or *haori*, and the wide petticoat-shaped trousers called *hakama*. Between them and the members of the foreign legations there existed no tie of any kind, for they were changed every fifteen days just like so many policemen, and mounted guard indifferently at all the legations.

It was not until 1867 that I managed to break through this rule and get a special body of men attached to myself. Small guardhouses were dotted about the legation grounds for their accommodation. As soon as it became known that a foreigner was about to go out on foot or on horseback, half-a-dozen were detailed to follow him at all hazards. It was impossible to escape their vigilance. They were to prevent our speaking to any person above the rank of a common citizen or to enter a private house.

On one occasion two members of our legation managed a visit to the father of a young samurai named Kotarō, who lived with us to study English. The fact was reported, and when the visitors went a second time they found the occupants of the house had removed to another part of the city. We were allowed to sit down in shops, and even to bargain for articles that took our fancy; but two kind of purchases were strictly prohibited, maps and the official list of *daimyō* and government officials. Anything we bought had to be sent afterwards to the legation, and delivered to the officials of the foreign department who lived within our gates, and payment was made to them.

On another occasion the Prussian representative, Max von Brandt, made a determined stand against this prohibition. Entering the shop of the bookseller Okadaya in Shinmei-mae, where we foreigners were in the habit of buying books, he inquired for the list of *daimyōs*. The bookseller replied that he had it not in stock. Von Brandt knew that he had, and announced his intention of remaining there until he was furnished with what he required. He sent a member of his party home to the legation to bring out the materials for luncheon, and sat determinedly down in the shop. The guards were at their wits' end. At last they dispatched a messenger to the castle and at last towards evening there came an order to say that for this once the foreigner was to have the book. So the day was won.

As a matter of fact, it was never necessary to proceed to this extremity, as we could easily procure what we wanted in the way of maps and printed books through our Japanese teachers. Manuscripts were always a difficulty. As nothing could be published without permission, any book that touched upon governmental matters had from of old to be circulated per copy. Amongst such works were the so-called "Hundred Laws of Ieyasu," which were supposed to embody the constitution of the Japanese government. The book contains references to offices of state that were instituted after his time, and the utmost that can be alleged in its favour is that it perhaps contains a few maxims from his lips and certain rules as to the appointment of high political functionaries that were observed in actual practice.

There was another book, of undoubted authenticity, containing a vast mass of administrative regulations, of which I never obtained a copy until after the revolution, when it was no longer of practical value. That manuscript is now in the British Museum. Another expedient for eluding the censorate was printing forbidden books with moveable types. It was frequently resorted to during the last years of the Bakufu and at the beginning of the new rule of the emperor, especially for narratives of political events during that period and for one or two important treatises on politics. Shinmei-mae was one of our favourite resorts in those days; here were to be had cheap swords, porcelain, coloured prints, picture-books and novels. I much regret that I did not then begin to collect, when the blocks were comparatively fresh; a complete set of Hokusai's *manga*, in perfect condition. They could be had for a couple of dollars, and his *Hundred Views of Fuji* for about a couple of shillings. But I had little spare cash for such luxuries, and all my money went in necessaries.

Two days after our arrival in Edo we paid a visit to the *go-rōjū*, or *shōgun*'s Council. The word means "August Elders." It was somewhat beneath the dignity of a foreign representative to use the prefix *go* in speaking of them, but the phrase had been caught up from the Japanese who surrounded the minister, and for a long time I believe it was thought that *go* meant five. I unveiled the mistake, and when I afterwards became interpreter to the legation we adopted the practice of giving them the bare Rōjū, except in addressing them directly, when etiquette demanded the honorific. I was unprovided with anything in the shape of uniform, and had to borrow a gold-laced forage cap from Applin. We came afterwards to look with much contempt on these gauds, and to speak derisively of brass caps, but in 1862 I was young enough to take considerable pride in a distinctive mark of rank, and after this occasion lost no time in buying a bit of broad gold lace to wear like my fellow officers. It was an imposing procession, consisting as it did of half-a-dozen "brass caps," the military train escort of twelve men under their gorgeous lieutenant, and a flock of about forty Japanese guards hovering about us before, behind, and on either flank. In these days a foreign representative may often be detected approaching the office of the minister for foreign affairs without any suite, and in the humble *jinrikisha* drawn by one scantily clad coolie.

The interview took place in a long room in the house of one of the *rōjū*. A row of small black-lacquered tables extended down each side, and chairs were set for the Japanese as well as the foreigners. On each table stood an earthen brasier, a black-lacquered smoking-stand, with brass fire-pot and ash-pit, and two long pipes, with a supply of finely cut tobacco in a neat black box. Three of the ministers sat on the right side of the room, and with them an *ōmetsuke*, whose title was explained to me to mean spy. I suppose "censor" or "reporter" would be nearer. Below them sat eight *gaikoku bugyō*, or commissioners for foreign affairs. We used to call them governors of foreign affairs, probably because the governor of Kanagawa was also a *bugyō*. In the centre of the room sat a governor on a stool, while two interpreters (one of whom was Moriyama Takichirō) squatted on the floor. The four higher Japanese officers alone were provided with tables and chairs, the governors sitting on square stools, with their hands in the plackets of their trousers. After some complimentary talk about the weather and health, which are *de rigueur* in Japan, a double row of attendants in light blue hempen robes (we used to term the upper part "wings") came in bearing aloft black lacquer boxes full of slices of sponge cake and *yōkan* (a sweetened bean paste), and afterwards oranges and persimmons. Then tea was served in two manners, simply infused, and also the powdered leaf mixed up with hot water and frothed.

The conversation proceeded at a very slow pace, as it had to be transmitted through two interpreters, ours who spoke Dutch and English, and theirs who spoke Japanese and Dutch. This gave rise to misunderstandings, and the Japanese ministers seemed every now and then to profit by this double obstruction to answer very much from the purpose, so that Neale's observations had to be repeated all over again, interpreted and re-interpreted. Often the ministers would seem at a loss, whereupon one of the governors would leave his stool and glide up to whisper something in his ear. This proceeding reminded one of the flappers in Laputa. The principal topic was the murder of the sentry and corporal at Tōzen-ji which has already been related. To all the demands made by Neale, in accordance with the instructions he had received from Lord Russell, the *rōjū* objected, and when he informed them that the British government required the payment of £10,000 in gold as an indemnity to the families of the two murdered men, they opened their eyes very wide indeed. They offered $3000. Neale at last lost all patience, which no doubt was what they were aiming at. He gave them a piece of his mind in pretty strong language, and the interview came to an end, after, I suppose, a sitting of about three hours length, without anything having been settled. I forget whether it was on this occasion that Siebold literally translated the epithet "son of a gun" by *teppō no musuko*. The adjective that preceded it he did not attempt to translate, as it has not even a literal equivalent in Japanese. The way in which the ministers contradicted themselves from time to time was something wonderful, and the application of the good unmistakeable Anglo-Saxon word for him who "says the thing that is not," was almost venial.

Of course Neale did not omit to complain of the ferryman and the guards at Kawasaki, who had run away instead of putting us over the river, and Eusden in translating used the words "*zij sloopen alle weg*," which excited my laughing muscles kept at too great a stretch through these tedious hours.

I whispered to my neighbour, "they all sloped away"; a terrible frown from the old gentleman rebuked my indecorous behaviour, and I was afterwards informed that I should never be allowed thenceforth to be present on one of these solemn occasions. That was a relief to me, but I confess I ought to have felt more contrite than I did. At the age of nineteen and a half a boy is still a boy, but I ought to have manifested more respect for my elders.

Early in February we received news that the legation buildings in Gotenyama had been destroyed by fire on the night of the 1st. Many years afterwards I learned on the best possible authority that the incendiaries were chiefly Chōshū men belonging to the anti-foreign party. Three at least afterwards rose to high position in the state. These were Count Itō, minister President of state (1886); Count Inoue Kaoru; who the third was I forget. It need scarcely be said that they long ago abandoned their views of the necessity of putting an end to the intercourse of their country with the outside world, and they are now the leaders of the movement in favour of the introduction into Japan of whatever Western institutions are adapted to the wants and wishes of its people.

Willis and I were now living together in a wing of the legation house at No. 20 on the Bund, and a young Japanese samurai named Kobayashi Kotarō messed with us. He had been placed under Willis' charge by the Japanese government in order to acquire the English language, and was a nice boy, though perhaps not endowed with more than average abilities. He disappeared to his home about the time that the ultimatum of the British government was presented to the Council of the *shōgun* in the spring of 1863, and we never heard of him again. I had the teacher Takaoka Kaname now all to myself, and was beginning to read Japanese documents. Across the hills south of the settlement lived a priest who knew something of the Sanskrit alphabet as used in Japan, and I used to go once or twice a week to him for instruction, but these studies were interrupted by the rumours of war that soon began to prevail. The lessons from the American missionary, Brown, also came to an end, as I was now able to get on alone.

Demands for Reparation

A very complete account of the murder of Richardson, and the failure of the Japanese government to afford satisfactory redress either for that injury or for the attack on the legation in June, had been sent home to the Foreign Office, and in March 1863 Neale received instructions to demand ample reparation from both the *shōgun* and the lord of Satsuma. On the 6th April he sent Eusden up to Edo on board the gunboat *Havoc* to deliver a note, demanding the payment of £10,000 in gold for the wives and families of Sweet and Crimp, an ample apology for the other affair, and the payment of £100,000 as a penalty on the *shōgun* for allowing an Englishman to be murdered in his territory in open daylight without making any effort to arrest the murderers. He warned the Council that refusal would have very deplorable consequences to their country, and gave them twenty days to consider their reply.

This lengthened period was allowed on account of the absence of the *shōgun* and his chief advisers, who had left for Kyoto on the third. If at the conclusion of the term allotted no answer was returned, or an unsatisfactory one was given, coercive measures would immediately be taken. It was also intended that on the return of the *Havoc* from Edo, the *Pearl* should be despatched to Kagoshima to demand of the lord of Satsuma the trial and execution of the murderers of Richardson in the presence of one or more English officers, and the payment of £25,000 to be distributed to the relatives of Richardson, to Marshall, Clarke and Mrs Borradaile.

On the 10th Eusden came back from Edo, bringing a receipt for the note and a refusal on the part of the Council to send an officer down to

Kagoshima to advise the lord of Satsuma to admit the demands to be made upon him. So the idea of despatching the *Pearl* was abandoned for the moment, as it was impossible to foretell whether the Council would give in. If they were obstinate, reprisals would at once, it was thought, be commenced, and all our available force would be required to coerce the *shōgun*'s people. Satsuma must be left to be dealt with afterwards. So the colonel waited until the 26th. By the 24th April we had in the harbour the *Euryalus*, 35 guns, bearing the flag of Admiral Küper, the *Pearl*, 21 guns, *Encounter*, 14 (commanded by the brave Roderick Dew), *Rattler*, 17, *Argus*, 6, *Centaur*, 6, and 3 gunboats. The despatch boats *Racehorse* and *Ringdove* were employed in travelling backwards and forwards between Yokohama and Shanghai with the mails, and the *Coquette* was daily expected from Hongkong.

But as was to be anticipated, the Council begged for further delay. They asked for thirty days, and Neale gave them fifteen.

My teacher Takaoka, who had private relations with the *yashiki* of the lord of Kishū, said they had never expected to get more than a fortnight, and as they felt certain the English chargé d' affaires would cut down their demands, they asked for double. He believed that the only motive for the delay was to gain time for preparation, and that war was certain. In the native quarter it was rumoured that the English had asked for the delay, which had been graciously granted by the Council; otherwise we should have been attacked the very day after the term elapsed. The inhabitants of Edo expected war, and began to remove their valuables into the country. Young Kotarō had been carried off by his mother about the 20th. At Uraga, the little junk-port just outside the entrance to the bay of Edo, there was a panic, and the people were said to have decamped with all their movable property to Hodogaya on the Tōkaidō.

On the other hand, there was some alarm felt in the foreign settlement. Meetings were held at which resolutions were passed to the effect that it was the duty of the executive to provide for the safety of the European residents. At the same time the merchants declared their intention of not leaving the settlement unless specially called on to do so by Neale, as they believed that if they deserted their property without such an order, they would not be able to recover its value afterwards in the event of its being destroyed. The precedent of the opium surrendered to Captain Elliot, the

British superintendent of trade at Canton in 1839, was of course in their minds, and they acted prudently in throwing the responsibility on the authorities.

On May 1, 1863, the Council asked for another delay of fifteen days. Eusden was sent up to Edo with a message to the Council that before the colonel could grant their request they must send down to Yokohama one of their number to receive an important communication which he had to make to them. The native population now began to be seriously alarmed, and the shopkeepers of Kanagawa removed their effects to Hodogaya so as to be out of reach of a bombardment, and to secure a further retreat into the interior, if necessary, by the cross-country paths. The second of May was the last day on which the Yokohama people were permitted by the authorities to send away their property to Edo. The government circulated a sensible proclamation from door to door telling them not to be alarmed as there would be no war. At the same time notice was served on the peasants within two miles of Yokohama to be prepared to give up their houses to the troops, but as yet no soldiers had appeared on the scene.

On the fourth and fifth of May long conferences took place between the English and French representatives and admirals and two commissioners for foreign affairs, Takemoto Masatsune and Takemoto Hayato no Shō, who had been deputed by the Council to explain the reasons why a further delay was necessary. They probably represented that the difficulty in acceding to the English demands arose from the opposition of the *daimyō*, for it seems that an offer was made to them that the English and French forces should assist the *shōgun* to quell the resistance of the anti-foreign party, in order to enable him to carry out the promises to which he was bound by treaty. They offered, it was reported, to pay the money indemnity, disguising it under the ingenious fiction of payment for a man-of-war ordered in England, and wrecked on its way out. Finally an extension of time was accorded until May 23, in order that the personal consent of the *shōgun*, who was expected to return by that date, might be obtained to the English ultimatum.

I rode out to Hodogaya on the afternoon of the fifth and met the train of the wife of a *daimyō* going westwards, but saw very few armed men other than those who accompanied her. A rumour had got about that ten thousand men were in the village and its neighbourhood, but the report was obviously without foundation.

During the night of the fifth of May there was a general exodus of all the native servants employed in the foreign settlement. When Willis and I rose in the morning and called for "boy" to bring breakfast, there was a dead silence. I descended to the pantry and found it empty. Servants and cook had gone off, carrying with them a revolver, a Japanese sword, several spoons and forks which they doubtless imagined to be silver, and the remains of last night's dinner wrapped in a table-cloth. This theft was the more curious, as I had the day before entrusted my servant with a considerable sum of native money to change into Mexican dollars, which he had faithfully delivered to me. But we ought to have suspected their intentions, as they had asked for an advance of half a month's wages, and had contentedly received wages up to date. Takaoka and my groom were faithful, so was also the messenger who went into fits of congratulation on learning that the petty cash-box, of which I had charge, had not disappeared. It is much to the credit of the latter class that they have often stuck by their masters on occasions of trouble and even danger, when everyone else has deserted the foreigner.

With some difficulty we procured some eggs and sponge cake, and I went off to the customhouse to report the robbery. The officials, of course, promised to find the thieves, but we never heard anything more of them or of our property. All day long the townspeople continued to depart at a great rate. I went down to the native town, where I found many of the houses shut up, and at others everything packed for removal. Among the rest my friend the bookseller, at the corner of Benten-dōri, had taken to his heels. But during the afternoon a proclamation was issued by the customhouse to tell the people that there would be no fighting, and many of them returned. The excitement was great throughout the town, both among foreigners and natives, and a lamentable instance of hastiness occurred on the part of a Frenchman. A native merchant, accompanied by two others, went to ask payment of a small debt that he claimed, and on its being refused, tried to obtain the money by force. Thereupon the Frenchman shot him, and two others, including the vice-consul, also fired their revolvers. Four bullets passed through the body of the unfortunate man, but without killing him. The French admiral was excessively angry. He at once arrested the merchant and had him conveyed on board the flagship. Two Americans were likewise attacked, and one of them was carried off halfway across the swamp by eight men, who frightened him with a spear and an iron hook which they held over his head. He was rescued by the tall sergeant of our legation guard, or else he would probably have been severely beaten, if not killed, for the Japanese were unable to distinguish between foreigners of different nationalities.

On the eleventh my teacher told me that a messenger had come to him from Edo, sent by a personage of high rank, who desired to learn confidentially the intentions of the English chargé d'affaires, and whether he was disposed to await the return of the *shōgun*, which would not be for three or four months, before taking hostile measures. In that case the high personage, who was superior in rank to the Council, would agree to issue a proclamation that a delay of a thousand days had been agreed upon, which would have the effect of restoring tranquillity at Yokohama. That if Neale, getting tired of these repeated delays, should change the seat of the negotiations to Osaka, the high personage would have to perform *harakiri*, which he rather wished to avoid, as a penalty for failing to induce the foreigner to listen to his representations. I communicated this to Neale, and the reply sent was that he could not consent to wait so long as three months.

The Council had announced the return of the *shōgun* for May 24, and Neale had replied that under the circumstances he would give time for "His Majesty's" settling down again at home, but on the sixteenth a note was received from them stating that circumstances had arisen which prevented their fixing any date whatever for his arrival at Edo. This seemed to point to an indefinite postponement of a settlement, but the Colonel's patience was not even yet exhausted. This accorded with what my teacher had told me. The high personage turned out to be the lord of Owari. Takaoka now said that having transmitted Neale's answer to Kyoto, he would no longer be under the necessity of committing suicide, as he had been able to show that he was not responsible for the foreigner's obstinacy.

Up to the sixteenth the general feeling was that the Council would give way, but the demand for a further postponement of the Japanese answer did not tend to encourage the hope of a peaceful settlement. A Japanese friend told me that the *shōgun* could not by any means accept the assistance of foreign powers against the *daimyō*, and that the abolition of the emperor's dignity was impracticable. If we attacked Satsuma the *shōgun* and *daimyō* would be bound to make common cause with him. I suppose the idea of the foreign diplomatic representatives at that time was to support the *shōgun*, whose claim to be considered the sovereign of Japan had already been called in question by Rudolph Lindau in his "Open Letter" of 1862, against the anti-foreign party consisting of the emperor and *daimyō*, and if necessary to convert him into something more than a mere feudal ruler. For we had as yet no idea of the immense potency that lay in the mere name of the sovereign *de jure*, and our studies in Japanese history had not yet enabled us to realize the truth that in the civil wars of Japan the victory had as a rule rested with the party that had managed to obtain possession of the person of the emperor and the regalia. There has probably never been any sovereign in the world whose title has rested upon so secure a basis as that of the ancient emperors of Japan.

On May 25, another conference took place between the English and French diplomatic and naval authorities on the one side, and Takemoto Masatsune and a new man named Shibata Sadatarō on the other. The latter began by thanking the foreign representatives in the name of the *shōgun* for their offer of material assistance, which he was compelled to decline, as he must endeavour to settle the differences between the *daimyō* and himself by his own unaided forces and authority. As to the indemnity, the *shōgun*'s government recognized that the demand was just, but they were afraid to pay immediately, as their yielding would bring the *daimyō* down upon them. But they offered to pay the money by instalments in such a manner as not to attract public notice, and the further discussion of the details was put off to a future occasion. Probably Neale did not care very much how the matter was arranged, provided he could show to Her Majesty's government that he had carried out his instructions. So the basis of an understanding was arrived at, and it was further conceded that the foreign representatives, that is those of England and France, should take measures to defend Yokohama from attack by the anti-foreign party.

Neale had written to Major-General Brown, who was in command at Shanghai, applying for a force of two thousand men, but a despatch now arrived from the general stating his inability and objections to furnishing any troops. It was said that he had ridiculed the idea of a military expedition against Japan long before Neale proposed it to him. Nevertheless the establishment of a garrison of English troops at Yokohama was merely delayed by this refusal, and after Sir Rutherford Alcock's return to Japan in the spring of 1864 good reasons were given to the same general why he should change his mind.

All this time there existed considerable alarm with respect to the aims and intentions of a somewhat mysterious class of Japanese called *rōnin*. These were men of the two-sworded class, who had thrown up the service of their *daimyō*, and plunged into the political agitations of the time, which had a twofold object, firstly, to restore the emperor to his ancient position, or rather to pull down the *shōgun* to the same level as the great *daimyō*, and secondly, the expulsion of "the barbarians" from the sacred soil of Japan. They came principally from the south and west of the country, but there were many from Mito in the east, and a sprinkling from all the other clans. About the end of May there was a rumour that they designed to attack Kanagawa, and the Americans still living there were compelled to transfer their residence to Yokohama, though not without "compensation for disturbance."

The *shōgun*'s people were naturally keen to conciliate their domestic enemies, and turned such rumours to account in the hope of being able to confine the foreigners at Yokohama within a limited space, such as had formed the prison-residence of the Dutch at Nagasaki in former times. Incidents, too, were not wanting of a character to enforce their arguments. One of the assistants of the English consulate was threatened with personal violence by a couple of two-sworded men as he was entering a teahouse on the hill at Kanagawa. He pulled out his pistol, and pointed it at them, on which they drew back. Taking advantage of the opportunity he ran down to the landing place, where he got a boat and so returned in safety to Yokohama. It was reported that the officials at the guardhouse tried to prevent the boatmen from taking him across the bay, but however this may be, they pacified his assailants, one of whom had half-drawn his sword. In those days we were always told that a samurai might not return his sword to the scabbard without shedding blood, so that the affair was entitled to be ranked as very alarming.

At the beginning of June, in consequence of a report that half-a-dozen *rōnin* were concealed in the place, the *bette-gumi* (a body from which the legation guards at Edo were supplied), together with some drilled troops, came down to Yokohama, and took up their quarters at some newly erected buildings under Noge hill, and from that date until long after the revolution of 1868 we had constantly a native garrison. I recognized among the former several men with whom I had become friends during the visit to Edo already narrated. Fresh additions were made to the British squadron in the shape of two sloops, the *Leopard* and the *Perseus*. The rumours of warlike operations had died away, and it was given out that the intention of directly enforcing our demands on Satsuma had been abandoned, as the *shōgun* had undertaken to see to that part of the business, and it was believed also that to insist upon them at present would give rise to a civil war.

On June 14, there arrived at the legation in Yokohama Kikuchi Takayoshi and Shibata Sadatarō, commissioners for foreign affairs, to complete arrangements for paying $440,000 (representing £110,000) in seven instalments extending over six weeks, the first to be delivered on the eighteenth. But on that day came a note of excuse from one of the Council stating that unavoidable circumstances had arisen which prevented the agreement being carried out, and that he himself would in a day or two arrive at Yokohama to discuss matters with the English chargé d' affaires. Neale very properly refused to hold any more communications with the *shōgun*'s ministers, and after a couple of days' consideration, finally placed the solution in the hands of Admiral Augustus Leopold Küper. The latter, it was said, did not know what to do. He had never seen a gun fired in action, and hardly appreciated the colonel's suggestion that he should at once proceed to seize the steamers lately purchased in such numbers by the Japanese. The Council at Edo now became thoroughly frightened; they had temporized as long as possible, and had worn out the patience of the English authorities. But they left no stone unturned to avoid openly giving way, and Ogasawara Nagamichi himself came down to Yokohama to bring the French chargé d'affaires and admiral to intercede. The latter refused. He insisted on the demands of Great Britain being satisfied and claimed that the defence of Yokohama should be entrusted to them. Ogasawara had just returned from Kyoto with an order from the *shōgun*, dictated to him by the emperor and the anti-foreign element in the ancient capital, to make arrangements with the foreign representatives for closing all the ports! For himself he seemed to dislike his instructions, and even gave hints to the French chargé d'affaires as to the nature of the reply which had best be given. A pageful of notes of exclamation would not be sufficient to express the astonishment of the foreign public of Yokohama when this extraordinary announcement was made, but the presence of the combined squadrons in the harbour relieved them from any anxiety as to the manner in which the diplomatic representatives would reply to it.

The Japanese government, having completely failed to persuade the French authorities to intervene on their behalf (which would have indeed been impossible when the request was accompanied by the preposterous demand that foreigners should forthwith clear out of Yokohama), sent a message to Neale at one a.m. on the morning of June 24 to say that the money should be paid, and requesting to be informed at what hour he would receive it. The reply was that the original agreement to pay in instalments, having been broken by the Japanese government, was now null and void, and that the whole must be delivered in the course of the day. This was accordingly done. At an early hour carts laden with boxes containing each a couple of thousand dollars began to arrive at the legation. All the Chinese shroffs (men employed by merchants and bankers in the Far East to examine coin to see whether it is genuine) were borrowed to do the shroffing and counting. The chancery was crowded with the intelligent Chinamen busily employed in clinking one coin against another and putting them up into parcels, to be replaced in the boxes and carried off on board the squadron. The process occupied three days. But already on the same day Neale had addressed a letter to the admiral relieving him of the unwelcome task of undertaking coercive operations.

The note, dated on the very day on which the indemnity was paid, in which Ogasawara Nagamichi had conveyed to Neale the orders of the *shōgun* to close the ports and expel all foreigners from the country, was the first on which I was called to exercise my capacity as a translator. Of course I had to get the help of my teacher to read it, but my previous practice in the epistolary style enabled me to understand the construction, and to give a closer version perhaps than either of the others which were prepared in the legation. This, to me supremely important, document ran as follows:

I communicate with you by a despatch. The orders of the *shōgun*, received from Kyoto, are to the effect that the ports are to be closed and the foreigners driven out, because the people of the country do not desire intercourse with foreign countries. The discussion of this has been entirely entrusted to me by His Majesty. I therefore send you this communication first, before holding a Conference as to the details.

Respectful and humble communication.

It is perhaps a little too literal. The opening phrase is simply equivalent to the "Monsieur le chargé d'affaires," and the sentence with which the note concludes is about the same thing as the "assurance of high consideration," which we have borrowed from the French. But the rest of it is accurate, and the allusion to the emperor which appears in the version made from the Dutch translation furnished by the Japanese (*vide* the Bluebook) had nothing to support it in the original text. I cannot forbear from quoting the reply of Neale, though as far as possible I intend in these "Reminiscences" not to rely on published sources of information. It ran thus:

Lieutenant-Neale to the Japanese minister for Foreign Affairs.

Yokohama, June 24, 1863.

The undersigned, Her Britannic Majesty's chargé d'affaires, has received, in common with his colleagues, and with extreme amazement, the extraordinary announcement which, under instructions from the *shōgun*, His Excellency has addressed to him.

Apart from the audacious nature of this announcement, which is unaccompanied by any explanations whatever, the Undersigned is bound to believe that both the Spiritual and temporal sovereigns of this country are totally ignorant of the disastrous consequences which must arise to Japan by their determinations thus conveyed through you to close the opened ports, and to remove therefrom the subjects of the treaty powers.

For himself, as Representative of Her Britannic Majesty, the Undersigned has to observe, in the first instance, that the Rulers of this country may perhaps still have it in their power to modify and soften the severe and irresistible measures which will, without the least doubt, be adopted by Great Britain most effectually to maintain and enforce its treaty obligations with this country, and, more than this, to place them on a far more satisfactory and solid footing than heretofore, by speedily making known and developing any rational and acceptable plans directed to this end, which may be at present concealed by His Majesty the *shōgun* or the emperor, or by both, to the great and imminent peril of Japan.

It is therefore the duty of the Undersigned solemnly to warn the Rulers of this country that when the decision of Her Majesty's government, consequent upon the receipt of Your Excellency's announcement, shall have in due course been taken, the development of all ulterior determinations now kept back will be of no avail.

The Undersigned has in the meantime to inform Your Excellency, with a view that you may bring the same to the knowledge of His Majesty the *shōgun*, who will doubtless make the same known to the emperor, that the indiscreet communication now made through Your Excellency is unparalleled in the history of all nations, civilized or uncivilized; that it is, in fact, a declaration of war by Japan itself against the whole of the treaty powers, and the consequences of which, if not at once arrested, it will have to expiate by the severest and most merited chastisement.

With Respect and Consideration.

Edward St. John Neale

With the exception of the lapse from the third person to the second, in the second, third and fourth paragraphs, this note is well constructed, and its periods nicely balanced. The language is perhaps rather stronger than more modern taste would approve, but with a powerful, almost overwhelming squadron of men-of-war at one's back, the temptation to express one's feelings with frankness is not easy to resist.

What the writer meant by "rational and acceptable means" directed to the end of placing the treaty obligations of Great Britain with Japan on a more "satisfactory and solid footing than heretofore" can only be conjectured. I think it is an allusion to the plan that had been mooted of our affording material assistance to the *shōgun* in suppressing the opposition of the *daimyō* of the west and south to the pro-foreign policy of the Japanese government, and perhaps to a formal agreement between the *shōgun* and the emperor that the latter should ratify the treaties. Certainly the successful execution of such a plan would have placed the *shōgun* firmly in the seat of his ancestors, and have forestalled the revolution of 1868 by which his successor was upset, but it would not have been effected without enormous bloodshed, and the Japanese people would have hated the ruler who had called in foreign aid to strengthen his position. He could then only have maintained himself there by the adoption of the severest measures of repression, and the nation would have been subjected to a terrible and lasting despotism. It is certainly a thing to rejoice at that the *shōgun*'s council had sufficient patriotism to reject such an offer. The Japanese were left to work out their own salvation, and when the revolution did at last break out, the loss of life and property was restricted within narrow limits, while the resulting benefits to the Japanese nation in the establishment of civilized and comparatively free institutions have been such as would have been for ever precluded had the suggestions of certain Europeans been listened to.

Bombardment of Kagoshima

Thus one portion of the instructions sent out from home had been carried into effect, and there now remained only the exaction of reparation from the lord of Satsuma. The demands to be made included, it will be remembered, the trial and execution in the presence of English officers of the murderers of Richardson, and the payment by the lord of an indemnity of £25,000 as compensation to Richardson's relatives and to the three other members of the party who had been attacked. Marshall and Clarke had recovered from their wounds, which in the case of the latter were serious enough, as he had received a dangerous sword cut in the shoulder, and Mrs Borradaile, who was not wounded, had returned to China. The *shōgun's* people were naturally desirous of having the settlement with Satsuma left in their hands, but I suppose Ogasawara, when pressed on the point by Neale, acknowledged that the government were impotent in the matter, and the British chargé d'affaires consequently assumed the responsibility of requesting the admiral to convey him and his staff to Kagoshima, in order to present the demands he had been instructed to formulate.

The admiral had at first been unwilling to send more than a couple of ships, but it was finally determined that the squadron should consist of HMS *Euryalus*, *Pearl*, *Perseus*, *Argus*, *Coquette*, *Racehorse*, and the gunboat *Havoc*. The whole staff of the legation, from Neale down to myself, embarked on board the various ships, Willis and myself being in the paddle-sloop *Argus*, Commander Lewis Moore. The weather on the voyage down was remarkably fine, and the squadron arrived at the mouth of the Bay of Kagoshima, where it anchored for the night, on the afternoon of August 11, 1863. Early on the following morning we proceeded up the bay, and came to an anchor off the town.

A letter had been prepared beforehand stating the demands, which had somehow or other been translated into Japanese by Siebold and his teacher. It was a difficult document, and I fancy the Japanese version did not read very well. A boat at once came off from the shore with two officers, to whom the letter was delivered. In the afternoon of the following day some other officials visited the flagship, and stated that it was quite impossible to say when the answer would be given. The name of the principal official who visited Neale on this occasion was Ijichi Shōji. I knew him very well afterwards in Edo. He and his retinue of forty men came on board, after having exchanged a parting cup of *sake* with their lord, with the full design of making a sudden onslaught upon the British officers, and killing at any rate the principal ones among them; they intended in this way to make themselves masters of the flagship. It was a bold conception, and might have been successful but for the precautions taken on our side. Only two or three were admitted into the admiral's cabin, while the marines kept a vigilant eye upon the retinue who remained on the quarter deck. While they were still on board another boat arrived, whether with reinforcements or orders to countermand the intended slaughter I do not know, but Ijichi, after communicating with the men who came in her, said he must return to the shore. In the evening a written reply was received, the bearer of which was told to return on the following morning to learn whether it was considered of a satisfactory character.

The letter on examination proved to contain a *fin de non recevoir*; it said that the murderers could not be found, blamed the *shōgun* for having made treaties without inserting a clause to prevent foreigners from impeding the passage of the lord along the highroads; spoke of delay until the criminals could be arrested, captured, and punished, after which the question of an indemnity could be discussed, and practically referred the British chargé d'affaires back to the Edo government. When the messenger arrived on the morning of the 14th, he was informed that the reply was considered unsatisfactory, and that no further communication would be held with the Japanese except under a flag of truce. The admiral then made a little trip up the bay to reconnoitre some foreign-built steamers lying at anchor and take some soundings at the head of the bay beyond. On his return in the afternoon the commanders of the various ships were summoned on board the flagship to receive their instructions from the admiral. There was no intention on our part of immediately attacking the batteries, but the admiral probably supposed that by adopting reprisals, that is taking possession of the steamers, he would induce the Satsuma men to give some more satisfactory reply than that already received.

In pursuance of this plan, Captain Borlase in the *Pearl*, with the *Coquette*, *Argus*, and *Racehorse*, proceeded to seize the steamers at dawn of the 15th. We were, of course, very excited, and busily engaged, as we approached, in estimating the probability of their offering resistance. But as the *Argus* was laid alongside the *Sir George Grey*, we saw the crew rapidly disappearing over the other side into shore boats with which they had already provided themselves. No attempt was made by us to take any prisoners, but two remained on board the *Sir George Grey*, who gave their names to me as Godai Tomoatsu and Matsugi Kōwan. On being transferred to the flagship they adopted the aliases of Otani and Kashiwa. The former was a remarkably handsome man, with a noble countenance, and was, I believe, the captain of the steamer. The profession of the second was that of a physician. He had been to Europe with the first Japanese embassy in 1862, and had in fact only just returned. Both of them were afterwards well known, the first as a rather speculative man of business who established indigo works at Osaka with capital borrowed from the emperor's government, the second was for a short time prefect of Yokohama in 1868, and afterwards minister for foreign affairs under the name of Terashima Munenori, and he still (in 1887) holds office at Tokyo.

We returned, with our prizes lashed alongside, to the anchorage under the island of Sakura-*jima*, whither the squadron had removed on the afternoon of the 12th in order to be out of range of the guns in the forts before the town, the *Euryalus* and *Pearl* lying about mid channel, between us and the forts. Here we awaited the development of events, which came sooner than was expected. The Japanese made no sign, and we could not divine their intentions from the slight glimpses obtainable of the movements on shore. But at noon the report of a gun was suddenly heard, and immediately all the batteries opened fire upon the squadron. Although it was raining and blowing like a typhoon, the admiral at once gave orders to engage, and made a signal to us and the *Racehorse* and the *Coquette* to burn the prizes. On this we all rushed on board our prize and began to plunder. I secured a Japanese matchlock and a conical black war hat (*jingasa*), but some of the officers found money, silver *ichibu* and gilt *nibu*. The sailors seized hold of everything portable, such as looking glasses, decanters, benches and even old pieces of matting. After about an hour of this disorder the steamer was scuttled and set on fire, and we went to take up our order in the line of battle.

Some time elapsed before we returned the fire of the Japanese, and it was said that the tardiness of the flagship in replying to the first shot of the Japanese (two hours) was due to the door of the ammunition magazine being obstructed by piles of boxes of dollars, the money paid for the indemnity being still on board. The *Perseus*, which was lying close under fort No. 9, had to slip her cable, and the anchor was months afterwards recovered by the Satsuma people and returned to us. Owing to this delay she had to take the last position in the line. It was a novel sensation to be exposed to cannon shot, and the boisterous weather did not add at all to one's equanimity. The whole line went a little way up the bay, and then curving round to the left returned along the northern shore at a distance of about four hundred yards, each vessel as she passed pouring her broadside into the successive forts. About three quarters of an hour after the engagement commenced we saw the flagship hauling off, and next the *Pearl* (which had rather lagged behind) swerved out of the line. The cause of this was the death of Captain Josling and Commander Wilmot of the *Euryalus* from a roundshot fired from fort No. 7. Unwittingly she had been steered between the fort and a target at which the Japanese gunners were in the habit of practising, and they had her range to a nicety. A ten inch shell exploded on her main-deck about the same time, killing seven men and wounding an officer, and altogether the gallant ship had got into a hot corner; under the fire of thirty-seven guns at once, from ten inch down to eighteen-pounders. The *Racehorse* having got ashore opposite fort No. 8, the *Coquette* and *Argus* went back to tow her off, which we succeeded in doing after about an hour's work. During this time she kept up a constant cannonade, and the gunners in the fort were unable to do her any mischief. But at one moment it was feared that she would have to be abandoned and set on fire.

I shall never forget the interest and excitement of the whole affair, from the bursting of the shells high in the air against the grey sky all round the flagship as she lay at anchor before we weighed, till we came into action ourselves and could see first the belching forth of flame from the middle of a puff of smoke, and then, strange to say, a round black thing coming straight at us. This black thing suddenly rose high into the air just as it seemed about to strike us, and passed overhead. The *Argus* was struck only three times, first in the starboard gangway, then by a shot which went right through the mainmast, but left it standing, and thirdly by a round shot near the water line which penetrated about three inches, and then fell off into the sea.

By five o'clock we were all safely anchored again under Josling point, except the *Havoc*, which went off to set fire to five Ryūkyū junks that were lying off the factories. Probably the latter were set on fire by sparks from the junks, but credit was taken for their wilful destruction. Under the impression that a large white building in the rear of the town was the lord's palace, every effort was made to destroy it, but it turned out afterwards to be a temple, and we learned that during the engagement the lord and his father had not been within range. Rockets were also fired with the object of burning the town, in which we were only too successful. The gale had increased to such a height that all efforts on the part of the townspeople to extinguish the flames must have been unavailing. It was an awful and magnificent sight, the sky all filled with a cloud of smoke lit up from below by the pointed masses of pale fire.

Our prize was still burning when we came back to our former anchorage, and as she had 140 tons of coal on board she made a good bonfire. At last she gave a lurch and went to the bottom. It was no doubt a great disappointment to the sailors, for the steamers alone were worth $300,000, and everyone would have had a good share of prize money if we had been able to carry them off. It was rumoured that the prizes were burnt at Neale's instance, who was very anxious, like the old warrior that he was, that every ship should go into action unhampered. It was also said that Captain Josling urged the admiral against his better judgment to fight that day, in spite of the adverse weather.

On Sunday morning, August 16, the bodies of Captain Josling, Commander

Wilmot and of the nine men who had lost their lives in the action were buried at sea. In the afternoon the squadron weighed anchor and proceeded down the bay at slow speed, shelling the batteries and town at long range until we left them too far behind. We anchored for the night at some distance from the town, and on the 17th proceeded to return to Yokohama. Most of us on board the *Argus,* and I believe the feeling was the same on board the other ships, came away bitterly discontented.

The Japanese guns still continued firing at us as we left, though all their shot fell short, and they might fairly claim that though we had dismounted some of their batteries and laid the town in ruins, they had forced us to retreat. Had we maintained the bombardment until every gun was silenced, and then landed, or even lain off the town for a few days, the opinion was that the demands would have been acceded to. Rumour said that Neale was very anxious that the admiral should land some men and carry off a few guns as trophies of victory, but that he declined to send a single man on shore. And men said that he was demoralized by the death of his flag-captain and commander, with whom he was talking on the bridge when the shot came that took off their heads. But none of this appears in the official correspondence. I believe the real explanation to be that differences had arisen between the diplomatist and the sailor, the former of whom interfered too much with the conduct of the operations. No doubt the etiquette was for him to remain silent after he had placed matters in the hands of the admiral, but this the impetuosity of his nature would not permit him to do. It is also possible that insufficiency of the supply of coals, provisions and ammunition may have been a factor in the determination that was come to.

The admiral in his report, which was published in the London *Gazette*, took credit for the destruction of the town, and John Bright very properly called attention to this unnecessary act of severity in the House of Commons; whereupon he wrote again, or Neale wrote, to explain that the conflagration was accidental. But that, I cannot think, was a correct representation of what took place, in face of the fact that the *Perseus* continued to fire rockets into the town after the engagement with the batteries was at an end, and it is also inconsistent with the air of satisfaction which marks the despatch reporting that £1,000,000 worth of property had been destroyed during the bombardment.

After the return of the squadron to Yokohama we settled down quietly again, and the trade went on pretty much as usual. There were some complaints that the *shōgun*'s council were laying hands on all the raw silk destined for exportation, with a view doubtless of forcing up the price and so recouping themselves out of foreign pockets for the indemnities they had been forced to pay to the British government. But on a strong protest being made to them by Neale, the embargo was removed. Rumours reached us of disturbances at Kyoto, where the retainers of Chōshū had been plotting to take possession of the palace, and seize the person of the emperor. Failing in their plans, they had been dismissed from their share in guarding the palace, and had departed to their native province, taking with them seven court nobles who had been mixed up in the plot. Amongst them were Sanjō Sanetomi, Higashikuze Michitomi and Sawa Nobuyoshi, who afterwards held high office in the government of the restoration.

The ill-success of the Chōshū clan, which had been one of the foremost in demanding the expulsion of the foreigners, was a turn of luck for the *shōgun*, and the result was the withdrawal of the circular of Ogasawara Nagamichi proposing the closing of the ports. Ogasawara himself was disgraced. Foreigners at Yokohama began to breathe freely again, and to renew their former excursions in the neighbouring country.

On October 14, a fresh outrage completely upset our tranquillity. A French officer of chasseurs named Henri Camus, while taking his afternoon's ride at a distance of not more than two or three miles from the settlement, and far from the high road, was attacked and murdered. His right arm was found at a little distance from his body, still clutching the bridle of his pony. There was a cut down one side of the face, one through the nose, a third across the chin, the right jugular vein was severed by a slash in the throat, and the vertebral column was completely divided. The left arm was hanging on by a piece of skin and the left side laid open to the heart. All the wounds were perfectly clean, thus showing what a terrible weapon the Japanese *katana* was in the hands of a skilful swordsman. No clue to the identity of the perpetrators of this horrible assassination was ever discovered, but it made a profound impression upon the foreign community, who after that were careful not to ride out unarmed or in parties of less than three or four. Not that we were able to place much confidence in our revolvers, for it was pretty certain that the samurai who was lying in wait to kill a foreigner would not carry out his purpose unless he could take his victim at a disadvantage, and cases of chance encounters with peaceably inclined Japanese were not known to have occurred. Excepting perhaps the Richardson affair, from the very first all these murders were premeditated, and the perpetrators took care to secure their own safety beforehand.

It was an agreeable surprise to us a month later, when there appeared at the legation two high officers of Satsuma, who undertook to pay the indemnity of £25,000 and gave an engagement to make diligent search for Richardson's murderers, who upon their arrest were to be punished with death in the presence of British officers, in accordance with the original demand. We may give Neale credit for knowing that there was no genuine intention on the part of Satsuma to carry out this promise, but on the other hand there was strong reason to suppose that Shimazu Hisamitsu himself had actually given the order to cut down the foreigners, and it could hardly be expected that the Satsuma men would ever consent to do punishment upon him. The actual doers of the deed were merely subordinate agents. We could not with justice have insisted on their lives being taken, and at the same time suffer the principal culprit to go scot-free. In order to succeed therefore in enforcing the whole of the demands made by Her Majesty's government, it would have been necessary to invade Satsuma with an over-whelming force and exterminate the greater part of the clan before we could get at their chief, who would never have fallen alive into our hands.

We had bombarded and destroyed the greater part of the forts and town, probably killed a good many persons who were innocent of Richardson's murder, and had thereby elevated what was in the beginning a crime against public order into a *casus belli*. There would indeed, it seems to me, have been no justification after that for taking more lives by way of expiation. The Satsuma envoys formally acknowledged that their countrymen had been in the wrong, and they paid the fine demanded by the British government. No one therefore can blame the British chargé d'affaires for having made peace on these terms. It should be mentioned that the Satsuma men borrowed the money from the *shōgun*'s treasury, and I have never heard that it was repaid.

75

Shimonoseki

Sir Rutherford Alcock returned from Europe early in March 1864, and Edward Neale took his departure. The members of the legation gave him a farewell dinner, at which he prognosticated about the future of those who had served under him. For me he prophesied a professorship of Japanese at an English university, but so far his words have not come true. The new chief was liked by everyone, and he was particularly gracious to myself, relieving me from all chancery work, so that I could devote the whole of my time to my Japanese studies. Willis and I occupied a wooden house in a back street between the native town and the foreign settlement, and there I worked industriously with my three teachers. Sir Rutherford had brought with him very ample powers, which he determined to make use of to chastise the Chōshū clan for its hostile attitude. We had, it might be said, conquered the goodwill of Satsuma, and a similar process applied to the other principal head of the anti-foreign party might well be expected to produce an equally wholesome effect.

In the summer of the previous year the Chōshū people, acting upon the orders which they had extorted from the emperor for the "expulsion of the barbarians," had fired upon an American merchant vessel, a Dutch corvette and a French despatch-boat as they passed through the straits of Shimonoseki. The corvette had returned the fire, and in the other two cases satisfaction of an incomplete kind had been obtained by the United States sloop *Wyoming* and the French squadron under Admiral Jaurès respectively. The batteries had been destroyed, but as soon as the foreign men-of-war quitted the scene, the Chōshū men set to work to rebuild the forts, to construct others, and to mount all the guns they could bring together. So the hornet's nest was after no long interval in good repair again, and more formidable for attack and defence than before. That no foreign vessels could take their way through the straits of Shimonoseki, which they had been in the habit of passing from time to time after touching at Nagasaki in order to make a pleasant and easy passage to Yokohama, instead of encountering the stormy Cape Satano, was felt to involve a diminution of Western prestige. Nothing but the complete subjugation of this warlike clan, and the permanent destruction of its means of offence, would suffice to convince the Japanese nation that we were determined to enforce the treaties, and to carry on our trade without molestation from anybody, irrespective of internal dissensions.

Sir Rutherford Alcock therefore lost no time in diligently setting to work in order to bring about a coalition with the representatives of France, Holland and the United States. In this he succeeded. The *shōgun*'s government were warned that if they did not within twenty days give a satisfactory undertaking to reopen the straits, the foreign squadrons would be despatched to bring the lord of Chōshū to reason. By a curious coincidence there had just returned to Japan two out of a band of five young samurai of Chōshū, who the year before had been smuggled away to England to see the world, and learn something of the resources of foreign powers. Their names were Itō Hirobumi and Inoue Bunda. The other three who remained in England while their companions, armed with the new knowledge, set forth on their journey to warn their fellow clansmen that it was no use trying to run their heads against a brick wall, were Endo Kinsuke, Inoue Masaru and Yamao Yōzo. They made themselves and the object of their return known to Sir Rutherford, who promptly seized the opportunity thus offered of entering into direct communication with the *daimyō* of Chōshū, and while delivering a sort of ultimatum, of affording him the chance of abandoning his hostile attitude for one more in accordance with the treaties. He obtained the consent of his colleagues to the despatch of two men-of-war to the neighbourhood of Shimonoseki in order to land the two young men at a convenient spot, and delivered to them a long memorandum for presentation to their lord.

A French officer (Commandant Layrle) and a Dutch naval officer, besides Major Wray, R.E., were sent at the same time to gain what information

77

might be obtainable as to the present condition of the batteries, and to my great joy I was lent as interpreter, along with my colleague, James Joseph Enslie. On the 21st July we left in the corvette *Barrosa*, Captain Dowell, and the gun vessel *Cormorant*, Commander Buckle, and passing up the Bungo channel, anchored off Himeshima Island after dark on the 26th. We ran ashore, but managed to get off again, smashing the jib-boom of the *Cormorant* as we did so. Early on the following morning we landed our two Japanese friends Itō and Inoue (who at that time went by the name of Shiji), after promising to call for them on August 7 at the island of Kasato, off the coast of Suō. On the way down I had talked a good deal with them, and between us, with the aid of my teacher, Nakazawa Kensaku (a retainer of the Ogasawara, who had to seek his livelihood in consequence of his master's disgrace), we had managed to put Sir Rutherford's memorandum into Japanese. They were to cross over in an open boat and land at Tonomi in Suō. At eight o'clock we saw them leave the shore. In Nakazawa's opinion the chances were six or seven out of ten that their heads would be cut off, and that we should never see them again.

We landed later on in the day at Himeshima and found the people very friendly. They sold to us a plentiful supply of fish, but there were no vegetables, beef or chickens to be had. Cattle were pretty plentiful and fat, but the people looked poor and half starved. The population was about 2000. The island was not fertile. I tried to buy some beef, but the pretext that it was wanted as medicine for sick sailors (a Japanese idea) was useless. Half the population was engaged in salt-burning; 1/2d and 1d banknotes were current, and very little coin was to be seen. At one place we gave a man an *ichibu*, worth say 10d. He pretended to turn it over and look at it carefully, and then said "these are very rare things here."

Next day we went round to the north side of the island and anchored there. Here we again landed to visit the salt pans, and met with the same friendly reception as before.

On July 29, we crossed in one of the ship's boats to Imi in Iyo, where the villagers refused to have anything to do with us, but at Takedatsu, a mile or two further west, they made no difficulties, and we were able to lay in a supply of pumpkins and brinjalls.

On August 1, we weighed anchor before sunrise, and stood away towards the straits. The *Barrosa* anchored about ten miles on this side of Shimonoseki, and we went on in the *Cormorant*, steaming towards the coast of Buzen and then up to Isaki Point. When halfway across the mouth of the straits we saw signal guns fired all along the north coast from Chōfu to Saho. After going nearly up to Dannorua, keeping carefully out of the range of the batteries, and cruising backwards and forwards for a while, in order that the situation of the batteries and the number of guns might be accurately noted, we finally returned to Himeshima. We used to go on shore there for a walk every day, and found the people inquisitive but friendly. On one occasion as we were returning through the village to our boats, we met a party of four samurai, who appeared to form part of a detachment sent over from Kitsuki in Buzen to protect the island against a possible attack from us. I spoke civilly to them, and asked where they had come from, but they answered in a surly manner, "from a distance." They looked as villainous a set as one could wish to see, and remained at the water's edge watching our movements until we got on board.

On August 6, we made another trip to Shimonoseki in the *Cormorant* to reconnoitre, going in a little further than before in the direction of Dannorua. On this occasion, in addition to the signal guns, the batteries fired a round shot and a shell as a warning, which fell in the sea about a mile ahead. When we got back to the *Barrosa* at half-past ten in the evening we found Itō and Shiji had already returned. After dinner we had a long talk, and received the lord's answer. They brought with them a single retainer, but said they had been accompanied down to the coast by a guard of soldiers given them by their lord. They commenced the delivery of the communication with which they were charged by saying that they had found him at Yamaguchi, and had handed over the letters of the four foreign representatives to him in person. He had then consulted with his chief retainers and come to the following conclusion: that he entirely acknowledged the truth of what was stated in the letters, and was conscious of his own inability to cope with the forces of Western nations. But he was acting under orders which he had received, once from the *shōgun*, and oftener from the emperor, and not on his own responsibility, and it was out of his power to reply to the foreign representatives without first receiving permission. It was his intention, therefore, to proceed to Kyoto in order to impress his own views on the emperor, which he calculated would take about three months. He begged therefore that the powers would postpone operations for that period.

They brought no written documents with them, not even a letter to certify that they were the accredited agents of their lord, but told us they could procure one if the vessels were delayed for two or three days. They were informed that a mere verbal reply such as they had brought could not be expected to satisfy the foreign representatives. They then inquired whether they should send a written reply to Yokohama with copies of the orders of the *shōgun* and emperor, but Captain Dowell replied that their lord might do as he liked about that. His instructions did not go so far as to enable him to express an opinion.

In private conversation they afterwards told me that their lord had originally been favourable to foreigners, but had gone too far now in the opposite direction to be able to retract, and they did not believe that the matters at issue could be settled without fighting. They suggested that it would be a good measure for the foreign representatives to throw over the *shōgun*, and proceeding to Osaka, demand an interview with the emperor's ministers in order to conclude a direct treaty with him. They spoke with great bitterness of the *shōgun*'s dynasty, accused them of keeping all the trade, both foreign and native, in their own hands, by taking possession of every place where trade was likely to develope, such as Nagasaki and Niigata, and they said these feelings were shared by most of the people. The way in which they delivered their message made me suspect that it was couched in far more uncompromising terms than those which they made use of in communicating it.

This was the first occasion on which I had been in full and frank communication with men belonging to the anti-*shōgun* party. Their proposal that we should at once try to enter into negotiations with the emperor was a bold one, and calculated, if it had been adopted, rather to injure than help their cause. The time was not yet ripe, for the *shōgun*'s authority, though much weakened, was still admitted and obeyed by a large majority of the *daimyō*. His troops had not as yet exhibited their inferiority in arms, and as a matter of fact almost at this very moment the forces of the lord of Chōshū were suffering an overwhelming defeat in their attack upon Kyoto, which was defended in the *shōgun*'s interest by Aizu and Satsuma. By the time we returned to Yokohama, and before the idea could have been even considered by the foreign representatives, Chōshū's principal men were either fugitives or dead, and the *shōgun* was temporarily master of the field.

Itō and his companion left again during the night. I could not help feeling sorry for their failure to impress on their lord the warning which they had come all the way from Europe to impart. But there was no help for it. We weighed anchor early on the following morning and arrived at Yokohama on August 10.

As soon as it became known that Chōshū would not give way preparations were actively made for carrying out the resolutions previously agreed upon by the representatives of the four powers. They held a conference with the ministers of the *shōgun*, in order to impress on them that the moment had now come when the naval forces must be charged with the duty of opening the straits, but before the meeting had separated there came like a thunderbolt on their deliberations an announcement of the return from Europe of a mission that had been despatched in the month of January to treat with Great Britain and France. They brought with them a convention concluded with the latter power which provided for an indemnity in respect of the attack on the French gunboat, for the removal by the *shōgun*'s government within three months of the impediments to the navigation of the straits of Shimonoseki, for a modification of the import tariff in favour of French manufactures, and for the payment of an indemnity of $35,000 to the relatives of Lieutenant Camus.

This news seemed to Sir Rutherford Alcock to threaten an utter collapse of his plans, for if the convention were ratified, the French at least would be compelled to withdraw from the coalition. But it was of course clear to those on the spot that the second article could not be possibly carried out by the *shōgun*'s government, and never could have been seriously intended, at least on the Japanese side. Pressure was therefore put on the council to make them declare that they would not ratify the convention, and a note from them to this effect reached the foreign representatives on the 25th August. On the same day they signed a memorandum declaring the necessity of a resort to force, which was then communicated to the naval commanders-in-chief, and four days later the allied squadrons put to sea to carry into execution the plans decided on before the return of the envoys had for a moment seemed to threaten the disruption of the diplomatic union so strenuously worked for by our chief. It was an immense responsibility that he had assumed. There was no telegraph in those days to any point nearer than Ceylon, but a despatch dated July 26 was already on its way to him positively prohibiting the adoption of military measures in the interior of Japan, and limiting naval operations against the Japanese government or lords to defensive measures for the protection of the life and property of British subjects. By the time it reached his hands, his schemes had already been accomplished with the happiest possible results, and he was able to console himself with the conviction that he had done the right thing, even though he might be censured for acting contrary to the wishes of Lord John Russell, and have incurred the penalty of a recall from his post.

The United States steamer *Monitor* had been fired at as she lay at anchor in a bay on the north coast of Nagato on July 11. This afforded fresh justification of the action adopted by the foreign representatives.

Naval Operations

To my great satisfaction I was appointed interpreter to Admiral Küper, and, packing up a few necessaries, embarked on board the *Euryalus*. I was messed in the ward room, and as there was no cabin available, slept on a sofa. The officers were a very pleasant set of fellows. Among them I especially remember Tracey and Maclear, both of them now post-captains. The former is a very distinguished officer, but what particularly attracted me towards him was his love of books, and his wide knowledge of modern languages, acquired by dint of sheer perseverance amid all the noisy distractions of life on board ship.

The *Coquette* was sent off to Nagasaki to bring up Sir Rutherford's stepson, Fred. Lowder, to be additional interpreter. The only other civilian on board the flagship was Felix Beato, the well-known photographer, who, making his first start in life with a camera in the Crimean War, had also accompanied the Anglo-French expedition to North China in 1859, and had subsequently settled in Japan, where his social qualities had gained him many friends. My teacher Nakazawa had been secretly taken away from me by the *shōgun*'s government as a punishment for having accompanied me on the visit to Himeshima. It only years afterwards that I was made acquainted with the treachery of the foreigner who had denounced him to the commissioners for foreign affairs. But Willis lent me his Japanese instructor and pupil in medicine, Hayashi Bokuan, and I was able to make shift with this faithful man, though as a scholar he was greatly inferior to Nakazawa.

The English squadron consisted of the flagship *Euryalus*, 35, commanded by Captain Alexander; the corvettes *Tartar*, 21, Captain Hayes; *Barrosa*, 21,

Captain W. M. Dowell; the two-decker *Conqueror*, 48, Captain Luard; the paddle-sloop *Leopard*, 18, Captain Leckie; the paddle-sloop *Argus*, 6, Commander Moresby; the *Coquette*, 14, Commander Roe; and gunboat *Bouncer*, 2, Lieutenant Holder. The French frigate *Sémiramis*, 35, bearing the broad pennon of Admiral Jaurès, and the American chartered steamer *Takiang*, carrying a Parrot gun and its crew from the United States corvette *Jamestown*, under the command of Lieutenant Pearson, accompanied us. The French corvette *Dupleix*, 10, and despatch boat *Tancrède*, 4, with the Dutch corvettes *Metalen Kruis*, 16, Captain de Man; *Djambi*, 16, Captain van Rees; *Amsterdam*, 8; and *Medusa*, 16, Captain de Casembroot, left the bay of Kanagawa on the 28th August, and the remainder of the ships on the following day.

We had calm weather and a smooth sea on the way down, sighting the south-west corner of Shikoku on the 1st September. About 5 p.m. we fell in with the *Perseus*, 17, Commander Kingston, towing a collier, and bringing the admiral's mail. The *Perseus* had met Commander Buckle in the *Cormorant* on his way to Shanghai for the mail, who, having started from Yokohama about the time of the return of the Japanese embassy, reported that the expedition was indefinitely postponed. She had therefore cast off the collier and steamed away at full speed for Yokohama, but falling a little later in with the *Coquette* on her way to Nagasaki, learned a very different tale, and turning round, had picked up the collier again and brought her on. On the following day we reached Himeshima and anchored a little after noon. Here we found the *Djambi* and *Metalen Kruis*. Shortly afterwards the *Medusa* and the three French ships appeared, and by midnight every ship of the allied squadron had arrived. We had still to wait for the *Coquette*, and either the *Cormorant* or *Osprey*.

In the afternoon the admiral, Captain Alexander, with other officers, went ashore for a walk, and I acted as their guide. The poor village mayor made his appearance in a great state of alarm. He was indeed in an uncomfortable position, uncertain of the disposition of the strangers, and sure of punishment from his own countrymen if he manifested too great friendliness towards us. He promised to send us off some fish, "quite privately," but was positive that he could sell no bullocks. He had despatched a messenger to Kitsuki to inquire whether the islanders might hold intercourse with the squadron and furnish us with what supplies they had.

During the night we took in 150 tons of coal, and the 3rd of September was spent by the rest of our squadron in replenishing their bunkers. In the afternoon I went ashore to the mayor's house, where I found three of the garrison from Kitsuki. They were very reticent, not to say sulky, and only one of them, who was evidently afraid of his companions, could be induced to open his mouth. It was a grand sight to see the master of the collier and his wife parading along the beach with a couple of dirty little village urchins running ahead of them. The common people were friendly enough, except when the eyes of the two-sworded men were upon them.

On September 4, 1864, we weighed anchor at nine o'clock and proceeded towards the straits of Shimonoseki, the eight British ships in the centre, with *Euryalus* leading, the French squadron and the *Takiang* in a line on the left, and the four Dutch vessels on the right. It was a beautiful show as the allied squadrons steamed calmly across the unruffled surface of this inland sea, which lay before us like a glassy mirror in its framework of blue hills. Towards half past three we anchored at a distance of about two miles from the mouth of the straits, and prepared for action. Everything was in readiness by the time we had got halfway through our dinner, but to the disappointment of the more eager spirits, we remained where we were without firing a shot. Everyone was naturally anxious that no new complication should arise to delay the longed-for encounter with the enemy. Early on the following morning two Chōshū men, common soldiers, came on board to inquire why all these men-of-war had come to the straits, but the admiral refused to hold any parley with men of evidently inferior rank, and they were told to return on shore at once. One of them told me very innocently that if we intended to go through he must go on shore to make preparations for us, and when I asked what preparation, he said "for fighting."

I was then sent in a boat to overhaul a couple of junks that had meanwhile been stopped as they were entering the straits. One was the *Ise-maru*, of Matsuyama in Iyo, going to load coals at Hirado, the other belonged to Kurume in Chikugo, and was returning from Osaka with a miscellaneous cargo. As they did not belong to the enemy we let them go.

About two p.m. the two men who had previously visited the ship came on board again to announce the arrival of a *bugyō* or commissioner of some sort, accompanied by Inoue Bunda (he had now laid aside his alias of Shiji). But signals had already been made to the captains to take up the positions allotted to them for shelling the batteries, and when my friend Inoue and his companion reached the flagship the only answer they received to their request that hostilities might be deferred with a view to negotiation was that the time for a peaceable arrangement had passed.

We went into action at ten minutes past four. The *Barrosa*, *Tartar*, *Djambi*, *Metalen Kruis*, *Leopard*, and *Dupleix* moved along the southern coast of the funnel-shaped entrance to the strait, and took up their station in front of Dannorua, as shown in the annexed plan, while a light squadron consisting of the *Perseus*, *Medusa*, *Tancrède*, *Coquette*, and *Bouncer* passed along the northern shore, the *Amsterdam* and *Argus* being held in reserve. The *Euryalus*, *Sémiramis*, *Conqueror*, and *Takiang* anchored out of range of the enemy's batteries, at a distance of about 2500 yards from the central cluster at Maedamura,[1] and consequently near enough to reach them with our 110-pounder breech-loading Armstrong gun on the forecastle.

The first shot was fired from the *Euryalus*, and the whole of the Dannorua squadron then followed her example. The light squadron speedily silenced the three-gun battery on Kushi Saki Point, but not before it had managed to pitch a shot pretty near the British flagship. Then the *Sémiramis*, which had been occupied in getting springs on her cable, opened fire from her quarter-deck guns with terrible effect, scarcely a shot falling short. The *Takiang* did her best with her single gun, and the *Conqueror* fired three shells, one of which burst beautifully among the great cluster of batteries. The *Euryalus* fired only sixteen rounds between ten past four and ten past five p.m. from her 110-pounder, which was pretty good work, considering that the vent piece got jammed once and a considerable time was lost in digging it out with handspikes. Another time the vent piece was blown up into the fore-top owing to its not having been screwed in tightly enough. The six vessels anchored south were soon engaged in a sharp conflict with the batteries opposite, while the light squadron, having silenced the batteries on the north, came to their aid, enfilading the 4, 7, and 9-gun batteries. The furthest shot fired from the *Euryalus* was at 4800 yards, and it went plump into a battery.

1 Today's Yukuhashi city, Fukuoka.

86

By ten past five, the principal batteries had been silenced, and a signal was made to discontinue firing. A fire now burst out among the buildings in the Maedamura batteries and a magazine exploded, making the third blow-up during the afternoon. We continued firing a shot now and then up to six o'clock. The quarter-deck 40-pounder Armstrongs were fired once only, as their range proved to be too short, and none of the smooth-bore guns on the main deck were brought into action, to the great disappointment of the bluejackets, who had probably not forgotten the slaughter made amongst their comrades at Kagoshima, and burned to avenge it. It must be admitted that the Japanese fought well and with great persistence, for I attach no value to the story that was told that the gunners were only allowed to fire once, and were then replaced by fresh men. At first many of our shot fell short, but when the range was found, they struck the batteries every moment, as we could see by the clouds of dust that were knocked up. After the signal to discontinue firing had been made, Kingston of the *Perseus* and De Casembroot of the *Medusa* landed and spiked fourteen guns in the Maedamura batteries. At the small battery on the cape of Kushi-*saki* two out of the three guns had been dismounted by our fire. The entire casualties on our side this first day were six men wounded in the *Tartar*, which bore the brunt of the fire.

Early on the following morning one of the Maedamura batteries reopened fire on the squadron anchored off Dannorua, but was replied to with such effect that it was speedily silenced, and the barrack behind was set on fire. The *Dupleix* lost two killed and two wounded, while the first lieutenant of the *Tartar* was struck by a round shot on the posteriors and severely wounded. He recovered, contrary to the expectations of the surgeons. I slept through the noise, but was woke by somebody with a message that I had to land with Captain Alexander, who was to command the small-arms party of the *Euryalus*, 200 strong. From the *Conqueror* there landed the battalion of 450 marines under Colonel Suther, besides her own complement of 100, and some bluejackets, small detachments of marines being added from the other ships of our squadron. The French landed 350, and the Dutch 200. Another calculation showed that 1900 men were put ashore, of whom we furnished 1400.

We rowed straight for the nearest land, followed by a string of cutters and pinnaces so full of men that there was only just room to work the oars, and got on shore at nine o'clock exactly. The task assigned to Captain Alexander's party was to scale a bluff immediately to the east of the Maedamura batteries, and take a one-gun battery. It was a stiff pull up the steep grassy hill, but up went the bluejackets pell-mell, as if they were out on a picnic, every man for himself. On climbing over the earthwork we found that the gun had been either carried off or concealed. There were a score or so of the enemy on the platform, who retreated as soon as the first of our people showed his nose above the parapet, but they kept up a dropping fire from the other side of the hill. Here one of our men received a bullet wound in the leg, and a second was accidentally shot through the body by the sailor immediately behind him.

Passing through the battery, we clambered up the hill behind, through a tangled brake of ferns and creepers. The heat was intense. It was a difficult job to keep one's footing on the narrow path cut through the slippery grass. Our bluejackets were very eager to get at the enemy, but not a single one was to be seen. Descending the other side of the hill, we at last found ourselves in a sort of covered way, which ran along the side of a narrow valley. It was reported that the enemy were posted further up the valley in considerable numbers, but instead of pursuing them we turned to the left along the covered way, which brought us down past a magazine into the central battery of the principal group. It turned out afterwards to be a fortunate counter-march, for if we had proceeded in the other direction we should have stumbled on a stockade defended by three field guns, which would have played "Old Harry" with our small force.

The first battery we entered was already in the possession of the French landing party and some of our marines, who, having disembarked below the bluff, had marched along the beach, meeting with no opposition. This work was of earth, having a parapet about twenty feet wide, armed along the edge with a *chevaux-de-frise* of pointed bamboo stakes. In battery No. 7 the guns were mounted *en barbette*, on carriages with enormous wheels, and worked on pivots. They were of bronze, very long, and threw a 32-pound shot, though marked as 24's. They bore a Japanese date corresponding to 1854, and had evidently been cast in Edo. Besides these, there was a short 32-pounder, and on the other side of a traverse, containing a small magazine, was a single 10-inch gun, also of bronze. We upset them all, broke up the carriages, threw the shot and shell into the sea, burned the powder, and even dragged a couple of guns down on to the beach. This occupied us till three or four o'clock in the afternoon. During this time our men were perpetually firing musketry at the enemy on the hill, who every now and then showed themselves to give us a shot or two. In the 9-gun battery were a couple of heavy 11-inch bronze guns.

Afterwards we proceeded to the next battery, which was almost *à fleur d'eau*. It was divided into two by a traverse containing a magazine, on one side of which were one 10-inch howitzer, two 32-pounders, and one 24-pounder; on the other side were the same number, with the addition of a single 24-pounder. These likewise were overturned, and the carriages and ammunition disposed of as before.

The Japanese field battery up the valley, which had been advanced some little way from the stockade along a path leading towards Maedamura, Dannoura and Shimonoseki annoyed us considerably during this operation, firing shells over us and at long ranges into the sea, while their musketeers kept up a pretty constant fire, though no one was touched on our side. Part of our men were told off to keep them in check, but our aim was not much better than that of the enemy. The great thing in war, until you come to close quarters, seems to be to make as much noise as you can to put your foes in a funk, or in other words to demoralize them. You can't do much harm, and it was laughable to see how many of our men ducked to avoid the shot, and I confess I followed their example until reason came to my aid.

The *Medusa* moved up and threw a few shells in among them, while the *Perseus*, *Amsterdam*, and *Argus* fired over the hill from their station before Dannorua. This quieted the zeal of our warrior foes for a while, and we returned to the first battery we had dismantled, for the men to have their dinners. Crowdy of the Engineers, McBean the assistant-surgeon of the flagship and I divided a loaf of bread and a tin of sardines, which we opened with Crowdy's sword. There were no knives or forks handy, but that did not hinder us from satisfying our well-earned appetite as we sat on the steps of the magazine in the traverse. After dinner we helped the French to overturn the guns in their battery, which were four in number, very long

32-pounders, mounted on field carriages. The enemy still continued annoying us from their position up the valley, while some of our men kept up a fitful musketry fire in reply, without much damage on either side.

The afternoon being already far advanced, the signal to re-embark was made from the *Euryalus*, and the French and Dutch detachments, some of the marine detachment, and the *Conqueror's* small-arms men, were already in their boats, when about six o'clock we saw Colonel Suther's battalion of marines returning from the Maedamura 15-gun battery through a heavy fire from the Japanese. The Japanese on perceiving them threw a round shot in among them, but without doing any harm. Our men replied, and for fifteen minutes there was nothing but ping, ping, ping on both sides. At last the Colonel came up to Captain Alexander and said: "Where are these men who are annoying us. I've enough men to take any battery." "All right," replied Alexander, "I'll take the left side of the valley and you the right." So the marines clambered up into the French battery (the eastern-most one) and proceeded up the covered way, while the *Conqueror's* men disembarked again, and the advance commenced. Beato and I stuck close to Alexander, and followed the bluejackets across the paddyfields by the narrow "bunds," and then along the path on the western side of the valley. How the bluejackets shouted and cheered, each man running on by himself, now stopping to take aim at an enemy from behind one of the pine trees that lined the edge of the road, and then on again. There was no order or discipline. Some of them wasted their ammunition on imaginary foes on the hillsides. I passed several wounded men as I went up, some seriously hurt, and the corpse of a sailor who had been killed by an arrow.

At last we reached the battery, whence the gunners had been driven by our fire, dismounted the guns and threw them into the paddyfield close by, after destroying the carriages. Here Alexander was wounded by a ball which passed through the ankle-joint of his right foot, and he had to be carried to the rear on a stretcher. From this point the valley contracted rapidly, while immediately in front of us was a stockaded barrack into which most of the Japanese retreated, turning back repeatedly to fire. But I saw others in black armour and white surcoats retreating with great rapidity along the road to the left. Lieutenant Edwards and Crowdy of the Engineers were ahead with a middy named Boyes, who carried the colours most gallantly; he afterwards received the Victoria Cross for conduct very plucky in one so young. When I got up to the front of the stockade there were three or four dead Japanese lying about and one of our men, shot through the heart. He presented a most ghastly sight as he lay there, getting visibly bluer and bluer, without any exterior signs of blood to show how he had come by his death. Having directed some of the men to put his corpse into a huge oblong basket which was on the ground close by and carry him off, I passed on into the stockade whence the Japanese had already fled. In retiring they had set fire to some houses close to the magazine, with the amiable intention of blowing us up, but the train was discovered and the explosion prevented.

After ranging over the whole place and removing whatever was worth carrying off as trophies, such as armour, bows and arrows, spears and swords, and bayonets bearing a foreign maker's name, we set fire to the buildings and retired in good order. The loss of the enemy was about twenty killed, but they had carried off all their wounded. We had five killed and thirteen or fourteen wounded, two mortally.

What the marine battalion was doing all this time I cannot say, for the excitement about what was going on ahead left me no disposition to look elsewhere, but I rather think that having marched along the covered way with great steadiness they managed to arrive just as the more active and impetuous "jacks" had finished the business. And no blame to them either for going about their work in a business-like manner. If we had met with a check in our heedless, headlong advance, the marines would have saved us from destruction. It was lucky for us that the skirmish terminated as it did, for our loss in small-arms' men would have been much greater if the Japanese had been strong enough to stand to their guns, or had posted marksmen on the hills to take us in flank as we hurried up the valley. They had the advantage in position, besides possessing seven small field pieces, while on the other hand we had at least a couple of hundred men in excess of their number, which it was supposed was 600. But I fancy I remember having heard since from a Chōshū man who was present that their force was only one half of that. The bluejackets bore the brunt of the business, as they had to cross the line of fire and to advance along the outer edge of the horn-shaped valley, which curved away to the east out of sight of the shipping. The Japanese could not stand our advance, the sharp musketry fire threw them into disorder, and they had to run for it. In only one case was an attempt made to come to close quarters. One fellow had concealed himself behind a door with uplifted sword in both hands, ready to cut down a man just about to enter. But contrary to his expectation, his intended victim gave him a prod in the belly which laid him on his back and spoilt his little game. Our French companions in arms were disgusted at not having been present at the affair, and turned up their noses at it, as *pas grand chose après tout*. It was the fortune of war, and we commiserated them sincerely.

The marines who in the first instance marched on Maedamura had one man killed and two wounded. They dismantled fifteen guns in the battery there. During the day a boat belonging to one of the Dutch men-of-war, with two men in her, got loose and drifted down with the tide towards the town. They were immediately shot, though quite defenceless. Fred Lowder and his brother George, who had come up with him from Nagasaki "to see the fun," had a narrow escape as they were paddling about in a Japanese boat, which became unmanageable and was drifting off in the same direction. They jumped into the water and swam ashore, or they would probably have encountered the same fate.

The eastern end of the town of Shimonoseki (more properly speaking, I believe, Akamagaseki) was set on fire, but the number of houses burnt was extremely small. It was alleged that this was done by the French because some Japanese soldiers had fired thence on their men, but I do not know whether this is a fact. The *Perseus* ran ashore opposite the nearest batteries, and as the tide ebbed her bow was high out of the water, nor did she get off again until the following day.

I found myself on board again at half-past seven o'clock, very dirty, very tired, very hungry and very thirsty.

On September 7, 1864, working parties of bluejackets landed under the protection of some marines to take possession of the guns, ten of which they got into the boats. Others went up to the stockade and found some field pieces, which they destroyed, hove down wells, or brought away. We got together sixty, all but one of bronze, with two mortars and six cohorns. We blew up all the powder and threw the shot and shell into the sea. There was not a single hostile Japanese to be seen. The *Perseus* had to be lightened by discharging all her guns and coals, and so managed to get afloat by noon.

Our list of casualties during the two days' operation was eight killed and thirty wounded, of whom one or two were not expected to live. We landed at half-past one near Dannorua in the Bay of Beppu to bury our dead, the French having already buried two in the forenoon. In digging the graves our men found particles of a glittering substance which was at first taken to be gold dust, but turned out to be mica.

I met a party of two-sworded Ogasawara men, who asked how many dead we had, and how we had fared on the previous day. On learning what a complete thrashing we had given the enemy at the stockade, they expressed great satisfaction, and recounted how the Chōshū people had crossed over the straits in the previous year, cut down their crops, carried off their live stock, and driven the peasants away, after which they held possession of Dannorua for some time, until public opinion and the necessity of providing for the defence of Chōshū's own territories had compelled them to withdraw. The Ogasawara men feared that when Chōshū came to find out that communication had taken place between us and the Buzen folk, he would visit them again after the withdrawal of the squadron, but I boldly assured them that they need not alarm themselves, as we intended to destroy the batteries, and deprive Chōshū of his territory. For I knew that part of the plan entertained by Sir Rutherford and his colleagues was the seizure of a sufficient piece of territory near Shimonoseki as a material guarantee for the payment of an adequate indemnity, and to hold it until it could be conveniently handed over to the *shōgun*'s government.

Sir Rutherford contemplated nothing less than the complete subjugation of the Chōshū clan, and he had enjoined upon the admiral the necessity of attacking Hagi, which was supposed to be the stronghold of the *daimyō*. The admiral, however, who was a prudent commander, and by no means disposed to take orders from the civil representatives of Her Majesty further than he was obliged, came to the conclusion that the resources at his disposal did not permit of a permanent occupation of any portion of Chōshū's territory, and considered that as soon as the forts were destroyed and the straits opened, his task was accomplished. Fear had made the Ogasawara samurai wondrously polite. The villagers were also friendly enough, and I made them laugh good-humouredly with some commonplace jokes, but did not succeed in inducing them to sell any supplies. The officials, after hunting through the village, as they assured us, produced eight or ten eggs, which they said was all they could find. Our bluejackets brought me some papers which they had picked up in the stockade, and which appeared to contain proof of plots by Chōshū against the emperor, also quantities of pills made, or said to be made, from bear's gall, and banknotes for small sums, such as were commonly used in the territories of all the *daimyō*. I believe that silver coin was current at that time in the dominions of the *shōgun* alone.

On the 8th, fatigue parties landed again to bring off more guns; we got all but two from the group of batteries, which made nineteen, besides fifteen from Maedamura and an equal number from the batteries on Hikushima, the large island in the western entrance of the straits. I went on shore to Maedamura, and found a well-built battery, with a parapet twenty feet wide cased with stone towards the sea, and divided into four sections by traverses, between which the guns were planted in unequal numbers. In the rear stood a stone-built magazine, the roof of which had been smashed by a round shot that went right through it. The powder magazine, also of stone, which stood on one side of the valley behind, had been blown up the previous day. Further up was a stockaded barrack, which the French had burned. I went towards the advanced guard near the town, but as the enemy began to show themselves and fire at us, I made a prudent retreat.

Peace with Chōshū

Returning to the ship at noon, I found there my acquaintance Itō Hirobumi, who had come to say that Chōshū desired peace, and that a *karō* or hereditary councillor, provided with full powers, was coming off to treat. A boat was accordingly despatched to meet the great man, who shortly afterwards stood on the quarter-deck of the flagship. He was dressed in a robe called the *daimon*, which was covered with large light blue crests (the paulownia leaf and flower) on a yellow ground, and wore on his head a black silk cap, which he took off on passing the gangway. His queue was then seen to be loose, hanging over the back of his head like a tassel, and his white silk underclothing was a marvel of purity. His two companions, who bore a rank next only to his own, wore their hair in the same fashion, but were without mantles. They were conducted into the cabin, and presented to the admirals, the Abbé Prudence Séraphin Barthélemy Girard, Lowder and myself acting as interpreters.

They began by stating that the lord of Chōshū acknowledged his defeat, and desired to make peace with a view to the establishment of friendly relations. The admiral thereupon asked to see their credentials, and finding they had none, intimated that he would give them forty-eight hours to provide themselves with a letter from their *daimyō*. They were told that the letter must contain the substance of what they had said, acknowledging that he had committed a grievous wrong in firing upon foreign ships, and begging for peace, that it must be signed with his own hand and sealed with his seal, and that a copy must be addressed to each of the four senior naval officers in command.

The conditions imposed were—first, that we should continue to remove the guns and destroy the forts; second, that we would discontinue hostilities, they on their side doing the same, but that if they fired another shot we should burn everything we could lay our hands on in Chōshū's territories; third, they must deliver up intact the Dutch sailors and boat which had fallen into their hands on the 6th; and fourth, that they should endeavour to induce the villagers to bring off poultry and fresh vegetables for sale. In order that they might have a token of a peaceable disposition on our part, a white flag should be hoisted at the main until the expiration of the time fixed for their return. They gave as their names Shishido Gyōma, adopted son of Shishido Bizen, minister of Nagato; Sugi Tokusuke and Watanabe Kurata, councillors. They then returned on shore, leaving communications addressed to each of the commanders of the allied squadron, which they had been charged to deliver at Himeshima before the bombardment. They handed these over at the admiral's desire, remarking that we should perceive from the contents that the documents were useless now.

Itō gave me also transcripts of the orders received from the emperor and the *shōgun* to expel foreigners from Japan, which Shishido certified with his own hand to be true copies. The translations made of these papers were afterwards published in the bluebook on Japan, where the curious can consult them. There is no doubt that they were perfectly authentic. It was amusing to observe the change which manifested itself gradually in the demeanour of the envoy, who was as proud as Lucifer when he stepped on board, but gradually toned down, and agreed to every proposal without making any objections. Itō seemed to exercise great influence over him. After the truce was agreed to, the country people ventured freely along the road near the batteries, and passed on into the town, no doubt heartily pleased at the ter- mination of hostilities. It must be said to their credit that the terms were faithfully adhered to by the Chōshū people, none of whom, except Itō and Inoue, had supposed Europeans to be any better than mere barbarians.

On September 9, 1864, the *Coquette* took the two admirals through the straits to visit the batteries on Hikushima, and as usual I accompanied them to interpret. From the eastern side the strait contracts rapidly, between lofty well-wooded hills, to a width of no more than six cables' lengths, and then as quickly opens out again, with the long line of houses forming the town of Shimonoseki on the northern shore, while to the left the coast trends away southwards past the village of Moji and the town of Kokura. In front lay the broad undulating Hikushima. Passing right out through the strait till we reached the north-west corner of the island, we turned back again and came along its coast, passing a little cove crowded with junks, till we came to Lime Point. Here we disembarked to inspect the site of the batteries, from which the guns had already been removed by our people. One of the batteries, which originally had six guns mounted, was cut out of the cliff, and there had evidently not been time to complete it. Immediately below the parapet was a single gun in a pit. A little further east was a battery of eight guns mounted *à fleur d'eau*, and close by was a smaller battery with four embrasures which had never been armed. The only other sign of a battery on this island was an old earthwork to the west of Lime Point, also without guns. Kokura appeared to be strongly fortified, and it was reported that the Chōshū people had demanded, but unsuccessfully, to be allowed to work the batteries against us. The *Tartar*, *Dupleix*, *Djambi*, and *Metalen Kruis* had been stationed here since the 7th, chiefly for the purpose of dismantling the batteries.

Leaving them we steamed up to Kushi-*saki*, where three brass and four *wooden* guns had been taken. The latter were about four feet long, and were constructed of single logs with a bore about eight inches in diameter, having a chamber behind capable of holding about a pound and a half of powder. Bamboo hoops surrounded the gun from breech to muzzle, then came a layer of boards, and then more bamboo hoops; the wood itself was only about three and a half inch thick. The shot consisted of a small bag of pebbles fastened to a wooden disk, and was intended to act like grape at close quarters against a landing party. These curious weapons were simply laid on the earthen parapet, and were not calculated to be used more than once.

The Japanese had shown themselves very friendly to the working party, and had themselves carried down the guns for delivery. They were not improbably glad to get rid of the toys that had brought them into so much trouble. On returning to the flagship we found a couple of boats laden with fowls and vegetables which Shiji Bunda had sent on board as a present. There was a note from him saying that the common people were much too frightened to come near us to sell supplies, and complaining that one of the ships had been firing again, an action which, he said, would tend to endanger the friendly relations so recently established. But this was a mistake on his part, for no incident of the kind had occurred. The bumboatmen were shown over the ship, and expressed themselves much delighted with the novel and wonderful sight. We sent half of Shiji's present to the French admiral, and our share was divided among the officers and men of the flagship.

On the following day the envoys of the lord of Chōshū arrived punctually on board the *Euryalus*. Shishido and Sugi, however, did not make their appearance, their absence being explained to be caused by illness from want of sleep and the hot weather. Admiral Küper observed that it was singular how often this sort of thing happened, and ironically begged that if the negotiations were not concluded in one sitting, the delegates would take care of their health until everything was settled. Their names were Mōri Izumo, minister (*karō*) Yamada Uemon, Hirozawa Hyōsuke and Watanabe Kurata, councillors (*sansei*), and Isota Kenzō and Harata Junji of Chōfu, councillors, with Shiji Bunda.

We had looked up the Japanese "blue-book" in the meantime, and fancied we had reason to suppose the previous envoy had given an incorrect account of his position, but they were able to clear up the discrepancy in a satisfactory manner. The officer there called Shishido Mino had recently changed his name to Shishido Bizen, and retired from public life in favour of Shishido Gyōma, who now represented the family. They produced a letter from their lord which, on being read, was found to declare in satisfactory terms that he sued for peace. The admiral then said: "We quite agree with your lord in desiring peace. It was never our intention to fight your countrymen. We solely desire to cement amicable relations between Japan and foreign countries, and to carry on trade."

Mōri replied that these were entirely the views held by the lord.

Küper: "Do you wish us distinctly to understand that you will offer no further opposition to the free passage of the straits?"

Mōri: "We do."

Küper: "We should like very much to have an interview with the lord, for we could concede much to him that we could not perhaps concede to you. We are ourselves of high rank in our own country, but will come on shore to meet him at Shimonoseki."

After consulting among themselves they named September 14 as the date on which he should come down from his capital to receive the two admirals in the town.

Küper: "We will first state our demands, which can be ratified by the lord when he comes. We shall then be able to explain to him many matters connected with the customs of foreign countries which will prevent mistakes arising in future. In any case the transaction of business will be facilitated and time will be saved by the lord's coming, as in any case his ratification has to be obtained to the terms agreed on."

"In the first place, no batteries must be constructed in the straits until all questions between foreigners and Japanese have been settled by the *shōgun*'s government and the foreign ministers at Edo."

"Secondly, according to the custom of foreign nations in time of war, a ransom for the town of Shimonoseki must be paid, because we spared it when we had a perfect right to set it on fire, for our people had been fired on from the houses. The amount shall be communicated to the lord himself at the conference which is to take place."

"Thirdly, when foreign vessels passing through the straits are in need of coals, provisions, or water, they shall be permitted to purchase what they want."

These conditions were readily accepted by the envoy, who said that as the tides were very strong in the straits, and both wind and waves sometimes violent, persons in distress should be permitted to land.

The admiral then informed him that during our stay we should go on shore at Shimonoseki to buy whatever we required, and requested him to tell the townspeople to bring together for sale what they could, in fact to start a market for the fleet. To this they at first objected, on the ground that the town had been completely abandoned by its inhabitants, but eventually agreed to do what was desired. Then Mōri got up, and leaning over to me said confidentially that there was one thing about which he was very anxious. The peace they had obtained was a most precious and valuable thing, and they would greatly regret if any untoward event were to injure our present friendly relations. It might happen that an ill-disposed person would lie in wait to attack foreigners, and, to prevent anything of this kind occurring, he begged that those who went ashore would be on their guard. This was interpreted to Admiral Küper, who at once replied that we had no fear of any such evilly disposed persons, but that if a single European were hurt, the whole town should be burnt to the ground. The Japanese authorities, he added, were in the habit of saying this sort of thing, solely to prevent our landing, and it looked to him a little suspicious.

Mōri answered that he feared the purity of his intentions in giving this warning was not understood. He was sure the Japanese authorities would on their part take every precaution to prevent mishaps, and he had only mentioned this to prevent mistakes.

Küper: "Very well. We shall not go into the country at all. No doubt there is a governor in the town. You can give orders to him to keep out the ill-disposed, and if he cannot defend the place, we will land and do it for him."

Mōri: "We will give orders to the governor."

This finished the business part of the conference, but the admiral was curious to know the details of what had recently taken place at Kyoto, where it was reported there had been fighting between the Chōshū and Aizu men. Thereupon Shiji told us a long story, the gist of which was that after Chōshū had received the orders of both the emperor and *shōgun* for "the expulsion of the foreigners," and had acted upon them to the best of his ability, he got a great deal of abuse for having done so. Being both surprised and hurt at this treatment, he sent several times to Kyoto to inquire the reason, but his people were driven out of the capital, and he was forbidden to present himself there again. He became indignant at this injustice, and his retainers sympathized with him very strongly. At last a band of them, who could bear it no longer, set out for Kyoto to demand an explanation from the emperor's ministers. They took swords, spears, and other warlike weapons in their hands. Why? On a former occasion, nay twice, Aizu had put to death every Chōshū man to be found in Kyoto. So, they said, "Aizu may attack us also, and then we must defend ourselves; we will not be killed for nothing." The lord, happening to hear of their departure, sent three of his ministers (*karō*) to recall them, but they refused to return. Then the governor of Kyoto summoned Chōshū's agent at the capital to send the men home again, "for if you don't," said he, "I shall attack them." However, the agent refused, and a battle ensued. When the *Barrosa* came the first time to Himeshima with the letters of the foreign representatives, the lord despatched his son to communicate with the emperor, but owing to the disturbed state of affairs he was unable to effect anything. Shiji hoped we would not believe that the Chōshū clan harboured any treasonable intentions towards the emperor, and the whole truth was that they had simply tried to get an explanation of the manner in which they had been treated. He added that we ought not to put any trust in what was told us by the Kokura people or the junk sailors, who came from Edo and Hizen and all parts of the country, and were enemies of Chōshū.

Our visitors were then conducted over the ship, and after being entertained with some music by the band they went over the side, and we parted on very friendly terms.

A comparison of dates with the account given in Adams, chapters 25 and 26, of what had passed at Kyoto during the summer, shows that the Chōshū clansmen were marching from Osaka to Kyoto at the very time that Itō and Shiji landed from the *Barrosa* and reached Yamaguchi to convey the messages of the foreign representatives to the lords. From time to time other bodies of Chōshū men reached the capital, and the accumulated elements of civil war finally exploded on the 20th August, before the younger lord of Chōshū, who seems to have really started from home to calm the excited spirits of the clansmen with news of a new enemy in their rear, had time to arrive. The best fighting men were consequently absent when the allied squadron appeared at the straits, and our victory was therefore a much easier affair than it would otherwise have been. I doubt whether any of the fugitives from Kyoto got home in time to take part in the defence of the place.

Next day Captain Hayes of the *Tartar*, Major Wray, and I went ashore for a walk through Shimonoseki. The eastern end of the town had received a good many round shot on the September 6, and some of the houses were almost knocked to pieces. I believe the Chōshū men had brought out a field piece or two and fired from that point against the squadron lying in front of Dannorua. This had drawn on them our heavy artillery. The townspeople were flocking back, and had commenced to settle down again, but very few shops were open. The common people followed us in crowds, and appeared very friendly, but the prices asked by the shopkeepers were exorbitant. We were somewhat surprised, though of course without reason, to find that the proportion of *curio* shops was very small as compared with Yokohama. We saw several soldiers, some armed with rifles, others carrying swords and spears; they of course could not be expected to look very amicably at their late foes.

On September 12, Hadano and the two governors of the town came off to tell the admiral that a market would be opened at a wharf called Nabehama from ten to twelve in the forenoon for the sale of fresh provisions. We of course suspected them of having made this arrangement in order to have everything under their own control, and to keep the prices as high as possible. The admiral demanded a market from six to eight o'clock, to which after much discussion they agreed. I learned through my teacher that the people were told to sell dearly to us, in spite of the promise given to us by the officials that they would not interfere. The latter had begged that our men might be ordered not to purchase anything in the shops, on the ground that we should buy up all the provisions intended for the townsfolk.

On September 13, Captain Dowell transferred to the *Euryalus* as flag-captain, vice captain Alexander invalided. Next day I accompanied the two admirals on shore to the clean little village of Moji. On asking some Kokura men whom we met to show us the way up to the battery on the point where the strait sweeps round, they inquired whether we had permission from the guard established at a temple close by. The answer to this astounding query was that we were not in the habit of asking leave. "Was that the path?" "Yes, that's the path." So we toiled up a hill through the pine trees, turned to the left, and descended into the battery, which was constructed for three guns. It commanded a view right up and down the straits, from Manshū to Hikushima. It was a splendid position for guns, though a shell pitched in the line of the work would of necessity have fallen into it, unless passing very high, as it was cut out of the hillside. All about it there were places cleared for guns which would have a powerful effect against ships. The thick brushwood would prevent any attempt at escalade, and a single gun is not easily hit. I do not know what might be done with modern artillery, but it was the opinion of all our engineer officers that if the Japanese of that day had known the advantages of the position, they could easily have rendered it impregnable.

At two o'clock in the afternoon arrived the Chōshū delegates, who by agreement made earlier in the day were to represent the lord. The story they told us was that he had voluntarily shut himself up in order to await the will of the emperor, or as they phrased it, he had placed himself in an attitude of respectful attention (*tsutsushinde oru*). Lest it should be supposed that this is merely a joke, I must explain that in the old times, whenever a member of the samurai class had committed an act in person or vicariously which might be expected to bring down upon him the wrath of his political superiors, he at once assumed a submissive posture, and as it were delivered himself up, tied hands and feet, to the pleasure of his lord. It was a sort of voluntary self-imprisonment as a first-class misdemeanant. We did not accept the excuse, which it was natural to suppose had been invented to save him the trouble of travelling to Shimonoseki, but I now incline to think that horrorstruck at the violent proceedings of his followers who had dared to fight against the defenders of the palace (and also repenting of their failure), the old lord had hastened to atone for the crime of treason, as far as lay in his power, by declaring his readiness to undergo any penalty that might be decreed by the sovereign—if his retainers would let him.

Their names were Shishido Bizen, Mōri Izumo, Shishido Gyōma and Ibara Kazue, ministers; and Naozaki Yahichirō (*metsuke*, a secretary), Itō Hirobumi, Hirozawa Hyōsuke and another whose name I did not note down. Bizen, it appeared, had after all not completely retired from public affairs. Both the admirals were present. As soon as the conference was formed, Admiral Küper asked why they had not let him know earlier that the lord was in seclusion, as the truce had been granted solely that there might be time for him to reach Shimonoseki. They answered that the boat was slow, and they had only arrived late on the previous day. They had spent a long time arguing with the lord and using their best efforts to persuade him to come, but he always answered that it was an old custom from which he could not depart. He was in disgrace with the emperor, and was not able to see even his own confidential retainers, much less could he see the admirals. They regretted it very much, but it could not be helped. The lord would have greatly liked to meet the admirals.

After this question had been so thoroughly thrashed out that the Japanese could not but suppose that great importance was attached to a direct undertaking on the part of the lord, the admirals' demands were announced, as follows:—

Firstly: Foreign vessels passing through the straits to be treated in a friendly manner; to be permitted to purchase coals, provisions, water and other necessaries. If driven in through stress of weather, the crews to be permitted to land.

Secondly: Henceforth no new batteries to be constructed, the old ones not to be repaired, and no guns to be mounted in them.

This article caused some discussion, for as now put it deprived them of a loophole that had been left open on the previous occasion. But when they were asked for what purpose the batteries had been erected, they had but one answer—"for making war on foreigners." "Well then, those foreigners having destroyed the batteries, and taken the guns, will not permit any more to be put in the same place. The article is indispensable, and must stand as it is." So they agreed to it.

Thirdly: The town of Shimonoseki might justly have been destroyed, because it fired on our ships. But it was left unhurt, and therefore a ransom must be paid. Furthermore, the lord must defray the cost of the expedition. The whole amount will be determined by the foreign representatives at Edo.

To this our friends offered strenuous opposition. Chōshū and Bōshū were two very small provinces, and possessed a revenue of scarcely 360,000 *koku* of rice. Of this, 200,000 went to support the retainers, the balance having been spent in batteries, guns, and all other manner of warlike equipments. If the sum demanded were beyond their resources, they could not pay it. There were plenty of men in the province who cared nothing for their lives in comparison with the fulfilment of their duty towards the lord. It is he who wishes to make peace, and he has much difficulty in repressing their zeal. The admiral replied that they should have calculated the price beforehand. They had chosen to make war, and now that the bill was being presented to them, they must pay it. Finally they agreed to this article, but it struck me that their object was solely to let us know that their spirit was not entirely broken, and that if our demands were too exorbitant they would fight rather than yield.

Last of all we inserted in the draft a declaration that this was merely a treaty for the temporary cessation of hostilities, and was entirely independent of any questions connected with Chōshū which might have to be settled later on between the foreign representatives and the Japanese government. I imagine that this clause had reference to the indemnities which might be demanded on the part of France, Holland and the United States. At any rate, it was agreed to without any discussion. A fair copy was written out, to which two of the *karō* affixed their signatures, and a couple of days were given to them to go to Yamaguchi in order to obtain the lord's signature. Those who had not previously seen the ship were taken the usual round through the lower deck and engine room, and they left in a body.

On September 15 things seemed quiet enough for a little private exploration on my own account in company with my teacher. We went first to call on Ibara Kazue, one of the envoys who had negotiated the agreement of the day before, and asked him to come on board to be photographed by Beato. Then while Hayashi, whose crown was by this time black with a fortnight's bristly growth, went to a barber's shop to get himself clean shaved, I strolled about the streets alone, and turned into an eating-house where we had agreed to meet. The people received me civilly, and showed me upstairs to a room, one side of which was entirely open to the air, and overlooked a small courtyard. In the next apartment were some Chōshū two-sworded men leaning over the wooden balcony, who waved their hands to me to go away, but I called out, "What do you want!" in a fierce tone, and they collapsed immediately, so great was the prestige of our victory. When Hayashi joined me, we ordered an *awabi* (rocksucker) to be got ready, and while it was being cooked, devoured nearly the whole of a ripe water melon. The *awabi* was cooked with sugar and proved terribly tough. Two sorts of *sake* were served, and the waiting maid smoked all the while to perfume the room. We wound up with turtle soup and rice. During the rest of my stay at Shimonoseki, which lasted nearly a month, I was constantly on shore, and never had any trouble with the townspeople, who were always civil and friendly.

The treaty was brought down on the 16th, and found to be duly signed and sealed. At the same time the Japanese produced a paper which they wanted the admirals to sign, undertaking that the officers and crews should keep within certain limits, and above all, should not land at night. There was a good deal of misunderstanding about this document. The Abbé Girard's teacher maintained that it was a memorandum or note-verbale from the Chōshū authorities, and as I was younger and had not the prestige of the Abbé as a Japanese scholar, I had to give way. So we concocted a letter in reply, which I wrote out, and took on shore to the governor. Our letter said that the principal restrictions which the Japanese asked us to agree to had been granted already, and that as for the rest, the governor had on the occasion of his last visit said there were no complaints to make of our people trespassing on either guardhouses or temples, and therefore it was unnecessary for them to make such demands. In future, if they had anything to communicate, it must be done by letter, signed and sealed by Ibara Kazue. On reading this, the governor to my delight said, "Here's a mistake. What I brought to you was a draft of a letter for the naval commanders to write to us."

The object of the naval operations in the straits having been completely attained by the destruction of the batteries and the establishment of a good understanding with the lord of Chōshū, preparations were now made to withdraw the major portion of the allied squadrons, leaving only three ships to prevent the possibility of the passage being again fortified. I received orders to remain behind on board the *Barrosa*. A day before the admiral sailed a letter came from the governor asking him to give a passage as far as Yokohama to a *karō* and two officers. The request was at once granted, but the three passengers not arriving in time, word was left that they might apply to the French admiral, who was to leave a day later. But this they declined to do, having been instructed to ask for a passage in an English ship, and they would go by no other. Eventually the *Barrosa* took them.

On the 20th accordingly, all the British ships except the *Barrosa*, and all the Dutch ships but the *Djambi*, sailed away up the Inland Sea towards Osaka, the French, however, remaining. I went ashore afterwards with some officers of the *Barrosa* for a walk, and as we passed the guardhouse, its occupants called out, "Take off your hats." I replied, "What do you say." The man on guard, "Take off your hats. This is the honourable guardhouse of Shimonoseki." Answer from our side, "What folly do you talk! If you repeat it, the governor shall be informed." So we passed on into the town to the governor's house and laid a complaint in due form against the over-zealous guardhouse keeper. The governor promised to administer a reprimand, and was as good as his word, so that when some other officers came ashore and passed the same spot, the Japanese officers rushed out into the road to tell them that they need not uncap.

I found the townspeople very communicative about the exploits of the Americans and French in 1863, and from their relation it was easy to see that while Captain M'Dougall of the *Wyoming* had given a very modest account of his achievements in the way of sinking ships and firing houses, the French had greatly exaggerated their own deeds of valour. The *Wyoming* ran the gauntlet of all the batteries and sank the *Lancefield* and the brig right in front of the town, whereas the *Sémiramis* never ventured further than Dannorua. The common folk were all entirely convinced that the *shōgun* had given orders for the expulsion of the foreigners, and I overheard a man in the market say "the Bakufu is playing a double game." Bakufu was the most common term by which the *shōgun*'s government was then designated. I was asked whether the *shōgun* had asked us to come down and destroy the batteries, to which I answered "No; but he said he could not open the straits." Then I gave them our view of the case, which was that the *shōgun*, finding himself in a tight place between the *daimyō* and the foreigners, had to give assurances to both which were inconsistent with each other, whereupon they all cried out with one voice: "*Honma da,*" (indeed).

That evening there arrived from Nagasaki the steamer *Victoria* with the vice-governor of that port and an interpreter. Passing in front of the town they paid the French admiral a call, and then anchored near us in Dannorua Bay. Coming on board to make inquiries, they asked whether Chōshū had been beaten, and on our replying in the affirmative, they produced a copy of the lord's first letter begging for peace addressed to the Americans, which they said had been furnished to them by the Kokura people. That I told them bluntly must be a lie, but they would not confess the source from which they had obtained the document. They said their instructions were to ask the admiral not to believe the lies Chōshū was telling about orders received from the *shōgun* to expel foreigners, and also that having heard the fleet was going to Osaka, the governor of Nagasaki, who was afraid that the appearance of so large a force before the city, fresh from the destruction of the batteries of Shimonoseki, might cause a panic, had sent them to prevent any difficulties between the admiral and the governor of Osaka. They were very anxious lest a treaty had been concluded with Chōshū for the opening of Shimonoseki to foreign trade, which would have caused the commercial ruin of Nagasaki; but we declined to give them any information. Having beaten the Chōshū people, we had come to like and respect them, while a feeling of dislike began to arise in our minds for the *shōgun*'s people on account of their weakness and double-dealing, and from this time onwards I sympathized more and more with the *daimyō* party, from whom the *shōgun*'s government had always tried to keep us apart.

On September 21, the *Sémiramis* and *Dupleix* quitted the straits, leaving behind them the *Tancrède*. Some of us went ashore to the *honjin* to inquire whether we could obtain a supply of bullocks for the ship. The officials promised to do all they could, but said it would be difficult, as they killed none for themselves. We also asked them to change some Mexican dollars into Japanese money, which they promised to do at the Nagasaki market rate, but it was finally arranged that if we found ourselves in actual need of coin, they should lend us a thousand *ichibu*, to be returned to their agent at Yokohama. They proved so obliging that we could not help regretting that in order to gain their friendship it had been necessary to come to blows with them. And it is not a little remarkable that neither the Satsuma nor the Chōshū men ever seemed to cherish any resentment against us for what we had done, and during the years of disturbance and revolution that followed they were always our most intimate allies.

That day we walked the whole length of the town unattended by any guard, and got a glimpse of the Sea of China beyond the straits. We met, however, with a little show of insolence from a couple of two-sworded men, who motioned us back to our boats, but I discoursed to them in their own tongue, and they were speedily reduced to silence: the show of a revolver had something to do with the production of this effect.

Itō came on board one day with a couple of men who, he said, were merchants, but it was evident from the respect he paid to one of them, who wore two swords, that they belonged to the high official class. They were con- ducted round the ship and entertained with various liquors. He declared that in all the fighting they had only seven or eight men killed, and about twice that number wounded, but one of his companions told me that the number killed was nearly twenty. Itō said that trade could be done at Shimonoseki in cotton, wax and silk produced in Chōshū, as well as in all the productions of the northern provinces and Osaka. Probably they might manufacture paper for the English market. The lord, he added, wanted to open the port to foreign commerce, but just at present they expected an invasion of the combined forces of the *shōgun* and all the *daimyō*, and all their attention was directed to their own defence. The two vessels sunk by the *Wyoming* in 1863 had been raised and sent round to Hagi. I was surprised to learn that the batteries at Maedamura, as well as those at Kushi-*saki*, were within the territory of the *daimyō* of Chōfu, who was not in so far independent that he could stand aside when the head of the family went to war. Last year, at the time when the Dutch corvette *Medusa* was fired on as she passed the straits, batteries had existed on the low hills behind the town, and at two points on the sea front, but the guns had subsequently been removed to Dannoura and Maedamura, where they fell into our hands. The small three-gun battery on Moji Point within the Kokura territory was also the work of Chōshū men, who had levelled land and began to construct barracks, which were destroyed by the Kokura people when the failure of the lord's Kyoto schemes drove him to withdraw within his own boundaries for self-protection.

We went one day in our boats down to Kokura with the intention of landing there to walk through the town, but after keeping us waiting an hour and a half, and repeatedly promising to open the gate, they finally refused to admit us. They did open it, but only to let out a couple of fellows, who told us in the lowest of voices that Kokura not being a treaty port, we could not enter. I told them it was a great piece of ingratitude to treat us in so inhospitable a manner after we had thrashed their enemy for them. Crowds of people had collected to look at us, and doubtless we should have been mobbed if we had landed. There was no idea on our part of forcing our way in.

Towards the end of the month smallpox broke out on board, and W. H. Cummings, who had succeeded to the temporary command on Captain Dowell's transfer to the flagship, determined to leave for Yokohama as soon as the necessary arrangements could be made. On the 27th we applied therefore to the authorities for a pilot to take the ship through the Inland Sea, and gave notice that the commanders of the three ships would pay a visit to Ibara on the morrow in order to settle about the passage up to Yokohama which had been promised to him and two other officers.

I took the message on shore, and stopped to have a meal with Itō, who good-naturedly had made great efforts to get up a dinner in European style. He had built a table seven feet long by half that width, covered with a short cloth of some coarse foreign material. Four plates were laid, flanked by long knives, villainously sharp, attenuated brass spoons with flat bowls, and a pair of chopsticks. The first dish consisted of a boiled rockfish, which I found great difficulty in cutting, but accomplished the task at last by inserting a sharpened chopstick into the head, and using a spoon to remove the flesh. Soy, a large bowl of rice, and a small saucer full of coarse salt, were also placed on the table. The second course was broiled eels, and then came a stewed turtle, both of which were very good, but the boiled *awabi* and boiled chicken which followed were quite out of the question. It was a problem how to cut up a fowl with a knife that had no point, and whose blade threatened at every moment to part company with its handle. I abandoned the attempt, and served my companions with slices from the breast. Unripe persimmons, peeled and cut in four, with sweet rice beer (*mirin*) were now produced, and this was excellent. This was certainly the earliest attempt ever made in that part of Japan at giving a dinner in European style, perhaps the first in Japan.

It was finally determined that the party that was to visit Yokohama should consist of Ibara, a councillor named Sugi Tokusuke, a secretary, and Itō, with four servants, who were to be accommodated on board the *Barrosa* and *Djambi*. The *Tancrède*, which was to leave before us, could not find room for more than half the party, and as they did not wish to be separated longer than they could help, they elected to come with us. On October 4, the *Racehorse*, Commander Boxer, arrived to relieve us. Ibara and his secretary, Yamagata Keizō, and we sailed the following morning.

News of our successful result of the naval operations and of the conclusion of a convention with the lord of Chōshū was at once conveyed to the foreign representatives at Yokohama, who lost no time in calling the *shōgun*'s government to account for their apparent complicity with Chōshū, as evidenced by the copies of orders from Kyoto which Itō had given us. The explanation was feeble, and the representatives found no difficulty in obtaining from the ministers their consent to pay whatever war indemnity might be due from Chōshū, or else to throw open to trade a port in the

Inland Sea. Although in the sequel the receipt of the indemnity money by
us actually took place, it was in a manner forced upon the four powers and
their diplomatic agents, and certainly as far as Sir Rutherford Alcock is concerned, he may be entirely exonerated from the accusation of a desire to
exact an indemnity from either the defeated *daimyō* or the government
which assumed responsibility for him. The principal object he sought was
to obtain the sanction of the emperor to the treaties, so as to put an end
to the agitation against foreign commerce which had been carried on by
hostile *daimyō* in the emperor's name ever since the opening of the ports.
Now that Satsuma and Chōshū, the two ringleaders of the opposition, had
been brought to their senses, it ought to have been, he thought, an easy
matter for the *shōgun*'s government, if they sincerely desired to carry out
their treaty obligations, to assert their authority and compel the whole
country to accept the new policy of foreign intercourse. The fixing of an
indemnity was intended only to provide a means of pressure upon the
shōgun's government in order to procure the emperor's ratification of the
treaties, and the consequent extension of commercial relations.

Ibara and his companions reached Yokohama on October 10, and obtained
an interview the same day with Sir Rutherford Alcock and Robert Hewson
Pruyn, the United States minister. The reception accorded to them
convinced them that the foreign powers were not hostilely disposed towards
the *daimyō* of Chōshū, and it was no doubt with a sense of relief that they
learned the intention of the foreign representatives to claim the payment
of the indemnity from the *shōgun*. At the same time it was clearly understood
by both parties that the other engagements entered into by Chōshū
respecting the permanent disarmament of the straits of Shimonoseki and
the hospitable treatment of foreign vessels were to be faithfully adhered to,
and on these heads his subsequent conduct gave no ground for complaint.
It was a curious position for the retainers of a lord, declared a rebel against
the emperor and enemy of the *shōgun*, to land at Yokohama, a port belonging
to the latter, but as far as I remember, they confined their visit to the foreign
settlement, where they were safe from interference, and on the 14th the
Tartar left with them on board to return to their native province.

The Murder of Bird and Baldwin

It was about this time that Sir Rutherford Alcock received Lord Russell's despatches recalling him to England. Ostensibly for the purpose of consulting with him on the state of affairs, this summons to London was accompanied by the expression of an opinion that the passage of the Inland Sea was not necessary to foreign commerce, which amounted to a censure upon his conduct. It is seldom that an agent of the Foreign Office is told in so many words that he is recalled because his conduct of affairs has not given satisfaction, but inasmuch as leave of absence is usually granted upon the application of the minister, envoy, or whatever the title of the head of a mission may be, an invitation to return home is equivalent to the removal of a diplomatic officer from his employment.

Arriving just at the moment when his policy had been successful in every direction, and when all the foreigners in the country were united in a chorus of gratitude to him for his energetic action, he and all the members of his legation felt that the displeasure of Lord John Russell was not a matter of much moment. The crushing defeat of Chōshū by the foreign squadrons coming so immediately after the repulse of his troops from the gates of the palace at Kyoto restored confidence to the *shōgun*'s government, and enabled them to declare firmly to the emperor that the idea of expelling foreigners from the country and putting an end to trade was utterly and entirely impracticable, while the demonstrated superiority of European methods of warfare had converted our bitterest and most determined foes into fast friends. The vindication of his proceedings was no difficult task, and the despatch in which he justified the course he had taken was conceived in a style at once calm and convincing. It is only fair to Lord Russell to say that he lost no time in acknowledging that his agent had been in the right, and in conveying to him the Queen's full approbation of his conduct. But this solatium to his feelings did not reach Yokohama until he was already on his way to England.

The *shōgun*'s government voluntarily undertook to be responsible for whatever sum might be fixed upon as the indemnity to be paid by the lord of Chōshū. On October 22, 1864, a convention was signed by a member of the *shōgun*'s Second Council and the four foreign representatives by which three millions of dollars were to be paid in satisfaction of all claims, or as an alternative the opening of Shimonoseki or some other port in the Inland Sea, if the *shōgun* preferred to offer it and the powers were willing to accept. The division of this sum of money among the different powers was reserved for adjustment between the four governments. Advantage was also taken of the desire to conciliate foreign powers now manifested by the *shōgun*'s ministers to obtain the promise of various improvements at Yokohama calculated to add to the comfort and well-being of the foreign residents, and Sir Rutherford, having thus reaped all the fruits of his courage and per-severance was preparing to quit Japan in obedience to the instructions of Lord Russell, when a fresh and totally unforeseen event occurred which for a time delayed his departure.

After our successes at Shimonoseki, and the frank admission by the *shōgun*'s government of the necessity of maintaining the treaties, the confidence of foreign residents in the safety of the neighbourhood had so completely revived that they no longer feared to make excursions within the limits marked out by the treaties. But they received a rude shock on the night of November 20, when the governor of Kanagawa came to Charles Alexander Winchester, the British consul, and informed him that Major George Waler Baldwin and Lieutenant Robert Bird of the xxth regiment had been barbarously murdered at Kamakura, a well-known resort some twelve miles from Yokohama. Baldwin was killed on the spot, but according to the testimony of the inhabitants, Bird had lived for some hours after he was disabled.

The two officers had visited the famous colossal Buddha, and riding along the road towards the Tsurugaoka Hachiman shrine, were just about to turn the corner into the avenue when a couple of men sprang out upon them with their keen-edged swords and inflicted such ghastly wounds as brought them to the ground almost unresistingly.

The horror of the foreign community can be more easily imagined than described, and it was further deepened when as the result of the inquest it came to be suspected that the mortal wound to which Bird had succumbed had been inflicted some hours after the assassins had left the spot. This, in the opinion of the surgeons, was a wound in the neck completely dividing the spinal cord between the second and third cervical vertebrae, which clearly must have been followed by instant death. Now all the evidence went to show that the younger victim had lived until ten o'clock in the evening. If so, by whom was this wound given, and with what motive?

Those who implicitly relied upon the report of the regimental surgeons jumped to the conclusion that it was the act of one of the officials despatched to the scene of the murder by the governor as soon as the news was brought to him, which was no doubt some three or four hours before he himself went to communicate it to Mr. Winchester, and the motive was suggested to be a desire to prevent the wounded man from giving such information to his countrymen as might have led to the identification of the murderers. But I cannot believe that any Japanese, official or not, could ever have compassed such a treacherous deed. I believe on the contrary that the surgeons who dissected out the wound, not using sufficient care, themselves divided the spinal cord with a probe or some other instrument, and that Bird's death was caused in reality by the loss of blood from his numerous wounds. And this was the view taken by doctor William Willis of our legation and Griffith Richard Jenkins, then established as a general practitioner in Yokohama, neither of whom was invited to assist at the postmortem.

The two surgeons having made a hurried examination and enunciated certain views as to the nature of Bird's wounds, without foreseeing the inferences that might be drawn, would naturally, and probably with entire good faith, adhere to those views afterwards, especially as it would not appear to them at all incredible à priori that the countrymen of the men who had committed such a foul assassination should be capable of a deed, dastardly enough in itself, but no doubt justifiable in the opinion of any foreigner-hating Japanese official. There are many additional considerations suggested by the reports contained in the parliamentary papers which would corroborate the view here put forth, if I had space to discuss them. But as this book is intended to be a record of my own experiences and memories, and not a compilation from published materials, it is not the place to go into all these particulars at length.

The *shōgun*'s government made all the exertions in their power to trace the assassins, and before a month was over they had arrested one of the guilty persons, named Shimizu Seiji. Already on November 16, two of his associates named Gamaike and Inaba, accused of conspiring with him to murder foreigners, and of extorting money from a rich farmer, had been executed, though they were not actual accomplices in the Kamakura crime.

I was present at the execution of these two men, which took place in an enclosure outside the Japanese gaol in the afternoon of December 16, 1864. There was a large concourse of spectators, both foreign and native. A little after three o'clock a whisper ran round that the condemned were being brought out. A door opened, and a man blindfolded and bound with cords was led through the crowd. He was made to kneel down on a rough mat placed in front of a hole dug in the ground to receive his blood. The attendants drew his clothes downwards so as to lay the neck bare, and with the hand brushed his hair upwards, so as to give full play to the sword. The executioner secured a piece of cotton cloth round the handle of his weapon, and having carefully whetted the blade, took up a position to the left of his victim, then raising the sword high above his head with both hands, let it fall with a swoop that severed the neck completely. The head was held up for the inspection of the chief officer present, who simply remarked: "I have seen it," and it was thrown into the hole.

The second man being then carried in, the attendants seemed to have a little trouble in getting him to kneel in the proper position, but at last the arrangements were completed to their satisfaction. The neck having been bared as before, a fresh executioner advanced, took his place at the prisoner's left side, and raising the sword with a flourish, let it descend with the same skill as his predecessor. It was a horrible sight to see the attendants holding the headless corpse down to the hole, and kneading it so as to make the blood flow more readily into the hole, and I left the spot in all haste, vowing that mere curiosity should never induce me to witness another execution.

Capital punishment was much commoner in Japan in those days than it has been since the promulgation of the present humane penal code, and included transfixing with spears. Many of the foreign residents must have been present at such sanguinary spectacles, merely impelled by curiosity, and without the natural excuse of desiring to see the sentence of the law fulfilled upon an offender against their own blood.

The night before Sir Rutherford embarked for England news was brought to him of the arrest of Shimizu Seiji, one of the actual murderers of Baldwin and Bird. Owing to the reputed excellence of the native detective police, which under a despotic government is usually efficient, it was believed by us that the Japanese government could always have procured the arrest of the assailants of foreigners, if they had been determined to do so. The names of many of those who were engaged in the attack on our legation in 1861 were, as I learned some years afterwards, matter of common notoriety, but in the difficult political position that the *shōgun*'s advisers had created for themselves, they did not dare to convict the murderer of a foreigner. This then was the first instance of such a crime being brought home to its perpetrators. The British minister had good reason to feel gratified at this proof that his policy had been the right one, and it was a very natural movement that induced him to take off his watch and chain and throw them over the neck of the messenger of good tidings.

Shimizu Seiji was executed on December 28 at ten o'clock in the morning, in the presence of a detachment of the English garrison. Whatever doubts may have existed as to the complicity of Gamaike and Inaba in his designs against the lives of the foreign residents, there is none as to the fact that this man was one of the actual murderers of Baldwin and Bird. I was instructed to accompany Marcus Octavius Flowers, the acting consul, to the prison on the preceding day to hear the sentence pronounced. We waited some hours till he arrived from Edo in custody of a strong guard, and he was at once confronted with the witnesses, who examined his features in silence. They were then separately interrogated, and one and all recognized him, the most important witness being the boy who had seen the attack. Afterwards we proceeded to another room and questioned the prisoner, who acknowledged his guilt in the clearest manner possible. He was proceeding to say something more, but was ordered by the Japanese officers to be silent. But the best evidence of his identity was obtained by another member of the consular service, who after the murderer had been paraded round the town preceded by a banner on which his sentence was inscribed (this was part of his punishment), accompanied the procession back to the execution ground. Here Lachlan Fletcher overheard him say: "When I killed the foreigners, I expected one of them might be a consul," and everyone who knew our colleague will acknowledge that he was a man of the most exact truthfulness, who was not in the least degree likely to make a mistake in such a matter, or overanxious to believe that the Japanese government were in this instance departing from the bad faith which is the usual refuge of Asiatics in a difficult position.

On the morning of the 28th the garrison was marched over to the execution ground, and drawn up on one side. The prisoner was brought out about ten o'clock. The first words he uttered were a request for some *sake*. Being again questioned, he frankly acknowledged his guilt. I asked him what it was that he had been prevented from saying to us on the previous day, to which he answered that if Bird and Baldwin had got out of his way he would not have attacked them. Whether this was true or not I have no means of judging, but it does not accord with his written deposition. That, it must be recollected, is not in Japan a simple record of everything a prisoner says, but is a reduction in writing by an officer of the court of the final result of all the statements made by him on the different occasions when he was examined, and resembles much more the summing up of the evidence on a criminal trial in England by the presiding judge. He begged the Japanese officials not to bandage his eyes, and began to chant a verse which might be thus translated: "I do not regret being taken and put to death, for to kill barbarians is the true spirit of a Japanese."

As the attendants were drawing back the clothes from his neck to prepare it for the executioner's stroke, he bade them loosen his cords so that they might do it with greater ease, adding: "In after ages they will say, what a fine fellow was Shimizu Seiji." He also remarked, "I don't think the sword that cut off Gempachi's head will do for me," alluding probably to the thickness of his own neck, and begged that the blade might be well whetted. Then saying, "Cut neatly if you please," he stretched out his neck for the stroke. These were the last words he spoke, but just as the sword began to descend he turned his head to the left as if to address some further observation to the officials, so that the cut partly missed its purpose, and the executioner had to hack the head off—a most horrible sight. Simultaneously with the delivery of the first blow, a gun fired by the battery of Royal Artillery announced to all that the assassin had received the punishment of his crime, and we dispersed as quickly as possible. The head was taken to the bridge at the northern entrance of Yokohama and there exposed on a gibbet for three days. Copies of the sentence were posted up at Totsuka and at the scene of the murder, and a few days later I accompanied the legation mounted guard to see that this part of the undertaking given by the Japanese authorities had been duly performed. We found that they had fulfilled their promises to the letter, and thus ended one of the most dramatic incidents in the whole of my experience in the country.

It was impossible not to hate the assassin, but looking at the matter from a Japanese point of view, I confess that I could not help regretting that a man who was evidently of such heroic mould, should have been misguided enough to believe that his country could be helped by such means. But the blood of the foreigners who fell under the swords of Japanese murderers, and the lives which were sacrificed to avenge it bore fruit in later days, and fertilised the ground from which sprang the tree of national regeneration.

Ratification of the Treaties

Sir Rutherford having quitted Japan, the conduct of affairs was assumed by Winchester as chargé d'affaires. Before long despatches reached us from Lord Russell expressing the entire satisfaction of the British government with the policy pursued by our late chief, and we heard that he had been rewarded by promotion to the more important post of minister at Beijing.

He was succeeded by Sir Harry Parkes, who came to us invested with the prestige of a man who had looked death in the face with no ordinary heroism, and in the eyes of all European residents in the far east held a higher position than any officer of the crown in those countries. And whatever may have been his faults and shortcomings, especially towards the latter part of his career, it must be acknowledged that England never was represented by a more devoted public servant, and that Japan herself owes to his exertions a debt which she can never repay and has never fully acknowledged. If he had taken a different side in the revolution of 1868, if he had simply acted with the majority of his colleagues, almost insurmountable difficulties would have been placed in the way of the emperor's restoration, and the civil war could never have been brought to so speedy a termination. He was an indefatigable worker, entirely absorbed in the duties of his post, untiring in his endeavours to obtain a correct view of his surroundings, never sparing himself, and requiring from his subordinates the same zealous assiduity.

Of his personal courage I had the opportunity afterwards of witnessing one striking example, and brilliant as have been the achievements of many of our Indian civilians, I do not think that his coolness and fortitude in the moment of peril have ever been surpassed by any man not bred to war. He was strict and severe in service matters, but in his private relations gracious to all those who had occasion to seek his help, and a faithful friend to all who won his goodwill. Unfortunately I was not one of these, and the result was that from the beginning we were never friends, down to the very last, though he never had reason to complain of sloth or unreadiness to take my share of the work, and so it came about that before long I became one of his assistants, and in the end of 1866 was finally transferred from the Yokohama consulate (where I had been appointed interpreter early in 1865) to the legation.

The accomplice of Shimizu Seiji in the murder of Bird and Baldwin, named Mamiya Hajime, was executed on the 30th October 1865. I went out early with Flowers in pouring rain to question the prisoner on some points which had to be cleared up in connection with the crime. He was condemned to the same punishment as his confederate, and we went out again at one o'clock to be present at his decapitation. It was a pouring wet day, and the dull leaden sky overhead was in keeping with the melancholy occasion. Mamiya was a young fellow, and endowed with far less fortitude than Shimizu, and in order to enable him to face the executioner he had been allowed to stupify himself with drink. His head was taken off at a single blow. The usual doubts as to his identity were expressed by the local foreign press, but for myself I was convinced that he was one of the assassins. If the *shōgun*'s government had substituted any other criminal for a man whom they had not succeeded in capturing, the truth would have surely leaked out, and by this time we had sources of information which would have enabled us speedily to detect any trick.

Sir Harry Parkes reached Yokohama early in July, and Winchester took his departure for Shanghai, where he had been appointed to be consul. Francis Gerhard Myburgh was transferred at the same time from Nagasaki to the Yokohama consulate. In passing through Nagasaki Sir Harry had already learned from the agents of some of the *daimyō* that a civil war was expected at no distant date, the object of which would be the overthrow of the *shōgun*. He already in September began to speak to the *shōgun*'s council of the desirability of obtaining the emperor's ratification of the treaties, but the credit of the idea is in reality due to Winchester, who (I did not know it at the time) as early as April had suggested to the British government that the written adhesion of the emperor to the treaties, and the reduction of the import duties to a uniform tariff of five percent *ad valorem* might be obtained in return for the partial abandonment of the Shimonoseki indemnity, the *shōgun*'s ministers having stated they could not continue to make the quarterly payments of $500,000 at a time, as had been stipulated in the convention. In fact Sir Rutherford Alcock had begun to lay stress on the necessity of the emperor's ratification of the treaties almost immediately after the bombardment of Shimonoseki. This suggestion was approved by Lord Russell, who at once communicated it to the governments of Holland, France, and the United States, and sent despatches to Japan to the same effect which reached Sir Harry Parkes towards the end of October. He lost no time in consulting with his colleagues, and in proposing that they should proceed in a body to Osaka, supported by a considerable squadron of men-of-war, to negotiate directly with the main body of the *shōgun*'s ministers. I should have mentioned before that the *shōgun* was at Kyoto, having proceeded thither in the month of June, ostensibly for the purpose of taking command of the army which was to chastise the presumptuous rebel, the lord of Chōshū, and was still detained there by various intrigues and the insufficiency of his military means.

The French minister, who was at first strongly opposed to the abandonment of the indemnity in exchange for the opening of a port, had received instructions from his government which had induced him to come over to the views of the British representative, who found the United States chargé d'affaires and the Dutch political agent equally willing to follow his lead. As to the latter, we were accustomed to believe that Sir Harry had him "in his pocket," as the phrase goes, and the Americans had at that time partially abandoned the affectation of acting on different lines from the "effete monarchies of Europe." Unity of action being thus secured, the word was passed to the naval commanders to get ready for sea, and the legations having packed up a sufficient quantity of foolscap paper, silk tape, quill pens and bottles of ink, embarked on board the next day but one day after the signature of a protocol in which the four diplomatic representatives had recorded their views and projects. Sir Harry took with him John Macdonald, Alexander von Siebold and myself.

The squadron was an imposing one, though not so overwhelmingly strong as that which had destroyed the batteries at Shimonoseki in the previous year. Of British ships there were the *Princess Royal*, 73, flying the broad pennant of Admiral St George Vincent King; the *Leopard*, 18; *Pelorus*, 22; and *Bouncer*, 1; of French, the *Guerrière*, 36; *Dupleix*, 12; and *Kienchang*, 4; while the Netherlands contributed the corvette *Zoutman*. Our admiral was extremely good-natured, and had fitted up private cabins for us three civilians on the main deck. I was delighted to find myself on board with my friend A. G. S. Hawes, a marine officer recently transferred to the flagship from the *Severn*.

The foreign representatives, it was rumoured, proposed, in addition to the emperor's ratification of the treaties and the reduction of the tariff, to ask for the opening of Osaka and Kobe to foreign trade on January 1, 1866. By the treaty of 1858 these places were to have been opened on January 1, 1863, but the powers had in 1862 agreed to a postponement of five years, in order to give time for things to settle down. In return, the four powers were ready to forgo two-thirds of the Shimonoseki indemnity, and the option of deciding was to be left to the *shōgun*. This much was bruited about among the members of the foreign legations. Outsiders said that we were about to present an *ultimatum*, and that the creation of two new centres of foreign trade was to be demanded without alternative. The men in the service who expected appointments would of course have been eager to believe this version but for the glorious uncertainty that surrounds all diplomatic projects.

The Edo government were alarmed at the energetic step on which the representatives had resolved, and Mizuno Tadahiro, the only member of the first council who had remained behind in Edo when the *shōgun* went up to Kyoto, came down in the company of Sakai Tadaka, one of the Second Council, to exert all his powers of dissuasion with Sir Harry. It was the first time that a functionary of so high a rank had ever visited a foreign legation, and the evidence of anxiety thus afforded simply confirmed the resolution that had been taken to bring matters to a crisis. That Mizuno and his subordinate hoped their efforts would be successful there is no reason to suppose, and in fact they contented themselves mainly with offering some advice as to the best method of proceeding on the arrival of the representatives at Kobe.

We left on November 1, 1866, and proceeding in a leisurely manner along the coast, passed the Izumi Straits at 8 a.m. on the 4th. The guns were loaded and the men beat to quarters, but the garrison of the forts at Yura showed no signs of molesting us, and everybody soon quieted down again. At half-past eleven we came in sight of Osaka, lying on the low land at the mouth of the Yodo River. The mountains which enclose the bay on either side here appear to retire far into the interior, until they disappear in the haze. The *shōgun*'s castle was easily distinguished by its innumerable many-storied white towers, rising at the back of the city. But of the town very little was visible owing to the slight elevation of the houses and the distance from the deep water outside where we were passing. The allied squadron formed in one line, headed by the *Princess Royal*, and gradually rounded off in the direction of Kobe, where we anchored at half-past one. One by one the other ships came in and took up the positions indicated to them.

The bay was crowded with junks of all sizes, and we counted seven Japanese steamers lying at anchor. From one of these, belonging to the *shōgun*'s War Department, a couple of officers came on board to make the usual inquiries, and shortly afterwards some very inquisitive shore-going officials came off, who put a great many questions about the object of our visit and where we had come from. They got very little information in reply, but were told that some officers would be going by sea to Osaka on the following day, and that notice should be sent to the governor of the city in order that he might despatch somebody down to the landing place to meet them. They were also requested to provide pilots for the two vessels to be despatched to Osaka, but they declared themselves unable to promise anything we asked. However, as by their own rules they were under an obligation to send information to the governor, this refusal was not of any great consequence.

The Abbé Girard, who had acted as interpreter to Admiral Jaurès the previous year at Shimonoseki, was on this occasion replaced by Mermet de Cachon, a Jesuit attached to the French legation. He, with Messrs

Macdonald and Alexander von Siebold of our legation, and Henri Alexander Noordhoek Hegt, the clerk of the Dutch political agent, were despatched on the following day in the *Kienchang* to Osaka bearing letters from the foreign representatives. The *Bouncer* was to have taken our people, but her commander was not able to get up steam in time, so that the French flag alone made its appearance at the bar of Osaka—first point scored by the French. De Cachon had ingeniously prepared the French's minister's letter in Japanese, inserting at the end a long paragraph, which did not appear in the other three letters, empowering himself to state in outline to the *shōgun*'s council the objects of the foreign representatives, hoping thus to become the spokesman for all four.

On arriving at the mouth of the river, they were met by the two governors of the city (all officials were kept in duplicate in those days), who conducted them to a building close at hand, evidently prepared beforehand for their reception. On learning that Mermet and his companions desired to have a personal interview with one of the council, the governors started off immediately to fetch him, as they said, promising that he should be down by four o'clock. In the meantime Macdonald, Siebold and Hegt started off to walk to Osaka, intending to seek out the ministers there, but after wandering a long distance, they found themselves at three o'clock only just in sight of the city, and had to hurry back in a boat. The governors, however, did more than keep their promise, and instead of one, produced two of the council, namely Ogasawara Nagamichi and Abe Masato. The letters were delivered to them, and they listened civilly and even affably to the messages which Mermet and Macdonald delivered, but were unprepared of course to give any answer. It was agreed that Abe should proceed to Kobe on the 9th to meet the four representatives on board the *Princess Royal*, as sole negotiator on behalf of the *shōgun*, who, it was stated, had gone up to Kyoto.

For me had been reserved the less glorious task of opening up communications with the local officials, and in company with Captain W. G. Jones I went ashore to talk about beef, water, coals, and other ship's requirements. We also informed them that the officers would land, and requested that the townspeople might be ordered to treat them with civility. This they promised to do, but added that their duty to their chiefs, the governors of Osaka, would oblige them to detail one or two constables to watch over the safety of each party. After we had conversed awhile with the head constable, a young man of 19 or 20, some higher officials made their appearance and assumed the power. They promised to do everything we asked, and to help their memories made very full notes. In the afternoon accordingly, leave to go ashore was given to all the ships, and many of the officers availed themselves of the opportunity of visiting what was then a *terra incognita* to most Europeans. The admiral, Sir Harry and myself walked from one end of the town to the other, and found the inhabitants well-disposed, though they followed us in crowds.

This was a very different reception from what the *shōgun*'s officers had warned us to expect. They always talked to us of the hostility of the *daimyō* and the dislike and fear of us entertained by the common people, but we met with nothing but indications of goodwill from all classes. It became clearer to us every day that the Bakufu feared lest free communication between foreigners and those sections of the Japanese people who were outside its direct control would impair the authority of the institutions that had now lasted, with no small benefit to the Tokugawa family, for the last 260 years, and that consequently it could not be a desirable policy for Great Britain to endeavour to bolster up a decaying power. As an instance of the manner in which the *shōgun*'s officials endeavoured to obstruct intercourse, they published a notification in Osaka forbidding the townspeople to visit the ships, knowing full well that a closer acquaintance would make their subjects and foreigners better friends.

The next few days were spent in exploring the neighbourhood with a view to selecting a site for a foreign settlement, and there was a good deal of running up and down to Osaka by sea with messages for the council. Abe was not able to come on Thursday, and at first it was held out that another member of the council would replace him, but when the day arrived, the two governors of Osaka made their appearance with other excuses. Sir Harry spoke very strongly to them, and insisted on seeing someone on Saturday at the latest. But as he did not expect that his request would be complied with, he despatched Siebold, Hegt and myself early in the morning to Osaka. On approaching the anchorage, we saw a Japanese steamer coming from the opposite direction, and lowering a boat we went on board. We found that she was conveying Abe Masato to Kobe to see the foreign ministers. It was arranged therefore that Siebold should return with him, while Hegt and I went on with a couple of officials lent to us by Abe. But as soon as we anchored these men began to be obstructive, refusing to accompany us on shore until the port officers had first visited the ship. Seeing, however, that we were determined to go, without them if necessary, they at last stepped over the side into the boat with a very bad grace indeed.

We rowed in safely in the ship's gig, with four bluejackets well-armed, over the bar, which a few days before had been rendered impassable by a strong west wind, and landed in a small creek behind the battery at Tempōzan Point. We at once took possession of a house where Macdonald and Siebold had lodged on their last visit, disregarding the excuses of the officials, who said it was occupied by a sick person, but we were used to such subterfuges, and of course there was no sick man there at all. After a while we returned to the gig, and rowing up the river in half-an-hour, reached the outskirts of the city, where we landed to inspect a house that had been assigned for the accommodation of the foreign representatives. The latter intended to negotiate in Osaka itself, but this idea was subsequently abandoned.

As this one house was evidently not large enough for the representatives and their suites, I said I would go to the governor and ask him to provide other accommodation. The officials became alarmed at this, and at once offered to show us another house, to which they would take us in a boat. As we wished to see something of the city, I declined, and to their horror we proceeded to walk along the bank. A dense crowd of people gathered round us, but they were very quiet, and after passing the Ajikawa-*bashi*, the first of the series of bridges that span the river right up to the castle, we were shown a temple which, however, proved to be again insufficient for our needs. It being clear that our guides were not animated by goodwill, I again menaced them with a visit to the governor, but here they became utterly obstinate, and I had to give way. So we returned to our gig, and resolving to have a good look at the city, got on board and started to row upstream.

Before long we reached a barrier composed of native boats moored right across from bank to bank, with the evident intention of impeding our further progress. Some officials in a guardhouse on the bank shouted to us to go back, but we pushed straight ashore, and I ascended the steps to demand the reason of this obstruction. Orders from the governor was the reply. A somewhat heated altercation ensued, and I demanded that either we should be allowed to pass or that I should at once be conducted to the governor's house. At last they gave way and removed one or two of the junks, leaving just enough space for our gig. Taking one of the guardhouse officials on board, we proceeded up the river, not a little proud of our victory over the bumbledom of a city of 400,000 people, and fully determined to go right up to the castle. Dense crowds of people gathered on the bridges, sometimes yelling and abusing us, now and then throwing stones. Hegt began to lose his temper, and drawing his revolver, threatened to fire, but I made him put it back in his pouch. We were in no danger, and could not afford to commit murder for such a trifling reason.

At last, after grounding once or twice on the sandbanks, we reached the Kyō-*bashi* bridge just below the castle. On our left was a small boat full of officials who called to us to come and report ourselves, while on the right extended a grassy bank crowded with soldiers dressed in semi-European costume, among whom were a few men in plain dress, apparently noblemen's retainers. One of these came down to the water's edge, close to which we had approached, and shouted out to the Japanese who was with us for his name and office. Our man replied: "Who are you?" and they wrangled for about five minutes, while we kept a watchful eye on the straggling soldiery.

It was clearly unadvisable to land in the midst of a hostile armed crowd, and we reluctantly turned the boat's head down stream, which now carried us swiftly along. The same crowds still occupied the bridges, and shouted abusive epithets as we passed, to the great alarm of the Japanese official, who had not got over Hegt's fierce demeanour on the way up, and trembled for fear lest there should be a row. Landing the poor fellow, whose tone had become remarkably fainter and humbler since he first made our acquaintance in the morning, we pulled out across the bar to the *Bouncer*, and in a few minutes more were on our way back to Kobe, having seen a good deal more of Osaka than anyone else, and braved the wrath of multitudinous *yakunin*. I began to feel contempt for the weak-kneed officials who so easily allowed themselves to be browbeaten by a few Europeans.

A curious rencontre took place during our stay at Kobe. A Satsuma steamer was lying in the port, and one day the captain, Arigawa Yakurō, came on board the flagship with some of his officers. One of them remembered having seen me at Kagoshima, and we immediately fraternized very heartily. After drinking and smoking a good deal they took leave, promising to send a boat for me next day to accompany them ashore to a Japanese dinner. But they forgot their promise. The day after my expedition to Osaka, Siebold and I went on board Arigawa's ship to find him on the point of weighing anchor. He was very glad to see us, abounded in apologies for being unable to fulfil his engagement to give an *onna gochisō*, and showed us the cabin that had been fitted up for the entertainment. This gentleman was too civil by half, but still the contrast to the offishness of the *shōgun*'s officials was very agreeable. If I would like to visit Kagoshima and the Ryūkyū Islands he would be glad to give me a passage. We passed some time on board eating raw eggs and drinking *sake*. I rather think I here met Kawamura for the first time. A few days later when the steamer returned I again went on board and made an even more interesting acquaintance. This was a big burly man, with small, sparkling black eyes, who was lying down in one of the berths. His name, they said, was Shimazu Sachū, and I noticed that he had the scar of a sword cut on one of his arms. Many months afterwards I met him again, this time under his real name of Saigō Takamori. I shall have more to say of him hereafter.

Abe Masato had a *five hours'* interview with Sir Harry on the 10th, after which he went on board the *Guerrière* to see Léon Roches, the French envoy. I learned from Siebold that the conversation had not been of a satisfactory character. His answer to the three propositions of the representatives amounted to *a non possumus*. The *shōgun* would pay up the second instalment of the indemnity rather than run the risk of incurring unpopularity by giving way to our demands. *Jinshin fuoriai*, the popular mind very unsettled, was the excuse then, and for many a day after. Sir Harry had given Abe a piece of his mind, and said he had better return to his colleagues and get them to reconsider their answer.

On November 13, Abe was to have come down again, but feigning indisposition as an excuse (this is well-known in Japan under the name of *yakubyō*, or official sickness), he sent a member of the Second Council, Tachibana Taneyuki, to inform the representatives that the *shōgun* had hitherto never spoken to the emperor about acknowledging the treaties, but that now he had made up his mind to do so. But he required a delay of fifteen days for this purpose. The ministers up to this moment had believed, on the faith of assurances given by the *shōgun*'s council in 1864 after the Shimonoseki business, that the emperor had long ago been approached on this subject, and that Abe himself had been entrusted with a mission to Kyoto to that effect. They were therefore naturally both surprised and incensed, but consented to a delay of ten days. The prospects of the negotiation looked very dark indeed. The *shōgun* seemed either unable or unwilling to obtain the emperor's sanction to the treaties, and it looked like we should have to throw him over entirely. If the *shōgun* was controlled by a superior authority, he was clearly not the proper person for foreign powers to deal with, who must insist upon direct communication with the authority. For the present, it was too early to talk of going to see the emperor against his will. We had not sufficient men in the allied squadrons to force our way up to Kyoto, and even if we had, Sir Harry's instructions would not have enabled him to take such a step. So there was nothing for it but to wait.

An interesting visit was that of some Aizu and Hosokawa retainers, who came on board privately to talk politics and to pick up what information they could for their lords. The former was the commander of the *shōgun*'s garrison in Kyoto, the latter one of the more important *daimyō* in the island of Kyushu, nominally a partizan of the *shōgun*, but already beginning to consider whether it would not suit him better to go over to the other party. For by this time a definite issue had been raised between the *shōgun* and the court of the emperor. The former being the friend of foreigners and an usurping vassal, the war cry of the latter was "serve the sovereign and expel the barbarians." My visitors talked a great deal about the "unsettled state of popular feeling." They said the emperor had already given his sanction to the treaties in a general sort of way, and had consented to Nagasaki, Hakodate and Shimoda being opened to foreign trade. But Kanagawa had been substituted for the latter port without his approval. They felt quite certain that the emperor would not agree at present to the establishment of foreign merchants at Kobe. They maintained that the anti-foreign feeling was pretty general among the people, but admitted that Chōshū made use of it as a mere party cry with the object of dispossessing the *shōgun* of his power.

After an interval of five days Tachibana paid Sir Harry another visit. He reported that the *shōgun* had not yet started for Kyoto to obtain the emperor's ratification of the treaties, being detained at Osaka by a headache! Abe and Ogasawara were afflicted with indisposition which prevented their having the pleasure of coming down to call on the British minister. Sir Harry administered some home-truths to the unfortunate prevaricator, and demonstrated very clearly to him that as the council acknowledged the inability of the *shōgun* to carry out the treaty stipulations in respect of the opening of new ports without the emperor's consent, which they had little hope of obtaining and still less desire to get, they must eventually go to the wall, and the foreign powers would be compelled to make a demand for the ratification directly on the emperor. It was pitiable to see the shifts that the *shōgun's* officials were put to in face of his merciless logic; they were perpetually being driven into a corner and left without a leg to stand on.

The demands presented by the foreign representatives had created a considerable movement at Kyoto, and dissension followed among the advisers of the *shōgun*. In a few days we heard that Abe and Matsumai Takahiro had been dismissed from office. They were believed to be in favour of accepting our demands, and their disgrace seemed to threaten the failure of the negotiations. The representatives thereupon resolved on the important step of addressing a *note identique* to the *shōgun* himself, containing a repetition of the demands already made, and warning him that if an answer were not made within the period of ten days originally fixed, it would be assumed by them that their propositions were refused.

De Cachon and I went ashore together to deliver the letters of our respective chiefs, and I learned that the indefatigable little man had translated the French copy into Japanese and induced his minister to sign the translation. He had also addressed it to the council, instead of to the *shōgun*, though he told me otherwise. On our arrival at the governor's house, he wrapped it in a sheet of Japanese paper, in order that I might not see the address, but the officials who received the notes, of whom I afterwards inquired, voluntarily assured me that it was addressed to the council at Osaka. What De Cachon's object can have been I was not able to conjecture, and it is probable that he did it merely to keep his hand in—it is a dangerous thing for an habitual intriguer to get out of practice by acting straightforwardly, even in unimportant matters. We learned that the *shōgun* had presented a memorial to the emperor urging him to ratify the treaties as well for his own sake as for that of the nation in general. That on its being refused, he had resolved to return to Edo, but was stopped by an order from the court before he had got halfway to Osaka.

The dismissal of the pro-foreign members of the council seemed to forebode resistance and the probable outbreak of hostilities. Japanese steamers lying at Osaka got up steam and went off in every direction, some passing through Kobe on their way. Siebold and I pulled on board one of these which belonged to Satsuma, and learned that she was going to Yura in Kishū in order to be out of the way in case the emperor should issue such orders to the *shōgun* as might result in war-like measures being taken by the allied squadron. On the 24th, the last day, notice was given to the governor of Hyōgo that the ships would move on the morrow to Osaka to await there the answer of the *shōgun's* government. From him we learned that Ogasawara would surely be down next day with the reply, but as had already happened so often in the course of these negotiations, he was ill, and Matsudaira Munehide took his place.

The interview with the foreign representatives lasted several hours, but the gist of it was that the *shōgun* had at last obtained the emperor's consent to the treaties, by his own urgent representations, backed by those of his cousin Tokugawa Yoshinobu, who declared (so it was said) that he would perform disembowelment unless the emperor yielded. At last the latter gave way, saying "Well, speak to the nobles of my court about it." The opening of Kobe was to be still deferred until January 1, 1868, but the tariff would be revised, and the remaining instalments of the indemnity paid punctually. Thus the foreign representatives had obtained two out of the three conditions, and those the most important, while giving up nothing in return. It must, however, be acknowledged that the payment of the indemnity was never completed by the *shōgun*, and survived the revolution to be a constant source of irritation and ill-feeling between the emperor's government and the British minister.

Munehide, on leaving the *Princess Royal*, promised that a note embodying these arrangements should be sent off in the course of the evening. But as it had to be sent up to Osaka to receive the signatures of his two remaining colleagues, the document did not reach us before half-past two in the morning. I sat up till that hour in expectation of its arrival, and was called into the cabin to read it to Sir Harry and Léon Roches, and then make a translation. The emperor's decree to his vizier the *kanpaku* delegating the conduct of foreign affairs to the *shōgun*, a short document of only three lines, was enclosed in it. At Sir Harry's request Matsudaira Munehide added an engagement to promulgate the decree throughout the country. It was a proud night for me when I displayed my knowledge of written Japanese in the presence of the French minister, whose interpreter, De Cachon, even could not read a document without the assistance of his teacher.

Thus successfully ended the negotiations which up to the day before showed no signs of fruit. The foreign representatives had to congratulate themselves on having secured the means of tranquillizing the country, while at the same time consolidating the relations between the Japanese people and foreign nations. The opening of Kobe on the 1st January 1866 was a concession which few people had been sanguine enough to expect, but something had been secured which was of more immediate value, namely the solemn reiterated promise of the council to adhere to the London agreement of 1862. It was hoped also on good grounds that Sir Rutherford's convention of the previous October would also be carried out in its entirety. At dinner the following evening the admiral made a speech, proposing Sir Harry's health and giving to him the whole credit of the success achieved. He replied by disclaiming any merit, and attributing a far greater share of the achievement to Roches; "but after all," he added, "it was you who did it, admiral, for without you and your magnificent ship, we should not have made the slightest impression."

On our return to Yokohama we found that the wildest rumours had been flying about. The United States chargé d'affaires, Anton Portman, was said to have been killed, and Sir Harry taken prisoner, while Siebold and myself were also reported to have fallen martyrs to the cause. The *Japan Times*, a newspaper conducted by Charles Rickerby, affected to pooh-pooh the whole affair, and denied the authenticity of the emperor's decree, which, he said, ought to have been covered with seals. I wrote a letter to his paper, controverting his arguments, but without convincing him. There was one point about it that escaped notice at the time, namely that the existing treaties were not explicitly sanctioned. All that the emperor had given was a general authority to conclude treaties with foreign countries, and he had added a rider enjoining on the *shōgun* the cancellation of the undertaking to open Kobe and Osaka to trade. This was carefully concealed from the foreign representatives, and we only came to know of it later. But without seeing it, no one could have guessed that the document represented to the foreign ministers to be the emperor's sanction to the existing treaties had not that meaning, because of the absence of the definite article in Japanese. In English it makes a great deal of difference whether you say "the treaties are sanctioned," or simply "treaties are sanctioned," but in Japanese the same form of expression does for both, and we had no ground for suspecting the *shōgun*'s ministers of taking refuge in an ambiguity in order to play a trick on us and to gain time.

Fire at Yokohama

In pursuance of instructions from the chief, I proceeded to Edo the day after my return to find out if possible what had been the popular feeling about our doings at Kobe, but did not succeed in discovering anything of importance. A general curiosity prevailed, and the result of the negotiations was yet unknown. A meeting of the *daimyō*'s agents had been held on the receipt of the news that two of the council had been dismissed, and it was rumoured that the *shōgun* had asked to be allowed to retire, but that his petition had been rejected.

I stopped at the monastery of Daichū-*ji*, which had been temporarily lent to Sir Harry for a residence. It was in a convenient position, nearer to the centre of the city than our former location at Tōzen-*ji*, though the rooms were dark and scarcely numerous enough for the accommodation of the staff in addition to the minister and his family. A new building had therefore been already commenced in front of Sengaku-*ji*, about halfway between the two. Instead of being called the British legation, it was to be named the *setsugu-jō* or "place for meeting (foreigners)," in order to avoid the risk of its being burnt down by the anti-foreign party. Report said that the lord of Sendai, offended at not having been consulted on this matter, had retired to his castle in great dudgeon. Sengaku-*ji* is a well-known monastery containing the tombs and effigies of the celebrated Forty-seven Faithful Retainers. After a couple of days' stay at the capital, I returned to my duties at the consulate in Yokohama, where I now held the post of interpreter.

I was beginning to become known among the Japanese as a foreigner who could speak their language correctly, and my circle of acquaintance rapidly extended. Men used to come down from Edo on purpose to talk to me, moved as much by mere curiosity as by a desire to find out what foreign policy towards their country was likely to be. Owing to my name being a common Japanese surname (Satō), it was easily passed on from one to another, and I was talked about by people whom I had never met. The two-sworded men were always happy to get a glass of wine or liqueur and a foreign cigar, and they were fond of discussion. They would sit for hours if the subject interested them. Politics afforded the principal material of our debates, which sometimes became rather heated. I used to attack the abuses of the existing regime, and then explain that I liked them very much, but hated despotic institutions. Many of the men who visited me were retainers of *daimyō*, from whom I gained every day a firmer conviction that the *shōgun* ought not to be regarded by foreigners as the sovereign of the country, and that sooner or later we must enter into direct relations with the emperor. And the state papers, of which copies came into my hands through these men, proved that the *shōgun* regarded himself as nothing more than the emperor's principal vassal. At the same time the *shōgun*'s ministers still persevered in their endeavour to keep the conduct of foreign affairs in their own hands, and had succeeded in persuading Winchester that this was an ancient and indefeasible prerogative of the Tokugawa family. Sir Harry Parkes from the first, with clearer insight, held that this was untenable, and resolved to press matters to a definite solution, which should bring the sovereign face to face with foreign powers.

Sir Harry had gone over to Shanghai to meet Lady Parkes and his children, and immediately after his return set to work at the revision of the tariff on the basis agreed to at Kobe. The negotiations, which began about January 1866, took much less time than is usual in these days, and the new convention was signed in June. I had little to do with it beyond assisting in its translation into Japanese. In February he began to make use of me as a translator, in addition to my work at the consulate.

My salary as interpreter at the Yokohama consulate, which I had joined in April 1865, was only £400 a year, and after the Kobe business, where I had demonstrated my knowledge of the Japanese language, I began to think my services worth quite as much as those of the Dutch interpreters, who received £500. At an interview with the Japanese ministers they used to translate into Dutch what the minister said, and the native Dutch interpreters translated this again into Japanese. The reply had in the same way to go through two men. But when Siebold or I interpreted, the work was performed much more quickly and accurately, because we translated directly into Japanese.

It was the same with the official correspondence, for I was able, with the assistance of a native writer, and sometimes without, to put an official note directly into Japanese. Then I was able to read and translate into English all sorts of confidential political papers, which the Dutch interpreters could make nothing of. We took a bold resolution, and in August 1866, Sir Harry having given me a quantity of political documents to translate, we addressed letters to him asking that he would recommend us to the Foreign Office for an additional £100 a year. This brought down his wrath upon our heads, and I became convinced that my application would be refused. Under these circumstances I wrote to my father that the service was not worth remaining in. At that time the telegraph reached only to Ceylon, but in as short a time as possible I received a telegram from him telling me to come home at once, and that I should have an allowance sufficient to enable me to go to the university and afterwards to the bar. Armed with this, I approached Sir Harry again, and asked him to accept my resignation. I had received a telegram from home which necessitated my immediate return to England. After a little humming and hawing, he finally produced from a drawer a despatch from Lord Clarendon, which had been lying there for several days, granting the applications of both Siebold and myself, and I consequently abandoned my intention of quitting the service.

About March 6, 1866, a review and sham fight were held of the English garrison in combination with the Japanese drilled troops commanded by Kubota Sentarō on the dry rice fields between Jūniten and Honmoku. The enemy was entirely imaginary, his place being taken by a crowd of spectators. The marching of the Japanese was very good, and received all the greater praise because they had received no practical instruction. Their officers had got it up from books, the difficult passages being explained to them by ours. The English soldiers looked magnificent by the side of the rather dwarfish Japanese. The bluejackets from the fleet were very amusing; one or two got drunk and danced a hornpipe in the face of the supposed enemy, to the great wrath and disgust of their commander, a young lieutenant. There was the usual amount of firing with blank cartridge, which, when it comes from one side only, renders everyone so plucky and desirous of charging the foe. It was a wonder that no ramrods were fired away, nor was anyone hit by a wad. The day was universally voted a great success.

The 2/xx regiment was despatched to Hongkong about March 20, and replaced by the 2/ix.

The danger to foreigners had so much abated since the execution of the murderers of Bird and Baldwin and the ratification of the treaties by the emperor that we began freely to make excursions into the surrounding country.

On one occasion I went away for a few days with Charles Rickerby of the *Japan Times*, and having thus become intimate with him, was permitted to try my inexperienced pen in the columns of his paper. My first attempt was an article upon travelling in Japan, but before long an incident occurred which tempted me to write on politics. It was doubtless very irregular, very wrong, and altogether contrary to the rules of the service, but I thought little of that. A Satsuma trading steamer had come into the bay, and was ordered by the authorities to anchor far away on the Kanagawa side, so that there might be no communication between the foreign community and the people on board. Taking this for my text, I descanted on the insufficiency of the treaties concluded with the *shōgun*, which confined us to commercial intercourse with the inhabitants of his dominions, and thus cut us off from relations with a good half of the country. I called therefore for a revision of the treaties, and for a remodelling of the constitution of the Japanese government. My proposal was that the *shōgun* should descend to his proper position as a great territorial noble, and that a confederation of *daimyōs* under the headship of the emperor should take his place as the ruling power. And then I proceeded to make various suggestions for the improvement and modification of the existing treaties.

With the aid of my teacher, Numata Torasaburō, a retainer of the lord of Awa, who knew some English, I put them into Japanese in the form of a pamphlet for the perusal of his lord, but copies got into circulation, and in the following year I found myself to be favourably known through this means to all the *daimyō* retainers whom I met in the course of my journeys. In the end the translation was printed and sold in all the bookshops at Osaka and Kyoto under the title of *Ei-koku sakuron* (*English policy*) by the Englishman Ernest Mason Satow, and was assumed by both parties to represent the views of the British legation. With this of course I had nothing to do. As far as I know it never came to the ears of my chief, but it may fairly be supposed to have been not without its influence upon the relations between the English legation and the new government afterwards established in the beginning of 1868. At the same time, it doubtless rendered us more or less suspect to the *shōgun's* government while the latter lasted.

During Sir Harry's absence in July on a visit to the *daimyō* of Satsuma and Uwajima after the signature of the tariff convention, some of us at the legation made up a party with three or four officers of the ix regiment, and went for a trip to Hachiōji and Atsugi. In those days all the high roads were intersected at certain points by strictly guarded barriers, where all travellers had to show their passports. Beyond Hachiōji a few miles to the west was one of these, just at the foot of a hill known as Takao-*zan*, about 1600 feet high, with a good road to the top. Up this we rode on our sure-footed ponies, and after lunching under the shade of the lofty cryptomerias, descended to the high road again, but unintentionally reached it beyond the barrier. The guards, who were inclined to interpret their duties rather too strictly than otherwise, shut the gates and refused to let us pass. It was in vain that we explained our mistake; they had orders not to let foreigners through. One would have thought that as we were on the side where we had no business to be, and were desirous of getting back to the right side, the officers in command would have facilitated our wishes to repair our error. But nothing would move them. At last Willis, who stood six feet eight inches in his stockings and weighed then about twenty stone, made as if he would charge the gate on his pony. Seriously alarmed lest he should batter the whole thing down in a rush, they prudently flung it open, and we rode through triumphantly.

A similar incident occurred on another occasion when I was out with Francis Myburgh, Captain Jones, of the flagship, and Charles Wirgman. The limit of excursions from Yokohama in the direction of the capital was formed by the Tama River, which in the treaties is called the Logo (a corruption of

Rokugō) River. We had slept at Mizoguchi, and ascended the right bank on horseback to Sekido, where without difficulty we induced the ferryman to put us across, and rode into the town of Fuchū to visit a well-known Shintō temple. We were bound for a monastery on the other side of the river, where we had planned to spend the night. To do this it was necessary to recross further up to the Buddhist monastery of Renkō-*ji*. But on arriving there, and shouting to the ferryman, we got a blank refusal, accompanied by the information that we had no business to be where we were. "We know that we are, and want to get back where we ought to be."

Ferryman: "Can't help that. Our orders are not to ferry any foreigner over."

It was impossible to convince him that though he would be right in refusing to facilitate a breach of the law, he was bound to assist the repentant and contrite offenders in repairing such a breach, and we saw ourselves menaced with separation from our baggage and perhaps a cold night on the stones. Just above the ferry was a shallower spot, too deep to cross on ponies without getting rather wet. Charles Wirgman and I therefore took off our trousers, and tucking our shirts up as high as possible waded to the other bank, walked down to the ferry house, jumped into the boat before the ferrymen had time to recover from their surprise at our audacity, poled it across to our friends amid cries of *Kore wa rambō rōzeki* (about equivalent to "Robbery and murder") from the guardians of the posts, and so got the whole party across.

On November 26 occurred one of the most destructive fires with which Yokohama has ever been visited. One fourth of the foreign settlement and one-third of the native town were laid in ashes. The fire-bell began to ring about nine o'clock in the morning. Willis and I ascended to the look-out on the roof of our house and saw the flames mounting to the sky exactly to windward of us, maybe half a mile away. I rushed into a pair of boots (unluckily my oldest), and putting on my hat, hastened forth to find out the location of the fire. My servants said it was only a few doors off, but when I got that distance it proved to be further away, and I pursued my course for a quarter of an hour before arriving on the scene. From the lower end of a narrow street, usually well crowded but now absolutely crammed with people, there surged along an agitated multitude carrying such of their goods as they had been able to snatch from the devouring element that closely pursued them.

I approached as near as I could to the burning houses, but finding that the conflagration was rapidly advancing, beat a hasty retreat and made my way to the open space at the back of the settlement, where a terrible spectacle of confusion presented itself to my eyes. The portion of the native town where the fire was raging most violently was on a small island surrounded by a muddy swamp and connected with the rest of Yokohama by a wooden bridge, already crowded with fugitives; to wade or swim across to the firm ground was impossible. There were one or two boats available, but they were already overcrowded, and their occupants were so paralysed by fear that they never thought of landing and sending back the boats to take off others. Most of the inhabitants of the quarter were women. I saw a few poor wretches plunge into the water in order to escape, but they failed to reach the nearer bank. It was a fearful sight to see the flames darting among the roofs of the houses on the causeway, and sending forth jets here and there where the fire had not yet attained full mastery, when suddenly one half of the street nearest blazed up with a tremendous flash, and a volume of black smoke arose which obscured the sky. This was an oil merchant's shop that had caught fire.

I turned and fled homewards, for there was no time to lose. I knew my own house was doomed, as it lay directly to leeward from the fire, and a violent wind was blowing from the north-west. As I passed through the little garden I shouted to Willis to bestir himself, and called my servants to assist in packing up my movables. My first thought was for my manuscript dictionary; if that went I lost the results of two years' labour. So I put it into a light chest of drawers, and huddled some clothes in from the wardrobe. To get our things out we had to break down the high wooden fence round the garden. At this moment up came some friends, who plunged into the house and reappeared, some with books, others with half a chest of drawers, and we worked with a will until the building was cleared of everything but carpets, curtains, and the heavier furniture. My harmonium, a massive article, was also got into the street, and some men from the garrison carried it away to a place of safety.

By the time we had removed the salvage to what we thought was a respectable distance, the fire had reached the house, which five minutes later was a heap of glowing embers. It now became evident that the houses in the rear of the settlement had caught fire, and as my property was lying on the open space between the foreign and native towns, it had to be transported further. Here occurred a serious loss. Most of my books were in boxes which had been carried out bodily, but the rest, hastily wrapped up in blankets, had to be left. There were plenty of pilferers about, who, under the pretence of helping, carried off chests full of clothing that I never saw again. I lost a good many European volumes and a large number of Japanese books, besides some notes on Manchu and Chinese which were irreplaceable.

After we had deposited our property where we thought it would be in safety, it was threatened by the progress of the flames, and was therefore removed to a godown belonging to our friends Wilkin and Robison at No. 3 in the settlement. By this time the area of destruction had extended to the main street of the native town, and the houses where A. B. Mitford, Siebold, Walsh and Vidal lived, as well as our own, had already gone. A Japanese house lightly built of wood, with paper instead of glass, takes little time to burn. Next the fire spread to the nearest houses in the foreign settlement. Huge sparks and pieces of red hot wood flew across the intervening space, set the American consulate alight, ignited the roof of Jardine, Matheson & Co., and began to spread along both streets of the settlement. The supposed "fireproof" godown where most of our things were deposited caught fire, and nearly everything we had saved was destroyed. It was a scene of the wildest confusion.

Bluejackets were landed from the ships, and soldiers came down from the camp to work at the fire engines. There was no discipline among the men, and no organization existed for dealing with the disaster. After the final destruction of my own property I went about helping others to save theirs or to fight the flames, handing buckets, fetching water, pouring it on whatever seemed most inflammable. Some of the redcoats behaved disgracefully. They had managed to get hold of liquor, and stood by drinking and jeering, while we civilians did the work they had been brought there to perform. At the close of the day there remained to me only the clothes

I had on my back, and I was hatless. But the excitement had been so lively that I felt rather pleased at the idea of beginning the world afresh. I had saved the manuscript of the English-Japanese dictionary on which Ishibashi and I were then engaged, as well as that of an annotated edition of Sir Alcock's *Colloquial Japanese*, which was then in the press, though destined never to see the light. My loss came to between £300 and £400, a portion of which was afterwards made good to me by Her Majesty's government. The losses of the insurance offices amounted to $2,800,000, or about £700,000. The value of what was not insured was not great.

The conflagration raged so fiercely among the foreign warehouses and residences that before four o'clock in the afternoon it had made its way half down the bund, leaving only the club-house standing, and at one point it was thought that the whole settlement would be in a blaze before night. If that had happened the European community would have had to seek an asylum on board ship, but fortunately our fears were not realized. The flames seemed invincible by the side of our puny efforts.

The expedient was resorted to of blowing up houses in the line of fire, but not with great success, for some of those so destroyed were never touched by it at all, while in other instances the debris could not be cleared away, and only helped it to spread to the buildings beyond. One hundred and seven Europeans and Americans were rendered homeless, and many of those who had trusted in their so-called fireproof godowns were left without anything in the world but the clothes they stood in. Merchants whose goods were uninsured were devoured by a terrible anxiety, for the most solidly-constructed stone godowns seemed to offer little more resistance than the wooden houses of the Japanese.

Although the wind had fallen, much apprehension was entertained for the safety of what still remained unburnt, for owing to the damaged condition of the hose, all the fire engines had become useless, and nothing could be done to extinguish the smouldering embers. The fire was therefore left to burn itself out, and four days elapsed before the flames entirely died down. The price of clothing rose incredibly, as also did house rent. Yokohama was not as well supplied with hatters, tailors and bootmakers as it is in these days, and most men were in the habit of supplying themselves from home. For the next two years, consequently, I was reduced to a very moderate wardrobe. I had, for example, to pay $4, or 18 shillings, for five pocket handkerchiefs.

After the fire I took up my abode with my friend Tom Foster, then the manager of Gilman & Co.'s Yokohama branch, until December 9 or 10, when I migrated to the legation at Edo. The new buildings in front of Sen-gaku-ji were now completed, and enclosed by a lofty black wooden fence which imparted to the establishment somewhat of the aspect of a jail. There were two long wooden buildings, one of which was the minister's residence, the other being occupied by the members of the chancery. Eusden had gone to Hakodate as acting consul, and the staff consisted of Mitford as second secretary, Willis as assistant accountant and medical officer, Siebold and myself as interpreters, and Vidal as student interpreter. The infantry guard was commanded by Lieutenant Bradshaw. Sidney Locock, the first secretary, a married man with a family, lived at Yokohama, as did also Hiram Shaw Wilkinson, still a student. They were ramshackle buildings, all windows and doors, terribly cold from want of proper fireplaces and bad construction, which admitted draughts on every side. But I did not live there long.

After my transfer from the Yokohama consulate to the legation in the autumn of 1866, one of the first matters in which I was able to be of use to our new chief was connected with the wording of the treaty. In the English text the *shōgun* was spoken of as "His Majesty," and thus placed on a level with the Queen. In the Japanese version, however, this epithet was rendered by the equivalent of "Highness," and it was thus to be inferred that our sovereign was of lower rank than the emperor. Moreover, the word "queen" had been translated by a title borne by great-grand-daughters of an emperor. I recommended that a new Japanese version should be made, in which "Majesty" should be rendered by its proper Japanese equivalent, and "Queen" by the word *kōtei* (Hwang-ti), usually translated by "emperor" in all the Chinese-English dictionaries, but really meaning "supreme sovereign," and applicable to both sexes. The preparation of the new version was entrusted to my hands, and with the aid of my teacher I managed in about a month's time to complete an accurate translation, which was adopted as official. It was the keynote of a new policy which recognized the emperor as the sovereign of Japan and the *shōgun* as his lieutenant. We gave up the use of "*shōgun*," which my reading had taught me was properly a synonym for the emperor, in our communications with the Japanese government, though retaining it in correspondence with the Foreign Office, in order not to create confusion, but the most important result was to set in a clearer light than before the political theory that the emperor was the treaty-making power. As long as his consent had not been obtained to the existing treaties we had no *locus standi*, while after he had been induced to ratify them, the opposition of the *daimyō* ceased to have any logical basis.

Kagoshima and Uwajima

A few days after I had assumed my new duties, and had settled down, as I thought, for a period of uninterrupted study, Sir Harry informed me that he contemplated sending me down to Nagasaki in the *Princess Royal*, which was about to proceed thither through the Inland Sea, to collect political information at Kobe and elsewhere. I was to return in the *Argus* by way of Kagoshima and Uwajima. *Shōgun* Tokugawa Iemochi had recently died, and had been succeeded by his cousin Tokugawa Yoshinobu, whose position was not very clearly defined. Before his elevation to the headship of the Tokugawa family he had been regarded as a partisan of the "return to the ancient regime," now so much in men's mouths, and it was desirable to learn as much as possible of his probable line of policy. In Edo we were too far away from the political centre to learn much. I was greatly pleased at the prospect of visiting Nagasaki, but took care not to seem too desirous of being sent on the proposed mission, lest over-eagerness should defeat itself.

Next day I got a note from Sir Harry, who resided chiefly at Yokohama, telling me that he had not yet seen the admiral, but that he still thought I should have to go. So I packed up some clothes in a wicker basket such as the Japanese use when travelling, and went down to Yokohama in the gunboat which was our principal means of conveyance between the two places. In the evening I learned that the matter had been arranged, and that the *Princess Royal* would sail the next day but one. I wrote to Willis for his teacher Hayashi, whom I intended to put ashore at Kobe to collect news, and for a tin box containing some stationery, and a little money, but neither arrived in time. In despair I borrowed a few hundred *ichibu* from Foster, bought a box of cheroots, wrapped a few sheets of foolscap in a newspaper, and got on board on December 12 just in time.

We had fine weather for our start, but encountered a strong westerly wind outside, which prevented our passing between Ō Island and the mainland. For four days I lay in my cot, utterly unable to eat, but consoling myself with reference to previous experiences of the same kind. At last I was revived by a plateful of greasy beefsteak pudding that Admiral King sent me, and a glass of champagne. The gale had not abated, and the huge two-decker rolled terribly. At one time the betting was strong on Hongkong as our first port of anchorage, and Kobe was given up as quite unattainable. Hakodate, Yokohama and Nagasaki rose by turns to the position of favourite. We were blown right out of the chart of Japan, and at last, after many days of tossing to and fro, tacking and wearing, we sighted the Linschoten Islands, where we turned to the north, and steaming as fast as 400 horse power will carry a vessel of 3500 tons, got into Nagasaki on the evening of the 23rd.

The appearance of the town and foreign settlement, lighted up by innumerable lamps dotted all over the hillsides, reminded me of Gibraltar as I had seen it from the deck of the *Indus* a little more than five years previously.

At Nagasaki I made the acquaintance of some Uwajima retainers, the most important of whom was Iseki Sayemon, afterwards prefect of Yokohama in the first years of the emperor's rule. He came to call on me, and said that the proposed assemblage of a council of *daimyō* at Kyoto had been put off for the present. But it was sure to take place eventually, and one of the first topics of discussion would be the position of Chōshū. About half of Shikoku was in favour of Kobe being opened to foreign trade, but the Kyushu people opposed it, on account of the anticipated decline of Nagasaki. He thought that the visit of the admiral and Sir Harry Parkes in the *Princess Royal* to Uwajima had done immense good, by familiarizing the common people with the appearance of foreigners, and their ingenuity in the construction of ships and warlike appliances. Date Munenari, the *daimyō* of Uwajima and his brother the ex-*daimyō* (who was the leading spirit of the clan) had excused themselves on the ground of sickness from attending the council at Kyoto. Tokugawa Yoshinobu had not yet been invested with the office of *shōgun* and its attendant court titles, and the probability was that they would be withheld until he had settled the Chōshū difficulty, which would doubtless give him a good deal of trouble. When I met him again on the following day the conversation turned upon our relations with Chōshū. I told him that the British government had stationed a man-of-war at Shimonoseki to prevent merchant vessels frequenting the straits during the continuance of hostilities between Chōshū and the *shōgun*; we did not wish to interfere in any of the civil quarrels of the Japanese. We were at peace with Chōshū, who had agreed to let foreign vessels pass without molestation, and had undertaken to let them purchase wood, water, and other necessaries, while promising to build no more batteries.

The *shōgun*'s government had undertaken to pay the indemnity imposed upon the lord of Chōshū. The powers, however, did not care for the money, and would be willing at any time to abandon the indemnity if their doing so would tend to the improvement of relations with Japan. The *shōgun*'s people had asked for delay in making payment of the remaining instalments, and in consenting to this, the foreign ministers had obtained in return the concession of permission for Japanese to travel in foreign countries. It was to be supposed that the nation was desirous of having the ancient prohibition removed, and the government would have had, therefore, no excuse for maintaining it. Kobe would certainly be opened on January 1, 1868, in accordance with the undertaking entered into by the *shōgun*; the intention of the powers was to uphold the treaties in their entirety and get them carried out. We could not ask for the opening of Shimonoseki under the present treaties, as the *shōgun*'s authority did not extend so far. It would require a separate treaty with Chōshū. As long as the present treaties remained unchanged, no ports could be opened in *daimyō*'s territories.

At Kobe we had discussed matters with the *shōgun*'s Council, who, we now learned, had deceived us by concealing the emperor's injunction to them to negotiate for the abandonment of Osaka and Kobe as seats of foreign commerce. It was a pity we had not thrown them over, and negotiated directly with the emperor's court, from which we heard that a noble had been deputed to visit the foreign representatives.

During my stay at Nagasaki I made the acquaintance of officers from Tosa and Higo. One of the latter said that there never would be another *shōgun*, but that the emperor would be restored to the throne. Here was a clear glimpse into the future.

My instructions from Sir Harry were to proceed from Nagasaki to Kagoshima and Uwajima, and call in at Kobe on my way back. I embarked, therefore, on January 1, 1867, in the *Argus*, Commander Round, with my two servants, Noguchi Tomizō and Yasu. The former was a young samurai from Aizu, who had left his home and attached himself to Vyse, our consul at Hakodate, in order to study English. In the autumn of 1865 he came to live with me, to carry on his studies, and on the present occasion he had accompanied me to Nagasaki, from where he intended to sail for England as cabin-servant to Alexander Buller, the Commander of the flagship. But whether it was the tossing about on the way down, or the disagreeable servant's position, he now changed his mind, and begged me to take him back to Edo. Buller expressed himself as somewhat annoyed, but I could not help it. Noguchi eventually went with me in 1869 to England, where I paid for his schooling during a couple of years. After my return to Japan he stayed on awhile in London at the expense of the Japanese government, and eventually came back to Tokyo, where he obtained a minor appointment in a public office. In spite of his then comparatively elevated position, he never gave himself airs, or forgot that I had befriended him, and it was with great regret that I heard of his death about the beginning of 1885. He was honest and faithful to the end. Yasu was a young monkey belonging to the lower classes, and I don't remember that he had any virtues.

Round did not treat me very well, and made me sleep in the cockpit, a sort of common den in the bottom of the ship, where the midshipmen keep their chests and sling their hammocks. There was no privacy, and we were crowded together in a most uncomfortable manner. I got a cot to sleep in, but no mattress or pillow, and was forced to borrow a cushion off a bunk in the captain's cabin and roll up my greatcoat for a pillow.

We reached Kagoshima next day early in the afternoon. As soon as we dropped our anchor, some officers pulled off from the shore, bringing a flag for us to hoist while firing the salute in answer to theirs. Matsuoka Jūdayū came on board to explain that the lord and his father were in retirement owing to the recent death of the latter's mother. As neither was able to receive visitors, the duty of receiving the admiral's letter, of which we were the bearers, would be performed by the lord's second brother and two councillors. This was a letter thanking him for kindness shown to ship-wrecked sailors. Sir Harry and the admiral on their visit in the previous summer had seen and conversed with both the lord and his father Shimazu Hisamitsu, but I do not suppose that my being unable to meet them made much difference to the result of my visit, as the conduct of affairs was to a great extent in the hands of the principal retainers. I went ashore to stay at the factory with three Englishmen named Sutcliffe, Harrison and Shillingford. The last of these, an engineer by profession, had been engaged by the *daimyō* in connection with some cotton mills which he was erecting, the other two had come to Kagoshima in search of employment.

On January 3, Round came on shore with a party of officers to deliver the admiral's letter, and I accompanied him to interpret. We were met at the landing place by some high officials, who conducted us through the town for half a mile to the house, where we were received by Shimazu Hisaharu, a handsome youth, the second son of Shimazu Hisamitsu, Niiro Gyōbu, a councillor who had been in England, and Shimazu Ise, also a councillor. It was a house set apart for the reception of visitors. The lord's brother, 29 years years of age, seemed a perfect child as far as intelligence went. All the talking was done by the high officials who sat on his right hand. I interpreted the contents of the letter, which was then handed to Shimazu Hisaharu, the whole ceremony not occupying more than five minutes. We then sat down to an entertainment, which opened with a few courses of Japanese cookery with *sake*, but consisted in the main of an interminable succession of European dishes, moistened with sherry, champagne and brandy. I took my revenge upon Round by keeping up a lively conversation in Japanese, and translating none of it, so the poor man was driven to count the oranges in a dish which stood near, in order to keep off ennui. After the banquet, the officers dispersed themselves through the town, while I remained behind to assist in making a translation of the admiral's letter. Niiro also stopped. We talked about the proposed meeting of *daimyō*, which had been postponed *sine die*. Then I praised the composition of a letter which had been addressed to the emperor in the name of the lord of Satsuma some months back.

"Did you see it? What a stupid document it was," said Niiro.

"Not at all," I replied. "I thought it excellent, and the style was worthy of all praise."

"Had it not reference to Kobe?"

"No. I mean the memorial objecting to sending Satsuma troops to co-operate with those of the *shōgun* against Chōshū."

"Oh, yes. Shimazu Ise, who sat next to me today, was the writer of that letter. He was in Kyoto at the time."

"How is the Chōshū business getting on," I asked. "I hear the *shōgun* has withdrawn the greater part of his troops."

"Chōshū is very strong," he replied, "and he has right on his side. None of the *daimyō* will support the *shōgun*, and the latter has now no chance of beating him."

"Well, I think that if he had put his best troops into the field and attacked Chōshū energetically at first, he must have conquered him."

"No, never. He had not right on his side."

"You appear to be very friendly with Chōshū," I remarked.

"No," said he, "not friendly, but we have a natural fellow-feeling for one of our own class."

Niiro's reference to the letter of the lord of Satsuma, which he supposed I had seen, revealed that the Satsuma clan were opposed to the opening of Kobe. It was the presentation of this letter or memorial to the emperor during the visit of the foreign representatives in November 1865 that had encouraged the emperor to make it a condition of giving his sanction to the treaties that the *shōgun* should arrange for that port being given up. It was necessary, therefore, to impress on Niiro's mind, for the benefit of his fellow clansmen, that the foreign powers would not for a moment entertain the idea of giving up Kobe or any other part of the treaties.

At this moment there was lying in the bay a little steamer named the *Otentōsama*, belonging to Chōshū. She had brought down the leading man of that clan, Katsura Kogorō, afterwards known during the year of the revolution as Kido Takayoshi. I said to Niiro that I should like to call on him to inquire after some of my Shimonoseki friends. Niiro replied that Katsura was to have an interview with Shimazu Hisamitsu at ten o'clock the same evening, and a meeting afterwards with some of the Satsuma councillors at three in the morning. If I wished particularly to see him, I might go and sleep at his lodgings, and wait till he turned up. I declined the invitation, preferring a European bed, for at that time I was not so accustomed to Japanese ways as I afterwards became. It was weak on my part. But what Niiro said rendered it perfectly clear that an understanding was being negotiated between the two most powerful of the western clans, and that they would henceforth be united against the *shōgun*. Fortunate for us that they were on friendly terms with us, and fortunate also for the general interest of foreign powers, between whom and the revolutionary government of 1868 the British legation acted as mediators.

The French legation on the other hand supported the *shōgun*. Roches was projecting the foundation of the arsenal at Yokosuka, which would place the military organization of the Tokugawa family on a new and superior footing, and he had procured a distinguished staff of French officers to drill the *shōgun*'s troops. It was even rumoured that he had made, or was contemplating making, offers of material assistance to Tokugawa Yoshinobu. And this policy he pursued until the logic of facts at last demonstrated its folly, being followed by the North German chargé d' affaires, Max August Scripio von Brandt, and the Italian minister, Count Vittorio de la Tour. The Dutch political agent, Dirk de Graeff Polsbroek, adhered to Sir Harry, while the new American minister, General van Valkenburg, was neutral.

We had felt the pulse of the Japanese people more carefully and diagnosed the political condition better than our rivals, so that the prestige of the British minister in the years 1868 and 1869 was completely in the ascendant.

On January 4, the lord's reply was to have been delivered on board the *Argus*, but at noon Niiro presented himself to say that it was not yet ready. We therefore landed and inspected the glass factory, shot and shell foundry, gun foundry and pot and kettle foundry near the lord's garden at Iso. The letter now arrived in charge of Matsuoka, and after its formal delivery, we sat down once more to a banquet in European style. It was shorter than that of the previous day, and the dishes better cooked, but it was politeness rather than gastronomic satisfaction that caused us to praise it. For in truth the dinner was bad and ill-arranged.

About five o'clock I started off with Sutcliffe to call on Niiro, who had not been seen since the morning. After an hour's walking, we arrived at his house, darkness having already set in. Niiro received us very cordially, and entertained us with tea, oranges, beer, cakes and conversation for an hour and a half. He told me that in passing through Kobe lately he had heard that the French minister was shortly expected there with a letter from Emperor Napoleon III, and that there was to be a general gathering of foreign representatives. Tokugawa Yoshinobu had disappointed his friends by accepting the succession to the headship of the Tokugawa family, and was suspected of wishing to establish his power as *shōgun* with the aid of foreigners.

He gave me to understand that they regarded the French with dislike and distrust, and seemed to be all the more friendly with us because they had learned to appreciate the value of our enmity. The Satsuma people seemed to be making great progress in the civilized arts, and gave me the impression of great courage and straightforwardness. I thought they would soon be far ahead of the rest of Japan.

Shōgun, as I have said before, was the title given in the treaties to the temporal sovereign. The Japanese, however, never used it. Seiitai Shōgun, or "Generalissimo for the subjugation of barbarians," was his official designation, which delicacy prevented his ministers from employing in their official communications with the foreign representatives, while the common people spoke of him as Kubō-*sama*. The "opposition" *daimyō*, however, had adopted the term Bakufu, which most closely might be rendered by "military establishment," and it was this term that my friends and I used in conversation. In like manner, for the honorific designation *go-rōjū* (noble old men) applied in the east of Japan to the *shōgun*'s council of ministers, the expression *kakurō* (old ones) was substituted. The opposition refused to recognize that the government which they wished to upset was entitled to any mark of respect.

On January 5, 1867, we left Kagoshima and anchored in Uwajima Bay at eleven o'clock on the following day.

The beautiful bay is completely landlocked, and surrounded by hills of varying height up to 2000 feet. Close behind the town, on its east side, rises a high peak known as Oniga-*jō*, the "demon's castle." The lord's fortress was a conspicuous object to the right of the town. It stood on a low, wooded hill, close to the seashore, and consisted of a three-storied keep, surrounded by a double wall of stonework surmounted by white plastered walls, almost hidden by the trees. South of this lay the official quarter, the citizens' quarter being to the east and north, stretching for some distance along the shore, as the hills behind leave the town no room to expand. Close in shore the water is very shallow, and advantage had been taken of this to construct salterns and reclaim rice fields by building a dyke. There was a small battery on each side of the bay, more for show than for defensive use.

About an hour and a half after we anchored, a boat was noticed hovering about the stern, with a person in the stern-sheets busily engaged in examining the ship through an opera glass. Finding out that it was the lord, Commander Round sent a gig at once to invite him on board. He explained his curious behaviour by saying that he had wished to remain incognito. The admiral's letter wishing him a happy new year was produced, and after I had translated its contents, he took possession of it. He was aged 32, of about middle height, and had an aristocratic cast of countenance, with a slightly aquiline nose, on the whole a handsome man. As a matter of course he was shown over the ship. In the meantime I had some conversation with a gentleman-like young man of about twenty years of age named Matsune Kura, son of the principal *karō*. He said that Satsuma and Uwajima were on very friendly terms, which was natural, as the ex-*daimyō* and Shimazu Hisamitsu had been amongst the little band of lords who were disgraced for their opposition to the elevation of the lately deceased *shōgun*. Tokugawa Yoshinobu had not been appointed *shōgun*, and perhaps never would be.

When the lord returned on shore I accompanied him in the gig, and found a number of his women waiting for him on the bank with his children, the eldest of whom was a little boy of seven years of age. The others were mostly babies in arms, and each was attended by an undernurse bearing a small sword wrapped in gold brocade. The Japanese samurai was accustomed to the companionship of his weapon from his very infancy. The lord was extremely affable, and promised to repeat his visit on the following day, and to bring the *inkyo* or ex-*daimyō* with him. I said good-bye, and went into the town, where I met three officers from the ship engaged in "curio" hunting. An immense crowd followed us everywhere, examining our clothes

153

and asking all manner of questions, but behaving with the utmost civility. I felt my heart warm more and more to the Japanese.

On January 7, it rained violently and blew hard all day, but the weather did not prevent the *daimyō* and the *inkyo* from coming on board. The latter was a tall man with strongly marked features and a big nose, and reputed to be one of the most intelligent of his class, imperious in manner, and 49 years of age. He was not a born Date (that was the surname of the Uwajima *daimyō*), but had been adopted from a *hatamoto* family in Edo. After his adoption the present *daimyō* was born, and the relationship between them was that of brothers by adoption. But still the adopted son could not be set aside, and he eventually succeeded to the title and fief, but by way of compensation to the younger brother who had lost his birthright, he adopted him as his son. Consequently, when the lord was disgraced in 1858 the real heir succeeded. *Inkyo* (living retired) is a common term for the head of a family, whether noble or commoner, who has given up the active headship and the management of the estate to his son, a not unusual thing in old Japan for a father who had reached the sixties. Here the *inkyo* was manifestly the ruling spirit, and it was touching to observe the immense respect paid to him by the titular lord, who always addressed him as father, while he on his part used the depreciatory term *segare* (my youngster) in speaking of the *daimyō*. They stopped for a couple of hours talking and drinking some Moselle with which I had provided myself at Nagasaki.

The *inkyo* began to talk eagerly to me about the very suspicious intimacy that existed between the *shōgun*'s government (Bakufu) and the French legation, but as soon as old Matsune, the principal councillor, perceived that his master was becoming indiscreet, he hurried him away on the pretext that it would be too late to fire the salute. So away they went, amid the thunder of seventeen guns, which was returned from one of the batteries. After he left the wives and families of the two lords flocked on board. They were not in the least afraid of us, and conversed with as much ease and readiness as European ladies. There was a Japanese officer on board, afterwards Admiral Hayashi Kenzō.

Noguchi, who had been ashore to have a hot bath and get shaved, had brought me an invitation to dine with Irie, the captain of the battery. So I took a boat and went off in spite of the wind and rain. My host had not yet returned from his duties, but his wife asked me to come in, and in about a quarter of an hour he made his appearance. Soon afterwards another artillery officer named Mori came in, and then two more juniors. Dinner was at once ordered. It consisted of innumerable courses of fish and soup, and lasted from six o'clock till eleven. We talked, drank hot *sake*, and sang by turns, and I had to answer a multitude of questions on all possible subjects. This gave me numerous opportunities of uttering appropriate wise saws and proverbial sayings, which gave my hearers unbounded delight, and inspired them with no small amount of respect for the philosophy of the Western peoples. At half-past eleven the last guest retired, and after we had eaten a little rice, we went to bed in Japanese fashion. I was surprised to find that one could sleep comfortably without sheets.

On the following morning, after a good breakfast *à la Japonaise*, I rejoined the ship, and started in company with Round, and Wright and Dunn of the ixth regiment, who as I have hitherto neglected to mention, had come on board at Nagasaki, for the rifle range, in accordance with an engagement made on the previous day. A guard of honour of twenty-five men received us at the landing place, and we were escorted by an officer of the Uwajima navy. Halfway we found another guard, which fell in and led us up a pretty stiff hill to the ranges. Some of our small-arms men were landed to exhibit their skill. We had to walk a short distance and climb the hills. There is not sufficient flat ground in Uwajima for a proper rifle range, so the butts were placed on the side of another hill separated from us by a valley about 700 yards wide. Here we found tents set us, and the *inkyo*, his own son, and the lord awaiting our arrival. Our men, who were not accustomed to shooting across a chasm of unknown depth and width, showed themselves less skilful than the Uwajima marksmen, who had the advantage of knowing their ground.

We got the shooting over by half-past one, and the whole party then proceeded to the *goten*, or palace, which was outside the castle. It was an old building, dating from about 500 years back, but without pretensions to architectural style. We were not received at the great entrance, but at some temporary steps erected for the occasion which led up at once from the garden into the verandah. Here old Matsune met us and conducted us into a long room, which was shut off on all sides by handsome folding screens covered with gold leaf. At one end of the room was a particularly large screen, which the lord said was a present to his ancestor from the great *taikō-sama*, Toyotomi Hideyoshi. A table was placed down the middle of the room, with armchairs on the right side for the *inkyo*, the lord, and Matsune, while on the left were seated Round and his officers. I sat at the head of the table to facilitate conversation.

The dinner was beautifully got up, every separate dish prettily arranged and decorated, but the most tasteful of all was a wild duck with all its plumage perfect, and the roasted meat cut up small and laid on the back between the wings, elevated in such a way as to convey the idea that the bird was swimming and flying at the same time. Other dishes consisted of huge crayfish, and there was a large baked sea bream, as required by etiquette, for each person. Each of us had a large porcelain cup to drink from, and the warm liquor was handed round in pewter vessels with long spouts, like flat teapots. The ex-lord exchanged cups with Round, myself, and the two redcoats in turn, and the same ceremony was aftwards gone through with the lord and his minister, old Matsune.

There was a good deal of eating and saké drinking, and the *inkyo* presented me with a large shallow cup of red lacquer which I had first to empty. My companions left early, while at the *inkyo*'s request I remained behind for some conversation on politics. He began by speaking of Kobe, as to which he had expressed his opinion to Sir Harry Parkes in July last. But he was now in favour of opening the port to foreign trade, and so was Tokugawa Yoshinobu. He had heard that negotiations were proceeding with the French for its being opened next September, but he would prefer that the arrangements should be made with us rather than with the French, whom he did not like. I replied that I believed the French policy was based upon the belief that the country needed a recognized head, and that as they had a treaty with the *shōgun*, who apparently was the most powerful political personage, they thought it would be better to strengthen him as far as possible. The English policy was different. We regarded our treaty as having been made with Japan, and not with the *shōgun* in particular. If with the latter, then as there was no actual *shōgun* at the moment, our treaty would have to be regarded as being in abeyance. We did not wish to interfere, and were quite content that the Japanese should settle their internal disputes among themselves.

"But," said the *inkyo*, "if civil war becomes chronic, your trade will suffer, and you will have to put an end to it for your own sakes."

"No," I replied, "for if we interfered and took a side, matters would become ten times more difficult, and the foreign trade would come altogether to an end."

The *inkyo* then remarked that his idea was for Japan to become a confederated empire, with the emperor for its head, and that this idea was favoured by Satsuma and Chōshū. I said I thought there was no other way out of the difficulty, and I had written an article in a Yokohama newspaper to that effect. "Oh," said the *inkyo*, "I have read it," meaning the translation which has been already mentioned. At last the ex-lord said, "Let us send for the women and have some music. The captain will be jealous if he hears that I produced them to you after he had left, so don't tell him, but if he hears of it, you may say I was drunk."

Here the conversation was interrupted by the entrance of the ladies of the harem, such a bevy of pretty women, some wives and some not. All the children came in too. I had to drink *sake* with all of the ladies, till I began to fear my head might give way. Musical instruments were brought in, and a great deal of *sake* was drunk, greatly to the increase of friendliness and conviviality, but not to the advantage of the interchange of political views. In fact the *inkyo* gave himself up to enjoyment and would talk no more. He afterwards said in a casual sort of way: "You must not let it appear in the newspapers that I went on board the *Argus*, for I have declined attending the meeting at Kyoto on the ground of sickness, and I should not wish the government to hear of it. I should not like to be at Kyoto just now." After the music had begun, I looked round and saw one of the officers of the *Argus*, who had come in after the captain's departure, performing a Japanese dance. I proposed to him to dance a hornpipe, which he at once did, and the ex-lord, a man of the sober age of 49, got up, placed himself opposite, and tried to imitate the steps, holding up his loose trousers with both hands. The fun infected two of the ministers, who joined him in a three-handed reel.

After drinking a great deal of *sake* with the two lords and their ladies, I was carried off—no, led—to his own house by old Matsune, where more *sake* was produced, and I was made acquainted with the rest of his family. After about an hour's conversation, I was glad to get to bed, for the fumes of the hot *sake* were beginning to have some effect on my head. Hayashi, young Matsune, another Japanese and myself, slept in one room. Next morning I was roused before daylight by the report of a signal gun fired from the *Argus* to announce that she was ready to leave. I dressed hastily and went on board with young Matsune, to whom I presented my opera glass as a souvenir. Noguchi and my boy Yasu, who had also been sleeping on shore, had not yet made their appearance, but Round refused to wait for them. So I begged Matsune to send them somehow to Yokohama, and advance them any money which they might ask for, to be repaid to the Uwajima agent in Edo. At half-past six we weighed anchor, and steamed out of the bay, full of regrets at being obliged to part from our kind, hospitable friends.

We reached Kobe about noon on January 11, after visiting one or two unimportant places in the Inland Sea. I went on shore to inquire whether we could get coals, beef and vegetables. After arranging with the local officials to send some supplies on board, I walked about the town, and found the people quite accustomed to the sight of a foreigner. I met some two-sworded men, who protested that they were determined to prevent the opening of Kobe to foreign trade, but they were evidently joking. A Hizen man whom I came across declared that I was an old acquaintance, though I had never set eyes on him before. Afterwards Hayashi Kenzō and I went on board a Satsuma steamer that was lying in port, and made the acquaintance of her captain, Inoue Shinzaemon. She had brought up from Kagoshima one of the leading Satsuma men named Komatsu Kiyokado. He had gone up to Osaka to meet Saigō, the greatest of all the Satsuma leaders. I immediately proposed to go up to Osaka and see them, and letters were written by Inoue and Hayashi to Godai Tomoatsu (our captive of 1863 at Kagoshima) to make the necessary arrangements. Next day, however, I heard that Saigō was himself probably coming to Kobe, and in the meantime Hayashi took me ashore to have a hot bath and some luncheon.

Here for the first time I learned how to put on a cotton gown (*yukata*) after the bath, and enjoy the sensation of gradually cooling down. We had just sat down to eat when it was announced that Saigō had arrived, and hastily swallowing our rice, we sallied forth to the other house-of-call of the Satsuma men. Saigō, as I had all along suspected, turned out to be identical with the man introduced to me as Shimazu Sachū in November 1865, and he laughed heartily when I reminded him of his alias. After exchanging the usual compliments, I began to feel rather at a loss, the man looked so stolid, and would not make conversation. But he had an eye that sparkled like a big black diamond, and his smile when he spoke was so friendly. I began about the employment of foreigners in Satsuma and the difficulties which might, under certain circumstances, arise from the residence of British subjects outside the treaty limits and beyond the jurisdiction of the consular authorities. But this did not produce much in the way of response. So I bethought myself of another subject which was more likely to draw him, and inquired if Tokugawa Yoshinobu had not lately received in person a letter addressed to him by the emperor of the French. He replied "Yes." A short time ago he memorialized the emperor to the effect that there was a letter from the French emperor addressed to the *shōgun*, the reception of which had been delayed owing to the late *shōgun*'s detention at Kyoto in connexion with the expedition against Chōshū; that he now intended to summon all the foreign representatives to Osaka, and would profit by the occasion to receive the letter in question. Tokugawa Yoshinobu would accordingly come down to Osaka on the 17th of the Japanese month (January 22), and expected the representatives to arrive shortly afterwards. We (the Satsuma people) sent up a copy of the memorial to Sir Harry Parkes by the hands of Yoshii Kōsuke, but he had replied that he was uncertain whether he would accept the *shōgun*'s invitation, not having yet heard anything directly about the matter.

"But," I asked, "how can Yoshinobu receive a letter addressed to the *shōgun*. He is not *shōgun*, is he?"

"Yes; he received his commission the day before yesterday."

"Well," I replied, "that is very unexpected. I thought he had to settle Chōshū's affair first. But his influence must have increased immensely for him to have been able to manage this."

"Yes, indeed"—(emphatically)—"A man who was yesterday no better than a beggarly *rōnin daimyō* is today *seiitai shōgun*."

"Who," I asked, "contrived it."

"Itakura Katsukiyo" (a newly appointed member of the council). "Yoshinobu is in great favour now with the emperor, and he could become *kanpaku* (grand vizier) if he chose. He has made his brother Ninbutayu, a younger scion of the Mito house, head of the Shimizu family, which had become extinct, and he is going to send him as minister to France."

"On what business?"

"We have not the least idea."

"And for what is Yoshinobu going to summon the foreign representatives to Osaka?"

"We have not the slightest idea of that either," said Saigō.

"How odd that he should be able to do these things without consulting the *daimyō*."

"The *daimyō* ought to have been consulted, as we expected they would be henceforth on all political matters. The Bakufu have got on so badly of late years that my lord is of the opinion that they should not be left to ruin the country as they please. And when certain of the *daimyō* were summoned by the emperor to Kyoto, they expected to have a share in the government. Now they perceive that such is not the intention of the Bakufu, and they don't intend to be made fools of. So they have one and all refused to attend. Echizen stopped there as long as he could, but went away at last."

"Then everything is over for the present?" I said.

"Well, we shall be able to find him out in the next three years, I suppose."

"Three years is a long time. But this council at Kyoto, was it not connected with the latter part of the decree giving power to the *shōgun* to conclude treaties, where the emperor says, 'There are points in the existing treaties which I wish you to rectify in concert with the *daimyō*?'"

"Oh no!" said Saigō, "you are quite wrong there. It was intended, as I have said before, that the *daimyō* should consult with the Bakufu about government reforms."

"I suppose," I said, "that among other questions for discussion the Chōshū affair and the opening of Kobe were included. What is the position with regard to Chōshū? We foreigners cannot comprehend it?"

"It is indeed incomprehensible," Saigō replied. "The Bakufu commenced the war without justification, and they have stopped it equally without reason."

"Is it peace, or what?"

"No. Simply that hostilities have ceased, and the troops have been withdrawn. There the matter rests."

"For us foreigners it is a great puzzle why the Bakufu attacked Chōshū at all. It was certainly not because he had fired on foreign ships. If he really had offended the emperor, surely your lord, with his profound affection for the 'Son of Heaven,' could have lent assistance."

"I believe the Bakufu hated Chōshū all along," replied Saigō.

"It is a great pity the council did not take place, because it is of the highest importance that the affairs of the country should come to a settlement within this year. We have a treaty with Japan, not with any particular person, and we don't intend to interfere with you in the settlement of your domestic disputes. Whether Japan is governed by the emperor or the Bakufu, or becomes a confederation of separate states is a matter of indifference to us, but we want to know who is the real head. I confess to you that we have serious doubts about the Bakufu. We saw that they are not supreme, or rather not omnipotent when they asked us to let them off the opening of Kobe. Then the murder of Richardson and the impotence of the Bakufu to punish his murderers showed us that their authority did not extend as far as Satsuma. Then, when ships-of-war belonging to friendly nations were fired on by Chōshū, we had to go and punish them because the Bakufu could not do it. And we see now that Chōshū has got the best of the late war. These things make us doubt the supremacy of the Bakufu throughout the country, and we had hoped that the council would settle the difficulty. The Bakufu will again be in a difficult position next year when, as we intend to do, we demand the opening of Kobe, if the *daimyō* oppose it."

"My master does not oppose the opening of Kobe, but objects to its being opened after the fashion of other ports. We want it to be opened so as to be a benefit to Japan, and not solely for the private advantage of the Bakufu."

"But how would you have it opened?" I asked.

"By placing all questions regarding Kobe in the hands of a committee of five or six *daimyō*, who would be able to prevent the Bakufu from acting exclusively for its own selfish interests. Kobe is very important to us. We all owe money to the Osaka merchants, and we have to send the productions of our provinces to them every year in payment of our debts. Our affairs will be much thrown out of order if the place is opened on the same plan as Yokohama."

"I see now why you attach so much importance to Kobe. It is your last card. It is a great pity you cannot settle all your internal difficulties before the port is opened."

"When we sent Yoshii up to see Sir Harry Parkes, he told him if he came to Osaka to ask for us. We could not go to call on him for fear of incurring suspicion. And Sir Harry replied that he would ask not only to see the lord of Satsuma, but all the other *daimyō* as well."

Sake and *sakana* (*i.e.* its accompaniments) were now introduced, and we were waited on by a good-looking girl who was said to be a sweetheart of Godai's. Saigō excused himself and retired for a few moments with my companion Hayashi, who was apparently a confidential agent of the Satsuma people. After the second course, as he seemed in a hurry to get away, I rose to go, but he would not hear of my leaving so early. I begged him not to stand on ceremony, but to leave whenever he chose, as I knew he had a long way to go. After a few minutes more, he rose, and saying, "In case Sir Harry wants to communicate anything to us, he has only to send a message to our house at Edo, and we will despatch anyone he likes from Kyoto to see him," he took his departure. I thanked him very warmly for coming so far to see me, and we bade each other farewell. The feast was resumed, and after numerous courses, Hayashi and I went back on board the *Argus* by half-past seven. Next day we left for Yokohama. During our stay at Kobe we had walked freely about the town, and found the people perfectly civil. They were evidently becoming accustomed to the sight of foreigners, and scarcely took any notice of us as we passed through the streets.

First Visit to Osaka

On reaching Yokohama, on January 15, 1867, I duly made my report to the chief of all I had seen, heard, and said, and took up my quarters on the following day at Edo. The first news I learned was that the *shōgun* had invited all the foreign representatives to meet him at Osaka, and that they would probably accept. His object, it was explained, was to break through all the traditions of the past eight years and to make the treaties of friendship which had been concluded by Japan with foreign countries more of a reality than they had hitherto been. But Sir Harry, who had now learned enough of the internal political condition to convince him that the *shōgun's* power was fast decaying, still hesitated, and it was only when he found a majority of his colleagues determined to go, that he made up his mind to join them. But he persuaded them that it would be well to have inquiries made beforehand as to the kind of accommodation that would be provided, and consequently deputed Mitford and myself to proceed thither in the *Argus*.

Joined by Captain Cardew of the 2/ix, we reached Kobe on February 9, after a two days' run. A couple of subordinate officials of the *shōgun's* foreign department had accompanied us to make the necessary arrangements, and were landed at once to provide for our going to Osaka without loss of time. We determined to go by land. The *Princess Royal*, *Basilisk*, *Serpent*, and *Firm* were in port, having just arrived from visiting the lords of Chikuzen at Fukuoka, and the lords of Chōshū at Mitajiri. Lord Walter Kerr of the *Princess Royal* kindly gave me photographs of the four nobles and of two of the leading councillors of Chōshū. Among them was Kido Takayoshi, already mentioned.

On board the *Princess Royal* I met some native traders, who were greatly interested in the approaching opening of the port, and discussed various suitable sites for a foreign settlement. They also conveyed to me the news of the emperor's death, which had only just been made public. Rumour attributed his decease to smallpox, but several years afterwards I was assured by a Japanese well acquainted with what went on behind the scenes that he had been poisoned. He was by conviction utterly opposed to any concessions to foreigners, and had therefore been removed out of the way by those who foresaw that the coming downfall of the Bakufu would force the court into direct relations with Western powers. But with a reactionary emperor nothing but difficulties, resulting probably in war, was to be expected. It is common enough in Eastern countries to attribute the deaths of important personages to poison, and in the case of the last preceding *shōgun* rumours had been pretty rife that he had been made away with by Tokugawa Yoshinobu. In connexion with the emperor I certainly never heard any such suggestion at the time. But it is impossible to deny that his disappearance from the political scene, leaving as his successor a boy of fifteen or sixteen years of age, was most opportune.

Noguchi and my boy Yasu turned up here, having been forwarded from Uwajima. They were full of excuses, which were readily admitted.

We got away on the morning of February 11, and Lieutenant Thalbitzer, a Danish officer from the *Argus*, having joined us, we were a party of four. Ponies had been provided by the Japanese authorities, and we had an escort of nine men armed with swords from the corps which supplied the guards of the foreign legations at Edo. Our steeds were small, ill-fed, and untrained, but each had a splendid running footman, who kept up the pace in magnificent style. Troops had been posted along the road for our protection, and the whole number thus detailed cannot have been less than 1500. This gave us a novel and somewhat embarrassing sense of importance. The road is perfectly flat the whole way, and fairly straight until it approaches Osaka, when it begins to make zig-zags which lengthened it unnecessarily. This plan was formerly adopted nearly all over Japan in the vicinity of *daimyō*'s towns for strategical purposes. As the roads nearly always run through the swampy rice fields, a hostile force is unable to march straight at its point of attack, but must follow the road, being thus constantly exposed to a flank fire from the defending force occupying the other arm of the angle ahead.

Soon after passing Amagasaki we came in sight of the castle of Osaka, a conspicuous object in the landscape by its shining white walls and many-storied towers, visible for many a league. At last we reached the city. Although our guides missed the route at first, and here and there a break occurred in the troops which lined the narrow streets, the crowd quietly made way for us, and stood in front of the houses without uttering a sound. At every corner there was an immense concourse, and the side-streets were filled with eager, gazing faces as far as the eye could reach. We crossed the great wooden bridge over the river which runs through the city, turned to the left along the embankment, and bending again to the right proceeded down a long, apparently interminable street until we finally reached our lodgings at the Hongaku-*in* monastery. Here we found some officials of the foreign department, and received calls from a few of the local functionaries. Everything had been done to make us comfortable, and the locality was the best that could have been selected. It was impossible to avoid contrasting this generous hospitality with the reluctant, almost hostile, reception accorded to us on the occasion of our visit in 1865. The times had evidently changed since the accession of the new *shōgun*, and the recent death of the emperor did not appear to have made any difference in his plans and intentions for the carrying-out of a conciliatory policy.

Preparations had been made by the officials for our accommodation to the best of their ability. After washing off the dust of our long ride in a comfortable bathroom, we sat down to a dinner served in imitation of Western fashion, with French wines, including an excellent bottle of Larose. Alas, it was the only one. The seats were mere four-legged wooden stools, and I suffered a good deal from them during our stay. Afterwards we inspected the bedrooms. The bedsteads were mere makeshifts, but there was a plentiful supply of bedding, consisting of cotton quilts and stuffed silk coverlets. The toilet service was made up of two ludicrously small basins and, underneath the toilet table, a huge water pot; at the side were a cake of almond soap and a bottle of eau-de-cologne. But what seemed especially unusual was the deference of manner and language exhibited by all the officials with whom we came in contact. Hitherto I had experienced only familiarity approaching to rudeness at the hands of government officers.

On the following morning we were visited by Suzuki, an official of the Date clan, who came with a message from the resident *karō* to beg that we would not visit them at their *yashiki*, but at the same time he managed to convey the contrary impression. I sent Noguchi to the Satsuma *yashiki* to invite Komatsu Kiyokado to call on us, and to that of the Date to convey my thanks for the kindness exhibited to my two servants. In the afternoon we went out for a walk in the Shinsai-*bashi* Suji, which is the principal street of the city, preceded by a small band of one-sworded men, who emitted a cry like a crow—*kau, kau*—to warn the people out of the way. Dense crowds hovered on our footsteps, eager to catch a glimpse of the strangers, for no Europeans had been in Osaka since the last Dutch mission from Nagasaki had passed through a few years before. We were no less inquisitive, and made a great round, past all the booksellers' and mercers' shops, till dark.

Our next visitor was Yoshii Kōsuke, whom I have already mentioned. He reminded me that we had met at Kobe in the autumn of 1865 on board the steamer, when I had also seen Saigō for the first time. Yoshii was a little man, very vivacious and talked with a perfect Satsuma brogue. Every day we spent the greater part of our time in sight-seeing, and the officials proved obliging in every way. We had only to express a wish and it was immediately gratified. In a day or two we got Komatsu and Yoshii to tiffin. The former was one of the most charming Japanese I have known, a *karō* by birth, but unlike most of that class, distinguished for his political ability, excellent manners, and a genial companion. He had a fairer complexion than most, but his large mouth prevented his being good-looking. They partook heartily of *pâte de foie gras* and pale ale, and at last became so merry that we feared they might make indiscreet revelations in the presence of the Tokugawa servants who crowded the house.

On the next day Mitford and I returned their visit at the Satsuma *kura-yashiki*, or produce agency, near the river bank. Yoshii received us at the door, and ushered us into a room where we found Komatsu, the agent and Matsuki Kōwan. The latter was one of the two prisoners taken by us in 1863, and I had some suspicion that he was not altogether to be trusted, as he was reported to have been in the *shōgun*'s service during the interval.

So after the exchange of compliments I suggested that we might have some more private talk. It was a mistake on my part, however. Matsuki afterwards changed his name to Terashima Munenori, or perhaps merely reassumed it, and held office pretty constantly since the revolution of 1868, chiefly in connexion with foreign affairs. So Komatsu, Yoshii, Mitford and I retired together into an inner room.

They told us the emperor had died on January 30, though the date officially announced was February 3. He had been succeeded by his son, a youth of fifteen, who, it was thought, had in him the makings of a clever man if properly educated in foreign and domestic politics. But unfortunately the Bakufu would not allow him to be approached by any teachers who could improve his mind. During the new emperor's youth, the conduct of public affairs would be carried on in his name by the *kanpaku* (best rendered vizier). This officer is chosen from one of five noble court families, nominally of course by the emperor, but in reality by the *shōgun* and principal *daimyō*. The present *kanpaku* was a wise and good man, but too much disposed to listen to the counsels of the Bakufu. They thought the new *shōgun*'s idea in inviting the foreign representatives to Osaka was merely a countermove to the invitations which Sir Harry Parkes had accepted from the *daimyō* of Satsuma and Uwajima. The *shōgun* would probably talk a great deal about drawing closer the bonds of friendship, but would avoid treating about the opening of Kobe. The Bakufu did not wish that event to take place, because it would let a flood of light into the minds of the emperor and the court nobles. Komatsu said he had remonstrated with the Bakufu for delaying to hand over the land at Kobe and postponing the notification of the tariff convention of last June, their answer being that they had not yet made up their minds on those subjects. Satsuma, he said, had purchased some land near Kobe as a site for a *kura-yashiki*, of which they would be willing to let us have the greater portion for a foreign settlement. Satsuma wished to see the place opened to foreign trade, but wanted it to be done in a proper manner. Many of the court nobles were also in favour of the measure. These were men of liberal tendencies, but not in favour with the Bakufu, which had imprisoned some of them and refused them access to the emperor.

Affairs being in a critical condition, it was probable that the *shōgun* would stop a long time at Kyoto. Were he to return to Edo, he would lose his hold over the emperor, and Chōshū might make another dash at the palace. None of the *daimyō* had proceeded specially to Kyoto for the investiture of the *shōgun*, the absent ones being represented by their agents. Komatsu begged us to tell Sir Harry that it was not the desire of the lord of Satsuma and the other *daimyō* who acted with him to upset the Bakufu, but simply to restrain them from misusing their powers. They hoped, however, to see the emperor restored to his ancient position as *de facto* ruler of the country. All the plans and hopes of Satsuma tended to the benefit of the country, and not to a revolution against the *shōgun*. If Sir Harry on his arrival would propose to make a treaty with the emperor, the *daimyō* would at once give in their adhesion, and flock to Kyoto in order to take part in carrying out the great scheme. All that was necessary was for him to help them to this extent, and they would do the rest.

The conversation had now lasted so long that we thought it best to break off, for fear of exciting suspicion, and we returned to the other room, where a capital Japanese luncheon was spread out. To my great surprise we were joined by Inoue Bunda, whom I had not seen since the bombardment of Shimonoseki. His face was now disfigured by a huge scar, the vestige of one of several wounds which he had received in the course of a party fight down in Chōshū. He said his people had now got the steam up and would like to give the *shōgun* another thrashing. He brought a message from the lord to Sir Harry inviting him to visit the province at the earliest opportunity. When Sir Harry last passed through Shimonoseki, he said, the French minister was there, and that accident had prevented an intended interview. The Satsuma people expressed the hope that Mitford and I would visit Kagoshima as soon as possible.

We had a discussion with Shibata Takenaka, one of the commissioners for foreign affairs, about Sir Harry's public entry into Osaka, and settled all the details quietly and amicably. But when we came to the ceremony of presentation to the *shōgun* some difficulties cropped up. He wanted the British minister to make his bow outside the room in which the *shōgun* would be, and we could not allow this. Our object was to insist on the forms being as like those of European courts as possible.

Noguchi, as I have said, belonged to the Aizu clan, which furnished the best part of the *shōgun*'s fighting force at Kyoto. I had sent him there to see his people, and he returned with the news that some were coming down to call on me. Accordingly, late in the evening of the 17th, four of them appeared, named Kajiwara Heima (a *karō*), Kurazawa Uhei, Yamada Teisuke and Kawara Zenzayemon, bearing as presents rolls of light blue silk damask, and lists of swords and other articles to be hereafter given to Sir Harry, Mitford, and myself. In making official presents the custom was that a list written on thick, light cream-coloured paper called *hōsho-gami* should accompany the articles, and often, if these were not ready, the list was handed over beforehand. We had nothing to give in return, but entertained them to the best of our ability. Kajiwara in particular distinguished himself by drinking champagne, whiskey, sherry, rum, gin and gin and water without blinking or shrinking. He was a particularly handsome young fellow, with a fair complexion, and had perfect manners. We gave them a letter of intro-duction to Captain Hewett of the *Basilisk*, as they wanted to see a foreign man-of-war. This was the foundation of a close friendship between myself and the Aizu clan, which survived the war of the revolution and the completest possible difference of opinion on Japanese internal politics. But they never resented the part we took, clearly seeing that all the English wanted was the good of the Japanese as a nation, and that they were not partisans of any faction.

Our new friends came a couple of days later to tiffin, when they were regaled with champagne and preserved meats, greatly to the elevation of their spirits. It ought to be noted that in those days it was quite the proper thing to get drunk at a dinner party, and a host whose guests went away sober would have been mortified by a feeling that his hospitality had not been properly appreciated. One of them got very tight, and began to talk things unfit for the ears of boys or maidens, while another produced a packet of indecent pictures, which he generously distributed among the four of us. In return for this entertainment Kajiwara invited us to go and drink *sake* with him in the evening. We at once accepted, but had some trouble with the foreign department officials from Edo, to whom it appeared an improper violation of all precedent for members of a foreign legation to attend a feast given by a *daimyō's* man, even though the *daimyō* belonged to the *shōgun's* party. We could therefore trust them to make every effort behind our backs to prevent the entertainment coming off.

The afternoon was spent in visiting the boats in which it was proposed to bring the British minister and his suite to the temporary legation, and a long weary tramp of it we had, but at last we got to the place where they would leave the men-of-wars' boats. Embarking here, we made an experimental trip ourselves, and came to the conclusion that it would not do. To begin with, the distance was very great, and poling against the stream was a slow method of progression. Next, instead of showing themselves to the populace, the minister and his staff would be almost hidden from view, and would be taken through a succession of narrow, obscure, and not very clean canals, to a very short distance from their lodgings, to which they would have to proceed on foot. We found a dense crowd had collected at the landing place to see us, although it was quite dark. We had been more than a week in the city, and the curiosity of the inhabitants seemed not a whit abated, though we had traversed the city in all directions, and not a day passed without our taking a long walk. Noguchi, who had gone with the Aizu men to find out where the symposium was to be held, was not yet back, so reconciling ourselves to the idea that the officials had succeeded in putting it off, we sat down to a dinner of turtle soup and boiled turtles.

In the middle of the dinner, Noguchi appeared to announce that all was ready. The guard that usually dogged our steps when we went out had all retired to rest for the night, so we got away unaccompanied except by one man carrying a lantern. The streets were by this time quite deserted, and we hugged ourselves with the consciousness of an adventure. No European had yet been abroad in the streets of a Japanese city at night as a free man. We had to walk a couple of miles, and then turn down by the river till we came to a house close to the great bridge. Here we found our friends awaiting our arrival. Blankets were spread for us on the floor at the upper end of the room, while the Aizu men sat on cushions opposite to us, a row of tall candlesticks occupying the centre. Tea was served by some very ancient females, and we began again to fear a disappointment, for the invitation had been accompanied by a promise to show us some of the most celebrated singing and dancing girls of the city. However, when the *sake* was brought up, they descended from the upper storey, where they had been engaged in completing their toilette. Some of them were certainly pretty, others decidedly ugly, but we thought their looks ruined in any case by the blackened teeth and white-lead-powdered faces. In later times I became more accustomed to the shining black teeth which were then the distinctive mark of a married woman, as well as of every "artiste" old enough to have an admirer, so much so that when the empress set the fashion by discontinuing the practice, it was long before I, in common with most Japanese, could reconcile myself to the new style.

I have always thought Japanese dancing, or rather posturing, extremely uninteresting. It is a sort of interpreting by more or less graceful (or, as one may look at it, affected) movements of body and limbs, of the words of a song chanted to the accompaniment of a kind of three-stringed lute (*shamisen*). It is some help to know the words of the song beforehand; they are no more comprehensible when sung than the sounds given forth by the singers in Italian opera are to the majority of their audience. But no foreigner, unless he be an enthusiast, would ever take the trouble to educate himself to appreciate this form of art. He can enjoy the beautiful in other ways at much less cost of time and mental exertion. Then it takes a long apprenticeship to accustom the European ear to music constructed with a set of intervals that are different enough from ours to make nine-tenths of the notes seem out of tune. This form of entertainment is universal all over the east, in India, Burma, Siam, China and Japan, with local variations, and is, to my uncultivated taste, everywhere equally tedious. Our Edo officials had found us out, and did not cease to urge our return, until at eleven o'clock we gave way to their importunity and said good-bye to our hosts, after only a short stay. I daresay they kept it up to a much later hour. This was the evening before we left Osaka.

Audience with the Shōgun

On our return to Edo we were horrified to learn of the death by his own hand of poor Owen Alexander Vidal, the junior student interpreter. No motive was assignable for the terrible act, except ill health. Insane he certainly was not. A more lucid intellect it would be difficult to find. He had abilities of a very high order, but was a prey to a torpid liver, which seemed always to embitter his existence. His first nomination was to Siam, but before he had taken up his appointment he was transferred to Beijing. After a year or two there, finding the climate did not suit him, he obtained a change to Japan. But even there he was not content with his lot, and preferred annihilation.

The next few days were spent in visiting Atami and Hakone in company with some friends from Yokohama. There is nothing worthy of record about this excursion, except that Atami, which then contained only a couple of hotels, now (1887) possesses at least a dozen, and has become a fashionable winter resort, much frequented by the higher classes living in Tokyo (Edo). The cost of transport then was much less than it would be now. We paid the coolies who carried our baggage over to Hakone, a distance of about ten miles, 1-3/4 *ichibu* per man. At that time there existed a barrier at the eastern end of the village, at which all travellers had to exhibit their passports to the men on guard. The notice board at the guardhouse, among other provisions, stated that dead bodies, wounded persons, and individuals of suspicious aspect were not allowed to proceed without the production of a passport. A lady of our party accomplished the difficult feat of riding on a Japanese pony down the steep and badly paved road which descends from the top of the pass to Odawara.

We established ourselves in the official inn, where we were received with due respect and cordiality by the innkeeper. It was a one-storied building spread over a considerable area, and containing ten or fifteen rooms of the regulation size, namely 12 feet square, besides a huge kitchen and an entrance hall. Here we passed the night, and on the following day Noguchi procured for us packhorses and coolies at the government rates. The coolies were obliged to perform the labour as corvée, and if they were not in sufficient number, the population of the post towns had to hire men at ordinary rates to let them out at the government tariff. It was a heavy tax, and one of the first reforms of the new government established after the revolution was the abolition of this system.

At Hodogaya I parted from the rest of the party, who returned to Yokohama, and went on to Kanagawa, where I slept at the *honjin* or official hotel, occupying the best rooms, which were reserved for *daimyō* and high officials of the government. I rode in a *kago* or palanquin from Hodogaya, just five miles, and was two hours accomplishing that short distance. It was the ordinary rate of travelling in those days. One of the native legation guard went ahead, also in a *kago*, preceded by a big bamboo and paper lantern on a pole, then came my *kago*, followed by a coolie carrying my baggage in a couple of wicker boxes slung on a pole (*ryōgake*), and a second guardsman. Noguchi probably walked.

Next morning when I came to discharge the bill for my whole party, including rooms, *sake* and *sakana*, supper and breakfast, I found it amounted to about 8s 6d, and I gave one *ichibu* (say 1s 4d) to the hotelkeeper as *cha-dai* or tea money, which was considered quite enough. In Japan the charge for a night's lodging, called *hatago*, used to include everything, rice, tea, sleeping accommodation, fuel, candles, and use of the hot bath. The only extras were *sake* and *sakana*, which a liberal-minded traveller ordered "for the good of the house," but if he was of an economical turn, he contented himself with the regular two meals, which were quite enough to satisfy his appetite. *Sakana* (fish) is more played with than eaten, and is merely the excuse for *sake*. The comparison with a European hotel bill, with its charges for candles, firing and bath, is striking. Moreover, in Japan, you give no tips, for none are expected, and the tea money takes the place of the charge for the room you occupy.

It was after my return from this journey that Mitford and I moved to a little house outside the legation, situated in a pretty garden on the rising ground which overhangs the side road leading from the Tōkaidō to Sengaku-ji. It was in reality a small monastery named Monryō-in, and we occupied the guest apartments, having each a bedroom and one sitting room. No palisade surrounded it, and our only protection was a hut at the gate which held three or four of the *bette-gumi*. We thought ourselves very plucky in thus braving the risks of midnight assassination, when the legation grounds below us were patrolled all night, and sentries passed the word to each other as the hours struck. Here we spent several months together, living entirely on Japanese food, which was brought three times a day from a restaurant known as Mansei, much frequented by our friends the Satsuma men.

Mitford devoted himself with unflagging diligence to the study of the Japanese language, as he had before at Beijing to that of the Chinese, and made rapid progress. I began to compile for his use a series of sentences and dialogues which some years afterwards were published under the title of *Kaiwa-hen*. It was convenient to be outside the legation compound, because I could receive visits from the retainers of *daimyō* without obstruction. I used to go a good deal to the Satsuma *yashiki* in Mita to get political information from two men named Shibayama Ryōsuke and Nanbu Yahachirō. The former met his death towards the close of the year in a remarkable manner. The *yashiki*, having gained evil repute as the refuge of a number of *rōnin* and other disorderly political characters, was surrounded and set on fire by the *shōgun*'s police. There was a fight, many were killed, but Shibayama was made prisoner. When brought up for examination, he boldly avowed that he had been the ringleader, and then drawing a pistol from the bosom of his dress, shot himself through the head. He was a capital companion, and I had more than one agreeable adventure with him.

Towards the middle of April the foreign diplomatic representatives moved in a body down to Osaka. The French minister, Léon Roches, had already been there in March in furtherance of the special line of policy he was pursuing, and seen the *shōgun*; doubtless promises of support had been given; at any rate, counsel had been offered. In fact, as it afterwards turned out, Roches so far committed himself with the Bakufu that he found it impossible to remain one day longer in Japan after its final overthrow. On our side Sir Harry Parkes was resolved henceforth to treat the *shōgun* as of no more importance than a vice-gerent; henceforward he was styled by us His Highness, while for the Queen we used a Japanese title placing her on full equality with the emperor.

Sir Harry took with him to Osaka the mounted escort under Captain Applin, and 50 men commanded by Captain Daunt and Lieutenant Bradshaw. Lady Parkes was also of the party. The staff consisted of the secretary of legation, Sidney Locock, Mitford, myself (I was acting Japanese secretary), Willis, Aston and Wilkinson. We had persuaded Sir Harry to let Charles Wirgman come with us. We numbered about seventy Europeans, besides some thirty Chinese and Japanese, writers, servants and grooms. The *shōgun*'s government furnished all the fresh supplies required. Great offence was caused by this exclusive privilege, and Rickerby in the *Japan Times* poured out his wrath upon the head of our friend the artist. It was perhaps not an unreasonable complaint from their point of view that no representatives of the mercantile community were invited to accompany the foreign ministers, but it is quite certain that they would have been very much in the way.

The British legation occupied four spacious temples or monasteries at the further end of a street called Tera-machi, the other representatives being accommodated in perhaps somewhat inferior buildings nearer to its entrance. But the British minister had taken the trouble to send down two of his staff beforehand to make all the arrangements, while the others were ready to be contented with what was provided for them by the Japanese government. Mitford, Wirgman and I occupied one end of a temple (Chōhō-ji) overlooking the city, while at the other end were Sir Harry's office and the temporary chancery. The whole mission messed together in the temple on the other side of the street, where Sir Harry and Lady Parkes had their abode. Next door was a temple given up to the officers of the guard and two student interpreters, and the fourth was set apart for guests. I had a charming set of rooms on three floors. The bottom was occupied by the Japanese writers and my retainers, the centre floor, consisting of two rooms, served as a bedroom and "office," and the top was a sort of parlour where I received guests, only twelve feet by nine, but large enough to accommodate a dozen persons, as it did not contain a single piece of furniture.

It was a busy time. I was employed from morning till night translating and interpreting, and remember that on one occasion I had to talk Japanese for eleven successive hours, as the chief had Japanese guests both at luncheon and dinner. For this reason I found no time to keep my journal, and what follows is a pure effort of memory, aided only as far as the dates are concerned by reference to printed sources.

A great part of our time was taken up with the regulations under which settlements were to be formed at Kobe and Osaka, the conditions under which land was to be leased to foreigners, and the creation of a municipality at each place, and Sir Harry being the most practical man among the whole body of foreign representatives, the work fell in the main on his shoulders. The Japanese government were evidently desirous of conciliating the representatives, and the negotiations proceeded with unaccustomed smoothness and celerity. No more angry discussions and heated arguments (in which the heat and anger of our chief were opposed to the stolid calm of the imperturbable Japanese ministers) such as had characterized our official interviews at Edo. At the word of the new *shōgun* an entirely new line had been adopted, and a serious endeavour was made to convert the treaty of friendship into a reality.

Then we had visits from Satsuma, Awa and Uwajima men, and tried to ascertain what was likely to be the result of the political movement that had been in progress now for thirteen years. But on the whole everything seemed to point to the triumph of the *shōgun* over his opponents. And one of the principal objects with which he had invited the foreign ministers to Osaka was that he might make their personal acquaintance, and thus manifest his desire to cultivate friendly relations with foreign countries. Who put this into his head I do not know, but it does not seem *á priori* unlikely that a closer intimacy with the legations had been suggested to him by one of the representatives themselves. A good deal of time was consumed in discussing the etiquette to be observed at the audiences of the *shōgun*, but in the end it was arranged that it should be entirely according to European fashion.

The first interview was a private one. Sir Harry proceeded to the castle on horseback, accompanied by all the members of the mission, preceded by the mounted escort, and with a detachment of the infantry guard before and behind. A cloud of the Japanese guard called *bette-gumi* hovered on our flanks and kept back the crowd. A rather ludicrous incident was the presentation of arms by the soldiers who lined the open space in front of the castle to the officer in command of the escort, whose resplendent uniform had led them to mistake him for the minister. At the nearer end of the causeway crossing the moat there used to stand a wooden board inscribed with the Chinese characters for "alight from horseback," but as had been agreed upon beforehand, we took no notice of this and passed on through the gateway to the very door of the palace. If I recollect rightly, this was almost close to the gate. The palace unfortunately exists no longer, having been destroyed by fire during the retreat of the defeated Bakufu forces early in February 1868. But it was reputed to be the most splendid example of domestic architecture then extant in Japan. It certainly was far superior to the emperor's palace at Kyoto. Wide and lofty matted corridors, partitioned off by painted screens, of choice cryptomeria wood, ran along the front of a succession of large rooms and away to the right by the side of the three large apartments constituting the *ōhiroma* or hall of audience. The other apartments had each a specific name, and the *daimyō* were classified according to their right of waiting in one or the other for their turn of admission to the presence. Over these wooden screens were large panels of carved wood representing birds and animals surrounded by foliage, but somewhat too richly painted, very much in the style familiar to those who have visited the mausoleum of Tokugawa Ieyasu at Nikkō.

We were conducted along the matted corridor by the commissioners for foreign affairs, who had some difficulty in walking, as the court rules prescribed their wearing long wide trousers that extended far beyond their feet, so as to give them the appearance of moving on their knees, until we reached the farther room, where the *shōgun* was awaiting us. He shook hands with Sir Harry, and sat down at the head of a long table, with Sir Harry on his right and on his left Itakura Katsukiyo, who might be styled prime minister. The rest of the staff sat next to Sir Harry, and I had a stool between him and the *shōgun*. He was one of the most aristocratic-looking Japanese I have ever seen, of fair complexion, with a high forehead and well-cut nose—such a gentleman. I felt somewhat nervous, not knowing whether I had got hold of the forms of speech required by court etiquette, and remember making a ridiculous blunder over an observation of Sir Harry's that all that was disagreeable in the past relations of Great Britain and Japan was now forgotten. There was no business talk on this occasion, and after the conversation was over, the whole company adjourned to a smaller apartment where dinner was served in European style. The *shōgun* sat at the head of the table, and was very gracious. Round the walls hung paintings of the thirty-six poets, and Sir Harry having admired them, the *shōgun* made him a present of one. Whiskey and water were produced after the repast, and I had the honour of brewing toddy for the great man. It was dark when we left.

A few days later there was a formal audience, at which the captains of the men-of-war were presented. We had arranged beforehand the address of Sir Harry and the reply of the *shōgun*, who had been tutored also into saying a few words to each person presented to him. These somewhat resembled the Turkish Pasha's remarks as translated by the dragoman at the famous interview described in *Eothen*. To Captain Haswell, who had been on a polar expedition, for instance, he said what really amounted to "you had a long journey," but was interpreted in much more complimentary style.

I remember receiving a visit from Saigō and others of that party, who were not at all pleased at the rapprochement between us and the *shōgun*. I hinted to Saigō that the chance of a revolution was not to be lost. If Kobe were once opened, then good-bye to the chances of the *daimyō*.

The street in which the foreign representatives lodged was shut in at each end by solid wooden gates, at which a number of the *bette-gumi* were stationed on guard day and night, and it was impossible to get out into the city without an escort, as the guard had instructions to follow us wherever we went. This was very irksome to Mitford and myself, until we found a gap in the wall which surrounded one of the temples, and from that time we used to make nocturnal excursions to all parts of the town, accompanied by my retainer Noguchi. The sense of a certain peril to be encountered, combined with a sort of truant schoolboy feeling, rendered these explorations into the night life of Japan very enjoyable. On one occasion young Matsune joined us on an expedition to the quarter occupied by singing and dancing girls. It was a moonlight night, and the chance of detection by the guard was so much the greater. After getting through our gap, we doubled back, and passing behind the legations, got into a lower street running parallel to that in which we lived, where we ran along for some distance keeping close in the shadow of the houses, then darted into another street at right angles, turned to the right again until we felt sure of having baffled any possible pursuers, after which we walked on quietly, and crossing one of the long bridges over the river, found ourselves at our destination. A room had been taken in Matsune's name, and some of the bepowdered and berouged girls were awaiting the arrival of the Japanese party they had expected to meet, when to their surprise and horror three Europeans were ushered into their midst. We were at that time objects of more alarm than interest to the women of Osaka. The fair damsels starting up with a scream fairly ran away, and no assurances from our friend would induce them to return. The keeper of the house besought us to leave, as a crowd might collect, and if there was any disturbance he would get into trouble, and so we had to submit to our disappointment. But even the slight glimpse we had of the native beauties seemed to compensate for the risk run, for here in Osaka no foreigner had ever been admitted to the quarter.

On another occasion, when we were accompanied by some of the guard we had better success, and enjoyed the society of some *geisha* for several hours, the government officials having given their consent and even interfered, I believe, on our behalf. Matsune, being a *daimyō's* man, was looked on with much suspicion. It seemed a plucky thing on his part to spend so much time with us, and even to accompany us in broad daylight to the tea-gardens opposite to where the Mint now stands. Everything was new and delightful in Osaka, politics and diplomacy afforded unceasing interest and excitement, the streets, shops, theatres and temples were full of life and character of a kind thoroughly distinct from what we were accustomed to in Edo and Yokohama, and the difference of dialect and costume imparted additional piquancy to the women.

During the whole five weeks we spent there we had not a single dull day. There was always something to do in the intervals of our official work, visits to temples and theatres, tea-drinking according to the elaborate ceremonial of the *cha-no-yu*, an excursion to the large commercial town of Sakai, the existence of which in such close proximity to Osaka seems hard to explain. Near our residence was a florist's establishment, famous for its collection of orchids, which in Japan are cultivated more for their foliage than for their flowers. This taste is conditioned by the fact that in the Ryūkyū Islands, China and Japan there are very few species bearing conspicuous or fine blossoms, and the amateur makes the best of what is procurable. More attractive to the European was the exhibition of tree-peonies, which was going on during our stay. These flowers are now fashionable in England, but at that time were not much known; the magnificent pink or white blossoms of various shades, often as much as nine inches in diameter, are quite unsurpassable, and fully justify the Chinese title of "king of flowers." In Chinese and Japanese decorative art it is always associated with the lion, and has often been mistaken for the rose by European writers. Curio shops and silk stores also took up a good deal of our time, but the fabrics of the loom had not then attained the high artistic development of later years. We went about the city in every direction, and though frequently encountering men of the two-sworded class, never met with any instance of rudeness, while the common people were uniformly friendly to us.

The negotiations between the foreign representatives and the delegates of the Japanese government proceeded satisfactorily though somewhat slowly, and about the middle of May had reached a stage at which it was felt that nothing more could be done for the present. All the ministers, therefore, made their preparations for returning to Edo. Before leaving that part of the country Sir Harry made a trip across to Tsuruga, which had been talked of as a possible substitute for the port of Niigata, reported to be practically closed to commerce for one half of the year by the combined inconveniences of a bar at the mouth of the river on which it stands, and the persistent north-west gales that raise a most dangerous sea. It had been agreed between us and the Japanese that as a supplementary refuge for ships the harbour of Ebisuminato in the island of Sado should be opened if necessary, but only as an anchorage. If after an inspection of these two places the combined arrangement should appear unworkable, then some other port was to be substituted, either Tsuruga or Nanao.

Sir Harry was accompanied by Lady Parkes and some of the staff. He proceeded by way of Fushimi, along the western side of the Lake Biwa, and returning by the eastern shore. The anti-*shōgun* party made a great grievance of this journey, and fell foul of the government for having permitted the "barbarians" to approach so near to the sacred capital, Fushimi being practically a suburb of Kyoto, and the Satsuma people put in a written memorial on the subject, more to annoy the *shōgun*'s government than as a mark of real hostility to us. Of course we did not know of this until long after. I obtained leave to return to Edo overland, and Wirgman became my travelling companion.

A proposal was made to Sir Harry by the *shōgun*'s government through Kawakatsu Hiromichi to procure professors for English for a large public school to be established in Edo on the basis of the existing Kaiseijo. Dr Temple was asked by Her Majesty's government to furnish a sufficient staff at salaries which we in the legation thought adequate, but he took no trouble about the matter, and we thus lost the opportunity of giving an English turn to the higher class education of the country.

From Osaka to Edo

For centuries the interior of Japan had been closed to all Europeans, with the exception of the head of the Dutch trading factory at Nagasaki, who used to travel overland to Edo at fixed intervals to pay his respects to the *shōgun* and carry valuable presents to him and his ministers. Perhaps the best account of these tribute bearing missions is to be found in Kaempfer's *The History of Japan*. But in the new treaties a provision had been inserted giving to the diplomatic representatives of foreign powers the right of travelling throughout the country, and Sir Rutherford Alcock had availed himself of this privilege a few years earlier, as he has recounted in his *The Capital of the Tycoon*. As a guide to succeeding travellers it cannot be said that his description of the journey was of much assistance. But the Japanese are great travellers themselves, and the booksellers' shops abound in printed itineraries which furnish the minutest possible information about inns, roads, distances, ferries, temples, productions, and other particulars which the tourist requires. Then a fairly good map was easily procurable, not drawn to scale, but affording every geographical detail that can be of any real service, and there was a splendid illustrated guidebook to the Tōkaidō containing all the legendary and historical lore that an Englishman accustomed to his Murray can desire.

There are two great roads which unite the eastern and western capitals, namely the Nakasendō or road through the mountains, which, as its name implies, traverses the central provinces, and the Tōkaidō or road along the sea to the east, which follows the seashore wherever practicable. Properly speaking this is not the original name of the road, but rather of the administrative division through which it runs, but practically it came to the same thing. It was the latter which had been chosen for me as the principal highway in the country, and the best provided with inn accommodation. Ever since the third Tokugawa *shōgun* established the rule that each *daimyō* must pass a portion of the year in Edo, the great highroads had become important means of internal communication. Posting stations were established at every few miles for the supply of porters and baggage ponies, and at each of these were erected one or two official inns called *honjin* for the use of *daimyō* and high functionaries of government. Around these sprang up a crowd of private inns and houses of entertainment where the *daimyō*'s retainers and travelling merchants used to put up. The Tōkaidō was the recognized route for all the *daimyō* west of Kyoto, and of course for those whose territories lay along it. Then it was the main route for the pilgrims who flocked annually to the sacred shrines in Ise, and was the means of access to many other famous temples. Of all the roads in Japan it was the most frequented and the most important from every point of view. Who that collects Japanese colour prints is unacquainted with the numerous delightful series of views devoted to its illustration, which present such vivid pictures of Japanese life.

One of the most famous of all native novels is occupied with the adventures of a couple of merry dogs on their way from Edo up to Kyoto, and the list of its fifty-three posting towns was one of the first lessons in reading and writing which the youth of Japan had to commit to memory. On account of its historical and legendary associations, to say nothing of its famous scenery, it occupied something of the same place in the imaginations of the Japanese that the Rhine formerly did in the minds of English tourists before the Loreley rock had been tunnelled, and crowds of indifferent travellers were hastily whirled in a few hours along an iron track on either side of the great stream which at one time it was the fashion to "do" with dignity in a carriage and four. Carefully as one may study a map, there is no way of learning geography comparable to the pedestrian method, which, by a thousand associations of pleasure, fatigue and weather, fixes indelibly the minutest topographical facts, and enables the student of history to understand the vicissitudes of warfare.

Japan being a country where a peculiar political system had taken its birth from centuries of civil war, the more we saw of its interior districts, the more likely were we to arrive at a correct understanding of the problem which at that moment was being attacked by the rival parties. I do not pretend that any considerations such as these determined my application to the chief for permission to return to headquarters by land. Insatiable curiosity as to everything Japanese, a certain love of adventure, and dislike of life on board of a man-of-war were the real motives, the last perhaps as strong as any, and probably many persons would agree with me in preferring to spend a day in walking from Calais to Dover, if it were practicable, to taking their chance of rough weather in a steamer, even though it might not last for more than an hour and ten minutes.

Wirgman and I were by this time so accustomed to living on Japanese food that we resolved not to burden ourselves with stores of any kind, knives or forks, finger glasses or table napkins. Ponies were not procurable, so we bought a couple of secondhand palanquins, called *hikido kago*, such as were used by public officials, and had them repaired. They cost the small price of thirty-two *ichibu* each. The pole was a long piece of deal, called by euphemism paulownia wood. A cushion of silk damask, thickly stuffed with raw cotton, was spread on the bottom, and there was then just room enough to sit in it cross-legged without discomfort. In front was a small shelf above the window, and underneath a small flap which served as a table. The sliding doors also had windows, furnished with a paper slide to exclude cold, and another covered with gauze to keep out the dust while letting in the air. If it rained, blinds made of slender strips of bamboo were let down over the windows. The body of the palanquin could also be enveloped in a covering of black oiled paper, in which a small aperture was left for the occupant to peep out of, a blind of the same material being propped up outside. This arrangement was, however, only resorted to on days of persistent rain.

Each of us had a pair of oblong wicker-work baskets to hold our clothing, called *ryōgake*, which were slung at opposite ends of a black pole and carried by one man over his shoulder. My bedding, which consisted of a couple of Japanese mattresses covered with white crape and edged with a broad border of common brocade known as *Yamato nishiki*, and one of the huge stuffed bedgowns called *yogi* of figured crape with a velvet collar, with a couple of European pillows, was packed in a wicker box of the kind called *akeni*, and formed a burden for two men. To each package was fastened a small deal board on which my name and titles were inscribed with Indian ink in large

Chinese characters. As escort we had ten picked men belonging to the native legation guard (*bette gumi*), and a couple of officials belonging to the Japanese Foreign Department were attached to us, who were instructed to make arrangements for our accommodation along the road. Last of all, a list was made out of the places at which we were to take our midday meals and sleep at night, the journey of 320 miles from Fushimi being calculated to occupy sixteen days.

On May 18, 867, having exchanged farewell calls with the commissioners of foreign affairs, we got away from our temple lodging at nine o'clock in the morning. Willis, who was to join Sir Harry Parkes' party at Fushimi, accompanied us. We embarked at the Hachikenya wharf on the river side in a houseboat, the escort and officials in another, two open boats following with the luggage of the whole party. The stream was very strong, and our progress was correspondingly slow, but we felt that we were travelling in a dignified manner, and therefore repressed our natural impatience. Where the stream was deep enough close in shore, the boatmen landed, and towed us by a line attached to the top of a mast fixed in the front of the boat, while the steersman remained at his post to prevent us from running into the bank. When the towing path changed to the opposite side, the boatmen came on board and poled across to resume their labour as before. The river, which winds a good deal, is enclosed between lofty dykes, so that we had no prospect but the broad surface of the river itself and the tops of ranges of mountains peering over the bank. It was a fine day, and we were full of eager anticipations about the novel scenes we were about to pass through, every inch of the way being entirely new to us as far as Hakone, and for myself the prospect of a fortnight's holiday was especially exhilarating after the hard work of the past five weeks.

By one o'clock we reached Suidomura, a small village on the right bank about five miles above Osaka, and landed to take our lunch. There was nothing to be had but rice and bean-curd, which did not constitute a very palatable meal. But *à la guerre comme à la guerre*. We passed a large number of crowded passenger boats descending the river, and ten barges laden with bales of rice. At half-past six we stopped at Hirakata, a somewhat more important place than Suidomura. Here we landed to dine off soup, fish and rice, the ordinary constituents of a traveller's meal. The charge for our three selves and three servants was less than an *ichibu*, and a second *ichibu* was given as *chadai*. Noguchi was paymaster, and gave whatever he thought right under this heading. The charge seemed extraordinarily cheap, which was explained by a regulation binding innkeepers to supply persons travelling in an official capacity at one quarter of the rates charged to ordinary people. We started again by moonlight, and as the night advanced, a thin mist rose and covered the surface of the broad river, imparting to the landscape that mysterious, sketchy indistinctness which is so characteristic of Japan, that none but native artists whose eyes have been educated to it from their childhood have ever been able to seize and represent.

The air now became as cold as it had been hot during the daytime. We had blankets fetched from one of the baggage boats, and lay down to sleep in opposite corners of the boat.

At two in the morning I woke and found that we were lying off the guard-house on the right bank opposite to Hashimoto, which was held by troops of Matsudaira Munehide, a member of the *shōgun*'s Codfdfdfduncil, the other bank being in the charge of Tōdō Takayuki, the *daimyō* of Ise. We had been as far as Yodo, where they turned us back because our pass had not been vised here, and we did not reach Yodo again till four o'clock.

It was still dark, the moon having set during the night. The river is here joined by the Kizu River, and is divided into several channels by islands lying in its course. We kept along the right bank, and arrived at Fushimi about six, where we found Sir Harry on the point of starting for Tsuruga. Here a generous member of his party gave us a last cigar. Our stock had been completely exhausted during the long stay in Osaka, and for the rest of the journey we had to content ourselves with Japanese tobacco, smoked in tiny whiffs out of the diminutive native pipes, all inadequate to satisfy a craving nourished on something stronger. The worst of the Japanese pipe, with its metal bowl and mouthpiece united by a hard bamboo stem, is the rapidity with which it gets foul, necessitating cleaning at least once a day with a slender spill twisted out of tough mulberry-bark paper. Willis left us here, and joined the chief. Special precautions had been taken by the government to prevent Sir Harry turning aside to Kyoto, which it was thought his adventurous disposition might tempt him to visit.

After breakfast we started in our *kago* for the journey overland. A crowd of *machi-kata*, who were a sort of municipal officers of all grades, dressed in their Sunday best, escorted us out of the town. Our road lay for a mile or so between the banks of the Uji-kawa and low, fir-clad hills masked by clumps of graceful bamboo. Leaving the tea plantations of Uji to the right, we journeyed along a level road winding through the hills to Oiwaké, where we joined the Tōkaidō. A kind of stone tramway ran from Kyoto all the way to Ōtsu, our next resting-place, for the heavy, broad-wheeled bullock carts, of which we passed a couple of score laden with rice for the use of the *shōgun*'s garrison at the capital. Oiwaké was famous for pipes, counting boards (*abacus*), and a species of comic prints called *toba-e*, and lies at the foot of the hills separating the province of Yamashiro from the beautiful Lake Biwa. By the roadside we had an opportunity of inspecting some tea-firing establishments on a small scale, like every other manufacturing enterprise in those days. The fresh tea leaves were damped, then spread out on a flat table heated from beneath by fuel enclosed in a plastered chamber, and twisted by hand. This new tea forms a delicious and refreshing drink when infused after the Japanese method for the finer qualities, with lukewarm water. At each establishment there were not more than two persons at work.

At one o'clock we got to Ōtsu, and after lunch went to a monastery called Ryōzen-*ji* to enjoy the celebrated prospect of the lake, but the midday heat had covered its surface with a dull grey haze, and hid it entirely from view. We found everything nicely arranged for us at the Takajimaya, where we rested for the midday meal, while the escort and foreign office men in our train vied in accommodating themselves to our wishes. From Ōtsu a level road skirted the lake, and, soon after passing through Zeze, the castle town of the Honda clan, we got out to walk. In crossing the great double bridge of Seta we saw a couple of men in a boat spinning for carp. The shallows here are crowded with traps, irregular shaped enclosures of reeds planted in the mud, into which the fish enter when stormy winds agitate the surface of the water and deprive them of their equanimity.

Before reaching Kusatsu, where we were to put up for the night, we retreated into our *kago,* in order not to be overwhelmed by the crowd, and for the better preservation of our dignity, which required that we should not be seen on foot. At the confines of the town we were met by a deputation of the municipal officers and by the host of the official inn, who escorted us in with great pomp, keeping back the inquisitive multitude. Our bearers quickened their pace, not indeed to our satisfaction, for the *kago*, which is uncomfortable at all times, becomes almost uninhabitable when the men get out of a walk.

At last we turned round a corner, and passing through a black gate, before the posts of which were two neatly piled-up heaps of sand, flanked by buckets of water, were set down in the wide porch of the official inn. It was one of the most beautifully decorated buildings of its kind that I have ever seen. That implies woodwork of the finest grain, plaster of the least obtrusive shades of colour, sliding doors papered with an artistic pattern touched up with gold leaf and framed with shining black lacquered wood, and hard thick mats of the palest straw edged with stencilled cotton cloth. In the principal room, only twelve feet square, raised six inches above the rest of the house, lay two thick mats forming a sort of bed-place, where the distinguished traveller was expected to squat without moving. The baggage was deposited in the corridor which ran round two sides of the apartment. There was no view from the windows, which looked out on a small courtyard enclosed by a sulky-looking, black wooden fence. Etiquette prescribed that a great man should neither see nor be seen. Our host came in with a small present, and bowed his forehead to the sill. After a few minutes he returned to give thanks in the same humble manner for the gift of two *ichibu* which he had received as *chadai*. We went in turn to the hot bath, where a modest, not to say prim, young damsel asked whether she might have the honour of washing our "august" back, but not being trained from our youth up to be waited on by lovely females during our ablutions, we declined her assistance.

At dinner time we ordered a dish of fish and a bottle of *sake*, which had to be several times replenished before the artist had had enough. The people of the inn were astonished to find that we could eat rice, having been taught to believe that the food of Europeans consisted exclusively of beef and pork. When we went to bed, soft silk mattresses in plenty were spread on the floor, and the chambermaid placed within the mosquito net a fire-box with a bit of red-hot charcoal neatly embedded in white ashes for a last smoke, and a pot of freshly-infused tea. *O-yasumi nasai*, "be pleased to take your august rest," was the end of the first day.

In Japan travellers are in the habit of making an early start. A native usually rises before day, makes a hasty toilet by scrubbing his teeth with a handful of salt from a basket hanging over the kitchen sink, washes his hands and face without soap, swallows a hasty breakfast, and is on the road as soon as the sun is up, or even earlier. His principal object is to arrive at the town where he is going to pass the night at as early an hour as possible, in order to secure a good room and the first turn at the hot bath, there being only one tub and one water for the whole of the guests. In some out of the way places this is not even changed every day, and I remember on one occasion finding the bath absolutely green with age and odorous in proportion. We were not expected to do as the vulgar herd, and did not get away much before half-past seven. Our average rate of going was about three miles an hour, and the day's journey not over twenty miles, but there were so many interruptions that we rarely reached our evening's destination before six o'clock.

First and foremost there was the midday meal (*o-hiru yasumi*), which consumed at least an hour, and then our exalted rank required that we should stop to rest (*o-koyasumi*) at least once in the morning and once again in the afternoon. Then we stopped again at every point of view to drink tea, and to taste every dish of cakes or other comestibles of which centuries of wayfarers had been in the habit of partaking before us. Thus on the third day we stopped at Umenoki to take tea at a house commanding a fine view of the legendary mountain Mukade-*yama* (Centipede's Mount), and again for half-an-hour at Ishibe, where a big board was stuck up outside inscribed with "the little resting-place of the interpreter (the officer) of England." We lunched sumptuously at Minakuchi on fish, soup and rice, and so got through an hour and a quarter. At Ono, celebrated for pheasants' meat preserved in *miso* paste, we again drank tea, which was served out by pretty girls who made a great pretence of bashfulness. Wirgman's costume, consisting of wide blue cotton trousers, a loose yellow pongee jacket, no collar, and a conical hat of grey felt, gave rise to a grave discussion as to whether he was really an European, or only a Chinaman after all. At Maeno, a centre of tea production, we stopped for another half-hour to taste several sorts of leaf at a tea dealer's shop. This was a great act of condescension on the part of such distinguished personages, but we made up for this derogation from our dignity by having our purchases paid for by Noguchi, the real Japanese swell being supposed to know nothing about money, not even theoretically. The dealer declared that unless the leaf is picked and fired by virgins, it will not be drinkable, but I fear he was humbugging the innocent foreigner.

Many of the houses bore a notice-paper inscribed with Chinese characters meaning "Economy in all things," a laconic sentence which was interpreted to signify that the occupants had forsworn social entertainments and other unnecessary sources of expenditure. Wirgman made himself very popular by the sketches he threw off and gave away to the innkeepers, sometimes of ourselves as we appeared on the road, or of a bit of local scenery, or perhaps a pretty girl, whose bashful pride on discovering that her features had been perpetuated on paper was a pleasant sight to contemplate. It usually took some time before the waiting maids overcame what seemed to us to be their excessive modesty, but it was explained to us that women were not usually permitted to approach the dais-room, as noble swells had their own men-servants to attend on them. We regretted the exigencies of our lofty position, and pitied the *daimyō* who have always to be correct and proper—in public.

Another consequence of our supposed high rank was that in many towns the people knelt down by the roadside as we passed, being told to assume that posture by the municipal officers who preceded us beadle-fashion, crying out, "*Shitaniro, shitaniro!*" ("down, down!"). This honour used in those days to be rendered to every *daimyō*, no matter whether travelling in his own dominions or those of another nobleman, and also to the high officials of the *shōgun*'s government, as, for example, the governor of Kanagawa, to the great indignation of the European residents. The only reported instance of a foreigner ever submitting to this indignity was that of Eugene van Reed, who is said to have fallen in with the train of Shimazu Hisamitsu on the day fatal to poor Richardson, and to have then and there conformed to the native custom. The practice had its origin, perhaps, in the necessity of protecting the nobles from sudden attack, combined with the rule of Japanese etiquette that considers that a standing posture implies disrespect.

This impotence of etiquette was forcibly impressed on me at Fuchū, where I went to visit the public school for the sons of samurai. Having taken off my shoes and laid my hat on the floor at the entrance, I was escorted into a room where about thirty youngsters were squatting on the floor, with Chinese books before them which they were learning to repeat by rote from the mouths of older and more advanced pupils, under the super-intendence of half-a-dozen professors. I bowed and remained standing, but to my surprise no one acknowledged my salute. I had in my ignorance of propriety assumed what to the Japanese appeared an attitude of disrespect, and it was only on being admonished by one of the escort that I discovered my error, which being at once repaired, the professors returned my bow, made in proper form with head to the ground. I afterwards found it necessary to adopt Japanese manners, as far as was compatible with a certain stiff-jointedness that forbade my sitting on my heels for more than a very limited period, but could never resist the uneasy feeling that while I was pressing my forehead on the mats, the man opposite might perhaps be taking advantage of the opportunity to inflict a slight on the "barbarian" by sitting bolt upright. In fact, Japanese themselves were not exempt from a similar uncertainty, and they might sometimes be detected, whilst performing the obeisance, in the act of squinting sideways to ascertain whether the person they were saluting lowered his head simultaneously and to the same level.

Whenever we passed through a town of any importance, the population turned out *en masse*, eager to convert the occasion into a holiday. At Kaméyama, for instance, which is a *daimyō's* castle town, the streets were thronged with samurai and their children in gala dress, presenting a gay appearance. Some of the young girls were extremely pretty, in spite of the quantity of white powder with which fashion condemned them to bedaub their faces.

Some odd methods of locomotion were practised in this part of the country, such as children riding in nets of coarse cord suspended from opposite ends of a pole carried by a man on his shoulder, women riding in pairs on packhorses, and in the flat plain between Séki and Kuwana in small open omnibuses, not unlike the costermonger's carts in which fruit is hawked about the streets of London, but drawn by a man instead of a donkey. Perhaps half-a-dozen grown-up persons fitted in one of these small vehicles, the precursors of the *jinrikisha* which came into vogue in 1869. Wirgman, who was too careless of his dignity (for he was travelling not as an artist, but in the quality of a *yakunin* or government official), insisted in getting into one of these, and rode all the way from Tomida to Kuwana, a distance of at least five miles, for three *tenpō*. At a teahouse at Komuki we were presented by our host with some teapots of very inferior Banko ware. This is the famous unglazed pottery moulded by hand, and showing all over its surface, both inside and outside, the marks of finger tips.

On May 22, we reached Kuwana, a large town belonging to one of the principal hereditary vassals of the Tokugawa family. Here an enormous concourse of people had collected to see us make our entry, and we had some difficulty in making our way through the crush, until suddenly the procession turned aside through a gateway under a tower and traversed the outer enceinte of the castle, finally arriving at the official inn on the shore of the bay. Dealers in Banko ware, curious stones from Mino and fans from Nagoya came flocking in, and the evening was passed in bargaining.

The stage from Kuwana to Miya is by sea, across the head of the bay of Owari. Nowadays (1887) people perform the journey by steamer, but in 1867 we had to content ourselves with a rather dirty boat, roofed in with planks. We left at half-past seven and arrived at the termination of our voyage a little after eleven, but as the distance is estimated at seven *ri*, we were precluded from going further that day. I proposed, therefore, to devote the afternoon to visiting Nagoya, of which Miya is little more than a suburb.

It boasts a castle founded by Oda Nobunaga towards the end of the sixteenth century. It is famous throughout Japan for two huge golden dolphins which crown the *donjon*, and is one of the finest extant specimens of that sort of architecture. But the foreign department officials had no instructions to let us deviate from the high road, and did not venture to take on themselves the responsibility for making other arrangements. They promised, of course, to see the governor of the town and ask him to get permission, which they represented was required before they could take us into the castle town of a great noble like the lord of Owari, but it was all fudge. Shopkeepers flocked in laden with fans, metal work, lacquered porcelain and crape, with which we occupied the interval till an answer should be received from the authorities at Nagoya. A report of Wirgman's skill with the brush having spread, he was overwhelmed with quantities of Chinese paper and fans which, our host said, had been brought by the leading inhabitants who desired specimens of his art, and I wrote mottoes to his productions. The *sake* bottle furnished us with the necessary inspiration.

But we found out at last that the fans thus decorated were being sold outside at an *ichibu* a piece, and refused to be imposed on any further.

In the evening we had in some singing and dancing girls, and having got ourselves up in native costume, invited the two foreign office clerks and some of our escort to join the party. One or two of the latter became so merry that they could not resist a temptation to perform buffoon dancing, and Sano, the biggest and most good-humoured, gave imitations of famous actors. We did not get rid of our guests until nine o'clock, by which time they had taken a good quantity of *sake* on board.

In passing through Arimatsu on the following day, famous for cotton *shibori*, dyed in the same way as the Indian *bandhana*, we called at the shop where the heads of the Dutch factory at Nagasaki had been in the habit of stopping from time immemorial on the occasion of their annual journeys to Edo, and were shown a ledger containing records of the purchases made by them year after year. It was a matter of obligation to follow this time-honoured example, and we selected some pieces of the stuff, which oddly enough is called not by the name of the place where it is made, but by that of the last post town, Narumi. Noguchi and the two foreign department officials did the bargaining, while Wirgman and I looked on and smoked in dignified silence as if we were utterly unconcerned about the prices. The owner of the shop was a distinguished person, evidently invested with a municipal function, in consequence of which he was allowed to have a few stands of matchlocks in his hall. Many of the houses were of more substantial construction than usual, thus testifying to the prosperity conferred by the local manufacture.

At Chiryū the landlord of the inn where we lunched came privately to Noguchi and asked him for four *ichibu* as tea money, on the ground that Sir Rutherford Alcock had given that sum in 1861, but his request was refused, and he was forced to content himself with what we had paid elsewhere, namely, half an *ichibu*. I always left such questions to his discretion, and have no doubt that he acted rightly. In the afternoon when the train stopped as usual to give the palanquin bearers a rest, the people of the *tateba*, or halfway teahouse, presented us with buckwheat noodles, for which, as they assured us, the place was said to be famous. It was, however, inferior to what I have eaten in other places. Wirgman's fame having preceded him, paper, brushes and ink were brought, and he executed a masterpiece representing us eating noodles and drinking *sake* from a gourd which he had been careful to get replenished at Miya.

The bridge over the Yahagi-*gawa* being broken down, we crossed the river in a ferry boat, and were met at the entrance of the town by municipal officers and constables, the latter being furnished by the local *daimyō*, whose function was to walk at the head of the procession and to cry, "*Shitaniro, shitaniro!*" Down went the whole crowd of spectators, including men of the two-sworded class, all the more willingly perhaps because that was the only way they had of bringing their eyes to a level with the windows of our palanquins. For etiquette demanded that we should always ride in entering and quitting a town, the vulgar practice of proceeding on foot being allowable only in the more countryfied portions of the highroad.

The following day opened with what promised to be persistent rain, and we had to be fastened up in our palanquins with the oiled paper covering thrown over us. Through a small opening we could just manage to see a few yards to right and left. All day long we ploughed our way onwards along the almost level road, which in places was flooded nearly six inches deep. At Arai there was then a guardhouse close to the shore of the Hamana Bay, where all travellers had to alight from their palanquins and walk through, taking off their hats and shoes in order to show respect while submitting to a searching examination. Over the *sake* on the preceding evening there had been a good deal of chaff about our being obliged to subject ourselves to this rule, which was said to admit of no exceptions. I was inwardly resolved not to submit, and was much relieved when the time came to find that the warden was satisfied with the *kago* door being opened about halfway as we were carried past. This slight concession had been arranged overnight by the foreign department officers, in order that the letter of the rule enforcing inspection might be observed, and we were quite contented, as the door was opened by a third party, so that our dignity as Europeans was duly saved by our not having to alight.

Some years ago a series of dykes and bridges exceeding a mile in length was thrown across the shallowest part of the bay. We had to embark in boats so small that they would not hold more than a single *kago*. The spits which run out towards each other at the mouth gave the bay the appearance of

a landlocked lake, until we got halfway across and the breakers became
visible, though the sea at the point where we crossed was as smooth as a
mirror. Two miles on the western side of Hamamatsu we were met by some
retainers of Inoue Masanao, the local *daimyō*, wearing black hats as flat as
a pancake, who, being himself a member of the *shōgun*'s Council, had no
doubt given special orders regarding our reception, and at the entrance of
the town they were joined by more. The procession was now formed in the
following order. Two *machi-kata*, in green mantles with one in brown
between them, marched a long way ahead to clear the street, followed by
a couple of aldermen (*shuku-yakunin*) in single file on each side of the road,
and a couple of *seishi* or heralds, whose fierce demeanour was delightful to
behold, who roared out "*shitaniro, shitaniro!*" and warned some young samurai
who displayed a disposition to approach too close that they must keep at
a respectful distance. Then followed our *kago*, with one of the native escort
(*bette-gumi*) walking on each side. Then a constable (*dōshin*) carrying a spear,
and behind him the rest of the escort, servants and baggage.

On arriving at the inn, we received visits from the head merchants and
were told that we were to be specially cared for, by orders of the *daimyō*,
some of whose retainers kept watch and ward in the kitchen throughout
the night, this being very spacious and situated in the front of the house.
In leaving on the following day the procession was arranged in the same
way, and as we passed the castle gates a high official stationed there handed
his card to one of the *bette-gumi* to present to me. At the end of the town
the escort was changed, and we were placed again in charge of the four
black-hatted *seishi*, who did not leave us until we arrived at the boundary
of Inouye's, the *daimyō*'s, territory.

After the rain of the day before yesterday the country looked especially
beautiful; ripe fields of barley behind the rows of tall pine trees that lined
the road stretched right away to the foot of the nearer hills, behind which
rose range after range in the blue distance. We met yesterday and today
soldiers of the 3rd regiment of the *shōgun*'s drilled troops marching to Kyoto
to support the new policy of the head of the government, and perhaps to
defend him against an armed confederation of the leading *daimyō* of the west.

As soon as the local escort had turned back we descended from our palanquins to pursue our way on foot to the Tenryū-gawa, which we crossed by

means of ferry boats. The river here is very wide and the current swift, and except during freshets is divided into two branches by a sandbank which occupies the middle of the stream. Wirgman had stopped behind to sketch, and I waited with one of the foreign office officials, who confided to me that we should probably meet a "barbáre" on the road. By this I understood the *reiheishi*, a high official of the emperor's court who was returning from a mission to the tomb of Ieyasu at Nikkō. He was of higher rank than any Japanese *daimyō*, and everyone on meeting him had to get out of his palanquin and go down on his knees. My informant hoped we should manage to avoid him, and I hoped so too. The rest of the party having at last come up, we proceeded by a shortcut through the fields, which saved us a couple of miles walking. We got to Mitsuke, where we were to lunch, some time before noon. The streets were crowded with pretty girls, who had turned out to see the foreigners. Our host, who had put on his robes of ceremony, made his appearance, bowing low and bearing a gift of dried white-bait fry, which when toasted and dipped in soy is very palatable. Handsome Turkish carpets had been spread in the bedroom. Two charming little boys about ten years of age, with perfect manners, were told to wait on us.

The *reiheishi* was the principal topic of discussion. He had not yet passed, and our followers were full of anxiety. Noguchi said that all Japanese of rank, down to the lowest two-sworded man, got out of his way, because his followers were in the habit of extorting money on the pretext that the proper amount of respect had not been paid to the great man. I was quite ready to follow the example of the Japanese in avoiding if possible the chance of an encounter. We were told that the *reiheishi*, whose rank by this time had been much diminished in the mouths of our informants, was to stop the night at Fukuroi, the very next town, only four miles further, so we hurried away hoping to get to our own destination early in the afternoon. Two miles over the tableland, then zig-zag down a beautiful hill covered with pine trees, then two more over the rice field flat to Fukuroi, where we changed the palanquin and baggage porters and hastened on without stopping.

Today, May 27, the peasants were cutting barley and planting out the young rice. I did the six miles more to Kakegawa in two hours, including the last stoppage, which was considered very quick going. A young Satsuma man who was on his way to Nagasaki called at our inn and gave me an account of the *reiheishi* and the doings of his retainers, for whom he professed the greatest contempt. He said they were wretched citizens of Kyoto hired for the occasion, and dressed in a little brief authority. At Shinagawa, the last suburb of Edo, they had seized eighteen people and fined them for exhibiting a want of respect towards the emperor's messenger. It was rumoured that he would pass through about six o'clock, and spend the night at Fukuroi. Six o'clock came, but no *reiheishi*. We passed the evening in expectation, and went to bed—still no *reiheishi*.

Wirgman and I slept in separate rooms, Noguchi in a third, and all the escort but one were quartered at another house a little way off. At a quarter past one I was roused from sleep by a Japanese saying to me: "Mr. Satow, Mr. Satow, get your sword; they've come." My sword was an old cavalry sabre, not good for much but to make a show. I got up and groped my way through the black darkness to the sword-stand in the alcove and got the weapon. The Japanese led me by the hand, and we stood together in a corner of the next room, wondering what was going to happen. He said: "I wish the escort would come." Meanwhile violent noises were heard, as if of people breaking in. Bewildered by the darkness, I imagined them to be coming from the little garden at the back, on to which my bedroom looked. We remained still and breathless. In three minutes all was silent again, and I heard a voice cry "Mr. Satow." It was Noguchi, who appeared with a light, and reported that the enemy had fled. Wirgman and my chancery servant Yokichi were nowhere to be found. The Japanese who had woke me proved to be Matsushita, the youngest of the escort.

We proceeded then towards Noguchi's room. The wooden door opposite was lying on the floor, where the assailants had broken in. As we stood in the passage, others of the escort came in, all dressed in fighting mantles, with drawn swords in their hands and wearing iron forehead pieces. Seeing my scarlet sleeping trousers, they begged me either to hide myself or take them off, but the danger being past, I only laughed at them. Two of them went in search of Wirgman, and found him in an alley leading to the back of the house—they narrowly escaped being shot.

We began to feel cooler, and Noguchi narrated what had happened. He heard the noise of the front door being broken down, jumped up, tied his girdle, and stood in the doorway of his room, a sword in the right hand, a revolver in the left. Some men approached and asked for the "barbarians," to which he replied that if they would only come in, he would give the "barbarians" to them. They took fright at his attitude and determined tone, and fled. Altogether there were, he thought, about a dozen, two armed with long swords, the rest with short ones. On looking about, we discovered that the mosquito nets in the room diagonal to Wirgman's had been cut to pieces, the occupants having escaped. It was lucky for us that we had put out the lamps before going to bed, so that the assailants could not find their way.

Wirgman explained that on being awakened by the noise of people breaking down the doors and shouting for the "barbarians," he followed the people of the house, who took to their heels. A lantern that had been dropped by one of the ruffians led to the conclusion that they belonged to the *reiheishi*'s suite. No one was hurt, except one of the assailants, who in the hurry-scurry of running away was accidentally wounded by a companion. After everyone had related his own experiences, I retired to bed, while Wirgman called for *sake* and *sashimi*, with which he and the escort regaled themselves until daylight.

On getting up in the morning my first step was to send for the two foreign office officials, and endeavour to obtain redress through them. The escort, who had not appeared on the scene till the danger was past, were now very anxious to distinguish themselves by some act of valour. I told the officials, with the full support of the escort, that they should either get the guilty men delivered up to me, or that I would go with my escort and take them by force. This was the attitude maintained until midday. I verily believe that if I had given the signal, the escort would have attacked the *reiheishi*'s lodgings.

At last the official came back and said that the *reiheishi*'s people refused to give the men up to me. As an alternative they proposed to obtain a written apology, coupled with a promise to punish the assailants on their reaching Kyoto. To this I expressed my willingness to assent, in the hope that we should be able to pursue our journey before night set in. But the negotiations lingered, and this was not to be. So we sent for some musicians, and invited the two officials and the escort to a banquet. Wirgman and one of the escort entertained the company with dancing. Another of the escort got very drunk, and begged me to take him into my personal service on the same terms as

Noguchi. We heard that the townspeople were delighted at the *reiheishi* and his blackguards being so bothered by a couple of foreigners. No emperor's messenger was ever before stopped on his road and talked to in our imperious manner. Four or five of the escort, when full of *sake*, started up the street in their fighting mantles and created great alarm in the minds of the *reiheishi's* retainers, who, thinking they were to be attacked in earnest, begged for a guard from the *daimyō* of the town. The captain of the escort and two others in particular behaved in a delightfully swaggering manner. But in spite of all this, nothing was settled, and we had to stop a second night.

On the following morning on getting up, I was told that matters were nearly arranged, that the men who had attacked our lodgings were to be left behind in the custody of the *daimyō*, the people at the castle giving a receipt on his behalf. The morning wore on without the desired document making its appearance, and I feared they would slip through my fingers altogether. I got tired of waiting and went to sleep, from which I was awakened by one of the foreign office officials, who had been acting as go-between, bringing me a certified copy, signed by the governor of the town, of a written undertaking given by a leading retainer of the *reiheishi* to remain there with three of the assailants. Another copy was given to him, and he started at once for Osaka with it, accompanied by one of the escort. I was now asked whether I would permit the *reiheishi* to depart, to which I gave my assent. We saw him and his retinue pass the inn; there were two large palanquins, half-a-dozen smaller ones, and about fifty ruffianly-looking fellows in green coats. We had thus remained on the field of victory. As soon as the *reiheishi* was clear of the place, we started in the opposite direction about three o'clock in the afternoon. The *daimyō's* people offered to give us a body of men to escort us out of the town, but I replied that my escort was sufficient to ensure our safety. A guard of honour was drawn up in front of the inn as we left, and eight policemen accompanied us to the exit of the town.

Ultimately, some months later, these men and three others implicated in the affair were brought to Edo and put on trial. Two were condemned to death, and four more to transportation to an island. Sir Harry wanted me to be present at the execution of these two men, but I persuaded him to send someone else instead. To look on at the execution of men who have tried to take one's life would have borne an appearance of revengefulness, which one would not have liked. But I think that under the circumstances of those times the punishment was rightly inflicted.

Our next stage was to Nissaka, a pretty little town lying in a basin of hills. Beyond rose a steep ascent, which we climbed not without fatigue, to find ourselves on the top of a tableland running away to the sea on our right, while on the left hills rose ever higher and higher above the road, being cultivated up to their summits in tiny level plots cut out of their sides. At the highest point of the road we rested at a teahouse, where a kind of soft rice cake, bedaubed with a substance resembling extract of malt, was served to us by a diminutive girl. Though fifteen years of age, and consequently nearly full grown, she did not measure four feet in height.

On the further side of the tableland lay Kanaya, the next post town, and beyond that the Oi River, which had to be crossed before we could gain our stopping place for the night. A hundred naked porters hurried forward to carry our palanquins and baggage to the other bank. For ourselves there were a sort of square stretcher, carried on the shoulders of twelve men for greater safety, who made a point of plunging into the deepest part of the torrent to give us a greater idea of the difficulties they had to contend with. For the idea then entertained by every Japanese was that the force of the stream was too great for a boat to live in it, and that a bridge was impossible. As it has since been successfully bridged, the probability is that this belief was purposely inculcated on the people on the principle of divide and rule, and what more effectual means of division could be found than a river which was not to be passed but by taking off your clothes and running the risk of drowning in it while effecting the passage, to say nothing of the inconvenience of emerging half-naked on the other side—that is to say, unless you could pay to be carried.

Following the economical practice we had observed all along of limiting our tips to the smallest respectable sum, we threw a *bu* to the men, who clamoured loudly for its division. We did not get to the inn till eight o'clock. Our host was particularly polite, and thanked us profoundly for doing him the honour of stopping at his humble abode. We were still under the influence of the excitement produced by our recent adventures, so *sake* and fish were ordered in, and the liveliest of the escort were bidden to the feast.

Someone distinguished himself by adding a new verse to the popular ballad then in vogue, expressive of our contempt for the "turnip-top" coated retainers of the *reiheishi*, which was sung over and over again to the accompaniment of a lute played by an exceedingly ugly red faced damsel who waited on us.

The next day brought us to the large town of Fuchū, formerly the residence of Ieyasu after his retirement from the active government of the state early in the seventeenth century, and since re-christened Shizuoka. It is an important centre of the tea and paper trades, and at the time we passed through was the seat of one of the principal universities of Japan, but greatly fallen from its ancient grandeur. On our way we had to taste various local delicacies, among which was a horribly tenacious kind of gruel, resembling bird-lime in appearance, made from the powdered root of the *yamato-imo*, a species of wild potato. We found the streets so full of spectators that it became necessary to get into our palanquins to avoid the crush of curious sightseers. The town is also noted for a variety of articles of cabinet work and lacquered ware of the ordinary sort, and the room next to our apartment had been converted into a kind of bazaar in expectation of our arrival. The articles were of the class common enough at Yokohama, and not much cheaper; in fact the prices were such as befitted the supposed exalted rank of the travellers. In those days in Japan it was a well observed doctrine that "noblesse oblige" in the matter of payments.

Next morning when we rose at six, we got a beautiful view of Mount Fuji, the "Peerless One," springing from the ground as it seemed almost behind the inn, and lifting its beautiful head into the pale blue sky, above horizontal wreaths and stretches of cloud. After breakfast we paid a visit to the university, where we found about thirty youngsters seated on the floor in one room, with copies of some Chinese classic before them, learning to read by rote from the mouths of older and more advanced pupils. This instruction was given for about two hours each morning, and six times a month explanations of the text were imparted by professors. The headmaster, who was from the Confucian College at Edo, used to be changed annually. And this, with the addition of learning to write with a brush, constituted the education of a young Japanese in the olden time. The system was one that cultivated the memory, but failed altogether to appeal to the reasoning faculties. Of course all this has long ago disappeared, and it is possible that this system of instruction is as obsolete in Japan as the dodo.

The great mountain having at last appeared on our horizon, we were to have its company for nearly every step of the rest of the journey. Near Ejiri we caught a delicious view of the summit appearing over the lower mountains on the left hand. At one o'clock we reached Okitsu, where we were to lunch. The inn stood close to the seashore, and possessed an upper room commanding a magnificent view, in favour of which we abandoned the dignified glories of the *jōdan* or dais. On the left the blue promontory of Izu stretched away far into the ocean until it became almost invisible in the haze. On the right hand the low hills of Kunō-zan terminated in a low spit of sand covered with irregular growth of pine trees, the famous Miyo no Matsubara of the Japanese poets. From the back window we had a glimpse of the snowy peak of Fuji-*san* peeping over the tops of the intervening hills, and by craning our necks out sideways the double-topped head of the Futago-*yama* near Hakone.

On leaving this spot, which we did with reluctance, we followed the base of the cliffs for two or three miles along the shore, when suddenly we turned a corner and Fuji-*san* came full in view. In front, the base of the great mountain was hidden by the low range which runs down into the sea near Kambara, and a white cloud encircled its middle. Wirgman sat down to make a sketch, from which he painted a picture which is still in my possession. Next we reached Kurazawa, famous for Venus-ear (*awabi*) and *sazai*, a big whorl with a curious spiral operculum. Of course we rested here awhile to eat of the local dish, washed down with repeated cups of *sake*, in which the guard joined us. Since the affair of Kakegawa we had become great friends, as men usually do who have shared the same perils. The road followed the sea-shore here to Kambara, and would be one of the most picturesque in Japan, but for the dirty uninteresting fishing villages which line nearly the whole of its length.

Next morning we were astir early, and crossing the low intervening hills, reached the banks of the Fuji River at eight o'clock. Extensive preparations had been made at the official hotel for our reception, mats laid down to the entrance and red blankets spread on the floor of the dais. At the urgent entreaty of the innkeeper we turned in for a few minutes, and discovered that Wirgman was an ancient acquaintance of our host, having seen him when he travelled overland from Nagasaki to Edo in 1861 in the suite of Sir Rutherford Alcock.

We were shown into the best room with much ceremony, and when we had taken our seats on the floor, piled-up boxes (*jūbako*) were brought in full of chestnut meal cakes, the speciality of the village, with a bit of pickled radish on the top. Other *meibutsu*, or "famous things," sold here are ink stones, bits of crystal with green streaks in them supposed by the common people to be grass, also agates.

We crossed in a boat the narrow turbulent Fuji-*kawa*, running between wide beds of shingle. Nowadays you cross the river by train. We then had a view of Fuji-*san* almost rising out of the sea and drawing its skirts up gradually behind it, curious but not so beautiful as when it is partly concealed by lesser summits which afford a standard of comparison.

On the road we met two little boys of twelve and fourteen years of age, who, having begged their way as pilgrims all the way from Edo to the sacred temples of Ise and of Kompira in Sanuki, were now on their way home, carrying slung across their backs huge packages of temple charms done up in oiled paper. The road was terribly sandy and hot, and passing for the most part between the bamboo fences of cottagers' gardens, was the reverse of picturesque.

We had intended to sleep at Hakone, but owing to delays for sketching, to say nothing of a huge feast of broiled eels and *sake* at Kashiwabara, did not manage to get beyond Mishima, at the western foot of the hills. Next morning we started at half-past six to ascend the pass which climbs the range of mountains by an excellent road paved with huge stones after the manner of the Via Appia where it leaves Rome at the Forum, and lined with huge pine trees and cryptomerias. At a tiny hamlet more than halfway up some hunters came to present us with eggs, according to immemorial custom. Three hours brought us to Hakone, the little mountain village standing on the southern border of the lake, surrounded by steep grassy hills. The warmth of the day tempted me to take a bath in the lake, which at first was strenuously opposed by the foreign official with us. It appeared that no boats were allowed on the lake, nor was anyone permitted to swim in it, lest he should take the opportunity of swimming round at the back of the barrier gate, and so avoid the necessity of showing his passport. With considerable trouble I persuaded the objector to withdraw his opposition, by representing that my natatory powers were altogether insufficient for the purpose.

After a couple of hours spent in this charming spot, which nowadays has become a fashionable summer retreat of foreigners residing at Yokohama, we resumed our journey down the eastern side of the pass, already described in a previous chapter, and got to our inn at Odawara by five, little dreaming of what lay before me.

A letter from Sir Harry Parkes was at once delivered to me urging me to hasten my return, as there were important negotiations on foot. On conferring with the leader of the escort, I learned that by starting at once and travelling post-haste through the night, I might get to Edo next morning. Eight porters in relays of four would be able to carry the palanquin at the rate of about four miles an hour. So the men were ordered without delay. The Japanese on these occasions, to save themselves from being too severely shaken, wind a broad piece of cotton cloth tightly round the waist, and tie another piece round the temples. A third is suspended from the ceiling of the palanquin, to which the traveller clings with might and main. I had to adopt this arrangement, and in addition stuffed my palanquin full of bedding and pillows. Noguchi and two of the escort accompanied me to negotiate the changes of coolies at the various posting stations on the way, and by seven o'clock we were in motion. The porters maintained a constant crying "*eeya-oy*," "*eeya-oy*," in order to keep step with each other and render the swinging of the palanquin less unendurable. To sleep was impossible, as this noise continued all night. When the day broke we had done twenty-six miles, which was slower than I had expected. So we urged on the fresh men we got here, and accomplished the remaining twenty-two miles by ten o'clock. From sitting cross-legged so many hours I was almost unable to stand upright when I got to the legation. And the vexatious part of it all was that the important conference, which I had hurried to attend, turned out to be a mere complimentary visit of a crowd of officials for whom anyone could easily have interpreted.

Sado Gold Mines

Our relations with government officials from this time onward suddenly assumed a character of cordiality which formerly would have been thought impossible. This was, of course, in consequence of very explicit instructions given by the *shōgun* to his ministers to cultivate the friendship of the foreign missions, and especially of the British legation, in order doubtless to counteract the intimate intercourse carried on between ourselves and the retainers of Satsuma and Chōshū. Each of the commissioners for foreign affairs in turn invited me to dine with him in Japanese fashion, and as I was extremely ignorant of Japanese etiquette, Noguchi used to accompany me on these occasions to be my tutor.

An exchange of presents was always an important part of the entertainment, and this was a very troublesome business on account of the difficulty of buying anything at the foreign stores in Yokohama that was worth giving away as a specimen of English productions. Most of these officials lived in a very modest way. The rooms in which they gave their entertainments were usually upstairs, perhaps not more than twelve feet by fifteen, but as there was no furniture, there was plenty of space. On arriving at the house we were shown up a very narrow staircase, and through an equally narrow door. Down we plumped on our knees immediately, and bowed our heads to the mats to the host, who did the same. Then ensued a contest of politeness, our entertainer trying to get us nearer to the top of the room, and we protesting that we were very comfortable where we were. Of course it ended in my being put down in front of the recess (*tokonoma*), which is the seat of honour, while Noguchi remained where he was, just inside the door. Usually I was then allowed to cross my legs in tailor fashion, owing to my joints not having yet acquired the lissomness of the Japanese. Then Noguchi with great solemnity unwrapping the present, would slide across the floor and deposit it between the host and myself. In Japan you don't use brown paper for parcels, but every household possesses a set of cloths of different sizes, silk or crape for the smaller, of cotton dyed green for the larger, which fulfil the same purpose as paper. Then I pushed the present gently towards my entertainer, saying "This is really a very shabby article, but as it is a production of my contemptible country, I …" To which he would reply, "Really I am quite overpowered. What a magnificent article. I am really ashamed to deprive you of it." And then all women folk, the servants, and the children who were peeping in at the door or round the corner of the balcony which ran along the front of the room would crane out their necks to get a glimpse of the precious rarity from the far west.

Then the other guests, three or four in number, would begin to arrive. If they were strangers, the following dialogue would take place. Each person putting his hands together on the mat in front would bend over and almost touching them with his forehead, say "I have the honour to present myself to you for the first time. My name is so-and-so. I hope to enjoy your friendship in perpetuity." To which either may add that he has often heard of the great fame of the other, and longed for an opportunity of meeting him.

When these bowings and prostrations are over, a small apparatus for smoking (*tabakobon*) is brought in and placed before the guest, after which tea and sweetmeats are served. Perhaps an hour passes in this way, for the entertainment is provided from a restaurant, as the domestic who performs the office of cook in a household only knows how to boil rice and make commonplace stews. In those days at least neither clocks nor punctuality were common. If you were invited for two o'clock, you went most often at one or three, or perhaps later. In fact, as the Japanese hour altered in length every fortnight, it was very difficult to be certain about the time of day, except at sunrise, noon, sunset and midnight. At last you began to hear a gentle clatter of dishes below stairs. The teacups, cakes and sweetmeats were removed, and a covered lacquered basin was set before you on a square tray, with a pair of chopsticks, the ends of which were neatly wrapped in paper. At the same time a girl put a basin half full of water down on the middle of the floor, with a small pile of diminutive flat cups by the side. Your host took one of these, held it out for a little of the hot *sake*, which is poured from a slender porcelain bottle, and having drunk it, slid forward to the basin to wash it. Having well shaken it, he crawled to where you were sitting, bowed profoundly, and presented the cup to you on his crossed palms. You bowed, and taking the cup between your own two hands deposited it on the floor, after which you were bound at once to present it to the damsel to be filled for yourself.

If your host, or one of the guests who has offered you the cup, wished to be very polite indeed, he waited before you with his hands resting on the floor in front of him while you emptied the cup, or at least took a good sip. When this ceremony had been gone through with all the guests, your host lifted the cover off his soup-basin, and invited you at the same time to follow his example. You drank a little of the soup, just dipped the end of the chopsticks into it by way of pretending to touch the meat, and laid down the bowl again; usually you replaced the cover. A number of dishes were brought in piled up with fish-cake, white beans boiled with sugar, raw, broiled and boiled fish, perhaps some boiled fowl or roast wild duck, cut up in small pieces, and these were served on small plates or saucers, and each person received a bowl containing a sort of pudding made of eggs, loach and the large seeds of the maidenhair tree. The raw fish, which was usually either *bonito* or sole, was sliced up very thin, and eaten with soy, raw laver (seaweed) and grated *wasabi*, which is the root of a plant belonging to the same order as the horse-radish, and resembling it in taste.

Towards the end of the feast a second water *souché* was brought in, and perhaps some broiled eels. The courses were not removed as each succeeding one was brought in, and the plates collected on your tray and the floor close by you till all the extent of the feast was exhibited. You ate very little, picking here a mouthful, there a mouthful, but you drank as much *sake* as you could stand, and sometimes more. After two or three hours of conversation, perhaps enlivened by some music and singing performed by professionals hired for the occasion, and you felt that you had had enough liquor you bowed to your host, and said that you would like some rice. This was the well-understood signal. A fresh tray was brought in with a large lacquered bowl for rice, and a couple more containing soups, accompanied almost invariably by the fish of ceremony called sea-bream, and the bigger it was the greater the honour. You had your bowl filled with rice, of which you were not able to eat much, as your appetite had been nearly destroyed by the repeated libations of warm *sake*, so after a few mouthfuls you handed the bowl to the maid, who filled it half full of very weak tea, or on very formal occasions with hot water, and thus you managed to swallow the contents, aided by a piece of salted radish or vegetable marrow pickled in the lees of *sake*. That over, you carefully replaced the covers on their respective bowls, pushed the tray a foot or two away from you, and executed a bow of profound gratitude to your entertainer. The feast was then removed downstairs, where all the portable parts of it were packed into a box of white wood-shavings and delivered to your servant, if you had one in your train, to carry home. Freshly infused tea was brought in, after which you thanked your host for the feast, and took your leave, being accompanied to the door of the house by the whole family, to whom you made as low a bow as possible before mounting your pony or entering your palanquin.

For the next six or seven weeks we were very busy arranging with the Japanese the details of a scheme for organizing their navy, with the assistance of a body of English officers who were to be sent out from England, as a counterpoise to the French military mission, which had been at work since the beginning of the year, and for the establishment of a college to be super-intended by a body of graduates from English Universities. The former plan was successfully carried out, and some months later a mission under the command of Commander, now Admiral, Richard Tracey, arrived in Japan. The educational proposal, however, came to nothing. Ultimately the Japanese obtained the assistance of a leading American missionary residing at Nagasaki, and the present (in 1885) educational system was established by teachers from the United States.

Sir Harry, as I have said before, had already visited Tsuruga, which was suggested as a possible alternative to Niigata as the port to be opened on the west coast, but before deciding this question, it was necessary to make a careful examination of Niigata itself. So in the latter part of July he started off on a voyage of inspection, taking Mitford and myself with him. I had Ono Seigorō, one of the legation writers, and my trusty Noguchi with me. We left Yokohama, on July 23, in the *Basilisk*, commanded by Captain, afterwards Sir William, Hewett, V.C. In less than four days we reached Hakodate, where the usual visits were exchanged with the governor, a little dark-faced man named Koide Hozumi. A good deal was said about the coal mine at Iwanai on the west coast of Ezo, where they had started to extract coal under the superintendence of my friend Erasmus Gower. Admiral Keppel was already here in the yacht *Salamis*, and, on August 1, we left again for Niigata, arriving there after a prosperous voyage of thirty-six hours.

From the sea the view of Niigata is very fine. In the background the mountains of Aizu rise at some distance inland, stretching far away to right and left. In front lies a level plain, consisting mainly of rice fields, fringed with trees. The foreground is a sandy shore, rising into sandhills to the right of the river mouth, and at some distance to the west the prospect terminates in the lofty peaks of Yahiko-*yama*. I landed immediately with Dr Wilson of the *Basilisk*, and the sea being quite smooth we crossed the bar without difficulty. Inside the water is very deep, and some eighty junks were lying there at anchor. The town is situated a little way upriver, not quite close to the bank. We chose what seemed a convenient landing place, and pushed ashore. Immediately a number of two-sworded officials made their appearance, and forming themselves into an escort, led the way to a Buddhist temple, the reception rooms of which had been prepared for the use of foreigners.

After we had waited for a few minutes the governor came in. He proved to be Shiraishi Chiwaki, an old acquaintance of mine when he held a similar post at Yokohama in 1864 and 1865. In those days we used often to have serious disputes about the claims of British subjects against defaulting Japanese merchants and questions of customs' duties, but I found him now in quite a different mood. He was very polite and cheery, and alluded with regret to the ridiculous arguments which in former days under a different regime he had been obliged to maintain against me. Now that the foreign ministers had visited the *shōgun* at Osaka all was to be changed, and our intercourse was to be really friendly. He had himself received from Kyoto a copy of instructions to that effect. After some further talk about the possibility of Niigata being made an open port, I arranged for him to call on Sir Harry on the following morning on board the *Basilisk*, bringing all the maps in his possession, and took my leave.

On our way back to the ship we stopped at a new hotel, where we dined in Japanese fashion, and made some purchases of the curious lacquered articles called *mokusa-nuri*, which are manufactured in Aizu, and China grass cloth woven in the villages further inland. This was not to be had in the shops, but was hawked about the town by people from the country. Here for the first time I saw the frozen snow, which in those days was the Japanese substitute for ice, and we found it a great luxury at that season of the year. Niigata was laid out in the form of the truncated segment of a circle, and intersected by canals, the banks of which were lined with willow trees, suggesting a Dutch model. The canals were narrow and dirty, and better deserving perhaps the name of ditches. At this moment the feast of Tanabata was at hand, and the streets were crowded with little boys carrying paper lanterns of all sizes and colours, many of them adorned with clever sketches in colour representing Japanese historical traditions and popular customs.

On the following day the promised interview came off on board, and we returned the governor's visit in the afternoon at his official residence. He had hastily had some benches constructed, which were covered with red cloth, the best substitute procurable for leather-bottom chairs.

Old Shiraishi renewed acquaintance with me some twelve years later at Tokyo, and used to give me lessons in the interpretation of the *utai* plays. His son became my librarian, and died in my house.

After a two hours' talk we started off to inspect an island in the river which it was proposed should be converted to the uses of a foreign settlement. Sir Harry, who was of an active inquisitive temperament, here signalized himself in the eyes of the natives by scrambling up to the top of a large shed, under which a junk was being constructed, to get a view of the surrounding country, much to the horror of Mitford and myself, who were so orientalized by this time in our notions that we longed to see our chief conduct himself with the impassive dignity of a Japanese gentleman. This exploit being over, he dragged us all, including Hewett, about the town till half-past six, not to the improvement of the tempers of that gallant officer or of his boat's crew, who thus lost their dinner. I remained behind with Noguchi, dined again in Japanese fashion, and spent the night on shore, in the enjoyment of a few hours' perfect freedom. In fact, I did not return to the ship till the following afternoon, and then had some difficulty in getting off, as there was a heavy swell on the bar, though outside there was neither wind nor rough sea.

From Niigata we crossed over to the island of Sado, the site of gold mines that have for a long period been famous. The Japanese proverb is that the "soil of Sado is the most effective of love-philtres." We had been told by the governor of Niigata that there was a good port here, where foreign vessels could lie, when the bar at the mouth of the Shinano River was too rough to cross owing to the northwest winds that prevail during the winter.

A letter had been sent off from Niigata on the previous day to announce the visit of the British minister, and as soon as we let go our anchor some of the local officials came off to call. The mines however lay at Aikawa on the other side of the island, where the governor resided. He had sent over his own *kago* for Sir Harry to perform the journey in, but the chief did not relish either the idea of locomotion after this fashion, nor yet of walking across the island and of passing the night on the floor of a Japanese house in native quilts, and with nothing better than rice and fish to eat. So he decided to send me across in his stead, and proceeded round to Aikawa in the *Basilisk*. This arrangement suited me down to the ground. It was much jollier to travel by one's self than to play second fiddle to one's chief always. The distance was about sixteen miles to Aikawa, and the officials made me extremely comfortable for the night.

Next day Sir Harry and a large party, including some of the officers of the *Serpent*, Commander Bullock and William George Aston our interpreter, landed at Sawane, where I went to meet them, and we walked over the hills to the village near the mines, where I had put up. On his arrival at the house where I had lodged, which in fact had been prepared for his reception, one of those scenes occurred which were not infrequent in those days, when the Japanese tried to treat foreigners with indignity, and it became necessary to resent their impertinence. At the door he was met by one of two vice-governors, who ushered him into a side room, where the idea was that he should do "ante-chamber" till the governor deigned to receive him. But Sir Harry was equal to the occasion, and promptly turning round without saying a word, walked out of the house. I overtook him at the gate, and having found out what was the matter, was on my way back to tell the alarmed officials that the governor must receive the British minister at the door of the house, when I met the two vice-governors hurrying after us with some ridiculous excuse. So we turned back, walking with immense dignity so as to give him time, and by the time we arrived back again the old fellow made his appearance beaming with smiles, as if nothing had happened. He was at once forgiven, and led the way into a large room where a long row of chairs extended down one side for ourselves, faced by three others for himself and the vice-governors.

We speedily became great friends and drank a quantity of *sake* together, Sir Harry and the governor vying with each other in the manufacture of the most high-flown compliments. After this the whole party adjourned to visit the gold mines, which were then, whatever they may be now, low-roofed burrows half full of water, and those who ventured in returned to the outer air again looking more like half-drowned rabbits than humans. I had never been able to see much pleasure in this sort of subterranean excursion, and carefully stayed outside. We got on board that night, and weighed anchor in order to proceed to Nanao on the Noto Peninsula. There a fine harbour was said to exist, which we thought could perhaps be substituted for Niigata.

Early on the morning of August 7, we came in sight of the lofty mountains of Etchū, which centre round the volcanic peak of Tateyama, nearly 10,000 feet high, and at eleven o'clock reached the southern entrance of the harbour, which is formed by a considerable island lying opposite to a bay. The *Serpent* led the way, in discharge of the functions appertaining to her as a surveying ship, but we had to take great care on account of the numerous patches of shoal water, and did not come to an anchor in front of the town till half-past twelve. Nanao, or Tokoro no kuchi, at that time containing from eight to nine thousand inhabitants, was rising into importance as a port for the few steamers belonging to the *daimyō* of Kaga, and was administered by a *machi bugyō* or prefect named Abe Junjirō. He was a young man who had been to Nagasaki and knew a little English, both of which facts in those days gave him a title to be considered travelled and learned, but he had no authority to speak on behalf of his lord. We therefore waited until the arrival of some more representative officials named Sano and Satomi, who were expected from Kanazawa, the capital of this fiefdom. They turned up on board the *"Basilisk"* on August 9, and sat talking, or rather being talked to, by Sir Harry for five mortal hours. The chief topic was the question of the suitability of Nanao as a substitute for Niigata. What the Kaga people feared was that this would lead to its being taken away from them by the *shōgun*'s government, as in former times had happened in the case of Nagasaki and Niigata. But they did not venture to state this openly, and alleged therefore various other excuses, such as that the inhabitants were not accustomed to see foreigners, that the majority would object on account of the general rise in prices which would follow on the exportation of produce, and the *daimyō*, however willing to see the place opened to foreign trade, must of course act in harmony with the wishes of the people.

Sir Harry then gave up pressing the point directly, enlarged on the inconveniences of the anchorage at Niigata, the need of a port of refuge, and the "fact" that none existed nearer than Nanao. He said nothing of our having inspected Ebisu Minato in Sado with the view of using it as an alternative anchorage to Niigata. Would the *daimyō* object to foreign vessels anchoring at Nanao when the weather was bad at the bar of Niigata? The reply was that for the sake of humanity and of our friendly relations he would be unable to refuse this. Well then, as ships could not afford to lie a long time at Nanao doing nothing, would there be any objection to their cargoes being landed and stored till they could be transported to Niigata? No, probably not, in the interests of humanity. Who then, asked Sir Harry, should undertake the construction of the necessary warehouses? The reply was that either foreigners or the Kaga administration could do this as seemed most convenient. Well then, supposing that the people of Nanao should wish to buy any of the goods so stored by foreigners, would it not be a hard thing to prevent the sale? They said perhaps it might be, but to give such permission would lead to converting Nanao into a foreign trading port. Nevertheless, if all the articles required were ordered beforehand, and not selected from those stored with a view to their transportation to Niigata, there could be no objection. But in actual fact, to speak frankly, they thought they could undertake the regulation of the port and the storage of goods without the assistance of the *shōgun*'s government. The territory of Nanao had belonged to the Maeda clan from very early times. It was the only good port in the three provinces of Kaga, Etchū and Noto, and could ill be spared. They would dislike to share the local administration with the government, nor could they give it up to them altogether.

Sir Harry expressed his concurrence in these views, and then proceeded to talk about the means of transport for himself and his party overland to Osaka. This subject had been discussed in the legation before our departure from Edo, though when the governor of Niigata had asked Sir Harry whether it was not his intention to return by land from Nanao, our very diplomatic chief had replied that such an idea had never entered his head. They received his suggestion with no marks of cordiality, and drew on themselves a severe rebuke for their want of friendship towards foreigners, so different to the feelings displayed by certain other clans. This plain speaking completely spoiled their temper. They became very sulky and silent, and alleging hunger, probably with much truth, took their departure.

As soon as they had left the ship Sir Harry made up his mind to send Mitford and myself overland to Osaka, while he went round by way of Nagasaki in the *Basilisk*. It was, of course, evident that we could travel through the country in a much less formal style than would be necessary for him, and on our part of course we were only too delighted to get the opportunity of seeing a part of the interior where foreigners had never been before. I was therefore sent on shore to get hold of the prefect. Bullock was ordered to remain behind with the *Serpent* to make a complete survey of the bay. The admiral, who had arrived from Niigata the day before us, got up steam in the *Salamis*, and was off at half-past three, the *Basilisk* following a couple of hours later.

The chief, who liked to keep us by him till the last moment, took us as far as the entrance of the harbour, where we put our traps into a boat belonging to the *Serpent*. But just as we were pulling away, the *Basilisk* got ashore in a shallow place, and they signalled to us to return to her. Eventually we were released from dancing attendance on him, and reached the shore at eight o'clock in the evening.

We proceeded to a house where I had more than once passed the night, and shortly received a visit from Sano and Abe, who were to make all the arrangements for our journey. Thither came also two officials of the Edo

Foreign Department, who had come from Yokohama with Sir Harry, and whom he had left behind with injunctions to facilitate the survey of the harbour by Bullock. But as soon as they heard that we were going overland, they conceived the plan of offering that one of them should accompany us, to spy upon our movements. They alleged that although everything might go well with us in the territories of the *daimyō* of Kaga, we should meet with difficulties further on. We should be unable to procure baggage and palanquin coolies; we might be attacked and killed. They had instructions to accompany us wherever we went on shore, and that it was a law of Japan that foreigners must not travel without foreign department officials to look after them. To this I replied with equal weight that they were bound to respect the injunctions laid on them by Sir Harry, to whom they had been lent by the *shōgun*'s Council. He had told them to remain at Nanao for a specific purpose, while we had positive orders from our chief not to take them. We felt assured that the *daimyō* of Kaga and Echizen, the territory that lay immediately beyond, would do everything to smooth our way. As regarded the rest of the line of road, they might write to the *shōgun*'s people at Kyoto to send down the necessary instructions, and even take on themselves the responsibility of transmitting the orders directly to the authorities of the towns we should have to pass through.

As for the law they mentioned, I felt convinced that it had no existence. At best there was only a custom to that effect, which we could decline to abide by at our option. These considerations proved to them that argument would not help them, so they tried to work upon my feelings by saying they would get into hot water with their superiors in Edo if they suffered us to depart alone. But this also failed. Finally they washed their hands of the business and begged to be excused from all responsibility for any difficulties we might encounter. This request was most readily granted, and they retired with a secret intention of getting Commander Bullock to dispense with their services, while we went to bed with the sense of a victory achieved.

From Nanao to Osaka

Next morning Sano and Abe presented themselves with the welcome news that everything was ready for our journey and made many apologies for the inconveniences we should have to put up with. They had provided a handsome palanquin for each of us and ordinary ones for Noguchi and Mitford's Chinese servant, the philosophic Lin-fu. A guard was furnished of twenty two-sworded men carrying long staves, under the command of an officer named Tominaga. We got away at half-past eight. Looking out to sea, we perceived that the *Basilisk* had departed, and that the *Serpent* was lying peacefully at anchor. The foreign department officials did not show up, and we concluded that they had made up their minds to submit. So we were perfectly free, away from our chief, from *shōgun*'s officials, from any other Europeans, embarked on an adventure in a totally unknown part of the country, which might end anyhow for aught we cared, but at any rate was of an altogether novel character.

As soon as we were clear of the town we got out and walked. It was a piping hot day. Each man of the twenty who formed the escort as he went along fanned himself with one hand, and wiped the perspiration from his brow with a towel carried in the other. It soon became evident that we were to be treated with great distinction, for we had not travelled more than an hour and a half before we were invited to rest and refresh ourselves with delicious water melons and tea. Nectarines were also offered, but of such fearful unripeness that we dared not make their close acquaintance. An hour further we had again to rest. Everyone was excessively polite; the peasants whom we met were made to crouch down and take off their hats.

This was much more than could have been expected after the scolding Sir Harry had given to Sano and his colleagues on the previous day. The road lay up a gradually narrowing valley, cultivated principally with rape and hemp. At a quarter past one we stopped for lunch at a clean inn where they gave us a capital meal. After a nap we resumed our way at three o'clock down another valley, stopped to rest at half-past four, and reached our night quarters at half-past six, having accomplished eighteen miles. This was the village of Shio, prettily situated on the banks of a tiny stream, and close to the mouth of a valley, the view up which into the hills growing ever higher and higher was one of the charming prospects in which Japan abounds. After the hot bath, they served an excellent dinner with many polite apologies for its badness.

The next day brought us some sixteen miles further to Tsubata, where we joined the high road which traverses the dominions of the *daimyō* from one end to the other at no great distance from the coast. Here our escort left us, and a new set of men took their place. We were now passing through a more populous part of the country, and were objects of intense curiosity to the inhabitants. At Morimoto the front rooms of the houses on both sides of the street were filled with spectators sitting in rows three or four deep or on mats placed at the side of the roadway.

Shortly after leaving this place we caught a glimpse of the white castle walls of Kanazawa peeping through the pine trees. As soon as we came in sight of the town itself we got into our palanquins, and were carried to one of the first houses, where we met Satomi and another official named Tsunekawa. Crowds of spectators had assembled, and some of them were so eager to gratify their curiosity that they even stood in a muddy lotus pond which commanded a view of the back of the house where we were. Here delicious melons and apples were served with frozen snow from the mountains behind the town. Gold paper screens lined the walls, there were tables piled high with fruit and cakes, and in the recess behind the seat of honour a beautiful writing box of the finest gold lacquer, in case we wished to sit down and write letters. A most unnecessary piece of ceremonial preparation, one would say.

The officials asked us to proceed from here on foot in order that the people might see us better, but we preferred making use of our palanquins, as we had on our travelling garments, and were somewhat dusty and way-worn. The streets were thickly lined with spectators of all ranks and ages, among whom were some very pretty girls. Another charming resting place had been prepared for us, into which they obliged us to turn aside, although we had previously expressed our wish to go on straight to the inn. Continuing thence along the street, thickly filled with inquisitive but perfectly orderly townspeople, we crossed a bridge and, after turning a few times to right and left, at last reached our inn, rather tired with all the fuss and ceremony.

At the porch we were welcomed by Satomi, who had hurried on ahead to superintend our reception. He conducted us through several rooms into an inner room of great size, spread with a huge velvet-pile carpet and furnished with Chinese tables and scarlet-lacquered chairs such as the high priests of Buddhist temples occupy on grand ceremonial occasions. The host immediately presented himself, bowing his head to the floor as if he were saluting a pair of kings. Each servant who brought in the tobacco trays or tea bowed low to the ground, then advanced holding the article high in both hands, deposited it on the table, and then retiring backwards to the edge of the carpet, knocked his head on the floor again before withdrawing. We were conducted in turn to the bath with great ceremony, and then put on our best clothes (which were neither new nor good) to receive visitors.

The first to call was a special messenger from the *daimyō*, to express a hope that we had not suffered from the heat and rejoicing at our fortunate arrival. Mitford replied with great dignity that we had not felt the heat. We were deeply grateful for the hospitality and kindness shown to us and said we would like to call on the *daimyō* to thank him in person. "My master," said the messenger, "is unfortunately indisposed, otherwise he would have been delighted to make your acquaintance." Mitford expressed a hope that he would soon recover. The real truth I imagine to have been that an interview between a *daimyō* and two foreigners would have involved far too important and complicated decisions on questions of etiquette for it to be lightly con- templated. The messenger added that he had been commanded by his master to offer us a small entertainment, and to accompany us in partaking of it. Mitford rose to even greater heights of flowery speech than before, and invented a message from Sir Harry Parkes (which if the chief did not actually charge us with, the omission could only be attributed to inadvertence), expressing his desire to swear eternal friendship with the *daimyō* and people of Kaga, which gave very great satisfaction to the messenger and everyone else present. Doctors were also introduced, whom the lord had deputed to attend on us in case we felt any ill effects from the heat.

To this exchange of compliments succeeded a feast resembling in character what has already been described but far surpassing it in magnificence and the number of courses. Observing that our Japanese entertainers were not comfortable on their chairs, we proposed to banish the furniture and squat on the floor after the manner of the country, and thus facilitate the passing of the *sake* cup. After a considerable time had been passed in general conversation, and everyone's head was more or less heated, we introduced political topics, which were discussed very confidentially in the presence of a crowd of people.

The structure of a Japanese house is such that no secrets can be whispered; there is always someone listening behind a paper partition or on the other side of a screen, and if you wish to hatch a plot, your best way is to transfer your deliberations to the middle of the garden, where you can keep off eaves-droppers. However, as we could not do that on the present occasion, it seemed better to take all who chose it into our confidence. The gist of the conversation amounted to this—that the Kaga people wished to trade with foreigners, but did not wish avowedly to make an open port of Nanao, because the *shōgun*'s government would then try to deprive them of it; but they would agree to its being an anchorage for foreign vessels, ancillary to Niigata, and to goods being landed there, in which case everything else would naturally follow. If the *shōgun*'s government were to inquire what view they took of the question, they would reply ambiguously. Our answer was that of course we desired to act in harmony with the wishes of the *daimyō*, and would do nothing that could possibly be prejudicial to his interests. This proved very satisfactory to our entertainers, who declared the warm feelings of friendship for us that animated them, and a stratagem, the details of which I do not recollect, was agreed upon for keeping up secret and confidential communications with them after our return to Edo. Both sides bound themselves to secrecy, and the party broke up.

The bedding, which was of the most magnificent description, was then brought in, piles of soft, quilted mattresses covered with silk or crape, and stuffed with silk wool, and a large net of silk gauze was hung up to keep off the mosquitoes. Then a freshly-infused pot of green tea, with teacups, on a small tray, and the necessary apparatus for smoking, were gently slid under the bottom of the mosquito curtain, and the people of the house wished us a good night's rest. In the morning, the very first thing before we were awake, the same elements of a comfortable existence were provided in the same unobtrusive manner.

The forenoon was spent in choosing lacquer and porcelain. On the previous evening an arrangement had been made for our visiting the neighbouring hills, but some hitch had occurred, and we were now asked to accept instead an excursion to Kanaiwa, the port of Kanazawa. It lay at a distance of about five miles, so we started on horseback about three o'clock. Our steeds were rather shabby-looking ponies, unshod, with saddles in the European fashion covered with thick black paper instead of leather, and painfully stiff bridles of badly tanned leather. Noguchi was mounted on a pony splendidly caparisoned in the native style, and the philosophic Linfu, who could not ride, was put into a palanquin. Though we had such a very short way to ride, it was supposed that delicately nurtured persons like ourselves would feel the fatigue, and three resting places had been prepared, two on the road and one at Kanaiwa itself. The so-called port proved to be an open roadstead at the mouth of an insignificant stream, quite useless except in perfectly calm weather.

At dinner that evening we had some further talk with a couple of officials. They had come to the conclusion, after thinking over the conversation of the previous evening, that it would be their wisest course to admit to the *shōgun*'s government the probability of a certain amount of trade taking place at Nanao. In that way no danger would arise of their getting into trouble for what would otherwise be smuggling. We approved of this proposal, and suggested their sending to Edo someone authorized to treat with the government and the foreign representatives. In the course of conversation on the domestic politics of the country, they said that in their opinion the *shōgun*'s government ought to be supported, and not done away with altogether, as the Satsuma and Chōshū people, with other clans, were believed to be advocating. But at the same time limits ought to be placed on its authority. They had read my pamphlet, and entirely approved of the suggestions it contained. After that, all one could say was that we entirely concurred in the views of the Kaga clan. As a matter of fact, these people were rather too remote from the main centre of political thought to be cognisant of or sympathise with the aspirations of the southern and western clans. They lay in an isolated position on the northern coast, in a part of the country that had always been looked upon somewhat as the home of ignorance and want of culture. They cared only for themselves. The lands held by the *daimyō* of Kaga were assessed at a much greater annual value than the fief of any other lord, which gave the clansmen an importance in the eyes of the rest of the world with which they were thoroughly satisfied. An alteration in the political organization of the country could hardly benefit them, and they were at bottom disposed to be contented with the status quo.

The British legation, on the contrary, was determined that so far as their influence went, the emperor should be restored to the headship of the nation, so that our treaties might receive a sanction that no one would venture to dispute. For this purpose it was necessary that the constitution of the *shōgun*'s government should be modified in such a manner as to admit the principal *daimyō* (or clans rather) to a share in the distribution of power.

Our hosts would have been contented to keep us longer, but we were due at Osaka at a fixed date, and could not stay with them. We resumed our journey, therefore, on the morning of August 14. The landlord was very urgent with us that we should call in passing at a shop for patent medicines kept by a relation, to lay in a stock of a preparation called "purple snow" (*shisetsu*), composed chiefly of nitre and perfumed with musk, and believed to be a remedy for most of the ills to which flesh is heir. The streets were again crowded with eager spectators. When just clear of the town we were forced to alight from our *kago* for a parting feast at a restaurant on a height commanding a picturesque view of the castle, which planted plentifully with trees presented a park-like aspect very unlike the grim fortresses that in Europe usually go by the name. Here we spent an hour eating fish and drinking *sake*, vowing eternal friendship with the Kaga clansmen, with whom previous to this visit we had had no intercourse whatever.

We lunched that day at Mattō, where I had a long talk with the mayor on things in general, in the presence of a vast and attentive crowd, and reached Komatsu in the evening, having accomplished twenty miles. This was very fair going, considering the numerous delays and stoppages for refreshment. The next day we passed the boundary line between the territories of Kanazawa and Daishōji, where the escort was changed. At the latter town we found the streets entirely cleared, and crowds of people quietly sitting in the front rooms of the houses, among them many daughters of the best families in holiday garb, with wreaths of silver flowers on their heads, their faces nicely powdered with white lead, and their lips stained with the safflower dye which imparts such a curious metallic lustre to the skin. Here we took a formal farewell of Okada and Shinbō, two Kaga gentlemen who had accompanied us during the previous days. Mitford's Chinese servant came in for a share in the general leave-taking, and philosophically remarked that he did not understand Japanese etiquette, which appears to consist chiefly in the performance of the *koto*.

About three miles farther we finally quitted the domains of the Maeda family, and passed into the territory of Echizen. There was no guard to meet us, only a couple of policemen, and it was proposed that we should retrace our steps to a teahouse half a mile back, to wait till an escort could be procured. To this we objected, saying that we were willing to go on without a guard. The *rusui* or head bailiff of the *daimyō* of Daishōji said that it would not be correct for his men to undertake our protection beyond the limits. Finally we reached a compromise. Okada and Shinbō, who in spite of the formal parting that had taken place at Daishōji, were still of the party, borrowed ten men from the bailiff on the distinct understanding that they were not any longer a guard, and walked on with us.

Shortly afterwards we met an Echizen official of low rank (he was a *metsuke* or assistant clerk), and our Kaga friends took their final leave of us, not without expressing the opinion that the Echizen people showed very little courtesy in not deputing someone of more exalted rank to offer us a welcome. But the fact was we were not welcome at all, as we speedily found, for although every possible pains had been taken to provide us with good food and quarters, the whole Echizen clan held aloof from us. For instance at Kanazu, where we passed the night, the whole town was illuminated with coloured lanterns, and the spectators who crowded the main street went down on their knees in the usual respectful manner.

Very beautiful guest rooms had been prepared for us at a monastery, chairs and tables had been provided, and a couple of good little boys, of preternaturally solemn demeanour, sat on the floor behind us to fan away the mosquitoes. The superior civilization and resources of the country, as compared with Kaga, were exhibited by the production of beer and champagne. Next day we reached Fukui, the capital of the province, a town of about forty thousand inhabitants. Here again the streets had been cleared; spectators in their best were seated in rows in the shops, and looked just as if they had paid for their places, like the people who go to see the Queen open parliament. I never saw so many pretty girls together anywhere. White brooms and buckets of water stood before each house, as a sign that the road had been swept clean and the dust laid.

We were conducted to the Hongan-ji, a new and handsome building, where a large room had been prepared for us, and hung with silk crape curtains dyed with the Echizen crest. In the recess stood a beautiful vase containing a huge bouquet of lotus flowers, standing quite six feet tall. The table was loaded with piles of fruit and cakes, and the usual Japanese luncheon was served, with champagne. No one approached us, with the exception of a young Japanese who had been in the service of a foreigner at Nagasaki and spoke a little English; but numbers of officials, some of high rank, collected in the passages to stare at us. We took no notice of them, adopting the perfectly cold and impassive manner of Orientals on their dignity. This was bad, but worse came behind.

Although on our quitting Fukui, they sent men before us to sweep the road ahead, our guards were rude, and chaffed about us among themselves. At Fuchū, the town where we stopped for the night, a noisy crowd pursued us from the entrance of the town to our lodging, running along the other side of the stream which lay along the middle of the street. Arrived at the inn, we found the dais room shut up, and the matted floors spread with *shibukami*, a sort of thick, tough paper in sheets, which is laid down when any particularly dirty household business is to take place. It is the correlative of the dust sheets used in England to cover up furniture when a weekly cleaning takes place. We were, of course, indignant, but I think these, to us, offensive precautions had been taken in the belief that we were ignorant of Japanese manners and customs, and would walk in with our shoes on.

The day after this we crossed the boundary on the top of a hill called the Tochinoki-*tōge* (Horse-Chestnut Pass), where we said good-bye to the rude Echizen escort, and were taken charge of by men belonging to Ii Naosuke, the *daimyō* of Hikone. A very moderate bill was presented to us for our board, lodging and coolie hire, which we paid, and we offered payment also for the extras in the shape of beer, champagne and fish, but could not induce the officials to accept it.

It is not very easy to explain why the Echizen people showed such an utter want of cordiality, but I think it may perhaps be attributable to the difficult position in which the clan then stood. Its head was closely allied to the *shōgun*'s family, being in fact descended from one of the sons of Ieyasu, the founder of the Bakufu. Although perfectly well aware of the difficulties in which the *shōgun* was involved, he was not prepared to side with the Satsuma and Chōshū party, which aimed at the restoration of the emperor, and was probably acquainted with the policy of the British legation, as supposed to be set forth in my pamphlet. Intimacy with foreigners had never until quite lately been a part of the government programme, and the Echizen people likely thought it wiser to hold aloof from us, in spite of the recent change of attitude on the part of the *shōgun*, especially as the south-western *daimyō* had never openly adhered to the policy of friendship with foreigners. The "expulsion of the barbarians" was still their ostensible party cry. So that on the whole I incline to the opinion that extreme caution was the keynote to the want of cordiality displayed by the Echizen folk.

We stopped that night at a little village among the hills called Naka no Kawachi, where we could get nothing to eat but rice and tea. In ordinary years there are no mosquitoes here, owing to its elevation, and we had therefore considerable trouble in procuring mosquito curtains. The general aspect of the country reminded me closely of Scawfell Pass in Cumberland. At the further foot of the hills we passed one of those barriers, curious relics of a past full of suspicion, where no woman was allowed to pass, and where every man had to exhibit a passport. At Nagahama we met an official of the *shōgun*'s government named Tsukahara Kanjirō (brother of Tsukahara Masayoshi), with eighteen of the foreign guard, who henceforward charged themselves with our protection. Sir Harry Parkes had passed through here in May last in returning from his visit to Tsuruga, and we found the people disposed to be familiar and careless of our comfort. We felt that we were now little better than prisoners; farewell all jollity and all politeness on the part of the inhabitants. We hastened on as rapidly as possible, being now as anxious to get over the rest of our journey as we had in the beginning been disposed to loiter among a friendly population.

At Takamiya, where we lunched, we found the dais room closed against us, but I took the innkeeper and his servants roundly to task, and made them open it. After this, they recognized that we understood Japanese etiquette, and for their previous rudeness substituted perfect courtesy. As we were now about to quit the territory of Ii Naosuke, we offered to settle our bill for lodging and coolie hire, but the official in charge refused to accept payment, alleging that he had received reiterated orders not to take anything from us. So we contented ourselves with addressing to him a letter of acknowledgment, and told him we would thank the *daimyō's* people on our return to Edo. The local escort left us at Nakajiku, the boundary, and we were consigned to the care of the foreign guard, who concerned themselves very little on our behalf. The consequence of this was that the people crowded in upon us at every village, and were extremely rude in their behaviour. On our arrival at Musa I administered a quiet blowing-up to the commander of the guard, who promised that things should be better arranged for the morrow.

Next day we reached Kusatsu, where, to our surprise, we fell in with a couple more of the *shōgun's* officials, whom I knew very well, Takabatake Gorō and a young fellow named Komeda Keijirō, the latter of whom spoke English remarkably well. They told us that they had come overland from Edo with Hirayama Seisai, one of the *shōgun's* Second Council, and had been dropped here by him to look after us. He had charged them to say to us that the temple of Ishiyama, just below the Seta bridge, which had been closed to Sir Harry in May, would be shown to us, and was well worthy of a visit. This temple in fact lay on the route which Tsukahara had already persuaded us to adopt. We were to embark at Kusatsu, descend the river which flows out of Lake Biwa as far as the rapids, then walk for about a couple of leagues (five miles), and embark again to Fushimi. This, he said, was a much shorter and pleasanter route than that which Wirgman and I had taken in May. We therefore jumped at the offer made on the part of Hirayama, whom we voted a capital fellow, and some amicable conversation followed on Japanese politics, in which they tried to persuade us that the positions taken up by my pamphlet were all wrong, but without success.

After they left, Noguchi came to me and said that the road over the hills to Uji, instead of being only ten or twelve miles, as had been represented to us, was in reality much nearer twenty-five, so that we could not possibly get there by midday. A misgiving immediately arose in my mind that there was something concealed behind all this solicitude about our seeing temples. Probably the *shōgun*'s officials wanted to get us away from Ōtsu, which lay on the direct route, and the vicinity of Kyoto, in order to prevent trouble with the anti-*shōgun* party, such as had occurred in May when Sir Harry passed through there. I therefore despatched Noguchi to probe Tsukahara, and sent for the posting officer to inquire about the distances. What he told me only confirmed my suspicions, which I then mentioned to Mitford. We therefore resolved to go by Ōtsu and to run all risks.

We had invited Takabatake Gorō and the other man to dinner. Just before our guests arrived Noguchi returned, and I imparted my suspicions to him. He thought I was wrong. As soon as they came in, I announced to Takabatake our intention of taking the usual route. He was greatly disconcerted, and declared it would be very inconvenient, nay impossible. I replied that we were indifferent to temples and scenery, but extremely fond of saving time in travelling; and as the road by Ōtsu was the shorter, we would take it. Seeing that we were very firm in our resolve, he retired from the room, and got hold of Noguchi, whom he begged to use his influence. Noguchi thereupon called me outside for a private conversation, and urged me to adhere to the original arrangement. I replied that it was useless; we wanted to go by the shorter route, and if altering the arrangements as to boats, etc., cost money, we were willing to pay it. I returned to the dining room, and my answer was communicated to Takabatake, who thereupon called out Komeda. Komeda came back, and begged me in turn to come out. As soon as we were alone, he said that he wished to have a friendly talk, and confessed that the whole thing was a plant. I said that we knew it before, and had felt convinced that Tsukahara had been sent down from Kyoto by the *shōgun*'s prime minister (Itakura Katsukiyo) to hoodwink us. If they had told us the truth in the beginning, we would have complied with their wishes; but that now it was too late to talk to us of going so far out of our way merely to oblige them. We then returned to the dining room again, and tried to proceed with our meal.

The three Japanese were very crestfallen, and became still more so when Mitford suddenly turned to Komeda and said to him in English that if the private secretary (*ōmetsuke*) who had been sent down from Kyoto on this particular business would address to him a letter stating explicitly the reasons why they wished us to change our route, we would fall in with their wishes; otherwise we would go by Ōtsu, even if the guard should refuse to accompany us. After a little demur, they accepted his offer as the easiest alternative, and Takabatake went off to prepare the letter. We had great difficulty in obtaining a document to our minds. Takabatake produced three drafts, one after the other, which had to be rejected, because it was alleged in them that we were travelling without the permission of the government, and the phraseology was so confused that it became impossible to make head or tail of it. At three o'clock in the morning they at last brought the fair copy of what we had insisted on being put down in black and white, namely that great complications had arisen at Kyoto in the previous May on account of Sir Harry's passing through Ōtsu, which was only six miles from the emperor's capital, and begging Mitford as a favour to go by way of Uji. Great victory for us and corresponding defeat for the Japanese officials.

I had very little sleep that night, for we were on the move by a quarter to seven. We went in palanquins as far as the bridge of Seta, and embarking in a boat, proceeded down the river to Ishiyama-dera. As soon as we were sighted by the priests in charge, they ran to shut the gates in our face. So much for Hirayama's promise of admission. It was a very hot day. We left the river to ascend and descend a series of little hills for four miles, and then came out by the river again. Here we got a scanty meal of rice and tea, all that was procurable in such an out-of-the-way spot. Then along the path for a mile or so by the river, which roared over its rocky bed between steep schistose hills, and then climbed a very stiff ascent, trying in the extreme under the burning August sun. At every peasant's hut they told us that it was still four miles to Uji. Frequently we had to stop and wash out our mouths by some scanty stream trickling from the rock. But at last we reached the summit, and gained a magnificent view of the great plain below, in the centre of which lies the mysterious and jealously guarded Kyoto, like a Japanese Mecca, in which it was death for the heathen foreigner to set his foot. To the left lay Fushimi, with its network of canals and rivers, far away in front the sacred top of Atagoyama.

At four o'clock we reached Uji, hot and tired, having trudged our weary way almost unceasingly since noon. We rested for a couple of hours at a charming teahouse on the bank of the river close to the broken bridge. At six we embarked in a comfortable houseboat, and drifted rapidly down stream to Fushimi, where we got a bath and dinner at the official hotel. Noguchi afterwards told me that he had overheard some men there talking about the advisability of murdering us. However, they lacked the courage to carry out their idea, and we got away safely at nine in a large boat. It was too hot to sleep inside, so I lay all night on the gangway which ran along the gunwale, overhanging the water.

Early in the morning we reached Osaka, washed our faces in the stream, dressed, and betook ourselves to the temple we had occupied in the spring. Sir Harry turned up in the afternoon, with the news of the murder of two sailors of HMS *Icarus* at Nagasaki, as they were lying in a drunken sleep on the roadway in a low quarter of the town. Before this new outrage the tale of our experiences paled altogether in interest.

Osaka to Tokushima

The next few days were occupied almost exclusively with the question of what measures were to be adopted for the detection and punishment of the murderers of the *Icarus* sailors at Nagasaki. Sir Harry, as was very natural, took up the matter with great warmth, and used some extremely strong language to the principal minister of the *shōgun*, a good-natured, yet not by any means weak, old gentleman named Itakura Katsukiyo. He seemed to be old, though probably not over forty-five. The rumour at Nagasaki had been that the perpetrators were Tosa men, and the suspicion was strengthened by the fact that a sailing vessel and a steamer belonging to Tosa, which were lying in the harbour, suddenly left before dawn, a few hours after the murder. It was suggested that the perpetrators had escaped in the sailing vessel, as she left an hour and a half before the steamer, and that they were transferred to the latter somewhere outside the harbour. As far as we could judge, the *shōgun*'s government seemed to entertain the same suspicions. The Tosa men had always had the reputation for being more savagely disposed than any other Japanese. The government promised to dismiss the two governors of Nagasaki, and to send a body of five hundred men from Edo to patrol the foreign settlement at Nagasaki to prevent anything of the kind recurring. Upon this Sir Harry accepted an invitation to see the *shōgun*, who had come down from Kyoto to give an audience to the French minister, Roches, about the recent arrest of some native Christians at Nagasaki. Sir Harry, Mitford and I went accordingly to the castle in palanquins, as the weather was very hot, and no good ponies could be procured. We were received in the private drawing-room (*shiro-in*). The *shōgun*, who looked a little worn, had with him Itakura and Hirayama; the latter was a little old man of rather low origin with sharp cunning features, who had lately been promoted. We nicknamed him the fox, and he deserved it well.

After an hour's talk, on indifferent matters, we were joined by Admiral Keppel and his staff. This led to some conversation on naval affairs, but I came to the conclusion that His Highness took very little interest in the subject. After a while the *shōgun* sent for Matsudaira Kansō, the ex-*daimyō* of Hizen, an oldish-looking man of forty-seven, and introduced him to Sir Harry and the admiral. He had a sharp countenance, and spoke in a fitful, abrupt manner, constantly winking with both eyes. He had the reputation of being a time-server and a great intriguer, and certainly, up to the very moment of the revolution, which took place in 1868, he never allowed anyone to guess what side he would take. He sat next to the *shōgun* on his left, and the only other mark of respect, other than that due to equals, which he employed in speaking was the word "*kami*," for "you." Sir Harry endeavoured to get an invitation out of him to visit his place at Saga, but he was too wary, and merely expressed the expectation that they might meet some day at Nagasaki; but that never came to pass. When the *shōgun* was tired of talking we adjourned to the next room, where a Japanese luncheon was served, with cold *sake*, which was a sign that no one was expected to take more than enough.

Early that morning I had received a call from Saigō Takamori, and here I insert a translation of a letter which he afterwards wrote to Ōkubo Toshimichi giving an account of our conversation. The original was found many years afterwards among the papers of Iwakura Tomomi, and a copy was given to me in 1906, as I was passing through Tokyo on my way home from Beijing, by my old friend Matsugata Masayoshi:

To Ōkubo Toshimichi

Yesterday morning at 6 I arrived at Osaka, and on inquiring where was the lodging of the English, I learned that it was at the temple where they were in the spring. So I at once sent to Satow to inquire at what time today it would be convenient for me to call. The answer was that I should come at 7 o'clock. I went at that hour, and found he had just woke, and I was shown upstairs. I said that hearing of the minister's arrival at Osaka, I had been, as you know, sent as a special messenger to inquire after his health. The ordinary compliments having been offered, he said the mail to England was being despatched about ten o'clock, and that at half-past eleven the minister was going to the castle. I said that I had no particular business, but had only come to call in order to congratulate him on his arrival at Osaka. As he must be very busy, I would not trouble him with a personal interview, and begged him to say so to the minister. He replied that the minister particularly wished to meet me, but as he was so much occupied he would ask to be excused that day. He said the minister would remain two or three days at Osaka, and particularly desired to meet me, and he thought he would be able to give me an interview in two or three days. He said he would sail from here on the 2nd of next month in order to return to Yokohama (or probably Edo).

When I saw Satow, he said things were exactly as before and that there had been no change of any importance, and the position being just as before, it was entirely different from what Shibayama had suspected. Therefore I told him that the Osaka Commercial Co. has, as I said to you the other day, agreed with the French, and is planning to make great profits. [An obscure passage follows.]

I said I should like to try to discuss the settlement of Japanese affairs by the French, on which Satow replied that he would very much like to argue it. I told him the French said Japan must have a single concentrated government like all Western countries, and the *daimyō* must be deprived of their power. Above all it was desirable to destroy the two provinces of Chōshū and Satsuma, and that it would be well to join in subduing them. I asked what he thought of this. Satow then answered that it might be seen from the two previous attempts at subjugation, that a government which had not been able to beat Chōshū alone would certainly not be able to deprive all the *daimyō* of their powers. I said: How could such weak people be helped. He replied that not a word could be said to that, and the argument was impossible. If such an argument were publicly brought forward, there was no doubt that they would help the government to destroy the *daimyō*. It was heard that the idea was that in two or three years' time money would be collected, machinery be provided, French assistance be invoked and war begun. As the French would then send troops to give assistance, it would be dangerous unless an opposite great power were got to assist. If a report were then spread that England would also send out troops to protect, it would be impossible for French auxiliary troops to be set in motion. He said that therefore it was necessary to come to a thorough agreement beforehand. In the first place the English idea was that the sovereign of Japan should wield the governing power, and under him the *daimyō* should be placed, and so the establishment of the constitution (or national polity) would be similar to the system of all other countries. This was the first [word omitted here] thing of all. The sovereign of England had lately sent to the Bakufu a letter addressed to the sovereign of Japan. This was a letter of condolence on hearing of the death of the late emperor. This was to be delivered to the emperor by the Bakufu. It would be improper if no reply were made to it, but up to the present no reply had been received.

Although that was what they had declared with respect to the emperor of Japan, at Kyoto H.M. did not take that view at all. It was maintained that the admission of aliens into the capital would be a defilement. As that sort of thing was undesirable, it would be necessary that a definite form of government vis-a-vis all countries carried on ordinary relations. If it was desired to consult with England, he would like to be informed, and as he was disposed to undertake the assistance asked for I replied that we would exert ourselves for the transformation of the Japanese government and we had no justification [?] vis-a-vis foreigners.

The French grabbed profit at Yokohama and entered into agreements for their own pleasure. England was a country based on commerce, and would strenuously oppose any attempt to hinder commerce, and was therefore extremely indignant.

The culprits who had killed two English sailors at Nagasaki were not yet known. We had heard it was rumoured to be the act of Nagasaki [Substituted by Saigō for Tosa] men. He heard that Nagasaki was very badly spoken of. When Satow and others travelled overland from Echizen, Nagasaki men lay in wait for them at Fushimi. It was also said by many that they committed acts of violence at Kyoto, and gathered gamblers together. If it was Nagasaki men who had killed aliens at Nagasaki, it was to be much regretted as doing a great injury.

When they came to Echizen no one came to meet them. Though local governors came to meet them in the country, no one came to see them at the castle-town, but they were entertained hospitably with *sake* and *sakana*. Satow said he could not understand this.

The above is a summary of the important points. Satow says he will come here tomorrow at ten o'clock, and I think there will be more conversation. I propose to stay two or three days longer, so please understand that. Satow's language about the Bakufu is very insulting. I will tell you all in detail. Good-bye. 27th of the 7th moon.

Saigō Takamori

P.S. Note by penman: This copy of the letter contains obscurities, and some incorrect transcriptions.

Next day I went to see Saigō at the Satsuma agency, in order to learn from him how things were going on at Kyoto. He talked a good deal of a parliament of the whole nation, to be established as a substitute for the existing government of the *shōgun*, which I found from my young friend Matsune was a very general idea among the anti-*shōgun* party. To me it seemed a mad idea. Saigō also revealed to me a plan conceived by the government for monopolizing all the trade of Osaka and Kobe by placing it in the hands of a guild of twenty rich native merchants, which was no doubt copied from the old arrangement at Canton before the opium war of 1840.

This piece of news, when it was brought to him, inflamed the chief's wrath, who immediately got hold of the prime minister and insisted upon the scheme being abandoned. A new proclamation was issued, annulling the previous one establishing the guild, but as it was extorted by dint of great diplomatic pressure, I had very little belief in its being acted on. It was, and always has been, a Japanese idea to regulate commerce, both domestic and foreign, by means of the guilds, who pay for their monopoly, and make the most of it. Whatever may be the abstract merits of such a system, it is not altogether in accordance with Western ideas, and we have never ceased to make war upon it whenever it crossed our path in Eastern countries.

Another matter about which we had to speak very strongly was the wording of the *shōgun*'s reply to the queen's letter, conveying the usual expressions of condolence on the death of the late emperor. The ministers apologized very humbly for having made use of discourteous forms, and promised to take great care for the future. The style of official documents addressed to the British minister was also a subject upon which we had never-ending disputes with the Japanese officials, and it was only after the revolution that I succeeded in getting these things done in proper form. Their object was always by the use of particular forms and turns of phraseology to convey to their own people the belief that the foreign representatives were the inferiors of the *shōgun*'s ministers. Doubtless they did not in their own country hold a rank at all approaching that of the high functionaries they had to deal with, most of whom were *daimyō*, and it was a difficult matter, as it always has been in every Eastern country, to induce them to recognize the official position of a diplomatist representing his sovereign.

I have said in an earlier chapter that one of my teachers at Yokohama had been a retainer of the *daimyō* of Awa. During the spring, when we were first at Osaka, there had been some talk about my going to pay the *daimyō* a visit at his capital, which lay not far from that city, but owing to a misunderstanding it came to nothing. On the present occasion the Awa people had sought me out again, and renewed the invitation, which I persuaded them to transfer to Sir Harry and the admiral. It had been already agreed that the British legation should proceed to the province of Tosa in company with some special commissioners of the *shōgun*, in order to discover, if possible, the murderers of the two sailors belonging to HMS *Icarus*. Our wily old friend Hirayama was selected, along with a couple of other officials, for this business, and they wished to precede us by a few days in order to make a preliminary inquiry. So when the projected visit to Awa came to the ears of the ministers, they pressed Sir Harry to accept it, as Tokushima lay in the direct route to Tosa, and also because they believed that the *daimyō* was not a dangerous opponent, but rather inclined to be a partisan of the *shōgun*, if he took any side at all. Sir Harry was pleased, because he liked these entertainments, and so the matter was settled to everyone's satisfaction. I took care to keep to myself the fact that the invitation had really been intended for myself alone, the *daimyō* having heard about me from my teacher, and being curious to see the writer of the pamphlet on "English policy."

Sir Harry and Mitford went off in the *Basilisk* with Hewett, the *Salamis* remaining behind to pick me up on the following morning. She was to leave at eleven, so I had to pack up overnight, and start very early. I hurried off with the legation writer Ono, leaving Noguchi in charge of the baggage, and as usual he was late. I waited some time, but still he delayed. I became impatient, and started in a boat with only the writer. Just as we were passing the proposed site of the foreign settlement, Noguchi came alongside in a tiny skiff, without the baggage. Further down, near the mouth of the river, we changed into a larger boat, built to cross the bar, and got on board half an hour late. Two Awa officials had joined just before me, and to my great joy and relief the baggage boat came alongside a quarter of an hour afterwards. We weighed anchor precisely at noon, and steaming southward through the Yura Straits, got to the little harbour of Nei in Awa about six o'clock in the evening. The *Basilisk* was there already. Apparently no one awaited our arrival. Sir Harry therefore despatched me to Tokushima to find out what sort of reception he might expect. I got into a big native sailing boat with one of the Awa officials, while the other man hastened on ahead in another.

There was a fresh breeze, and we rushed along under the cliffs at a good pace until we found ourselves approaching the bar at the mouth of the river on which Tokushima is situated. It was already dark, and the breakers extended right across the entrance. The other boat, which had preceded me, now turned back, and as she passed the people on board shouted out that the passage was no longer safe. My pilot however disregarded the warning, and pushed boldly on. The passage was extremely narrow, between widely extended sandbanks on either side; the huge waves tossed about the boat, big as it was, like a child's toy. At last after some anxious minutes we got inside, and were now in comparatively smooth water, without having shipped a drop. A great deal of apparently unmeaning shouting and hallooing took place, and our boat was allowed to surge hither and thither, till we drifted back again to the sandbank, where we found the other Japanese. They had run their boat ashore in the most reckless way, narrowly escaping a drowning in the surf.

After mutual congratulations, we got into a houseboat and proceeded up the river to the landing place, where I had to wait some time till a guard of soldiers could be brought down. This gave time for a crowd of spectators to collect, in spite of the advanced hour. At last the guard arrived. It consisted of cavalry, in long boots and conical hats, with white plumes of horsehair, commanded by a grizzled old warrior named Hachisuka Mimasaka, a descendant of the robber chieftain who founded the House of Awa, but a retainer for all that. They escorted me in solemn procession to a temple that had been prepared for our accommodation, by laying down red felt carpets and furnishing it with hastily constructed tables, chairs and bedsteads. It was evident that they had expected only a small party of three or four Europeans, but I explained to them that Sir Harry would not land without the admiral, and neither of them could come on shore without the whole of his staff. So they had to make the best of it, and greatly extend their preparations before I would acknowledge myself satisfied. They had written up our official titles over the doors of the rooms intended for us, and mine had been rendered by "tongue-officer," a euphemism for interpreter. This I immediately had done away with, and my name substituted, for in Japan the office of interpreter at that time was looked upon as only fit for the lowest class of domestic servants, and no one of samurai rank would ever condescend to speak a foreign language. I had often to fight pretty hard with Japanese of rank in order to ensure being treated as something better than a valet or an orderly.

My good Awa friends, anxious to make me as happy as possible, had racked their brains in order to produce a dinner in European style, and a most dismal banquet it was: inedible fishes in unsightly dishes, piles of unripe grapes and melons, heavy and tasteless sponge cakes, with coarse black-handled knives and forks to eat with. A wretched being, who had been to the United States as a sailor and had picked up a few words of low

236

English, was put forward prominently to wait upon me, as if I were so ignorant of Japanese as to need an interpreter. It was explained that he was the only person in the clan who understood European manners and customs. I found him disgustingly familiar, and had to address a private remonstrance to one of the officials who had come down with me, who said that he was a privileged person "on account of his great learning." Nevertheless he administered a rebuke to the individual in question, who thereupon reverted to his native Japanese good manners.

I had entirely lost my appetite, owing to having been without food since the middle of the day. We proceeded to discuss various points of etiquette connected with our proposed visit to the *daimyō* at his castle. It was the first occasion on which foreigners of rank had been received within the walls of a native baron's fortress. It was finally decided that we should ride past the place where the notice to dismount stands, and get off our horses at the inner gate. The question of precedence at table was also decided. On one side were to sit the *daimyō*, his eldest son and a *karō* named Mori Arinori, Commander Suttie of the *Salamis*, Major Crossman of the Royal Engineers, Lieutenant Stephenson (flag lieutenant); on the other Sir Harry Parkes, Admiral Sir Harry Keppel, Captain Hewett, Mitford and Risk, the admiral's secretary. I was to sit at the head of the table between Sir Harry and the *daimyō*. Separate and special individual presents were to be given to Sir Harry Parkes, to the admiral and to myself, and a general present to all the others, to be divided among them as they liked. After all these knotty points had been disposed of, at a late hour I got to bed.

On the following morning I left early and went down to the mouth of the river to see whether it was possible to cross the bar in order to meet Sir Harry, but found that it was still impassable owing to the heavy swell that continued to roll in from the open sea. After wasting a good deal of time in this vain attempt, I returned to the town and procured nine horses, with which I started off overland to Nei, where the ships were lying. The road was pretty good in places, but at times very narrow, and wound in and out among the hills. The ponies were sturdy little animals, and though unshod trotted over the stones without stumbling, but they had hard mouths, and would not obey the snaffle. At Nei I got a small boat and went on board.

From Sir Harry downwards everyone was willing to risk the ride to Tokushima, in spite of the weather. We started at four, and in a couple of hours reached the town, in a heavy storm of rain and wind. The streams, which had been quite dry when I passed in the middle of the day, were now so swollen that the water came up to the ponies' girths. We were wet through. If we changed at the temple, there was the risk of getting wet again in riding to the castle. It was arranged therefore that we should go on as we were, and dress in an ante-room. Mitford and Aston were engaged in drying their clothes. I had got into a pair of pyjamas, and could not ride in that costume. So I tried to procure three palanquins for us, which took an unexpectedly long time to produce. Sir Harry lost his temper, and swore he would not be kept waiting for all the "damned *daimyō*" in Japan.

Numata (my old teacher) and the other Awa people manifested the most stoical indifference to all this wrath. Mitford volunteered to go on horseback, so they set out. Aston, as a punishment for not being ready, was forbidden by Sir Harry to join the party, a prohibition which caused him the intensest joy. At last my palanquin arrived, I got in, and the bearers went off at such a pace that I reached the castle at the same moment as the others. In the dark, for it was now nine or ten o'clock, the walls of cyclopean masonry, as we entered the gates and wound through the outer fortifications, seemed very imposing, though they were not so in reality. We had to alight outside the point at which I had agreed with the officials, but luckily no one seemed to be aware of the alteration. We got into the palace and were shown into rooms where we changed our dress. The different garb worn by the various members of the party was very curious, no proper uniforms or evening dress at all. I could only muster a shirt, a white coat and trousers, no waistcoat, and no cummerbund. Sir Harry was the only one who kept his shoes on, as everyone had got his feet wet in riding from Nei.

Everyone being at last ready, we were ushered through a series of wide passages into the banqueting room, and were met by the lord, who according to the agreement was clad in the ordinary costume of a gentleman, wide trousers, gown and mantle of silk. The introductions followed in the proper order of rank, and the lord led the way to the tables. The top one was oval, having been made months ago when it was expected that Mitford and I would be the only guests; the others were square. For the lord and his son there were elaborately carved chairs of old-fashioned style, for the rest of us there were three-legged chairs with semi-circular seats, very rickety and badly balanced. We were placed with our backs to the alcove (*tokonoma*), this being the seat of honour, on which the presents were laid out, a magnificent bronze about two feet high occupying the centre.

Sir Harry and the admiral gave the lord a couple of revolvers, which seemed to afford him much pleasure, and the return presents, consisting of rolls of brocade, crape and so forth, were then announced by one of the attendants. Sir Harry, who had by this time quite recovered his equanimity, made himself very agreeable to the lord, talking on general topics, instead of dwelling on the "relations of friendship which happily unite our respective countries" and the usual diplomatic commonplaces. The lord, Katsu Kaishū, was a man of about forty-seven years of age, of middle height, and with a refined countenance, slightly pock-marked. His manner was abrupt and imperious, but his good humour without limits. Koroku, the son, was about twenty-two, a little taller than his father, with a mild, fat countenance, a gentle and subdued manner, and he exhibited great deference towards his father.

The usual order of a Japanese dinner was reversed, the rice, soup and baked fish being first placed on the table. When this course had been removed, drinking commenced, a red lacquer cup being handed first to Sir Harry. I whispered to Sir Harry to call for the bowl to dip it in, and he returned it to the lord, who then offered it to the admiral and to Captain Hewett, and then it travelled down the line to Stephenson, from whom it was returned to the lord. There was a good deal of picking at the various dishes of the banquet which was placed before us, and a great quantity of *sake* was drunk. After a while a play was announced, and in order to get a better view of the acting we moved our chairs down to the other end of the room, where tables with our plates and drinking cups were placed before us. The actors were retainers of the lord wearing the long trousers belonging to the court costume, but not otherwise dressed for their parts. In the first piece there was three characters—master, servant, and guest. The master tells the servant to imitate him in all things, which injunction he takes literally, and addresses the guest in exactly the same style as his master employs to him. This enrages the master, who cuffs the servant, and he in turn the guest. This sort of fun continues with variations until the master's patience is quite exhausted, and he kicks the servant out of the room.

The second piece is a well-known one, entitled *The Three Cripples*. A rich and benevolent person advertises for cripples to enter his employ, and there enter successively a lame, a blind and a dumb man, gamblers who having become beggars have adopted these disguises in order to impose on the charitable. They are accepted, and having placed them in charge of three storehouses, their employer goes out. Then the three recognize each other as old comrades, and agree to open one of the storerooms, which is full of *sake*, after which they will rob the other two. However, they get so drunk that when their master returns each forgets the part he had previously played; the blind man assumes dumbness, the lame one blindness, and the dumb pretends to be deaf. Their detection of course follows, with the natural consequences.

After the play was over we drew round the little tables, and the *sake* cup passed freely from hand to hand. Kaishū vowed that the admiral was his father, and Sir Harry his elder brother, while Koroku expressed himself to me in a similarly affectionate manner. It was arranged that we should have a review of the troops on the following day, and about midnight the wind and rain having moderated we took our leave, getting back to our lodging at one in the morning. I found that even our servants had not been forgotten, presents having been sent to each one of them; not a single person was passed over. This was truly lordly hospitality. I forgot to mention that before we started for the castle, a polite message of welcome was brought to Sir Harry from the lord, accompanied by a box three feet long, one deep and one wide, full of eggs, another of the same size full of noodles and a basket of fish. The trouble that had been taken to make us comfortable was very great, even after they had heard of the increased number they would have to entertain. They had gone to work to make bedsteads and tables, and even to build bathrooms.

The morning turned out finer than could have been reasonably hoped for after the storm of the preceding day, and after breakfast we started for the parade ground. Our way lay through the castle, and over a considerable stream which washed one side of the fortress. It was a very good ground, though rather small, but the lord explained that he could not enlarge it without pulling down some Buddhist temples, which would shock the religious feeling of the townspeople. Some five hundred men, divided into five bodies of varying strength, were put through their drill. Their uniform was in imitation of European style, black trousers with red stripes down the side, and black coats. Happy the soldier who could muster a pair of boots, the rest had only straw sandals. On their heads they had hats of papier-maché, either conical or of dish-cover shape, with two horizontal red bands. They used the English infantry drill, with the quaint addition of a shout to indicate the discharge of their firearms. In the opinion of those who were competent to judge, they acquitted themselves very creditably. We viewed the evolutions from a sort of grand stand, with tables before us piled up with various delicacies. *Sake* of course formed part of the entertainment, and Hewett was singled out by the lord as assuredly the best toper of us all, on account of his jolly red face. Everyone this morning had remarked what a capital liquor is *sake*, it leaves no bad effects behind, from which it may be inferred that we had returned home on the previous night in a happy frame of mind and body.

About noon we took our leave. Sir Harry presented a ring to the young lord, and the admiral put another on the finger of Katsu Kaishū, to their intense delight. On our way back from the drill ground we were taken to a temple on a hill commanding an extensive view, where we were entertained with a luncheon washed down with bad champagne procured in Yokohama for the occasion. The lord whispered privately into my ear that he intended to abdicate and pay a visit to England. To Sir Harry he said all sorts of friendly things about the opening of Kobe to foreign trade. The admiral promised to bring the *Ocean* and *Rodney* to Nei in the coming winter to show him what English men-of-war were like.

After returning to our lodgings we had a substantial lunch off the provisions brought from the ships, but our entertainers were not contented till they had made us sit down to a final feast prepared by themselves, just for five minutes, to drink a farewell cup and receive a parting message from the lord. At last we got away, some on horseback, others in palanquins, and in three hours after leaving Tokushima we were safely on board ship. Sir Harry was accompanied by four principal officials to the *Basilisk*, where

Hewett gave them some excellent champagne, and they went over the ship's side full of affectionate regrets at having to part from us. The *Salamis* left at once for Yokohama with the admiral, Mitford, Aston and Crossman, while we remained to pursue our voyage to Tosa on the morrow in the *Basilisk*.

Tosa and Nagasaki

Early on the morning of September 3 we anchored outside the little harbour of Susaki in Tosa. Inside were lying the *shōgun*'s war steamer *Eagle* (*Kaiten-maru*) and a smaller one belonging to the lord of Tosa. We had fully expected a hostile reception, and preparations had been made for action. Shortly afterwards Takabatake Gorō and Komeda Keijirō came on board to say that Hirayama, the chief commissioner, was up at Kōchi. Gotō Shōjirō, the leading Tosa minister, also paid us a visit, but we told him to go away till we could get the ship inside the bay. Then arrived the other two commissioners (Togawa and an *ōmetsuke*) to tell us that no evidence implicating any of the Tosa men had been discovered. The little schooner *Nankai*, in which the assassins were supposed to have escaped from Nagasaki, was lying higher up the bay at Urado.

Later on Gotō came on board with two other local officers. They promised to do all they could to discover the murderers, even if they should not be Tosa men. Sir Harry, who had quite made up his mind that the Tosa men were guilty, tried to browbeat them, adding oddly enough that with Tosa he could have none but friendly relations, and that official discussions must take place with the *shōgun*'s government. After they left, Hirayama made his appearance. A long and stormy interview took place, in the course of which he heard a good deal of strong language, and was told that he was of no more use than a common messenger. He recounted to us in a plaintive manner the hardships he had undergone on the way down and since his arrival, for the Tosa people were extremely angry at the suspicions cast on them.

Sir Harry sent me ashore to see Gotō, and detail to him all the circumstances which seemed to us evidence against his fellow clansmen. He renewed the assurances he had given in the morning, and said he felt certain my writer Ono and Noguchi were neither more nor less than government spies. The next morning I saw Gotō again, who renewed his protestations, and complained of Sir Harry's rough language and demeanour, which he felt sure would some day cause a terrible row. I was myself rather sick of being made the intermediary of the overbearing language to which the chief habitually resorted, and told Gotō to remonstrate with him, if he really thought this; as for myself, I did not dare to hint anything of the kind to my chief. I also saw Hirayama, and arranged with him that I should be present at the examination of the officers of the *Nankai*, who were to be sent down from Urado. At three o'clock two small steamers arrived, yet it was seven before the *shōgun*'s officials reached the *Basilisk* to say that everything was in readiness. As dinner was now announced, the inquiry was put off till the next day.

On September 5, the examination was accordingly held in my presence. On the Japanese side the evidence went to show that the *Nankai* did not leave till ten p.m. on August 6, while Sir Harry's version was that she sailed at half-past four that morning, only an hour and a half after the schooner. It was on this alleged fact that the whole of the suspicion against the Tosa men was founded. (It was proved at the end of 1868 that the murderers belonged to the Chikuzen clan, which was rather an unfortunate conclusion for him.) I reported this to Sir Harry, who was of course greatly dissatisfied. Gotō afterwards came on board to see Sir Harry and there was the usual talk about cultivating friendly relations between the English and Tosa. Sir Harry said he wished to send me as his envoy to call formally on the retired *daimyō* of Tosa, to which Gotō replied that Sir Harry could himself see the ex-*daimyō*, if we were on friendly terms. Otherwise, it was useless to hold any communications even by messenger. I knew perfectly well that I could easily manage to visit Kōchi, if left to myself, without the chief taking a roundabout way to get me there under the pretext of a mission to the old lord.

By this time my relations with the Japanese were such that I could have gone anywhere with perfect safety. A visit from Hirayama and his colleagues came next. The evidence taken was discussed, and Sir Harry said the inquiry must now be removed to Nagasaki, and that Hirayama ought to go there to conduct it. Hirayama objected strongly, offering to send his two fellow commissioners, but it would not do, and he was finally forced to consent. The poor old fellow was almost at his wit's end. He became impertinent, and remarked that this murder case concerned Englishmen alone, while he had business to transact at Edo which concerned all nations. I was much astonished to find that Sir Harry did not get into a passion on being talked to in this somewhat unceremonious way by a Japanese, but simply replied to it in a quiet argumentative tone. But a more curious thing followed.

After dinner Gotō came on board to have a talk on politics. He spoke of his idea of establishing a parliament, and a constitution on the English model, and said that Saigō entertained similar notions. That we had learned at Osaka. Then followed a good deal of abuse of the *shōgun*'s government, especially with reference to the proposed formation of a guild to control the foreign commerce of Osaka and Kobe. We showed him the proclamation we had extorted from the government, intended to annul the previous one constituting these guilds. He replied that it was a mere blind, and I confess that I agreed with him. Sir Harry took a great fancy to him, as being one of the most intelligent Japanese we had as yet met with, and to my own mind Saigō alone was his superior by force of character. They swore eternal friendship, and Gotō promised to write once a month to report anything that might come to light in connection with the *Icarus* murder. Last of all he remonstrated with Sir Harry, at some length and in very explicit terms, about his rough demeanour on previous occasions, and hinted that perhaps others would not have submitted so quietly to such treatment. It was by no means a pleasant task for me to put his words into English, especially as Hewett's presence rendered the rebuke all the more galling, and Sir Harry at first seemed inclined to resent being thus lectured by a Japanese. Yet he managed to keep his temper, so no bones were broken.

Poor old Hirayama was made quite ill by the struggle he had had with the chief, but he did not venture to break his promise to proceed to Nagasaki and pursue the inquiry in person. I now received detailed written instructions from Sir Harry to follow the old fox, as we called him, to Nagasaki, to watch the proceedings and stimulate both the *shōgun*'s officials and the Tosa people to leave no stone unturned in their search for the murderers. Sir Harry himself was obliged to return to Edo in the *Basilisk*, and it was arranged that I should take a passage down to Nagasaki in a Tosa steamer, together with the incriminated officers of the *Nankai* and the officials named to conduct the inquiry. I was to be clothed with authority equal to that of the consul, but was not to interfere in any measures he might think fit to take. Sir Harry left on September 6, and I transferred myself to the Tosa steamer along with my writer and the faithful Noguchi.

There I spent the next day, after having seen the *shōgun*'s war steamer *Kaiten-maru* depart with Hirayama on board.

In the middle of the night I was woken up by a messenger from Gotō, bringing an invitation for me to go up to Kōchi and make the acquaintance of the ex-*daimyō*. They had sent down a tugboat for me, so I went on board at once at four, after a hasty meal of rice and tea, and falling asleep on a locker, woke up at daylight to find myself already some way from Susaki. We did not anchor at Urado till half-past nine. The view outside of distant hills and a belt of pine trees fringing the shore reminded me strongly of the Bay of Point de Galle in Ceylon, where the Eastern mail steamers used to call before the construction of the harbour at Colombo.

Kōchi Bay is in reality an estuary, with a very narrow outlet, much obstructed by rocks. We seemed to be running straight on to the sandy beach, when a sudden turn to the left put our head into the river, and we came to an anchor in fifteen feet of water inside a little cove. The river widens considerably above this point, but is so shallow that only boats drawing less than a foot of water can go up. I was transferred to a houseboat, which made very slow progress. At last, after traversing two or three broad lake-like reaches, we came in sight of Kōchi castle, rendered conspicuous from a distance by its lofty *donjon* four storeys high. Soon afterwards we turned up an embanked canal to the left, and touched the shore under a large new building on the outskirts of the town. Here I was met by Gotō, who told me that the ex-*daimyō* would shortly arrive. While waiting for his appearance I changed my dress, and was introduced to a host of Gotō's colleagues. At last the ex-*daimyō*, Yamauchi Yōdō, was announced, and I was conducted upstairs into his presence. He met me at the threshold, and saluted me by touching the tips of his toes with the tips of his fingers. I replied by a bow of exactly equal profundity. We then took our seats, he on a handsome Japanese armchair with his back to the alcove, and I on a common cane-bottomed wooden chair opposite, a little lower down to his right. Gotō and some of his fellow councillors squatted on the sill dividing the room from that next to it.

He began by saying that he had heard my name. I replied by thanking him for according me the honour of this interview. He then renewed the assurances already given through Gotō that if the murderers were Tosa men, they should be arrested and punished, and that even if it should appear that the guilty persons belonged to another clan, he would not relax his efforts to trace them out. He had received a letter from the *shōgun* stating that he had heard there was strong evidence against Tosa, and advising him to punish the offenders. This of course he would be ready to do, supposing that the murderers were men of his clan, but he did not understand what the *shōgun* meant by "evidence." I replied that we supposed the government to be in possession of proofs which they had not disclosed, as it was not likely that they were convinced simply by what Sir Harry had said to them. Perhaps, I added, they threw the suspicion on Tosa in order to get rid of an unpleasant discussion. This remark called forth from Gotō somewhat unmeasured expressions of indignation, and he announced his intention of giving the government a piece of his mind on the subject. Old Yōdō said that he had received a letter from a friend advising him to try and compromise the matter, as the English were greatly incensed at the murder of their men, but he would do nothing of the kind. If his people were guilty he would punish them; he could do no more; but if they were innocent he would declare their innocence through thick and thin.

Matsune Zusho (the chief man of Uwajima) had told Date Munenari that Sir Harry had said the *shōgun*'s government had assured him of Tosa's guilt. I replied again that from the language of the *shōgun*'s ministers we could not help inferring that they had independent grounds for their suspicions. Yōdō remarked that the only thing Hirayama had alleged was the supposed transfer of men from the schooner *Yokobue* to the steamer *Nankai*, which had never been proved. I answered that this was all we had to go upon, but I should consider that we had good reason to blush if after all we had said

the men should turn out to belong to another clan. At present I saw no
ground for supposing that we were mistaken.

An argument then ensued between Gotō and myself as to the nature of
suspiciousness in general, and what might be held to be sufficient
justification for that attitude of mind. In the end he admitted that we were
entitled, by our past experience, to mistrust all Japanese *à priori*, though
he maintained that in the present case the rule did not apply. After this Yōdō
and Gotō plied me with questions about the Luxemburg affair, the
constitution and powers of parliament and the electoral system. It was
evident that the idea of a constitution resembling that of Great Britain had
already taken deep root in their minds. Later on a proposition was actually
made to either Mitford or myself, I forget which, to enter the service of
the emperor and assist in organizing their parliament for them.

Huge dishes of fish were now placed on the table, and waiting women,
coiffées in the exaggerated style of the *daimyōs'* courts, poured out the *sake*.
While we drank and conversed, a pair of anatomical models of the male
and female human being, life size, were exhibited and taken to pieces for
my especial edification! Rice was afterwards served in the next room, Yōdō
excusing himself on the ground of indisposition. The fact was, he preferred
to remain alone with the *sake* bottle, of which he was notoriously fond. I
had once in my possession a scroll of Chinese verses from his brush, signed
"Drunken old man" (*sui-ō*).

Before taking my departure, I saw him once more for a few minutes, when
he presented me with seven rolls of white crape. Under the circumstances
I should have preferred to decline them, but Gotō argued that they were a
part of the entertainment, and I could not refuse without being ungracious,
almost discourteous. I therefore accepted, subject to the chief's approval,
and we parted, with the same exchange of formal bows as before.

Yamauchi yōdō was a tall man, slightly pock-marked, with bad teeth,
and a hurried manner of getting out his words. He certainly looked very
ill, and over-indulgence in *sake* would quite account for that. From some
of the remarks he made, I gathered that he was free from prejudice, and
not by any means conservative in his political notions. Still, it may be
doubted whether he was prepared to go the same lengths as Satsuma and
Chōshū in the direction of change.

It was not considered advisable or safe for me to promenade through the town, and I made no attempt to insist on doing the sights. As I returned to Urado in the gondola, multitudes of people followed in small boats, anxious to get a sight of the first European who had visited their part of the country since the wreck of the Spanish galleon in 1596, and even grappling with us in order better to satisfy their curiosity. No order was kept, and I was easily convinced that a walk in Kōchi itself might have given rise to a tumult.

Next day they took me to Susaki, and put me on board the *Shooeyleen*, the steamer in which we were to proceed to Nagasaki. For the past two days I had been suffering from a whitlow on one of the fingers of the right hand, and felt utterly indifferent to all that passed around me. Bad food, a dirty cabin, excessive heat, sullen fellow-voyagers were all accepted with the calmness of exhausted misery. The *Shooeyleen*'s boilers were old, and we steamed along at the rate of two knots an hour. Luckily the weather was calm, otherwise there was every reason to think we must have gone to the bottom. Passing through Shimonoseki, I went on shore to ask after old friends, and found Inoue Bunda, who was a perfect sink of taciturnity. There was no appearance here of guns or men-of-war, nothing to indicate that Chōshū was still at war with the *shōgun*; all around were signs of peace and prosperity. The Tosa officers also landed, one and all, on some pretext or other, and the whole day was spent at anchor. Towards evening we set forth again in the same leisurely fashion, and reached Nagasaki, on September 12, late in the afternoon. Here I put up with Marcus Flowers, the consul.

At dinner that evening I met for the first time the well-known Kido Takayoshi, alias Katsura Kogorō, who came to the consulate together with Itō Hirobumi, whom I had known since 1864. Kido was remarkable for his gentle suave manner, though under this there lay a character of the greatest courage and determination, both military and political. We had some talk after dinner about politics, but I think they mistrusted me. At any rate they thought it necessary to assert that their lord was a much wronged, innocent and harmless individual, who had never entertained any schemes for over-turning the *shōgun*'s government. But we had long been in possession of indisputable evidence that the abolition of the Bakufu was the cardinal point in the policy pursued by the western *daimyō* acting in concert.

On the following day Flowers and I went to meet Hirayama at the custom house. The two governors were also present. Though they had been severely blamed by Sir Harry, they did not appear to be particularly disturbed by his censures. The Tosa steamer *Nankai* had left, in fact she steamed out of the harbour just after Sir Harry went off in the *Basilisk*. On August 19, as she was about to leave for Kagoshima, she was stopped, and an examination was held, which lasted through the night until the afternoon of the 20th, but without any evidence of complicity in the murders being elicited. The officers and crew were then entrusted to the charge of Iwasaki Yatarō, Tosa's agent (*kikiyaku*), who undertook to produce them whenever they should be wanted. But she sailed the same evening, in defiance of Iwasaki's orders, at least so the Tosa people alleged. Nothing had been discovered with respect to the real criminals, and, as far as we could see, the governors had not exerted themselves to find out the guilty persons.

August 14, I spent with Itō and Kido at a teahouse called Tamagawa, away at the back of the town close to the stream which flows down through it. We had a long discussion on Japanese politics, domestic and foreign, ending with the conclusion that Europeans and Japanese would never mix, at least not in our time. On my way back I called on Hikozō (the well-known Joseph Heco), who told me of a document, said to be signed by Satsuma, Tosa, Geishū, Bizen and Awa, which had been presented to *shōgun* Tokugawa Yoshinobu, requiring him to resign his office and allow the government to be reconstituted.

On Sunday, August 15, I lunched with Hirayama. He said that Sasaki Sanshirō, the Tosa *metsuke* (equivalent to attorney-general, but not trained in law), was overruled by the Tosa society called the Kaientai, a sort of local navy league, who would not allow him to carry out the official orders received from his lord to have search made for the criminals. This was natural enough, as it was afterwards proved that the Tosa men were altogether innocent of the affair.

The 16th was spent at the custom house in the examination of the men of the *Yokobue*, a Tosa sailing-vessel. It appeared certain that the *Nankai* did not leave Nagasaki till the evening of August 6. Two of the Kaientai, one of whom was the captain of the *Yokobue,* were shown to have been at a house of entertainment opposite to the spot where the British sailors were murdered up to midnight. This looked suspicious, but I told the Japanese officials that if they did not disbelieve the statements that had been made, neither did I. The Tosa people did not want to make the *Yokobue* return, neither did the government officials seem to insist on her recall. As my plan was to throw on the government officials the responsibility of discovering the murderers, I did not urge it, but left it to Flowers, who was associated with me in the inquiry, to do so if he judged it necessary.

In the evening of August 18, I went to see Hirayama, and communicated to him my suspicions regarding a young fellow of forbidding countenance, who was with the captain of the *Yokobue* on the night of the murder at the house of entertainment referred to. I suggested that his companion should be sent for, and also the four men stated to have gone to Karatsu (in the north of Hizen, near the boundary of Chikuzen) in the *Nankai*, and to have landed there. I advised that the keeper of the house of entertainment should be examined, and asked for copies of all depositions received, especially of the two Tosa men. What had fixed suspicion upon men of that province in particular was their general evil reputation as being predisposed towards assassination. The depositions were sent to us by the governors in the afternoon of the 19th, and on discrepancies being pointed out in those of the two Tosa men, they promised to send for one of them whose further examination appeared to be especially desirable. The translation of the depositions occupied me for the whole of the succeeding day.

On August 21, I went to see Niiro Gyōbu, a Satsuma *karō*, and asked him to make an inquiry about the murder among his own people. He said this had already been done, and offered to give me a copy of the record. As he said that nothing suspicious had been discovered, I declined his offer with thanks. But I hinted to him the possibility of the exclusion of all two-sworded men from the foreign settlement after dark, unless the murderers were discovered and delivered up by the combined clans, a measure which had been recommended to Flowers and myself by Sir Harry, for if the discovery were made by the government, it would be taken as proof of the complicity of his clan at least. He did not at all like this suggestion. Then I went to Sasaki Sanshirō, with whom I had travelled from Tosa. He said that the governors had lent a steamer to fetch the captain of the *Yokobue* and another man, and complained of Hirayama's supposition that he was lukewarm, seeing that he had given money to all the detectives in the place, and had offered a reward of four thousand pieces of silver (worth £450) for the discovery of the murderer or murderers.

Next I went to Hirayama, to whom I proposed that he should order the Nagasaki representatives of all the clans to examine their men as strictly as the Tosa agents were doing. For as we had been ten days at work without being able to fix the responsibility on them, it was not unreasonable to admit the possibility of men of some other clan being guilty. I proposed that every two-sworded man should be called upon to give an account of his doings on the night of the murder, and that all the houses of entertainment should show their lists of guests on that date. There was, I said, no real difficulty in discovering the perpetrators. In consequence of all this one of the governors called the next afternoon. We proposed to him that the two-sworded men should be excluded from the settlement after dark, to which he added an amendment that if they had urgent business there in the evening, they should be escorted to and fro. The examination of all the clansmen and of persons who were in a house of entertainment close to the site of the murder was again urged by us. The governor also promised to have guard-houses erected at three points in the foreign settlement.

Two days later the same governor called again, and promised that the precautionary measures we had proposed to him should be taken. Nothing further was done until the 28th, when I attended at the custom house to hear the examination of two Tosa men who had been brought from Kōchi in the government steamer. It led to this result, that the governors declared that they found nothing to incriminate any of the men who had left Nagasaki in the *Yokobue* and "Nankai," and considered the Tosa people to be cleared of all suspicion as far as these two vessels were concerned. We rejoined that on the contrary we entertained very strong suspicions, not founded on any ocular testimony, but on circumstantial evidence, namely, that the murder was almost certainly committed by men in white foreign dress a little after midnight. That one of the two men with a companion were close to the spot where the murder was committed at the very moment, and that they were dressed in that fashion, and that no one else had been shown to have been in the brothel quarter in similar costume. We afterwards addressed a letter to the governors demanding the arrest of these two men on the above grounds, but we were not sanguine of obtaining their consent, as it was evident that the government officials were unable to exercise any control over the Tosa people.

Very little progress was made after this, as was natural enough, seeing that the Tosa people were entirely innocent of any share in the murders, as was afterwards proved. On October 6 I had an opportunity of conversing amicably with the vice-governor. I said that the Tosa people tried to throw obstacles in the way of discovering the criminals, instead of courting inquiry in accordance with lord Yamauchi yōdō's expressed wishes. That the government had lost much ground with foreigners in this affair. Firstly, the possibility of the murder being committed in such a manner showed the incapacity of the government to maintain order, and, secondly, it was not fitting that a body calling itself a government should allow *daimyō* to enjoy such rights of extraterritoriality to the extent that was shown by the recent examinations at the custom house. The vice-governor replied that he had nothing to do with these matters, to which I rejoined that this was precisely the reason why I had spoken to him about them. We received a refusal to our demand for the arrest of the two Tosa men.

A few days later a drunken Englishman was cut about the head and an American wounded slightly in the arm by a Tosa man, who straightway gave himself up to his own authorities, and they reported the affair. Having failed entirely in our attempts to bring the crime home to the Tosa people, Flowers and I agreed that it was useless for me to remain any longer, and accordingly I returned to Edo, leaving about midnight of October 12 on board HMS *Coquette*, which had been lent by the admiral to bring me back to Yokohama.

During my stay at Nagasaki we heard a good deal about the discovery and arrest of native Roman Catholic Christians of Urakami, a village near the town. Niiro Gyōbu of Satsuma, who came to see me on October 12, said that besides the Urakami people, some of the inhabitants of a village close by, belonging to Ōmura Sumihoro, the *daimyō* of Ōmura, had been converted, and were now in prison at Nagasaki. According to Japanese law this was a capital offence. The Ōmura officials had hitherto conformed to the practice of the Nagasaki government with respect to the punishment of criminals, and desired to act accordingly in the present case. It was, however, reported that the governors intended to pardon all those who were willing to abjure, because the number of offenders was so large. This offended the Ōmura officials, who held that believing in Christianity was a very grave crime. Further, that the proposal to let such criminals off on the pretext that they were too numerous to punish was revolutionary and subversive of good government, and they were endeavouring to induce all the *daimyō* of Kyushu to join in a representation in that sense to the government at Edo. This proposal was of course intended as a general manifesto against the *shōgun*'s government. I replied that he must quite well know that Christianity was not harmful to any country by whose people it was professed, and that even a Protestant government such as that of England would not be pleased to hear of Roman Catholics being persecuted on the ground of their religious belief, but if the only object of the remonstrance was to annoy the *shōgun*'s government, we should not disapprove of that by itself.

On the general subject of Japanese internal politics, he said he did not believe that civil war would break out, or at least he pretended not to, though at the same time he acknowledged its possibility. Hirayama, to whom I said good-bye on the same day, told me that all the Christians of Urakami had been forgiven on their promising "not to do so again," and that they would be permitted to believe what they liked, doubtless on condition of their not professing their religion openly. He thought the Ōmura officials would also forgive their Christians. This opinion of his was in contradiction to what I had heard from Niiro.

My stay at Nagasaki afforded me useful opportunities of making the acquaintance of samurai of various southern clans. I have already mentioned my introduction to Kido Takayoshi.

The 14th I spent almost entirely in the company of Kido and Itō. A few days later Kido called to offer me the use of a steamer to Osaka, if it suited me to return to Edo by that route, but I deferred accepting, as my plans were not yet settled. Eventually arrangements were made for my being conveyed to Yokohama in one of H.M. ships, so that I was able to decline his obliging proposal. When Itō came to say good-bye on September 23, he was accompanied by a young fellow-clansman whom he wished me to take to Edo, nominally as a pupil. This was Endo Kinsuke, one of the party of five Chōshū men to which Itō had belonged, who went secretly to England in 1863, as already narrated. He bore the alias of Yamamoto Jinsuke. Itō's pseudonym was Hayashi Uichi, and Inoue Bunda went by the name of Takada Harutarō.

Amongst other interesting information given to me by Itō was that my friend Yamagata Keizō, who was one of the Chōshū men that had accompanied me to Yokohama in October 1864, had been adopted by Shishido Bizen. It was his father, Yamagata Taiga, who wrote the pamphlet of which the title translated is the equivalent of "The present *daimyō* are not vassals of the lord," *i.e.* of the *shōgun*, and not Nagai Uta, to whom it was usually attributed. Itō was a pupil of the well-known patriot Yoshida Torajirō, the author of several books controverting the views of Yamagata and Nagai. He said there were two schools of Chinese philosophy in Japan, namely, of Teishi (Ch'êng-tzu) and Oyōmei (Wang Yang-ming), of which the first inculcates the duty of resisting tyrants, the second that of self-reformation. Yamagata belonged to the latter, hence his arguments against any attempt to disturb the existing political arrangements. (But the most widely diffused system in Japan was that of the philosopher Chu Hsi.)

Niiro Gyōbu I saw four times. I dined with him once at a Japanese restaurant, when he said that he knew nothing of the engagement of Frenchmen by Iwashita Sajiemon, a Satsuma man who had gone to Paris for the exposition of 1867, and there came under the influence of the Comte de Montblanc. As soon as he heard of it he wrote to Iwashita that the engagements must be cancelled, but his letter did not reach Paris in time. I said that of course we could not object to Satsuma employing Frenchmen, but as French views of Japanese domestic politics differed so widely from ours, and it was well understood that ours coincided to a certain extent with those of Satsuma, it was natural to ask whether this engagement implied a change of policy on the part of the Satsuma clan. Niiro replied that such a supposition would be quite natural, but that in fact no such change had occurred. Since the time when Shimazu Hisamitsu (father of the new lord of Satsuma, and virtual ruler of the clan notwithstanding his formal retirement from public life) had decreed the adoption of English methods, the whole province had become enthusiastic in their favour, and objected very strongly to the proposed introduction of Frenchmen. He was afraid he should have to send them home again.

A few days later Niiro dined with Russell Robertson (assistant at the consulate) and myself at Robertson's house, when we engaged a French cook to serve the dinner. On this occasion no political conversation took place, but he told us that Saigō was Shimazu Hisamitsu's confidential man, and Komatsu Kiyokado one of the seven *shussei* (administrators) of the Satsuma clan. The lord, Shimazu Tadayoshi, whose title was Shūri no Taiyu, was 29 years of age, and his brother, Shimazu Hisaharu, 28. Altogether there were ten brothers and sisters, besides the three girls of the late lord, Shimazu Nariakira. My last talk with Niiro was on October 12, when he gave me information about the native Christians, already recorded.

Last year I had met at Robertson's house a doctor belonging to the Kurume clan, and he now came with his son to ask permission to bring some of his fellow clansmen to call on me. This they did on October 8. Their names were Imae Sakai, said to be connected with the government of the clan. Nagata Chūhei, who was visiting Nagasaki for the first time in his life; and Tanaka Konoye. Originally a Kyoto clockmaker, he had developed into a skilled mechanical engineer, and had constructed engines and boilers for a couple of Japanese steamers. After drinking a bottle of champagne together, we sallied forth to a Japanese restaurant, where we had a little feast in the style of the country, and a great deal of political talk. They said their principal reason for objecting to Kobe being opened as a port for foreign trade was that the tea consumed at Kurume came from the provinces to the west of Kobe, and they feared it would be diverted to that place for exportation. With regard to internal affairs, I said I did not see how they could be settled without a war of some kind or other, as the *daimyō* could not agree among themselves. A civil war might last twenty or thirty years, and greatly impoverish the country, while it would afford an opportunity to foreign powers to appropriate bits of Japanese territory by aiding one party against the other. But a foreign war, in which Kyoto became the object of attack, would lead to the reconciliation of their internal differences, and when peace came, we could conclude treaties with the emperor, in which the constitutional position of the *shōgun* might be defined.

Nagata, who was already drunk, shouted out: "You must not attack Kyoto, but destroy the Bakufu." This was the term, meaning "military power," by which the adversaries of the *shōgun* were in the habit of speaking of his government. It appeared from this utterance that the men of Kurume shared what was evidently the general feeling in the west of the country. Afterwards we adjourned to another restaurant, where a grand feast was served. More of the Kurume clan came in, and the room was gradually filled with courtesans and musicians. Most of my friends got very drunk, so after about two hours of this festivity I left, and the party broke up. I also had a dinner with a Tosa man named Yui, who was captain of the *Yugao*.

Another acquaintance I made was that of Nagaoka Moriyoshi, younger brother of Hosokawa Morihisa, the lord of Higo, who came to call on Flowers. He had a fat round face, was about 25 years of age, and intelligent. He tried to pump me about the Tosa affair but failed, and when he proceeded to talk politics I held my tongue, for Higo was supposed not to belong to the Satsuma party. He then invited me to visit him on board his steamer and have a long conversation, but when I went at the appointed hour on the following day he was absent.

The next day two of his men called to apologize for his breaking the engagement, and he also appeared in person to tell me of the desire cherished by the Higo people to invite Sir Harry Keppel, the admiral in command of the China squadron, to some point off their coast to display naval evolutions. The clan having ordered an iron-clad man-of-war and two smaller war steamers to be built in England, now wanted to learn how they should be manoeuvred. He was at great pains to prove that he was on the best of terms with Kido (alias Katsura), and that the Hosokawa brothers loved the English more than they did any other nation, for all their steamers, besides 16,000 rifles of different patterns, had been bought from us. I replied that their inviting the admiral to a place off their coast and not to the castle at Kumamoto, was like sending for a troupe of tumblers to perform before one's house, into which one would not care to admit them. If a man were prevented from inviting a guest to his own house, it would be more courteous to go and call on him than to ask him to come halfway, and that Moriyoshi at least ought to come to Nagasaki and visit the admiral first of all. He said he intended going to Shimonoseki with one of the Higo *karō* (councillor) to arrange an alliance between Higo and Chōshū.

Endo presented himself on the 12th, but instead of coming straight to me, he sent in his card by my Aizu retainer Noguchi, who read it and at once discovered who he was. We embarked in the course of the evening, and steamed out of the harbour at eleven p.m. through the Inland Sea, and without calling anywhere, arrived at Yokohama at midnight on the 16th.

Downfall of the Bakufu

Before leaving Edo I had taken a lease of a house known as Takayashiki (high mansion) on a bluff overlooking the bay, at a monthly rental of 100 *ichibu*. It was the retired home of a Japanese gentleman of rank, who had abdicated his position in favour of his eldest son, and had bought a piece of ground to build himself a residence after his own taste. Consequently it was one of the oddest houses imaginable, consisting of a number of small rooms of varying sizes, and the garden was laid out in little hills and grass-plots, planted with trees and shrubs. The only flowers were those of the camellia and St John's wort bushes, for herbaceous borders are almost impossible to manage in Japan, owing to the heavy summer rains, which beat down all plants that have not woody stems. The whole covered about two-thirds of an acre.

There was an upper storey, where I had my bedroom and apartments for the entertainment of Japanese guests, and three staircases provided means of escape in case of attack from a midnight murderer. Downstairs was a room for the reception of European visitors, and two waiting rooms for callers, one more for the accommodation of my head man and my own study. This was nine feet square, with a circular window commanding a view of the sea, and a square one at the side overlooking the garden. It was fitted up with numerous small cupboards and shelves for books and papers. It held a writing desk, a small table, a chair for myself and one for my Japanese teacher, and a stool for the Chinese teacher attached to the legation. There were also a large bathroom, a kitchen, and a two-storeyed building beyond where my head man lived, and where the young Japanese to whom I intended to teach English were to be lodged.

My food was entirely Japanese, sent in from the well-known house called Mansei, but I continued to drink English beer. The household consisted of my head man (the Aizu samurai, Noguchi), whose function was to superintend everything, pay my bills, arrange for necessary repairs, and receive persons on business that did not require a personal interview with myself. Next to him came a small boy of fourteen who waited at table and acted as valet. He was of the samurai class and so entitled to wear sword and dagger when he went abroad. Then there was a woman of about thirty years of age, whose duty it was to sweep the floors, open the sliding shutters in the morning and close them at night, and sew on my buttons. As there was hardly any furniture, she had very little dusting to do. I was to engage a man to go, not run, on errands, perhaps cook the rice for the whole family, and make himself generally useful. Lastly came a gatekeeper, who had also the duty of sweeping the garden, and a groom or running footman. When I went out walking or on horseback, I was accompanied by a couple of the mounted escort that had been attached to me by the *shōgun*'s government since my journey overland from Osaka in the earlier part of the year.

Thus established as a householder after my own liking, able to devote myself to Japanese studies and to live intimately with Japanese and thus become acquainted with their thoughts and views, I was perfectly happy. In my journal I find noted down a dinner on November 6 with Nakamura Matazō at the Sanku-tei near Shimbashi, with *geisha* of course to pour out the *sake* and entertain us with music and bright conversation, and on the 7th a dinner of broiled eels and rice at the Daikokuya, Reiganbashi, with Yanagawa Shunsan, a teacher at the foreign language school (Kaiseijo). The political ferment threw a great deal of work on me in interpreting for Sir Harry in his talks with government people, and in translating official papers from and into Japanese, and these duties often occupied me from nine o'clock in the morning till nine in the evening, with only short intervals for meals.

In the dead of night on November 16 Ishikawa Toshimasa, one of the commissioners for foreign affairs, came to impart to Sir Harry the momentous news that the *shōgun* had resigned the direction of government into the hands of the emperor, and in future would simply be the instrument for carrying out His Majesty's orders. We had heard from other sources that he had abdicated, and that the office of *shōgun* would cease to exist. Already on the 14th Ogasawara Nagamichi had told us confidentially that the programme of the future consisted of a council of the great *daimyō*, decision by the *shōgun* subject to the approval of the emperor. The actual date of Yoshinobu's resignation was November 8.

At an interview with Sir Harry two days afterwards, Nagamichi read out a long paper explaining the causes which had led to the *shōgun*'s decision to surrender the government into the hands of the emperor. He went into a long retrospect of affairs from the commencement of the renewed intercourse with foreign nations. The blame was, of course, thrown on the agitators for political change. Yoshinobu, it said, had not resigned the chieftainship of the Tokugawa clan, but had simply abolished the office of *shōgun*. The new arrangement would not involve any change in the previous agreements about the opening of the new ports which had been entered into earlier in the year. Two of the Council of State, Matsudaira Norikata and Inaba Masami, were off to Kyoto.

Katsu Kaishū told us that he was afraid that the *shōgun*'s party would precipitate events, and cause the outbreak of civil war. Kaneko Taisuke, a retainer of Sakai Tadaka, told us that the *daimyō* were collecting troops at Osaka. Satsuma had five thousand men, and Chōshū and Tosa men, under the command of Mōri Nagato, were also encamped there, so that we should find ourselves in a hornets' nest when we went down to superintend the opening of the ports. The *shōgun* had ordered four or five thousand men to be despatched thither. The Council of State had informed his chief and Matsudaira Munehide that in future they might be *shōgun*'s or emperor's men as they liked. A secret circular had been sent round among the *hatamoto* (retainers of the Tokugawa chief holding fiefs assessed at less than 10,000 *koku* of rice) inciting them against Yoshinobu, by accusing him of having poisoned the previous *shōgun* Iemochi, and calling upon the faithful to assemble at Mukōjima, a suburb of Edo. The *sanpei* or drilled troops were clamouring for their pay. Civil war at Kyoto was inevitable.

Truly it seemed as if the end of the old regime had come.

A week later Nagamichi circulated another paper to be substituted for the first, in which he had vented a little too much abuse of the anti-*shōgun* party.

261

Matters had quieted down very much in the interval. Kaneko also came to us and confessed that there was no foundation for the rumours he had previously reported. Last night there arrived a letter from Gotō Shōjirō, brought by Gotō Kyūjirō, one of the aliases of him whom we afterwards knew so well as Nakai Kōzō, and a companion. They produced a copy of the Tosa memorial of last month, advising the *shōgun* to take the step he had since adopted, and proposing various reforms. Of these the most important were the establishment of an assembly composed of two houses, the erection of schools of science and literature in the principal cities, and the negotiation of new treaties with foreign powers. They asked me for detailed information about parliamentary practice, which I did not possess, so I put them off by promising that they should get it from Mitford when we went to Osaka for the opening of the ports. They were succeeded the following day by a messenger from Yoshii Kōsuke of Satsuma, to report that all went well, and that they hoped to be favoured with a call as soon as we reached Osaka. Saigō and Komatsu had gone down to Kagoshima to fetch either Shimazu Hisamitsu or his son Shimazu Tadayoshi.

We had now become acquainted with the Satsuma agents in Edo; the *rusui* (as the principal representative of a *daimyō* was called) Shinosaki Hikojirō scoffed at the notion that the *shōgun* had given up the reins of government because he thought it would be better for the country at large to be ruled by an assembly; the fact was that he could not help himself. Messages arrived by post from Tosa and Satsuma, the "two or three clans acquainted with the dispositions of foreigners" mentioned in the emperor's most recent edict respecting foreign affairs. This seemed to indicate a pretty strong desire to gain our support. We now prepared to start for Osaka.

On November 27, I went down to Yokohama with my little pupil, Tetsu, dressed like a drummer-boy. Mitford and I sailed on the 30th at daylight in HMS *Rattler*, Captain Swann. On December 2, as we were steaming up the Kii channel, we encountered a strong northwest breeze, against which the ship could only do two knots, so deficient in boiler-power were the British men-of-war of that period. We anchored off Osaka in the afternoon, and as no boats put off from the shore, we had to conclude that the bar was impassable. We managed to get ashore about noon, and proceeded to call on the governors at their official residence opposite the castle. It is a remarkable proof of Mitford's linguistic powers that he was able to carry on the conversation in Japanese entirely unaided, although he had been in the country no longer than twelve months.

Our mission was to find quarters for the legation, and after consultation with them we went to inspect a *yashiki* behind the castle, which had been occupied in the spring by Itakura Katsukiyo, Yoshinobu's principal minister. We arranged for its repair, and for the construction of a temporary barrack for the mounted escort and a detachment of fifty men of the 9th regiment, who were to arrive as a guard. Everything was to be ready by the 18th if possible. This peaceable and entirely commercial city was full of two-sworded retainers of *daimyō*. Finding that Saigō had not yet returned from Kagoshima, and that Yoshii Kōsuke was in Kyoto, we wrote to the latter asking him to come down to see us, but he replied that he was too busy, and recommended us to wait until Saigō came back. We visited the site of the intended foreign settlement, where we found bonded warehouses, a custom house, a guardhouse and a palisade being erected, the object of the latter being to cut off the foreign residents from the city. This proceeding was altogether contrary to treaty stipulations, and we lost no time in lodging a protest with the governors.

On December 7 we called on two of the Council of State and their colleagues of the Second Council (Inaba Masami, Matsudaira Norikata, Nagai Naokoto and Kawakatsu Hirokazu), who were on their way to Edo, and had orders from the *shōgun* to stop at Osaka to see us. They gave us no information worth mentioning, but asserted that he had long ago been intending to take the step of surrendering the government to the emperor. This of course we did not believe, our view being that he was tired of being badgered by Satsuma, Chōshū, Tosa and Hizen, and that in order to give unity to his own party, he had resolved to call a general council, which possibly might reinstate him by a majority of votes, and thus establish his authority more strongly than ever.

On December 12, having transacted all our business at Osaka, we started in palanquins for Kobe. Mitford walked as far as Amagasaki, which he reached in just under four hours, and I in a palanquin took half-an-hour more. By three o'clock in the afternoon, after travelling six hours, we had got only halfway. So we betook ourselves to Shanks' mare. Mitford's Japanese teacher

Nagazawa and our escort had to trot in order to keep pace with us, and we got on board the *Rattler* soon after six. Having dined with Captain Swann, we went ashore again, and took up our quarters for the night at the municipal office (*sōkaisho*). Next day we called on the newly appointed governor, Shibata Takenaka, to discuss various business details. He told us there had been a week of feasting at Kobe in honour of the anticipated opening of the port, with processions of people dressed in red silk crape, with carts that were supposed to be transporting earth to raise the site of the proposed foreign settlement. Its situation appeared to us entirely satisfactory. Fêtes at Kobe itself were also projected. These we took to be marked signs of goodwill on the part of both government and people, and to promise a great extension of friendly intercourse between Japanese and foreigners.

The same day we returned to Osaka by boat, accompanied by Noel (afterwards Admiral Sir Gerard Noel), first lieutenant of the *Rattler*. There we found the whole population occupied with festivities in honour of the approaching opening of the city to foreign trade. Crowds of people in holiday garb, dancing and singing "*Ii ja nai ka, ii ja nai ka*" (isn't it good), houses decorated with rice-cakes in all colours, oranges, little bags, straw and flowers. The dresses worn were chiefly red crape, a few blue and purple. Many of the dancers carried red lanterns on their heads. The pretext for these rejoicings was a shower of pieces of paper, bearing the names of the two gods of Ise, alleged to have taken place recently.

On December 14, we received a visit from our Satsuma friend Yoshii. He told us that the coalition, which was determined to push matters to the last extremity in order to gain their points, consisted of Satsuma, Tosa, Uwajima, Chōshū and Geishū. Higo and Arima were inclined to join, Hizen and Chikuzen indifferent. On the whole, it might safely be said that all the western clans were pretty much of one mind. Shimazu Hisamitsu (who suffered a good deal from *kakke*, a sort of dropsy of the legs) was too ill to come to Kyoto, and Shimazu Tadayoshi was to take his place, arriving in a few days. Saedani Umetarō, a Tosa man whose acquaintance I had made at Nagasaki, had been murdered a few days ago at his lodgings in Kyoto by three men unknown. The *shōgun* had about 10,000 troops at Kyoto, Satsuma and Tosa about half that number between them, part in Kyoto, part in Osaka. Other *daimyō*, such as the lord of Geishū, would also bring up troops. The

Chōshū question would be difficult to settle peacefully, as the *shōgun*'s party included a large number of men who wished to force on a renewal of the war in order to effect the complete destruction of that clan.

I took occasion to say that the murder of our sailors at Nagasaki was by no means disposed of, and that one of the first demands to be laid by us before the new government would be for the punishment of the murderers; that no money compensation would be accepted; and that the Japanese, if they wished to remain on good terms with foreigners and to avoid a disaster, had better prevent the occurrence of such incidents. Yoshii replied that if internal affairs were not placed on a sound footing on the present occasion, the *daimyō* would wreak their wrath upon foreigners, in order to provoke bad relations between the *shōgun* and the treaty powers. I responded that they would not gain their object, as we could no longer hold the *shōgun* responsible for the acts of persons over whom he had no real control.

On December 16, I received a visit from two Uwajima men, Sutō Tajima and Saionji Yukie, the former a man of high rank in his clan, the other an official whom I had met when I was at Uwajima in the spring of the year. They had come up to Osaka as precursors of Date Munenari, who was expected to arrive early in January. They represented him as greatly pleased with the prospect of the establishment of a parliament, regarding which the old lord had talked to me on more than one occasion. I mentioned the Nagasaki affair in similar terms to those I had used to Yoshii, and assured them that the question of reparation was by no means abandoned, but was simply in abeyance for the present, and I explained that we were on as good terms with Tosa as before.

No sooner had they gone than Nakai came in to say that Gotō had arrived the previous evening, but was too busy to call on us. We offered to call on him instead of his coming to us, a proposal which was joyfully accepted, and meeting Gotō in front of the Tosa *yashiki* (agency), we turned in there with him. Our first topic was the murder of our two sailors. We said that though the particular suspicion against Tosa was removed by the discovery that there was no foundation for the report of the *Yokobue* and *Nankai* leaving the port together on the night of the murder, the fact that our men had been killed by Japanese still remained, and that we should not rest until redress was afforded. Not in the shape of a pecuniary indemnity, which some people appeared to suppose would satisfy the British government, but by the punishment of the criminals, and that we were content to wait until the establishment of the new constitution gave us an opportunity for presenting our demand with effect. He replied that the recent murder of two of his own subordinates inspired him with sympathy for our feelings, and that both the former lord Yamauchi yōdō and he himself held that no stone should be left unturned to discover the criminals. I then asked him to take charge of a gun I wished to present to Yōdō as a small return, though not of any great value or beauty, for his kindness to me. We then discussed the constitution which he proposed for the new government, and particularly the senate he desired to see established. The upshot of the conversation was that he promised to come down from Kyoto to see the chief on his arrival, and to stay a few days at Osaka to learn more from Mitford and myself about the English form of government. All we could do on that occasion was to give him some information about the composition of the cabinet, and the method of carrying legislation through parliament.

Gotō said he wanted to employ a foreigner, such as myself, to collect information for him, and with whom he could consult. I replied that I was content to serve my own government, and could not take service under that of any other state, but that if the clan wanted the services of an officer they should apply to the minister for the loan of one. I did not like the idea of taking pay from a Japanese, however highly placed, and was resolved, in case I quitted Her Majesty's service, not to seek another career in Japan.

That evening we, that is, Mitford, Noel and I, devoted to a *dîner en ville* in the Japanese fashion at a sort of *Trois frères* called Tokaku, and about half-past six we started forth. It was expected that the streets would be full of merry-makers, and the two men of my escort who were detailed to accompany us wished that the rest of them should be summoned to attend us. But I threw the burden of decision on their shoulders by saying that I thought the two of them would be enough for anything, and no more was heard of that proposition. So we issued into the streets, and dived through all sorts of back lanes to find a shorter cut, for my instinct seemed to show the road, but our escort triumphed after all, and they brought us to the place of entertainment by what proved to be a circuitous route.

Some difficulty was experienced in making our way through the crowds of people in flaming red garments dancing and shouting the refrain *ii ja nai ka*. They were so much taken up with their dancing and lantern-carrying that we passed along almost unnoticed, but I was half afraid the escort (*bette*) would provoke a quarrel by the violent manner in which they thrust people aside in order to make way for us. But the crowd did not offer any rudeness to us, and let us pass without hindrance.

On reaching Tokaku we found the principal rooms occupied by festival makers and the rest of the house shut up. Our messenger had been just that instant turned away with a refusal to receive us. While we stood there trying to persuade the people of the house to give us a room, a herd of young men and boys trooped in, shouting and dancing, and tossing about in their midst a palanquin occupied by a fat doll clad in the most gorgeous robes. All the feasters in the house came out to meet them, one cannot say at the doors, for in Japan there are no doors, but on the thresholds in which the sliding screens run that divide the different parts of a house. After a violent united dance executed by all present, the troop disappeared again. The number of pretty girls who appeared as dancers was much larger than previous experience had led us to suppose Osaka could possibly contain. We could not prevail on the Tokaku people to take us in, but they gave us a guide to a house about five minutes walk distant. There we found the doors locked, the explanation being that all the inmates had gone to the dance. We began to despair of success, and contemplate the possibility of having to return to our quarters and sup on whatever cold food "the philosopher" (Mitford's Chinese servant Lin-fu) could give us.

Luckily the guide, a little man on sturdy legs, said he knew of a house called Shōōtei (Hall of the Old Man of the Pine Tree), where we might as well call, since it lay on our road home. So we went there, and after waiting a few minutes were shown into a very good room, where we had our meal, waited on by the women of the house, who carried on the conversation and passed the wine cup, offices usually discharged on such occasions by *geisha*. The entire absence of fear or dislike on the part of the Osaka women was very remarkable when compared with the cold and often hostile reception we were accustomed to meet with in Edo. Curiosity apparently triumphed over every other feeling. Besides, the attendants mostly had their teeth dyed black, a sign of mature age, instead of wearing them as they are naturally, and probably felt immune from attempts at flirtation. We got home early, very pleased with our adventure.

Noel returned next day to his ship, and we moved over from our lodgings in Tera-machi to the quarters prepared for the whole legation behind the castle. The main building was large enough to accommodate the minister and three or four members of what he delighted to call "the staff," a military term picked up during his campaigns in China. The outbuildings were given up to Mitford, the officers shared a second, guests were to be put up in a third, the mounted escort in a fourth, and the fifth I reserved for myself. A temporary shed was provided for the infantry guard.

After settling in, we went to call on Saigō, with whom we found Iwashita Sajiemon, just back from Europe, accompanied by his friend the Comte de Montblanc. The conversation turned on the murder of the two bluejackets of HMS *Icarus*. Saigō paid me the compliment of saying that I gave little hits, but hard ones. Opinion seemed to be divided as to the probability of more such murders being committed. I used to find that men who desired the progress of Japan, and were actuated by friendly feeling towards its people, maintained that the attacks on foreigners would cease, but that unprejudiced observers did not give one much encouragement to leave off the practice of carrying revolvers. We gave them clearly to understand that the *Icarus* affair could not be disposed of by the payment of a sum of money by way of "indemnity." They were anxious to disprove the possibility of there having been a plot on the part of Tosa and Satsuma men to murder Mitford and myself when we passed through Fushimi the previous August. (Fortunately we changed our route for other reasons.) But I had no doubt myself. Noguchi had told me when we reached Osaka that he had overheard some men, whom he believed to be Tosa samurai, expressing their regret at having failed to carry out their plan. When I told Gotō at Susaki that I had heard this story, he replied that being in Kyoto at the time he too had heard such a report, and took measures to prevent the scheme, if there were one, from being carried out. Saigō tried to show that it could not have been true, and asserted that Gotō was not then in Kyoto. We assured him that we did not think it probable that men of either Satsuma or Tosa would desire to take the lives of foreigners, but that the clans contained ruffians who sometimes took such ideas into their heads quite independently of their chiefs.

Ishikawa Toshimasa, a commissioner of foreign affairs, came to see us on December 18. He told us that no date had been fixed for the assembling of the *daimyō*, and no one of them could be blamed if he arrived at Kyoto later than the others. Even supposing that the few who were already there, or were about to arrive, should discuss matters and come to a decision, how could they enforce it? Objections would surely be raised. We came to the conclusion from this conversation that civil war was after all not unlikely to break out, and that the omission to fix a date for the assembly was part of the *shōgun*'s plan to embarrass his opponents.

Letters that arrived overland from Edo on the 20th reported the general impression to be that there was no more a *shōgun*, and that Yoshinobu was nobody. So much did distance and report by word of mouth change the look of the situation. Itō Hirobumi's opinion was that war would begin almost immediately, with the object of depriving the *shōgun* of a part of his domains, which were far too large for the peace of the country. He had only seven battalions of infantry in Kyoto, all reinforcements having been countermanded in the belief that no cause for war existed. Of course Kobe and Osaka would not be the most peaceful places of residence for foreigners if war did break out, and our legation, situated just at the back of Osaka castle, would be endangered, as that fortress was certain to be the centre of a severe conflict in arms. He wanted to know whether Sir Harry's arrival and the opening of Kobe and Osaka to foreign trade could not be deferred, and whether Saigō had written to the chief to make this proposal. I said "No, of course" (though I did not know). Then, said he, their object must be to open these two places, and so content foreigners, while the Japanese went on with their plans for the reformation of the government. Someone however must be appointed to represent Japan at Osaka and Kobe. I suggested the present governors, but he replied that they would immediately be expelled when the crisis arrived. I rejoined that as long as the insurgent forces did not attack the residences of foreigners, they might do as they liked with the *shōgun*, but that if they interfered with us they would have a couple of English regiments and all the foreign men-of-war to fight against, as well as the Tokugawa troops. Itō did not think they would wish to do this, and promised to let me know beforehand when the actual day for taking action became imminent. A body of Chōshū men was coming up under the command of Mōri Motoisa and Fukumoto Shima, Kido (*i.e.* Katsura) and Kikkawa Kenmotsu being obliged to remain at home to carry on the administration of the province.

Sir Harry arrived on December 24, took a look at the legation quarters, and then went back to the ship that had brought him down. There was a fine confusion all day. I received a letter from Shinosaki Yatarō comparing the present condition of the country to an eggshell held in the hand, and begging me to persuade Komatsu and Saigō to keep the peace. On Christmas Day Kasuya Yoshiaki, a commissioner of foreign affairs, called. He said that the *daimyō* of Hikone, Bizen and Geishū, all three men of importance, were in Kyoto, and he appeared to be doubtful what was going to happen. My old friend Hayashi Kenzō, who had made the cruise in HMS *Argus* with me in January, called on the 28th, and reported that 1500 Chōshū men had disembarked at Nishinomiya on the 23rd, under the command of Mōri Takumi. He also seemed uncertain whether there would be any fighting, but he thought that Saigō and Gotō were trying to keep the peace. My protégé Endo naturally went off to Nishinomiya to see his clansmen, and doubtless to report what he had learned in Edo to Mōri Takumi. The latter had the reputation of being a man of capacity, which was perhaps the reason why he had retired into a private position (*inkyo*) early in life. On the 29th Itakura Katsukiyo came to see the chief, accompanied by Nagai Naoyuki, who had the credit of being almost the only adviser of the *shōgun* at the moment, though of course Katsukiyo was admitted into their secrets. All the governors of Osaka and Kobe were present, and the only subjects of discussion related to the arrangement for opening these places to trade on January 1. "All the governors" is the phrase, because the practice in those days was to duplicate nearly every administrative office.

Next day the two great men came again, and the Nagasaki murders were the topic of conversation. It appeared unlikely that we should obtain any satisfaction. It was however agreed that old Hirayama should again go to Nagasaki, in spite of Gemba's efforts to get him let off this disagreeable errand. The Foreign Office had written approving Sir Harry's action, and he seemed inclined to keep this question hanging over the *shōgun*'s government as a perpetual nightmare. He told them in the strongest language that we would never desist from pressing the matter until the murderers were seized and punished. Our callers asked a great number of questions about the English constitution, just as Gotō had done, so that it appeared as if both parties were desirous of getting our advice. Then Sir Harry told them that unless they got all troops away from Osaka, where they might come into collision with foreigners, he would send for a couple of regiments. I could not help feeling that it was unfair of him to meddle in this way in Japanese domestic affairs and thus add to the *shōgun*'s embarrassments, for as the *daimyō*'s forces had taken Osaka merely as a stage towards advancing on Kyoto, where else could they go except to the capital?

Following on this move, Sir Harry sent me the following day to Koba Dennai, the Satsuma agent, to explain why he wished their troops to be removed. Koba replied that there were only two hundred and fifty, but doubtless they could be sent elsewhere, and he would write to Saigō on this point. From there I went on to see a Chōshū man named Nagamatsu Bunsuke, who had come over from Nishinomiya, and was stopping with the Geishū people. A proclamation was out announcing that the Chōshū forces, having been ordered to come up to the neighbourhood of the capital, were allowed to borrow the use of the Geishū *yashiki*, and to be quartered also at the Nishi Hongan temple. Nevertheless, they had no wish to come to Osaka, and thought it a great piece of luck that the English minister had proposed to the *shōgun*'s people what they themselves happened to desire most particularly. I found it impossible to get any explanation from Nagamatsu of the real reason for their coming.

Katsukiyo had told us that by a messenger who left Geishū on the 15th, instructions were sent ordering them not to come, but he went by sea, thus missing a Chōshū messenger who arrived there by land to report that they were starting in compliance with the orders previously given. (This was evidently a mere fiction.) He also said that on the 20th three Chōshū steamers full of troops put in at Mitarai in Geishū, and asked for Geishū officers to accompany them. This request was refused, and they were advised to return home, which they declined to do, alleging their lord's orders;

without a recall from him they were unable to go back to Chōshū. This was the Geishū story, which it was impossible to believe. I felt certain that it had been concocted between the two clans, and was simply in accordance with the general plan of campaign. That the *shōgun* should have sent orders to countermand the movements of Chōshū troops was pretty clear proof that when the original instructions were given (if they really were), the present change of policy on the part of the government was not contemplated—as Nagamichi had pretended to us—but in reality had recently been forced on them by the confederate *daimyō*s. It had been intended by the chief that I should go down to Nishinomiya to ascertain how the land lay, but having learned all that the Chōshū man was willing to tell me, I was relieved from the necessity of undertaking a toilsome journey.

That day, the last of the year 1867, despatches arrived from the Foreign Office sanctioning my appointment as Japanese secretary, with a salary of £700 a year, in succession to Eusden, transferred to Hakodate as consul.

Outbreak of Civil War

On new Year's Day, 1868, salutes were fired at Tempōzan, the fort at the mouth of the Yodo River, and at Kobe, in honour of the opening of the city and the port to foreign trade. Many Japanese had been under the impression that it had been deferred, owing to the notification about the west coast port, *i.e.* Niigata, which they took to mean Kobe because of its situation west of Kyoto. I conceived a plan for taking the chief up to Kyoto to mediate between the contending parties, and to prevent the Japanese from cutting each other's throats, and I proposed to go ahead of him to Fushimi in order to make the necessary arrangements with Saigō and Gotō. But this ambitious scheme was frustrated by the rapidity with which events developed at Kyoto.

Rumour was very busy during the next few days. First, we heard that the two lords of Chōshū had been reinstated in their titles. The Tosa *inkyo* (Yamauchi yōdō) landed on the afternoon of January 1, and went up to Kyoto at once without stopping at Osaka. It was said that the *shōgun*'s position was weak, for he had no support except from Aizu and one or two of the smaller clans. Chōshū's people had taken military possession of Nishinomiya, and were patrolling the surrounding country, as if afraid of being attacked. My man Noguchi told us that the Chōshū troops had left Nishinomiya, and marched ten miles to Koya on the road to Kyoto. All the Aizu men at Osaka had gone up to Kyoto. The lord was dissatisfied with the *shōgun*'s leniency in the Chōshū business, and intended to resign his office of guardian of the emperor's person (*shugo-shoku*).

On January 4, there were symptoms of a great disturbance at Kyoto. The ministers of the other treaty powers came to visit the chief and impart their views of what had passed. For the most part these were of very slight value, for they were very much in the dark as to the internal condition of Japan. Von Brandt, the chargé d'affaires of the North German Confederation, was so little acquainted with the geography of the country as to confound Geishū and Kishū. Endo, who had come back from Nishinomiya, told me that Mōri Takumi was already at Kyoto with part of the Chōshū force, and that another part had occupied Fushimi in conjunction with Satsuma troops. But more significant than anything else was the fact that Satsuma, Geishū and Tosa were guarding the imperial palace in the place of Aizu.

There was some talk of the *shōgun* intending to come down to Osaka, and boats were said to have been embargoed at Yodo to convey his drilled soldiers down the river. It was said that the object of the *daimyō* was not to fight the *shōgun*, but only to extort concessions from him. They proposed to deprive him of a million *koku* of lands as a punishment for the transgressions of the Tokugawa family. It was certain, Endo said, that the Chōshū question was settled, and that the guards of the palace had been changed. Noguchi's story was that the lord of Aizu, disgusted with the *shōgun*, sent in his written resignation, but that it was intercepted by Kuwana. The *shōgun* however had heard of Aizu's intention, of which he informed Itakura Katsukiyo directly after the return of the latter from Osaka, and sent him his dismissal. Then the three clans above-mentioned seized the environs of the palace. The *daimyō* thereupon proceeded to the palace to discuss the situation, but the *shōgun* refused to attend. He would neither fight nor take any decided action. His sole aim was to arrange matters peaceably. Noguchi evidently was reflecting the war-like disposition of his clan. Ishikawa Toshimasa gave a somewhat different account, but it was clear that up to that moment there had been no disturbance of the peace. The *kanpaku* Nijō, a nephew of the *shōgun* Ienari, who died in 1841 aged 52, was said to have been dismissed, and either Konoye or Kujō appointed in his place. Chōshū's troops had entered Kyoto on January 2.

Osaka was not perturbed by the events that had passed at the capital, and on the 5th I was able to entertain my Japanese escort at a restaurant in the city. We had two charming *geisha* to attend on the party, one looking as if she had just stepped out of a picture, the classical contour of the face, arched nose, small full underlip, narrow eyes, and a good-hearted expression of countenance. The other personally more attractive according to Western notions of beauty, but with a little of the devil in her eyes. Lastly, there was an old *geiko* or musician of twenty-six or eight, a clever woman. The streets were still illuminated at night for the festival, and crowded with dancers.

On the 6th the mystery was cleared up by Ishikawa, who came to tell me that on the 3rd Satsuma had proposed to abolish not only the *shōgun*, but also the *kanpaku*, *tensō* and *gisō*, the three offices intermediary between the emperor and the *shōgun*. The new administration would consist of *sōsai*, which sounded like secretaries of state; *gijō*, which he thought meant a cabinet; and thirdly *sanyo*, resembling our under-secretaries of state. This looked rather like what we had suggested to Gotō as the framework of the future executive. (This was not quite correct. The *sōsai* were to be a sort of partners in the office of minister-President, as we should call it, and *gijō* were to be the heads of administrative departments.) He said that this proposal had met with great opposition from others besides the *fudai daimyō*, who were afraid that the extremists might go further and abolish the emperor. I endeavoured to reassure him on this point. "It is not," he continued, "a proposal which can be discussed over the table, and fighting must decide." It seemed from his account that the *shōgun* personally did not object, but his followers objected for him, while he seemed willing to make every possible sacrifice in order to secure peace.

From a letter of January 4 to my mother, I find that on the 1st Locock, Mitford and Willis, the legation doctor, and I intended to go over to Kobe to dine with the admiral, whose steam launch would come to Osaka to fetch us. So we went down to the foreign settlement, and, having no other resource, got into a large Japanese boat managed by a single little boy with a paddle. At first we proceeded very slowly, but a sailing boat gave us a tow, after which we shoved off and had to depend again on the small boy. It was bitterly cold, with a north-east wind. I sat in the bows, holding up a railway rug with my teeth. Two of the others protected themselves with umbrellas, and Mitford's Chinese servant, the faithful Lin-fu, hoisted a mat on a pole. So we sailed down the river to the port at its mouth.

There were no signs of the launch, so we tried to hire a Japanese boat to carry us across the bay, the distance being only eleven miles and the wind fair, but one and all refused, on account of the gale they would have to encounter in coming back. So we were compelled to put our luggage into a boat and return. The distance from the fort to the legation was about seven miles and a half, but it took us several hours, as we had to call in at the newly established vice-consulate in the foreign settlement. We dined all together at the legation, the chief being confined to his room with a sharp attack of lumbago, which had not prevented his making a formal entry into Osaka on horseback, accompanied by the mounted escort and the guard of fifty infantry detached from one of the regiments stationed at Yokohama.

By January 7 all was over with the *shōgun*. That morning Moriyama Takichirō, the ancient Dutch linguist who used to interpret between the foreign ministers and the *rōjū*, came to communicate the news of Yoshinobu's withdrawal from Kyoto. At first I feigned to suppose that he was coming down to see the French minister. "Not at all, he is coming here, deprived of the office of *shōgun*." He had already made up his mind to do this four or five days before, but was persuaded to countermand the orders given for his departure, whereat the commissioners for foreign affairs stationed at Osaka had rejoiced greatly. But now the orders had been repeated, and would be carried out.

We sauntered out to look at the preparations made for his arrival. Small bodies of drilled troops were marching about headed by drummers, and field-pieces were placed so as to sweep the narrow streets. We saw men in all sorts of military costumes with their heads muffled up to protect them from the cold, not presenting a very martial appearance. We went on to the restaurant on the river bank, where in the spring we had been often entertained *à la Japonaise*, and found it full of Aizu men, whose arms were piled outside.

There was a *karō* inside, on whom I paid a call. He ascribed the *shōgun*'s withdrawal to his unwillingness to fight under the walls of the palace, and described the leading *daimyō* as being at loggerheads, Satsuma desiring to carry out their plans by main force, and Tosa preferring to rely on reason, though their objects were identical. It was not Kaga, but Tosa, that was endeavouring to negotiate an arrangement between Satsuma and the *shōgun*. He talked a good deal about forms of government, and thought that Gotō's plans would be delightful, if feasible, but the nation was not yet ripe for fundamental changes. I agreed with him that representative government would be a curious substitute for the despotic form of authority that had existed hitherto.

Mitford and I went out again about two o'clock to have another look at the preparations, and wandered over the Kyō-*bashi* bridge onto the road to Kyoto. Here it was evident that the *shōgun* was expected to arrive at any moment. There were wonderful groups of men in armour, wearing surcoats of various gay colours, armed with spears and helmets.

Here we found Kubota Sentarō, the commander of the *shōgun*'s drilled troops, with a couple of colleagues, one of whom told Mitford that they were very brave and intended to die. I whispered to Kubota that a brave man did not retreat in this fashion. He repeated the explanation of the *shōgun*'s objection to fighting at the steps of the throne, and perhaps endangering the person of the emperor. I replied that he should not have given up the guard of the palace. Kubota alleged the emperor's orders. I suggested that if the emperor ordered that there should be no fighting, that orders must be obeyed. The significant rejoinder was: "Yes, by the *shōgun*, but not by his retainers."

We had just got to the end of the street that ran by the castle moat when the bugles sounded to arms, and we saw a long train of drilled troops advancing. We stood on one side opposite to a man wearing a gorgeous red surcoat, till the troops should pass. On they went, followed by a herd of men in fantastic costumes (*yūgekitai*, "brave fighting men"), some wearing helmets with long wigs of black or white hair reaching halfway down their backs, others in ordinary helmets, basin-shaped war hats (*jingasa*), flat hats, armed, some with long spears, short spears, Spencer rifles, Swiss rifles, muskets, or the plain two swords.

Then a silence came over the scene. Every Japanese knelt down as a group of horsemen approached. It was Yoshinobu and his train. We took off our hats to fallen greatness. He was muffled in a black hood, and wore an ordinary war hat. What could be seen of his countenance looked worn and sad. He did not seem to notice us. Katsukiyo and Matsudaira Nobuyoshi, members of his council, who came next, on the contrary nodded gaily to our salute. The lords of Aizu and Kuwana were also there. They were followed by other *yūgekitai*, and the procession closed with more drilled troops. We turned round with the last of these, and hurried on to see the entrance into the castle. On the way we met the chief, who had come out to have a look at the *shōgun*, to whose downfall he had contributed as far as lay in his power. The defiling across the bridge over the moat was an effective scheme of colour, and the procession entered by the great gate (*ōte*). Everyone dismounted except the *shōgun*. Rain fell, in much accordance with the occasion.

The chief insisted, much against my own feeling, in sending to ask for an interview on the morrow. In the letter I sent, I spoke of Yoshinobu as *shōgun denka* (His Highness the *shōgun*). The reply which came back styled him simply Uesama, the title borne by the head of the Tokugawa family before his formal recognition as *shōgun* by the emperor's court.

Endo came back with the following information. Arisugawa and Yamashina, both lords of the blood, Ogimachi and Iwakura, court nobles, were appointed *sōsai*; the lords of Owari, Echizen, Geishū, Satsuma and Tosa were appointed *gijō*. Ohara (a court noble) and various others were to be *sanyo*, besides three from each of the great clans. Satsuma in this way was represented by Iwashita Sajiemon, Ōkubo Toshimichi and Saigō Takamori. Those of the other clans were not known to him. The titles of the lord of Chōshū and his son had been restored to them. The palace was guarded by Satsuma and Geishū, Chōshū's troops held the city of Kyoto. A Satsuma steamer had left for Chikuzen to bring back the five court nobles who had fled in 1864, Sanjō (afterwards prime minister for a series of years), Sanjō-Nishi, Mibu, Shijō and Higashikuze Michitomi (subsequently minister for foreign affairs).

It was difficult to accuse Yoshinobu of cowardice. No one had ever yet expressed such an opinion of him, and the probability was that he could not put confidence in the courage of his troops. How a new government that did not include the Tokugawa chief could hope to succeed one did not see. He must either join the *daimyō* or be destroyed. Perhaps the latter alternative was what his adversaries designed. Yoshinobu had declined to see the chief on the following day, and it looked as if the audience would have to be deferred. The policy advocated in the *Sakuron*, translated from my articles in the *Japan Times*, seemed to govern the situation. The opening

of Edo to foreign trade must evidently be postponed, as Locock had declined
the responsibility of superintending the execution of the arrangements.

On the morning of January 8 the chief became very impatient, and about
noon ordered me to prepare a note to the effect that Locock and I should
go to Osaka castle and arrange for an audience. Its despatch was delayed
by a private note from Koba Dennai asking me to name an hour for an
interview with him. At three o'clock our note was to have gone in, when
in came Tsukahara and Ishikawa to inform us that the French minister was
to see the *shōgun*, as we still called him, at once, and that Yoshinobu could
receive Sir Harry tomorrow at any hour he chose.

On hearing that he had been outstripped by his colleague, Sir Harry's
wrath was unbounded. He claimed priority on the ground of superior diplomatic rank, and ordered out the escort. We proceeded to the castle in
pouring rain. I was a little behind the others, and entered the audience
chamber just as Roches and Sir Harry were exchanging words about what
the former called a breach of *les convénances* in interrupting his interview.
But he got as good as he gave, and the audience proceeded, after the lords
of Aizu and Kuwana had been presented and ordered to retire. The lord of
Aizu was a dark-complexioned man with a hooked nose, about thirty-two
years old, of middle stature and thin. The lord of Kuwana was an ugly young
person, apparently twenty-four years of age, pock-marked and of dwarfish
proportions. The old fox Hirayama sat behind the *shōgun* and took notes.

Shioda Saburō, who spoke French well, interpreted for Roches and I for
Sir Harry simultaneously the words which fell from Yoshinobu's lips. He
gave but a lame account of the events of the last few days, professing at one
moment to have withdrawn his troops from the palace in accordance with
an imperial order, while refusing to recognize another such order, which he
felt was equally dictated by Satsuma. Perhaps this was natural on his part,
for it abolished his office and forbade him access to the palace. He had had
it hinted to him that he should also resign his rank of *naidaijin*, and offer to
surrender two million *koku* of lands. But he had resolved not to heed the
suggestion, on the ground that this property belonged to him apart from
his office, just as much as the lands of the lords of Chōshū, Satsuma and the
other *daimyō* belonged to them. He appeared to feel that the *daimyō* had

stolen a march on him by preparing their plans beforehand, instead of proceeding with the general congress of lords at which each should be free to speak his own mind—in other words, he was vexed at having been taken in by a stratagem. That the proposal of a congress was merely intended to throw dust in his eyes was pretty evident. He explained the order for the withdrawal of the Aizu palace guard by saying that other *daimyō*, amongst them Satsuma and Geishū, held some of the gates under Aizu, and that they introduced certain proscribed court nobles into the precincts after the *kanpaku* and other dignitaries had retired for the day on the morning of January 3, and that at noon the same day these persons issued the proclamation setting up the new government. This he said was a preconcocted matter; they had it all ready on paper, and took these measures without consulting anyone. At one time he seemed to say that the five great *daimyō* were divided among themselves, at another he spoke of the decrees as having been agreed to by them all beforehand.

After finishing his account, he asked the opinion of the two ministers. Both expressed admiration of his patriotism in surrendering power and the justice of his desire to settle all questions by a general congress, Roches in very flattering terms, Sir Harry more moderately, asking also some pertinent questions, which were answered without much frankness. Yoshinobu gave as his reason for coming down to Osaka his fear lest a tumult should arise in the vicinity of the palace, and his desire to appease the indignation of his followers. It was his intention to remain at Osaka, but he could not say whether the opposite party would attack him there. To another question as to the form of government that had been set up at Kyoto, he replied that the emperor ruled nominally, but that Kyoto was occupied by a set of men who did nothing but quarrel among themselves. Yet he did not appear to claim that he himself possessed any authority, and he did not know whether the other *daimyō* would rally to his support. Some of those who were at Kyoto had been disgusted at the congress not having come into existence, and had returned to their homes; others who were confounded by the audacity of the five still remained there. Our inference, of course, was that they were not of his party.

The *shōgun* finally said he was tired, and so put an end to the conversation. One could not but pity him, so changed as he was from the proud, handsome man of last May. Now he looked thin and worn, and his voice had a sad tone. He said he would see the ministers again in order to consult with them. The commissioners for foreign affairs gave us a paper announcing Yoshinobu's resignation of the office of *shōgun*, and the change of his title back to Uesama.

It turned out that what Koba Dennai wanted was to ask whether I could tell him what the *shōgun*'s plans were. Was he returning to Edo in order to gather his forces together? Or would he reimain at Osaka with the intention of undertaking a "ruffianly" expedition to the capital? I sent back a reply by Itō that I knew nothing of Yoshinobu's intended movements. To suppose that I would supply information on such points showed great simplicity.

The diplomatic body being intent on the observation of neutrality between the contending parties, held a meeting on the morning of January 9 at the Prussian legation to frame a declaration, and a request to be informed where the government was being carried on. The French minister did his best to make the former a declaration of non-partizanship with the *daimyō*. Shioda his interpreter and I had to translate it into Japanese, which we did separately. His version was very literal, and he rendered "divers partis" by a term which could only be applied to conspirators. I also wished the translation to be in free Japanese, not adhering slavishly to the wording of the original, and we had a quarrel over this point.

After Shioda left me, Ishikawa came in, to whom I showed my version, in order that whatever were the result, no doubt should be possible as to the attitude of the British legation. Up to a late hour at night nothing was settled, except that the interview with the *shōgun*, which was to have been immediate, was put off. On the following morning, after the two translations had been compared, the chief suggested an alteration in the French original which removed the cause of dispute. Then Locock and I went round to the other ministers and got them to accept my translation.

While we were at the French legation Hirayama and Kawakatsu came in, and took the paper with them to prepare the *shōgun*'s reply. A difference had arisen between Roches and Sir Harry as to relative precedence. The former was only minister plenipotentiary, while our chief was envoy extraordinary and minister plenipotentiary. According to all rules he was senior, but the other ministers held that Roches, having arrived first in

Japan, had precedence. This decision did away with Sir Harry's claim to be *doyen* and his reason for asserting a right to have audience before any of his colleagues. The latter pretension was, of course, one that could in no circumstances be upheld.

At three o'clock the whole diplomatic body assembled at the castle in the *o-shiro jōin*, all the other apartments being occupied by the lords of Aizu, Kuwana and Kishū. The same ceremony was observed as at a European court. Behind the *shōgun* stood his pages. At his left were the lords of Aizu, Kuwana, Makino Tadayuki, Matsudaira Nobuyoshi (two councillors of state), and a noble person whom I took to be the lord of Ogaki, then Hirayama Seisai and Tsukahara Kanjirō. On his right were a number of *ō-metsuke*. In Japan, as in China, the left was the position of honour. Close to Yoshinobu stood Itakura Katsukiyo, on whom devolved the task of reading the translation of the diplomatic body's address. The reply was a very long one, spoken by the *shōgun* himself.

Yoshinobu began by explaining his policy, vindicating his retirement from Kyoto, and expressing his determination to abide by the decisions of a general council. His reply to the particular question asked by the ministers was that foreigners should not trouble themselves about the internal affairs of Japan, and that until the form of government was settled he regarded the conduct of foreign affairs as his own function. The commissioners for foreign affairs, who were probably apprehensive that they might today become nonentities, were obviously relieved. They became joyful, and somewhat triumphant. The audience was over in an hour and a half.

After the delivery of his speech the *shōgun* went round the row of foreign ministers and spoke a few words to each. To Sir Harry he said that he hoped for a continuation of his friendship, and for his assistance in organizing the Japanese navy. The chief replied in florid style that his heart was the same as it had ever been towards him, and that he trusted the sun shining through the windows was an omen of his future, a metaphor which I found some difficulty in putting into Japanese. The *shōgun* pretended to take it all in. One of the private secretaries, Tsumagi Nakazukasa, came in the evening to assist me in translating the answer into English.

From Kuroda Shinemon I received the correct text of the Kyoto decrees. He told me that the *daimyō* were unanimously awaiting Yoshinobu's reply to the demand for two million *koku* of lands and the surrender of a step in court rank. They expected to be joined by the other western *daimyō*, and also by the northern ones. I advised that they should not fight if they could help it, but if they judged it necessary, to do it at once. He nodded assent. It was intended that in three or four days the *daimyō* would declare their intentions to the foreign ministers. It showed, I thought, a good deal of courage on the part of a Satsuma man to come all the way past the castle sentries to our legation, and to spare him this risky proceeding I promised to go and see him at his own quarters.

Ishikawa brought me a document purporting to be a protest of the retainers of Awa, Hizen, Higo, Chikuzen and other great *daimyō* against the violent proceedings of the Satsuma party, and insisting on the convocation of a general council. As far as could be inferred from their language, it did not appear that war was contemplated by either party. We heard that in a day or two Owari, Echizen and the court noble Iwakura would come down to receive the Tokugawa answer to the demands already mentioned. The troops of Sakai Tadaaki of Obama in Wakasa, a powerful adherent of the *shōgun*, had been sent to Nishinomiya, where there were probably Satsuma and Chōshū troops. Endo however was of opinion that war would certainly break out. He said that a hundred of Satsuma's people arrived from Kyoto last night to escort thither the five court nobles who had been recalled from exile.

On January 12, 1868, I went to see Kuroda Shinemon and Koba Dennai, and gave them copies of the address of the foreign diplomatic representatives to the *ci-devant shōgun* as well as of his reply. They acknowledged the authenticity of the protest of Awa and the other eleven clans, and said that there were others who had disapproved of his restoring the sovereign power to the emperor. From this it was evident to me that the reason why the five clans were in such a hurry to act was that they wanted to carry out their plans before the others arrived. The lord of Kaga was said to have left Kyoto in order to muster his forces for the assistance of Yoshinobu. It now became evident that the Tokugawa party were preparing for war. Kishū's men were at Tennōji, Sumiyoshi, and Kizu, close to Osaka. The lord of Aizu had occupied the castle of Yodo, a few miles south of Kyoto on the direct road, with 500 of his own troops, and three hundred of the Shinsen-gumi, a recently raised body of Tokugawa infantry, had also proceeded thither, while all along the road small detachments were stationed. Owari, Echizen and Iwakura were expected on January 18, but it was possible that the five clans might march on Osaka before that date.

Koba Dennai invited us to the Satsuma *yashiki* on the 14th, so Mitford and I went, and there we met Terashima Munenori (formerly known as Matsugi Kōan), who had arrived from Kyoto that morning. He explained that it was thought better to delay issuing the emperor's announcement to foreign countries of his having assumed the government until the question of a surrender of territory by the late *shōgun*, which Owari and Echizen had undertaken to arrange, should be settled. (It must be understood that in conversation with Japanese this title was never employed, as it was only invented for foreign use. Either Tokugawa, or the Bakufu, was the term we employed.) It had been originally proposed that only the lords of Aizu and Kuwana should come down to Osaka, in order to return by sea to their respective countries, but as they were unwilling to come alone, Yoshinobu was allowed to accompany them. The territory to be surrendered by him was to form the nucleus of a national treasury, and it had been proposed by Tosa and some other clans that each *daimyō* should sacrifice a smaller proportion for the same purpose, but Satsuma objected to this latter part of the scheme.

The emperor's notification would be in archaic Japanese (this was stated in reply to a question about the court language. When the document eventually was delivered, it was found, as far as my memory serves me, to be framed in classical Chinese). It would state that he was the head of the confederated *daimyō*, that he alone was the sovereign of Japan, that the office of *shōgun* was abolished, that the government was entrusted to a general council of *daimyō* subject to his supervision, and lastly that the treaties were to be remodelled in his name. We quite agreed with him that to issue the announcement in the present undecided state of affairs would be premature. A civil governor had been appointed for Kyoto, and a night patrol to arrest marauders and disturbers of the public peace. Of course Yoshinobu's plan of calling a general council of *daimyō* to deliberate on the state of the country was put forward because he was certain of securing a majority by the aid of those of them who were his own vassals, and that he would get a vote carried in favour of reinstating him in his previous position of authority.

This stratagem had been defeated by the bold stroke of Satsuma getting possession of the emperor's person.

Next day Sir Harry paid a visit to the castle with the object of pumping the *shōgun* about his plans for the general council and the new form of government, but he was anticipated by inquiries about the British constitution, which took up all the time available, and he was only able to get in a question or two at the end. These the *shōgun* adroitly parried by saying that the events he narrated on the last occasion of their meeting had upset all his arrangements. The escort was ordered, and we were obliged to leave. As we were going, the lord of Aizu came up and saluted the chief with great cordiality, who replied that he was very fond of making the acquaintance of *daimyō*, and already knew several. He hoped to know more of them. Could the lord of Aizu tell him whether the lord of Awa was at Kyoto or Osaka. The lord of Aizu replied that he did not know. The chief rejoined that last year he had been to Awa's place, and had been very civilly treated. This rather broad hint, however, produced no effect.

The same day there came to see me a young Tosa man, of Kishū origin, named Mutsu Yōnosuke, with whom I discussed the question of the recognition of the emperor's government by the foreign ministers. I explained that it was not for the foreign representative to take the first step. We had received assurances from the Tokugawa chief that he would continue to carry on the administration, and as no communication had yet come from the Kyoto side, we had to go on holding official relations with him. If the Kyoto government wished to assume the direction of affairs they should inform the Bakufu that they were going to notify their assumption of foreign affairs to the ministers, and then invite the latter to Kyoto. This would be to all the world a clear proof of the position held by the emperor.

The lord of Mutsu replied that he had not come as a messenger from Gotō, but was merely giving his individual views. He thought a lord of the blood should come down to Osaka and hold an interview at the castle with the foreign representatives, at which the Tokugawa chief should attend and resign the conduct of foreign affairs, on which the lord of the blood would deliver the emperor's declaration of policy. Of course he would be escorted by *daimyō* and their troops. I warmly approved his suggestion, and at his request promised not to divulge it to anyone.

The next day Mitford and I went again to the Satsuma *yashiki*, and found that a list of questions to be put to us had been sent down from Kyoto. We gave one answer to everything, namely, that it was only necessary for the emperor to invite the ministers to Kyoto, and compel the ex-*shōgun* to abandon his claim to conduct the foreign affairs of the country. They proposed to make Yoshinobu withdraw his answer of the 10th. I gave them copies of Sir Harry's note conveying the Queen's condolences on the death of the late emperor, and of Itakura's reply. But they were not able to say whether the note had been communicated to the court. The *daimyō* of Higo had arrived and proceeded to Kyoto. Bizen was to garrison Nishinomiya. The five exiled court nobles were expected to arrive that evening, and would go up to Kyoto by the river.

The *daimyō* of Echizen and Owari came down from Kyoto and went to the castle, as had been announced several days previously. The former sent a message through the Japanese Foreign Department to ask when his retainers might come to see our guard go through their drill. We replied that they did not drill. Perhaps they had heard of the mounted escort being exhibited to the *shōgun* on some previous occasion. We should have preferred to have this request made to us directly.

On the 23rd Ishikawa came to tell us that our Japanese guard was to be increased by one hundred men in consequence of disturbances that had occurred at Edo. On the night of the 16th, he said, some Satsuma men had attacked the Shiba barracks of Sakai Tadazumi, *daimyō* of Shōnai in the north, but were beaten off. On the next day but one Sakai's people went together with some troops which they had borrowed from the government, intending to demand the surrender of the men concerned in the violence of the 16th, but before they reached the Satsuma *yashiki* fire was opened on them with field pieces and small arms, to which they replied. In the end the *yashiki* was burnt to the ground. Some of the defenders were killed, others captured, and some escaped to a Satsuma war vessel that was lying in the bay. This at once attacked a government ship, but the result of the fight was unknown. At any rate, the other *yashiki* of Satsuma and of Shimazu Tadahiro had also been burnt. It was possible that the Satsuma people who had escaped might try to revenge themselves by creating disturbances at Osaka. Though it was not likely that they would attack the castle, it was thought prudent to station some troops where we were. The chief's answer was that they must first write all this officially to him and await his reply before sending a single man to the legation.

To alarm us still further Ishikawa told us a story of boatmen having reported that the student interpreters we had left at Edo had been fired at from the Satsuma *yashiki* in the street called Tamachi, the date of the letter which brought this news being January 14th. As this was two days before the Satsuma attack on the Sakai *yashiki*, we did not give credit to his tale. What we thought was that Yoshinobu had refused the ultimatum of the *daimyō*, and feared they would attack him at Osaka. The lords of Echizen and Owari returned to Kyoto that day, but we did not hear what had been the result of their mission.

On Janurary 24, the admiral arrived with news from Edo confirming all that Ishikawa had reported. His account of it was that on the night of the 17th the Satsuma people had contrived to set a part of the castle on fire, and carried off Tenshō-in-*sama*, a lord of theirs who had married the last *shōgun* but one. Thereupon the government people attacked all the Satsuma *yashiki* in Edo and burnt them, and the occupants getting on board their steamer put to sea. Meanwhile, the *Eagle* and other government vessels received orders to get up steam and attack her. A sea fight ensued, which ended by the *Eagle* and the Satsuma steamer disappearing in the offing. The former was met by HMS *Rodney*, the admiral's flagship, returning next day with her fore-yard gone, and the latter was seen off Cape Oshima, south of the province of Kishū, on the 23rd. The story that our student interpreters John James Quin and George Hodges had been fired at about the 12th as they were passing in front of the Satsuma battery in a Japanese boat was true, but no harm was done.

Hostilities at Fushimi

On the evening of January 27, 1868, a great blaze was seen in the direction of Kyoto. Endo said it was at Fushimi, three miles from the capital, and that the ex-*shōgun*'s troops and those of Satsuma and his allies were fighting there. The government ship *Kaiyō-maru* with others were blockading Satsuma vessels at Kobe. On the preceding day a couple of battalions had been seen parading for the march to Kyoto, and were probably among the troops engaged at Fushimi. Report said that Yoshinobu himself would take the field in a few days. Willis' servant, the faithful Sahei, who passed through Fushimi the same day, saw bodies of Satsuma men waiting about in the streets and warming themselves at fires, but he could not say for certain whether there were any other imperialists with them. A little on the nearer side of Fushimi were the *shinsengumi*, and behind them large bodies of infantry, all apparently eager for the fray.

During the succeeding night the Satsuma *yashiki* on the Tosa-bori canal, where we used to meet our friends, was burnt down. Some accounts said it was set on fire by the occupants before they stole away, others that the Tokugawa troops sent three or four shells into it and so caused the blaze. At any rate the Satsuma people got into boats and went down the river, pursued by the Tokugawa men, who fired at them from the banks, and killed two of the fugitives. Sir Harry went to call on Itakura, who told us that the town of Fushimi had been set on fire by Satsuma troops, who were opposing the entry of the *shōgun*'s forces into Kyoto. Fighting began at four o'clock, and the result was not yet known. Another detachment marching up the Toba road, which follows the right bank of the river, fell into an ambuscade and was forced to retire. He could not tell us when the *shōgun* would start. The troops that had been opposed at Fushimi were his advanced guard, destined to occupy Nijō castle in Kyoto, as he was returning there shortly, having been invited to do so by Echizen and Owari. All the other *daimyō* were tired of the arrogant conduct of the lord of Satsuma. Probably it was his troops alone which had fought at Fushimi. Ishikawa gave me a copy of a letter from the commandant at Fushimi, who writing to Tsukahara and Matsudaira Nobuyoshi mentioned that guns had been lent for the destruction of the Satsuma *yashiki*. It was reported that Tsukahara had dis-appeared, and it was conjectured that he had been shot during the imperialist attack on the official residence of the governor of Fushimi, but we could not ascertain that he had been seen farther on than Yodo.

Next day the chief went to Itakura's house just inside the Tamatsukuri Gate near our legation, where he saw Nagai Naoyuki. Nagai told us that up to last night the Tokugawa troops had been repulsed on both points of their advance, and were going to try another road, the Takeda Kaidō, further to the west. To us it appeared that they ought to have done better, as they were 10,000 to 6000. They reported the enemy force to consist of Satsuma and Chōshū men, assisted by *rōnin*, which probably meant the men of other clans, but the remaining *daimyō* appeared to be preserving a neutral attitude. The *shōgun*'s commander-in-chief was Takenaka Shigetaka. The denunciation of Satsuma's crimes was carried by the advanced guard, whom Naoyuki described as the *shōgun*'s "retinue." He still maintained that the *shōgun* had not wished to have recourse to arms, but was forced into it against his will. Still Naoyuki could not give a satisfactory explanation of the firing on the Satsuma steamer *Lotus* as early as the evening of January 26. The same evening reports came in that the Tokugawa troops had retired 7-1/2 miles from Fushimi, and had destroyed the bridge over the Kizu River below Yodo, to obstruct the further advance of the Satsuma forces. Seven boat-loads of wounded had come down the river.

From what we heard on the morning of the 30th, it appeared that the prospects of the Tokugawa party were not very encouraging. In the afternoon great fires were distinctly visible from the hill by the castle, in the direction of Hirakata and Nashimoto, about halfway between Osaka and Fushimi, which showed that the battle was getting nearer. A consultation was held by the chief with the legation staff, the result of which was that we were to hire as many boats as possible to convey the archives to the British squadron, and when they were placed in safety we should be able to await the development of events with calmness. After dinner Sir Harry went to see the French minister, and returned about half-past nine with information that a circular was to be addressed to the foreign ministers announcing that the *shōgun* could no longer defend them, and they must take their own measures for the protection of their flags. At eleven came an official messenger with the circular, who promised to get us as many boats as possible on the following morning to move our baggage, and after packing up the archives we went to bed.

At four o'clock in the morning, Locock woke me with the news that a note had come from the French minister to say that the enemy would enter the city early in the day, and that we must run off at daylight with what we could carry. So we all got up, frightfully cold though it was, and packed up our belongings. No boats had arrived. At daylight my Japanese escort came to say that with the greatest difficulty they had managed to procure one large boat. On this the archives were placed, and it started off about nine. Then came Ishikawa, who said he was powerless to help us. The imperialists had not yet appeared, but he considered it advisable for us to get off at once. So Sir Harry and I went off with him to look for the porters, whom we met outside the great gate of the castle. Just at that moment we saw a curious procession going in. It consisted of a palanquin like a *mikoshi*, one of those portable shrines carried in religious pageants, a large umbrella held over it and two men with lanterns on long poles in front. Ishikawa let out that he thought it was conveying a messenger from the emperor. He and I came back with the porters, and brought the greater part of the baggage down to the bank of the stream behind the legation, but still there were no boats. So we went off to the governor's residence and tried to interest the officials on our behalf. They appeared to be in a state of extreme perturbation, and declared that it was impossible to procure any boats. Ishikawa almost shed tears, and vowed that he would never again try to get boats and porters for the legation; it was none of his business. We agreed therefore to deposit the greater part of the baggage inside the castle. Luckily this proved unnecessary, for when I returned to our quarters I found the chief radiant with joy, five boats having arrived in the interval.

About ten o'clock therefore we were able to make a start for the foreign settlement, but I stayed behind with the six men of my Japanese escort, capital fellows who had stuck to me ever since we made the journey overland from Osaka to Edo in 1867. I had to procure boats for my own baggage, which by an oversight had been left behind, and to get the stores removed to the castle. However, more boats arrived than had been expected, so I put all the baggage on board, including even a huge pot of mince-meat. Unluckily, a fine gold lacquer cabinet of Mitford's, for which he had recently paid 800 *ichibu*, was overlooked.

About noon I started for the foreign settlement in great triumph. There was even a house-boat (*yakatabune*). I asked a man I had never seen before for whom this was intended, and was greatly flattered when he replied innocently that it was for Satow-*sama*. This enabled me to go down comfortably instead of walking the whole distance. On the way we all nodded and dozed, for we had had no proper night's rest. From time to time we were challenged by the posts on the banks, but no attempt was made to stop us.

On arriving at the settlement I found the wind was blowing too strongly from the west to allow of our passing the bar at the mouth of the river. The chief, Locock, Willis and Wilkinson were all fast asleep. Captain Bruce, commandant of the infantry guard, and the constable had gone off again to the legation to try to recover the remainder of our property that had been left behind, and I got Lieutenant Bradshaw a boat with the same object. Towards evening they returned. A steam launch from the squadron was lying off the settlement, and the legation was located at the vice-consulate there. It was bitterly cold, and we were glad to get to bed, after what was a very good dinner considering the circumstances. The other foreign representatives were at Tempōzan, at the mouth of the river, in miserable huts, and with very little to eat. We felt pity for them, mingled with pride, when we compared our situation with theirs. Rumours were flying about among the townspeople that Yoshinobu had been declared a rebel (*chōteki*).

About nine o'clock on the following morning, February 1, Locock and I took an escort from the 2/ix detachment and went off to the castle to see what was the state of things there. In front of it there was a great crowd, and all the gates seemed deserted. We knocked at the governor's door, but got no answer, a clear sign that he and his people had taken to flight. The crowd laughed. We sent in to the castle by one of my Japanese escort to inquire who was there, and were told in reply that Yoshinobu had departed, leaving it empty. We went on to the legation, where we found everything just as we had left it. We got back by noon, and as we were at lunch there came in a detachment of thirteen Frenchmen, who in return for being stoned by the crowd had fired and killed some eight or nine people. This was looked upon as a wholesome lesson to the rabble not to cry out abuse of foreigners, but nevertheless was much to be regretted, as it would tend to make the foreign colleagues believe Osaka unsafe for themselves. During our walk to the castle and back we had observed no signs of hostility, a fact which seemed to show that the population were able to distinguish between nationalities. The French legation had been pillaged and the furniture smashed.

After lunch, Sir Harry, Willis and I went down to Tempōzan, the chief to call on his colleagues, Willis to attend to the wounds of some Aizu men who had been brought down from Kyoto, where they had fought against the imperialists. The colleagues were furious with Sir Harry for having been so fortunate as to save all his baggage and archives, and for having had the pluck to remain four miles nearer the supposed danger than they had. A rather angry discussion ensued. Sir Harry declared that he would not leave Osaka unless he was able to carry off every atom of legation property, and he did not know when that might be possible. They, on the contrary, said that having struck their flags, it was their intention to move across to Kobe, and await the course of events.

I went to make friends with some of the Aizu wounded, who were waiting for boats to put them on board of Tokugawa ships. They asserted that they would have beaten the enemy if they had been properly supported, but Tōdō Takayuki had turned traitor at Yamazaki (on the right bank of the river, nearly opposite Yodo), which was the most important point of the defence, and Yoshinobu's general Takenaka had gone over to the enemy at Yodo itself. Moreover, the drilled infantry were useless; if one man ran the rest followed like a flock of sheep (as we should say). They estimated the Satsuma force at the low figure of 1000, but said the skirmishing of the enemy was very good, and they were armed with breech-loaders. Yoshinobu had run away, they knew not whither, but probably to Edo.

We found that the fort at Tempōzan, and one a little further up the river, which had hitherto been under the charge of Kōriyama (a Kyushu *daimyō*) had been dismantled, the guns in the former spiked, and the ammunition embarked in the Tokugawa warship *Kaiyō-maru*, which left at noon. Yoshinobu was believed to be on board. Old Hirayama was in the fort at Tempōzan, but studiously concealed himself. Chanoine and another officer of the French military mission had arrived the previous night from Edo, but had had to leave again, greatly disappointed that they had come too late for the fair. Obviously they had wanted to act as advisers to Yoshinobu's commander-in-chief. The town of Sakai was reported to have been burnt, and also the houses round the Namba-*bashi* bridge over the Yamato-gawa, but it was not known whether by accident or intentionally. No Satsuma men had yet entered Osaka. The French minister was our authority for a story that Yoshinobu, on finding that the majority of the *daimyō* were arrayed against him, had surrendered the castle and city of Osaka to Echizen and Owari, because they had been kind and polite to him when they came on their mission from the court!

The Aizu men were very grateful to Willis for the assistance he gave in attending their wounded, and apparently regarded the English as the best and kindest people in the world. Sir Harry decided to go to Kobe in order to avoid a quarrel with his colleagues, and I volunteered to remain at Osaka with Russell Robertson as acting vice-consul, and half the guard from the 2/ix under the command of Bruce, so that the honour of the flag might be maintained. I was certain that Noguchi and my Japanese escort would stand by me, and we were determined to fight to the last if we should be attacked, but that I did not anticipate. I despatched the Chōshū student Endo to Kyoto to urge that the *daimyō* should forthwith make their declaration of policy to the foreign representatives, as Mitford and I had given the draft of a notification to our Satsuma friends, and there was also my private understanding with Tosa on that subject. The Aizu soldiers at the fort said that Satsuma men had been found in the castle in disguise, and that there even were some amongst Yoshinobu's drilled troops—cunning devils they must have been if all we heard was true.

Accordingly, on February 2, the chief went away to Kobe to arrange for HMS *Rattler* to convey Locock to Yokohama, where he was to be in the charge of the legation, and also for his own temporary withdrawal to Kobe. About half-past eight in the morning we saw from the vice-consulate a puff of white smoke ascend in the direction of the castle, followed by dense clouds of black smoke. The report soon spread that the castle was on fire, and so it was. After breakfast Locock and I took forty of the 2/ix guard, with Bruce and Bradshaw, and went off to see the fire and find out whether our legation had been burnt.

We marched along the bank of the river to the Kyō-*bashi* gate of the castle, and turning in there, found that the granaries and the *honmaru* (inner circle) had been set on fire, but no one could tell us by whom this had been done. The wind was blowing from the north, and sparks had spread the conflagration to some of the huts previously occupied by the drilled troops on the south side. We walked round to Tama-tsukuri, where we found that the legation buildings were being plundered by people of the lowest class. We pursued some of them, but were not in time to put an end to the devastation. All the furniture had been destroyed, and the *kura* sacked. Unfortunately this contained Mitford's beautiful *étagère*, which had no doubt been carried off. There was an immense crowd in front of the castle, and men were pouring in and out of the gates but offered no opposition and did not stone us as we might have expected. The mob had, of course, destroyed the official residence of the governors as far as was possible.

We got back to the vice-consulate about midday, and found there Endo, who had already returned from his mission. He said that two or three hundred of the Chōshū folk were already in the castle, and that an official had been left behind to hand the place over to Owari, but the flames broke out before the ceremony could be completed. Whether the fire was started by the rabble or by Yoshinobu's followers he did not know. The only imperialists who had yet arrived were Chōshū men.

About two o'clock we left the foreign settlement in a lifeboat with Locock and Wilkinson, who were to be embarked on board HMS *Rattler* and proceed to Edo. Halfway down the river we met the steam launch, with two other large boats, bringing the chief and Captain Stanhope of HMS *Ocean*, who, seeing what they took to be a general conflagration of all Osaka, had come to take us away and haul down the flag. How angry I was! We were not in the slightest danger, either of being attacked by the victors or from the burning of the castle, and I would have answered with my life for the safety of every person left with me. Had I not received repeated assurances from Satsuma, Tosa and Chōshū that our legation would be respected? Yet there was no help for it; orders had to be obeyed. We found great difficulty in procuring barges, and had to send the steam-launch out to seize as many as we wanted. We secured three, into which we packed everything, including the vice-consul's furniture, the archives and the baggage of the 2/ix having been already started off. Everything was got away by half-past six, and we eventually crossed the bar in safety. The steam-launch, in which I was, grounded three times, and finally stuck fast, but Captain Bullock of HMS *Serpent* fetched me off in his gig. Willis, who, with the safe containing the legation funds, was in a boat towed by the *Serpent*'s pinnace, did not get on board till midnight. Then she took all the barges in tow, and steamed over to Kobe.

Next morning we landed there, and got the baggage on shore. Most of the party found accommodation at the consulate. I took possession of the district administrator's house, which had been occupied by some custom house officers. The caretaker objected. I insisted that as we had been turned out of Osaka by the Bakufu, we had the best right in the world to the abandoned accommodation of the Bakufu's officials. So I had my baggage carried in and set up house there. Our chief had quartered himself at the consulate, and the other five foreign representatives, French, Dutch, American, North-German and Italian, occupied the custom house, a large two-storeyed building in foreign style, which the officials would otherwise have set on fire to prevent it falling into the hands of the victors. The governor, an old acquaintance of ours named Shibata, had chartered the steamer *Osaka* at $500 a day (say £100) to convey himself and his staff back to Edo, whither he started the same afternoon.

Satsuma's man Godai Tomoatsu, I learned, had gone to Osaka the previous night, or early that morning, in order to assure the chief that he might safely remain there, but of course he came too late. The next thing one heard was that it had been intended to declare Yoshinobu a rebel if he did not withdraw his troops from Osaka, Kyoto and other points between the two cities, and that Satsuma, Geishū, Chōshū and Tosa were charged with the duty of using force to compel obedience if he refused to listen to the advice offered to him by Echizen and Owari in the first place. This seemed to explain his hasty flight, but from any point of view, European as well as Japanese, it was disgraceful. After informing the diplomatic representatives that he regarded himself as charged with the direction of foreign affairs, the only further intimation they received from his officials was that he could no longer protect the legations, but he never so much as hinted that he was about to abscond. I was also informed that it was intended to invite the ministers to Kyoto, and Yoshinobu had been ordered to transmit the invitation to them, which of course he omitted to do. In fact the policy of the Tokugawa government from the very beginning of their relations with the outer world of Europe had been to keep foreigners from coming in contact with the Kyoto party. In this they were heartily assisted by Roches, the French minister. I well recollect how, when we went to the castle to see Yoshinobu after his retirement from Kyoto, some of the commissioners for foreign affairs jeered at me, saying, "Of course you now expect to get to Kyoto, but don't be too sure," or words to that effect.

A report having been circulated that Satsuma or Tokugawa people were going to blow up the martello tower that stood at the end of the dry river bed near Kobe, boats were sent from HMS *Ocean*, the French flagship *Laplace* and the *Oneida*; the door was locked and the key taken away.

The Kōbe Incident

On February 4, 1868, Bizen troops were passing through Kobe from the early morning, and about two o'clock in the afternoon the retinue of one of their *karō* shot an American sailor who had crossed the street just in front, which according to Japanese ideas was an insult that deserved mortal chastisement. After that they attempted the life of every foreigner whom they met, but fortunately without any serious results. What at a later time became the foreign settlement was then an open plain. At the upper edge of it ran the high road, and as the Bizen people passed along they suddenly opened fire, apparently from breech-loaders. Then every foreigner was seen scurrying across the plain for safety. The American marines immediately started in pursuit, our guard of 2/ix was called out, and some French sailors were landed. Half of our guard under Bruce were despatched to occupy the entrance from Kobe into the foreign quarter, and the other half followed in pursuit.

On reaching the Ikuta-*gawa* stream bed, at the eastern extremity of the plain, we perceived the Bizen men marching in close column about six or seven hundred yards ahead, so we passed through the gap in the river bank and opened fire. There were at least half-a-dozen civilians with us, all armed with rifles, who likewise fired. Willis, Mitford and I had only our revolvers. At the first volley from our side, the enemy turned into a field by the side of the road, and fired at us from below a bank. On our returning their fire, they all took to flight. We pursued them, every now and then firing at one or other who had failed to get under cover, but finally they took to the hills and disappeared completely. Sir Harry, followed by his mounted escort of ex-policemen, galloped some distance down the road in the direction of Nishinomiya, but was unable to catch sight of the foe. If any of them had suffered from our fire, he must have been carried off by his comrades.

Willis found an old peasant woman lying by a bank with a bullet wound through both ankles, whom he brought back and cured of her hurt. Then we took prisoner a wretched porter, who escaped with his life by a mere miracle, for at least fifteen revolver shots were fired at him at close quarters as he rose from his place of concealment, without his receiving a single wound. We opened the baggage which had been dropped by the fugitives, but found nothing of value, only three small weapons, representing a cross between a matchlock and a howitzer, and a few carpenters' tools. From the porter, whom we led home as our prisoner, we ascertained that the detachment consisted of two Bizen *karō*, Ikeda Ise and Hiki Kiyokado, who were on their way with about four hundred men to reinforce the garrison of Nishinomiya, and that some of them had remained behind at Kobe.

On returning to the settlement we found a quantity more baggage which had been dropped in Kobe by the men whom Bruce had intercepted. Sentries were then posted along Kobe's main street as far as the first barrier gate, where a strong guard was stationed with a howitzer. A line of sentries was also drawn round the north and east sides of the plain. From some of these, American sailors or marines, an alarm was raised about ten o'clock. Great alacrity was displayed by the naval people, who landed field pieces and numbers of small-arms men. After all, no enemy made his appearance to justify so great a stir being made. I proposed to Sir Harry that we should issue a manifesto declaring that if Bizen's people did not satisfactorily explain their behaviour, the foreign powers would make it a quarrel with Japan as a whole. He induced his colleagues to agree to this, and I started our prisoner back to his people with a copy, though I did not feel much confidence in its reaching its destination.

About half-past one, a hundred Chōshū men sent down for the protection of Kobe against Tokugawa troops arrived just outside our post in the middle of the village, and were within an ace of being fired on by our guard. Luckily I came up at the moment, and went to an inn at which they had billeted their rank and file, to arrange that they should withdraw, which they did very readily.

During the afternoon, four steamers belonging to the lords of Chikuzen, Kurume, Uwajima, and one it was thought to the Tokugawa, were seized at Kyōgo and Kobe, to hold as a "material guarantee."

The morning of February 5 brought me again an invitation from Yoshii Kōsuke to visit him at Osaka and talk over affairs, but it was impossible, for I had too much on my hands. The *Whampoa*, a steamer belonging to Glover & Co., of Nagasaki, had arrived, and a rumour was invented and spread that she was conveying eight hundred Satsuma troops, so I was sent off in a boat to stop their landing. There was not a single Satsuma man on board. Some men of Awa in Shikoku had decamped in boats from Kobe, and our people pursued them, but as they were only few in number and very miserable in appearance, they were not molested.

We then issued proclamations, with the wording of which I was entrusted, explaining why we had seized the steamers, a second exhorting the people to go quietly about their business, and a third announcing that all unarmed persons would be allowed to pass our posts. About one o'clock a Dutchman (appropriately enough in accordance with popular notions) raised an alarm that the Japanese were advancing to the attack. The report spread as far as the quarters of the foreign representatives at the custom house, where Von Brandt was making a great fuss about a body of at least three hundred armed men that he asserted were menacing Kobe from the hills close by on the north side. I had a look at them through his glass, and certainly saw men, but if they were armed, I was sure they were friendly Chōshū men.

So I got leave to take Lieutenant Gurdon of HMS *Ocean* with ten men, and we started out to explore, and to paste up our proclamations wherever we found one of Chōshū's. The only people on the hills turned out to be peasants. The Chōshū troops were billeted at the Shōfuku-*ji*, a large temple, or Buddhist monastery, about two miles away among the hills, so it was manifest that they were keeping their engagement to us. We marched through Kobe, and pasted a copy of our first notification on the door of the Bizen official hotel (*honjin*), and the whole series of four on the house where their troops had passed the night of the 4th. Having accomplished all this, we returned to relieve the anxiety of our fellow foreigners.

Just as I got back I met Yoshii and Terashima Munenori, who had come down to have a talk. The chief gave them a short interview, at which he advised them to send off at once and get the emperor's messengers to come down with their notification to the foreign representatives. They wanted him to let three hundred Satsuma troops pass through our lines, but he refused, on the ground that as we did not know anything officially from the emperor, we could not recognize Satsuma as acting under His Majesty's orders. So they agreed to bring their men into Kobe by another route.

Then I went off with them to their *honjin* at Kobe, and they told me a good deal about the course of recent events. Theirs had been a continuous course of victory from the very first, for being like "rats in a bag," they had to fight hard for their lives, and were compelled to be victorious. At Fushimi they had had a desperate fight, but after that they pressed on and drove the Tokugawa forces into Yodo. This place, as well as the long bridge over the river, was fired by the retreating troops. Aizu's men fought very bravely.

The plan of the Bakufu was to get the Satsuma and Chōshū soldiers engaged with Aizu and the Shinsengumi (a body of armed samurai recently raised), and then to creep round to the imperialist right with the drilled infantry and seize Kyoto. The lord of Higo too was only waiting for signs that Satsuma was getting the worst of it, in order to seize the palace, but now he was very humble. The number of Satsuma and Chōshū men actually engaged was about fifteen hundred, the remainder being employed in the defence of the city. Anyhow, as the roads to be held were very narrow, large bodies could not have been employed to any advantage. They loaded their field-pieces with bags of bullets, which did great harm among the enemy. About twenty Satsuma men were killed, and the entire list of casualties did not exceed 150. They took a good many prisoners, and captured numbers of guns and small arms.

Tōdō Takayuki's defection was a great help to the imperialists. His men had been fighting against them, but when the emperor's standards, the sun in gold on a red ground and the moon in silver, were displayed, they lost heart and changed sides. Another of their advantages was their good skirmishing. Prince Komatsu Akihito was the commander-in-chief. They anticipated that all the clans as far as Hakone would submit, and that Sendai would join them. Kishū already showed signs of a desire to come to terms, and Ogaki had submitted, as indeed had nearly all the other clans who had fought, with the exception of Aizu. They said that Iwashita Sajiemon, Gotō Shōjirō and Higashikuze Michitomi, the latter one of the five runaway court nobles, would come down to Kobe to communicate the emperor's proclamation to the foreign representatives. It would be the desire of the new government to show perfect impartiality in its relations with foreign states, but as the English had been the good friends of the Kyoto party, they would always be regarded with particularly grateful and amicable feelings.

I remained with Yoshii and Terashima till half-past ten in the evening. They seemed to admit that we had acted within our rights in seizing the steamers, and while I was with them they wrote and despatched long letters to their own people at Osaka, explaining the affair and enclosing our notification. They also wrote up to Kyoto urging that no time should be lost in despatching the emperor's messengers with the announcement to the foreign ministers.

Early on the morning of the 6th Satsuma troops came over from Nishinomiya in large boats, and were landed at Kobe, in accordance with our agreement of the previous day.

Some retainers of Ōmura Sumihoro in Hizen, Watanabe Noboru and Fukuzaka Kōzō, came to inquire about our intentions with regard to their steamer which had been seized, and was now held by the French. The steamer belonged to Uwajima, and was only borrowed by them for this trip. So I gave them copies of our manifesto against Bizen, and another one explaining why the steamers were seized, and they declared themselves quite convinced that we had acted rightly. Our bluejackets, and the Americans and French also, were getting us a bad name by committing all sorts of petty pilfering.

I went to call on Katano, commander of the Chōshū troops, who said that the two Bizen *karō* had gone to Osaka or Kyoto, he did not know which, after the affray on the 4th, the rank and file remaining behind.

On February 7 the emperor's messenger, Higashikuze, accompanied by Iwashita, Terashima and Itō, with a small retinue, arrived at Kobe in a little steamer belonging to Geishū. As soon as I received the note informing me of this, I went over to the chief, on whom devolved the task of seeing his colleagues, and arranging with them the place and hour of meeting.

Apparently they were greatly annoyed, especially the French minister, at finding themselves as it were ignored, and that their English colleague had thus become the channel of communication between the emperor and themselves. They tried to pump him about the contents of the imperial message, but he did not tell them even the little he knew. It having been decided that the interview should take place at the custom house at noon on the following day, I went over to Kobe and informed Iwashita. There had been a report that three hundred Bizen men had entered the town, but I could not find a trace of them. All our marines had been withdrawn on account of the difficulty experienced in forming mixed posts, and the Americans now had charge of the gate in the middle of the town, so that they would henceforth be responsible for all the petty pilfering that went on. I found them most unpleasantly strict, and because I had no pass they obliged me to go a long way round in order to reach my destination and get back again.

So on February 8, the fateful communication was made by Higashikuze at the place and hour previously fixed. Higashikuze was a small man even for a Japanese, with sparkling eyes, irregular teeth, which were not yet completely freed from the black dye (*o-haguro*) worn by court nobles, and with a stutter in his speech. The document was drawn up in classical Chinese, and might be thus translated:

> The emperor of Japan announces to the sovereigns of all foreign countries and to their subjects that permission has been granted to *Shōgun* Tokugawa Yoshinobu to return the governing power in accordance with his own request. We shall henceforward exercise supreme authority in all the internal and external affairs of the country. Consequently the title of emperor must be substituted for that of *shōgun*, in which the treaties have been made. Officers are being appointed by us to the conduct of foreign affairs. It is desirable that the representatives of the treaty powers recognize this announcement.

> February 3, 1868

> Mutsuhito (L.S.)

This document was very ingeniously framed. It assumed as a matter of course that the treaties were binding on the emperor, and therefore only mentioned them incidentally, in saying that the emperor's title must be substituted for that of *shōgun*.

After the translation had been made and shown to all the ministers, a fire of questions was directed against the envoy, who answered them well. Roches asked whether the emperor's authority extended throughout the whole of Japan, to which he replied coolly that the rebellion of Tokugawa prevented that from being the case at present, but that it would gradually extend all over the empire. Roches' interpreter (who was a Tokugawa man) then made a wilful mistake by representing the envoy to say that "if all the people submitted to the emperor, he would be able to govern the country," whereas he really said, "the people will all submit to the emperor as a natural consequence of his taking the reins," as we ascertained on repeating the question. With regard to the Kōbe Incident, the emperor's government undertook to protect the lives and property of foreigners at Kobe for the future, and to satisfy the demands of the foreign representatives for the punishment of Bizen. On these conditions, it was agreed that the marines and bluejackets should be withdrawn to the ships, and the steamers released. Osaka was not as yet perfectly quiet, but normal conditions would soon be restored, and foreigners would be formally invited to return there.

On the part of the emperor's government the envoy desired to know whether the foreign representatives would report the announcement to their governments and proclaim it to their people. This was tantamount to asking for recognition. Roches became very angry, and said: "We must not throw ourselves upon the necks of these people," whereupon the Italian De la Tour and the German Von Brandt raised their voices against him, and replied that so far from doing anything of the sort we had waited till they came to seek us (not knowing, of course, of our secret negotiations at the Satsuma *yashiki* in Osaka). On this, everyone said he would report to his government, and this satisfied the envoy. A great deal of desultory conversation went on while he was waiting for the gunboat to convey him back to Kobe, but on no particularly important topic. Itō said to me that it was all right about our going to Kyoto, that there would be no difficulty. I pretended to be indifferent, though in truth I was very eager to get a view of the city and its famous buildings, from which foreigners had been so jealously excluded for over two centuries.

Next day Higashikuze, at his own request, went to visit *HMS Ocean*.

A joint note was sent in to him demanding reparation for the Kōbe incident, namely a full and ample apology and the capital punishment of the officer who gave the order to fire. The ministers, and especially Roches, insisted that the fact that they were under fire increased the gravity of the offence—as if their presence there could have been known to the Bizen troops passing through on the march. Itō seemed to think that the government would agree to make the Bizen *karō* perform *harakiri*. He said that Chōshū had relinquished to the emperor the territories he had conquered in Kokura (on the south side of the strait of Shimonoseki) and in the province of Iwami. Kido (*i.e.* Katsura) and Itō wanted him to go much farther, and resign to the emperor all his lands, retainers and other possessions, except so much as might be required for the support of his household. If all the *daimyō* would do this, a powerful central government might be formed, which was impossible with the existing system. Japan could not be strong as long as it was open to every *daimyō* to withdraw his assistance at his own pleasure, and each lord to drill his troops after a different fashion. It was the story of the North German Confederation all over again; the petty sovereigns must be swallowed up by some bigger one. The *daimyō* of Matsuyama and Takamatsu in Shikoku, who were partizans of the Tokugawa, would be destroyed, and their territories imperialized. Tosa was charged with the execution of this measure, having offered to undertake the duty. It was probable that Himeji, a few miles west of Kobe, would also be attacked by the imperialists.

A notification, signed by Iwashita, Itō and Terashima, as officers of the Foreign Department, was placarded about the town, informing the people that the emperor would observe the treaties, and enjoining on them proper behaviour towards foreigners. It was given out that Roches, with his interpreter Shioda, would leave that evening for Europe, Baron Brin, the secretary, remaining in charge. The official declaration made the day before by the Kyoto envoy had quite thrown him on his beam-ends, and he could not bear to stand by and see his policy turn out a complete failure. His intention was to proceed first to Yokohama, where I suspected that he would try to rehabilitate his reputation as a diplomatist by some of his artful tricks. However, he thought better of this idea, and remained in Japan until matters shaped themselves so that he could accept the emperor's invitation to Kyoto, and so decently recognize the new political arrangements. The other ministers behaved very correctly, having very little to do but to follow Parkes' lead.

The foreign ministers had another interview on February 10 with Higashikuze, who was accompanied by Iwashita and Gotō. They told us that Itō was to act temporarily as superintendent of customs and governor of the town of Kobe. It seemed curious, we thought, that a man of certainly not very high rank should be thought fit for this double post, and that the common people should be ready to obey him, but the Japanese lower classes, as I noted in my diary, had a great appetite for being governed, and were ready to submit to anyone who claimed authority over them, especially if there appeared to be a military force in the background. Itō had the great recommendation in his favour that he spoke English, a very uncommon Japanese accomplishment in those days, especially in the case of men concerned in the political movement. It would not be difficult, owing to the submissive habits of the people, for foreigners to govern Japan, if they could get rid of the two-sworded class, but the foreigners who were to do the governing should all of them speak, read and write the Japanese language, otherwise they would make a complete failure of their undertaking. But as the samurai were existent in large numbers, the idea was incapable of realization. Looking back now in 1919, it seems perfectly ludicrous that such a notion should have been entertained, even as a joke, for a single moment, by anyone who understood the Japanese spirit.

Gotō was to proceed to Kyoto with the joint note about the Kōbe incident, and there was every reason to expect that the court would agree to the infliction of the capital sentence, but they would probably desire to let the *karō* Hiki Kiyokado perform *harakiri* instead of having him decapitated. At least that was what I heard privately from my Japanese friends, who also asked that, until the question was finally disposed of, foreigners should abstain from visiting Nishinomiya, where Bizen men were stationed. Everything was now reported to be quiet at Osaka, and we looked forward to returning there in a few days.

Gotō Kyūjirō, as he had called himself previously, now resumed his real name of Nakai, and was attached to the Foreign Department. He was a very cheery and gay personality, always ready for any kind of fun and jollity, and when an entertainment had to be got up, it was to him that its organization and conduct were entrusted. In this way he earned the nickname of *gaimushō no taikomochi*, "jester of the Foreign Department."

On February 11, Higashikuze with his staff came to the consulate to talk business with Sir Harry and Von Brandt, a talk which lasted three hours. We exhibited to them all the treaties, conventions and agreements respecting the opening of the ports, all of which had to be confirmed by the chief minister for foreign affairs, Prince Komatsu Akihito, in the name of the emperor. There was much said by way of question and answer about the recent transactions at Kyoto, which ended in their promising to furnish a detailed narrative, rebutting the statements made by Ogasawara Nagamichi and other supporters of the former regime. The general council, which Yoshinobu complained had been violently anticipated by Satsuma, ought to have met on December 15. The western *daimyō* waited a considerable time after this date, but none of the others arrived, so they were compelled to take action.

The demands made on the Bakufu were that, together with the governing power, they should surrender as much territory as would suffice to maintain that power. They estimated that 2,500,000 *koku* of lands would then be left to the Tokugawa family, besides the territories of the *fudai daimyō* and most of the *hatamoto*. Yoshinobu had declined, but offered to surrender 800,000 *koku* of lands, and to continue his subsidy for the support of the imperial establishment. When leaving Kyoto however he had agreed to make the surrender demanded of him, though this was strenuously opposed by Aizu and Kuwana. Then when Echizen and Owari came down to Osaka, they invited him back to Kyoto to conclude these arrangements, but it was never intended that Aizu and Kuwana should form the van of his retinue, and that was how it happened that fighting ensued. At the date of this conversation nearly all the *daimyō* west of Hakone had been reduced, or had given in their adhesion, or would soon be compelled by force to submit to the emperor, and thus about seven out of the eight million *koku* of lands possessed by Tokugawa would be actually in the hands of the emperor. If

Yoshinobu then submitted, he would be left peaceably with the remainder of his possessions. It was feared however that he would endeavour to regain what he had lost, in which case the emperor's party would destroy him. Forces would be dispatched against him by the north-eastern road (which passes through the provinces of Echizen and Kaga), by the central road through Shinshū, and by the Tōkaidō. Ii Naosuke of Hikone and later adherents to the Kyoto party would be placed in the van of the imperial forces, in order that their fidelity might be tested. The *daimyō* of the north had nothing to thank Yoshinobu for, and there was no reason why they should support him. Awa had submitted, and was assisting in garrisoning Kobe. Prisoners taken in Kyoto during the recent fighting would be returned to their homes on the restoration of peace, instead of being put to death according to the ancient Japanese custom in civil war.

We understood that the emperor's party intended to call upon the foreign powers to observe strict neutrality.

A report went about that Nanbu Yahachirō and Shibayama Ryōsuke, old friends of mine in the Satsuma *yashiki* at Edo, had been put to death, the one by crucifixion the other by simple decapitation, and I felt that I should like to do something to avenge them, for to Western minds the idea of taking the lives of prisoners was revolting.

We heard that old Matsudaira Kansō, the retired *daimyō* of Hizen, Mr. Facing-both-ways as he was universally regarded, was expected to make his appearance shortly at Kyoto. Also that the governors of Nagasaki had departed, and that the town was occupied by Satsuma, Geishū and Tosa, Hizen holding the batteries.

The mail that reached us on February 13 brought a letter from Nagamichi to Sir Harry very diplomatically framed, in which Yoshinobu's failure to reach Kyoto was attributed entirely to the machinations of Satsuma, and a hope was expressed that a momentary success on the part of the latter would not cause the violation of engagements of long standing. He entirely dodged the question put to him by Locock, as to the course the chief should take in case the emperor sent an envoy to the foreign representatives. The news came from home that Mukōyama Kōson (while in Europe for the French Exhibition of 1867), had complained at the Foreign Office of Sir

Harry having applied the title of "Highness" to the *shōgun* instead of "Majesty."
To this Lord Stanley had replied that he understood there was a higher title
than that of *denka* in use in Japan, and that consequently *denka* could not
mean "Majesty," which was the highest designation applicable to any
potentate. It was also noteworthy that in this letter of Nagamichi *heika*
(which is synonymous with "Majesty") was reserved for the Queen, *denka*
being used of the *shōgun*. As modern slang would have it, this was giving
away the whole show.

Godai and Terashima came to see me, after which they had a long talk
with the chief on political matters. They told him that in three weeks or a
month's time affairs would have made sufficient progress at Kyoto to enable
the government to invite the foreign representatives in order to enter on
friendly relations. They also asked for the loan of a surgeon to attend to their
wounded at Kyoto. The chief replied that the alleviation of suffering in the
case of any human being was always a pleasure, and that as the legation doctor
had looked after the wounds of Aizu men, no objection could exist to his
treating others. But his consent would depend upon the nature of the reply
the ministers received about the Kōbe incident. The question of the legation
returning to Osaka was mooted, and Buddhist temples were offered for our
accommodation, as the buildings which we had occupied behind the castle
had been too much knocked about to be fit for a residence. This would not
matter much, as they would be occupied only temporarily.

Godai and Terashima were very anxious that I, and I alone, should visit
Osaka at once. (In fact I believed I could have gone anywhere I liked, for
instance to Kyoto the next day, by only expressing a wish.) Godai wanted
to buy an English man-of-war with which to attack Edo. It was a curious
notion that we had H.M. ships for sale. I advised them to get their note
demanding neutrality on the part of all foreign powers sent in at once,
because then they could request the American minister to prevent the
Stonewall Jackson being delivered to the Tokugawa people, as well as the two
iron-clads from France which were expected. Godai said further that Uesugi
and Satake, two *daimyō* from Dewa province, had asked to have the duty of
chastising Aizu entrusted to them, and their request had been granted.

Next day they brought notes from Higashikuze enclosing copy of the
instructions he had received from Date Munenari (Uwajima) and Sanjō

Sanetomi (one of the fugitive court nobles) accepting on behalf of the emperor's government the terms of settlement of the Kōbe incident laid down by the foreign representatives, namely the capital punishment of the officer who had given the order to fire on foreigners and the apology.

The ministers expressed themselves gratified with the promptness of the reply, which was received twenty-four hours before the expiration of the delay accorded. They said they would wait three or four days for the letters of apology and for the announcement of detailed arrangements for carrying out the execution. Godai and Terashima stated that if Bizen were to refuse to surrender the officer, the emperor's troops would compel obedience. They also brought a note from Prince Komatsu Akihito, ratifying the treaties and all subsequent engagements in the name of the emperor, and notifying his own appointment as chief administrator of foreign affairs, with Date, Sanjō and Higashikuze as his assistants. There was also a note demanding strict neutrality on the part of the British government and its subjects, and a like note to each of the other representatives. Facsimiles of the emperor's notification to the treaty powers were also handed to those ministers who had not yet received it. The request for Willis to go to Kyoto to treat the wounded was repeated and granted, and a proposal made by myself to accompany him was accepted with alacrity.

News was received that day from Nagasaki that the withdrawal of the governor Kawazu Sukekuni had been quietly effected on the night of the seventh, and a provisional government formed on the following day of all the *daimyō*'s agents in the port, thirteen clans in all. The direction of local affairs had been offered by the governor to Hizen and Chikuzen, but they declined to undertake such a responsibility without the cooperation of the other clans. All the subordinate custom house officials and interpreters, as well as five hundred troops raised at Nagasaki for defensive purposes, were taken over by the provisional government, so that the business of the port had not been interrupted for a single day. A few fires broke out, but were soon extinguished.

First Visit to Kyoto

The next day was taken up with our preparations for Kyoto, including the purchase of sufficient stores for a fortnight. Saionji Yukie of Uwajima called, and I offered him a passage to Osaka in the gunboat that was to convey Willis and myself to the starting-point of our journey. A Satsuma man named Ōyama Iwao, whom I had known in Edo, came to announce himself as commander of our escort. That European surgical skill was very necessary for the treatment of the wounded can be seen from the fact I find recorded in one of my letters home, that the Japanese surgeons had sewn up all the gunshot wounds, and some of their patients died from this cause. The prospect of visiting the city from which foreigners had been rigidly excluded ever since the ports were opened in 1859 was enticing, especially as we were now being invited by the very people who, we were told by the *shōgun*'s officials, had all along tried to keep us out.

Sir Harry was in high spirits and in very good temper. We had no more of the interviews with Japanese officials at which he used strong language, and interpreting for him, which used to be a painful duty, was changed into a labour of love. Success makes a man kind, and certainly Sir Harry had been successful. By the departure of the French minister he became the doyen of the diplomatic body, and the rest of his colleagues followed his lead with perfect unanimity, for they had begun to see that his policy was the right one to adopt. It was his influence that induced his colleagues to join him in issuing declarations of neutrality in the conflict between the emperor and the *shōgun*, which among other things prevented the delivery to the latter of the American iron-clad ram *Stonewall Jackson*, bought with

Japanese money. These declarations were subsequent to the departure of Roches to Yokohama, and while his secretary Baron Leon Jules Brin was in charge of the French legation.

We started about nine o'clock in the morning of February 16 on board the gunboat *Cockchafer*, having in our train Noguchi, a boy-pupil named Tetsu, one of my Japanese escort named Matsushita, and Willis' servant the faithful Sahei. Off the Osaka bar we found the Satsuma steamer *Keangsoo* and another engaged in disembarking a large body of troops. On landing at the city we found lodgings had been taken for us at a Buddhist temple close to a burnt Satsuma *yashiki* called Takamatsu. No sooner had we seated ourselves than a messenger arrived, in the person of Koba Dennai's secretary, to ask us to stop two or three days in Osaka so that Willis might see some men who were ill of fever, and to say that boats to convey us up the river were not obtainable. We replied that Willis had not made any preparations for treating fever patients, and had brought appliances for wounds only, that we supposed boats were as numerous at Osaka as they had been before the recent fighting up-river, and that we could not understand this delay, after we had been so urged and hurried by Iwashita and Terashima, who had wished us to start even a day earlier than we had found possible. So the secretary went out, and Yasuke after him. They stayed away a whole hour, and we came to the conclusion that the permission to bring us into Kyoto had been revoked, resolving to return to Kobe rather than waste our time at Osaka.

At four o'clock Ōyama returned, bringing with him an old, ugly, misshapen fellow named Ijichi Shōji, who appeared to be one of the Satsuma generals. After bestowing on us a vast quantity of complimentary phrases, this individual brought out in a jerky St Vitus' dance sort of way the same sort of excuses as had been made by Koba's secretary. To this we returned the same answer as before, with the addition that if they found it inconvenient to receive us in Kyoto, we would go back at once to Kobe. This decided attitude induced Ijichi to give orders at once for boats to be got ready, and we then went off to see the ruins of Osaka castle. There was a notice at the front gate refusing entrance to any but Satsuma and Chōshū men, but as we had one of the former clan with us we found no difficulty in gaining access.

Passing through the gate we came upon a wide scene of desolation. The white-plastered towers and wall of the inner moat were gone; all the barracks and towers of the outer wall to the south likewise; only the stones of the gateway to the right remained. We passed into the *hommaru*, or keep, through the gateway constructed with huge blocks of stone, the largest measuring forty-two by sixteen feet and thirty-five by eighteen feet. Nothing was left but the masonry, giving somewhat of the look of the ancient Greek Cyclopean walls of Tiryns. The magnificent palace itself had disappeared. All that there was to show where it had once stood was a level surface covered with half-calcined tiles. The way to the foundation tower of the *tenshi* remained clear, and we mounted to the summit. Here in the exfoliation of the stones were traces of a former conflagration. A plaster wall built right round had escaped not only the flames, but also the explosion of the great magazine close underneath. Four doors in this wall gave on to the outer parapet, from which the view of the river, with its three great bridges, winding through the city to the sea, and the hills on the further side of the bay surpassed anything I had ever seen. In the opposite direction the stream could be distinguished here and there as it meandered through the fields down from Fushimi.

The interior of the castle had been completely destroyed, with the exception of a few rows of storehouses, which had escaped through being situated to windward of the flames. The three concentric walls of masonry, including the one from which we looked, reminded one of the appearance that West's Tower of Babel would have presented if viewed from above. We sounded the well, whence is drawn the famous *ōgonsui*, or golden water, and found the depth to be 140 feet. Issuing again from the gate at the base of the *tenshi*, we came upon a quantity of burnt armour and helmets piled up round a storehouse which the flames had spared. Some had been melted by the violent heat into an irregular mass of metal. There were also piles of thousands of matchlock barrels, with a few rifles among them. Curious to see what had become of our temporary legation buildings, we took our way out of the ruined Tamatsukuri gate. The whole place, excepting the houses that had been occupied by Mitford and myself, was level with the ground, and even they had been gutted so completely by the rabble as to be quite beyond the possibility of repair. It was a melancholy sight.

On returning to our lodging we found Godai, who with many profuse apologies conducted us to a house close by which was better fitted for inhabitation by human beings. He explained that we could not start for Kyoto before the following morning. From what he said it appeared that delay in issuing the permission from the imperial court for our entrance into Kyoto was caused by Prince Komatsu Akihito's having unexpectedly gone there himself, but as he, Godai, had at once despatched a messenger, the pass would be received at Fushimi the next evening before our arrival there. This arrangement being accepted by us, *sake* and its accompaniments were ordered in, and half-a-dozen singing girls attended to help us pass away the time.

February 17, 1868, at ten o'clock in the morning, saw us start in a houseboat from the stairs below the burnt Satsuma *yashiki*. The party, seven in number, included our merry friend Ōyama, and another officer in command of a guard for our protection. Although we had only just breakfasted, *sake* and various dishes were soon introduced, and the entertainment was repeated all through the day at short intervals. It was a fine morning, and the scenery was as beautiful as on the previous occasion in May, when Willis, Wirgman and I had made the same journey.

Conversation naturally turned for the most part on the incidents of the recent fighting. The Tokugawa forces had been pressing all day along the Toba road until four o'clock, when they made an attempt to force the Satsuma position. The attack was met by a steady fire from a field-piece planted in the middle of the path (for the so-called road was very little wider), and from three others in position on the left, while troops concealed in the brushwood opened on them with musketry. This unexpected reception threw the Tokugawa men into confusion, and they retired precipitately leaving numbers of dead and wounded on the ground. The imperialists at Fushimi, on hearing the sound of firing in the direction of Toba, from which place they were about a mile distant, attacked the *shōgun*'s troops as they formed outside the governor's residence, and the fighting lasted till the middle of the night. The officers on the *shōgun*'s side set the example of flight, and their men could not resist the temptation, so that the rout became general. After Yodo was passed no more fighting occurred on the road to Osaka. At Hirakata the drilled infantry broke into the storehouses of the townspeople who had run away, and disguised themselves in the finest garments they could find. Other townspeople pursued the marauders and killed six of them.

We passed Hirakata at four, but did not reach our hotel at Fushimi till midnight. Tōdō was holding his old post at Yamazaki, and Kaga occupied Hashimoto. Dear old Yoshii was at our hotel to welcome us, and more respectably dressed and shaven than I had seen him for a long time past. A fresh supply of *sake* was produced, and we kept up the conversation till past two in the morning. These late hours did not prevent our being ready to start at ten o'clock, escorted by a company of eighty-eight men. Large palanquins of the sort called *kiribō kago*, that is "with a Paulownia-wood pole," used by personages of the highest rank, had been provided for us, but Willis, who was six feet three inches tall and big in proportion, was not able to double himself up inside, and preferred to walk. The route lay through Fushimi for some way, issuing on to the Takeda road, fifteen feet wide, then ascended to the top of a dyke constructed to keep the river within bounds, crossed a bridge and so into the city of Kyoto. At a temple by the roadside we fell in with Komatsu, who had followed us from Fushimi, and by one o'clock we arrived at Sōkoku-*ji*, a Buddhist temple close to the Satsuma *yashiki* at the back of the imperial palace.

Shimazu Tadayoshi, the lord of Satsuma, paid us a visit of welcome, accompanied by his confidential adviser Saigō. After shaking hands with us both, he sat down in a chair placed at the end of the table by the door, while we occupied chairs behind the table in a position of greater dignity. All his attendants squatted on the floor. After the exchange of a few complimentary speeches he took his leave, and we accompanied him as far as the door.

The grounds of Sōkoku-*ji* were extensive, and well planted with trees, the temple itself a fine example of wood architecture, the state apartments divided off by splendid gold paper screens decorated with landscapes in Indian ink, the coffered ceilings fifteen feet above the floor. To suit the convenience of us Westerners a table and chairs had been provided, and a luxurious feast was served immediately after the lord had taken his leave.

In the afternoon Willis went to look after the wounded, while I took a walk down to the bookshops in Sanjō-*dōri*, accompanied by an escort. It was not until I reached this point that the populace seemed to be certain that I was a foreigner. One little boy asked whether I were not a native of the Ryūkyū Islands. The Tokugawa Castle of Nijō struck me as insignificant compared with many a fortress belonging to a small *fudai daimyō*. It was then occupied by the troops of Owari. The *yashiki*, which had been the headquarters of Aizu as military governor of Kyoto, was tenanted by a few of Tosa's troops. The men who had accompanied me about the city took the liberty of sitting down with us to dinner and showed great want of good manners. It was evident that they took a departure from the polite social observances characteristic of the Japanese to be an evidence of what was held to be civilization, in their own words *hiraketa*.

Next day I went to ask Saigō about the settlement of the Kōbe incident. He replied that Hiki Kiyokado, the *karō* who was riding in the palanquin, could not be regarded as free from blame, and that he would be imprisoned in the charge of three clans. The officer who had been riding on horseback would be executed. The emperor's inspectors (*kenshi*) would attend, the sentence would be pronounced, and a copy would be furnished to the foreign representatives. Afterwards the sentence and an account of the proceedings would be circulated throughout the country for the information and warning of others.

Saigō said the emperor's government hoped to keep the whole of Japan in order, so as to prevent the necessity ever arising for foreigners to take the law into their own hands. I said that this view was shared by Sir Harry; that in regard of the Kōbe incident he had felt confident that an envoy would be sent from the emperor, and he had therefore resisted the solicitations of those around him, who had urged that a force should be despatched against the Bizen people at Nishinomiya; he preferred to leave the opportunity open to the emperor. Saigō also explained the reference in the emperor's proclamation regarding the observation of the treaties, to the "reform of abuses," to mean that the new government would propose a revision of those agreements. I mentioned three points on which changes were desirable. Firstly, the residence of the foreign ministers being fixed at Edo (for it was naturally supposed that the government of the country would in future be conducted from Kyoto). Secondly, the confinement of foreigners to a radius of ten *ri* (245 miles) round treaty ports. And thirdly, the circulation of all foreign coin throughout the country. While abolishing the ten *ri* limit, it should be made obligatory on a person travelling about the country to carry a passport signed either by the minister or the consul, and countersigned by the governor of the port from which he set out. This last proposal was in fact one made by the Japanese themselves.

In the afternoon we went to return the call of the lord of Satsuma. As during his visit yesterday, he scarcely opened his lips. But Willis said that he had treated Sir Harry in the same way when he went to Kagoshima in 1866, and that it was supposed he was advised by his councillors not to talk, lest he should make a fool of himself. It was a probable though not very charitable explanation. We spent the afternoon in exploring the city, which had been little more than half rebuilt after it was burnt in 1864 in the Chōshū attack on the palace.

Next day I went with Yoshii to call on Gotō, to whom I spoke about the Kōbe incident. He told me pretty much the same thing as Saigō, but less decisively. He talked of executing the man who used his spear before the firing began. Then he discussed the new constitution, and said he despaired of getting a deliberative assembly, because the majority would always be stupid and wrong-headed. I advised him to make the experiment nevertheless; if the members ran their heads against a block of stone, they would learn reason from the blow. He seemed to favour the idea of governing by a *junta* composed of the prime minister and the cleverest men in the country, in default of one man of heroic mould, who should rule autocratically. Of course he included himself among "the cleverest men" (*jinketsu*).

During this part of our conversation Gotō had excluded Yoshii, as well as Saionji of Uwajima, who happened to be calling on him, and Yoshii expressed his annoyance to me afterwards at having been treated with so little confidence. I pacified him by saying that we had been discussing the settlement of the Kōbe incident. After these two were admitted some general conversation ensued among them, from which I gathered that it was by no means decided as yet who was to be what, and that the chief men of the different clans found it difficult to manage each other, that mutual jealousy, and especially jealousy of Satsuma, prevented their pulling together. I gave them a hint to use in revising the treaties, namely, the establishment of mixed courts for trying cases between foreigners and Japanese, instead of deciding them according to the laws of the defendant's nationality.

I also called on Kido (Katsura), but we did not meet till the next day, when he came to our lodging in company with a Chōshū naval captain named Shinagawa, who for some time past had been living in Kyoto as a Satsuma man. Yoshii also turned up, but the conversation flagged until Willis came back from the hospital, and during lunch a heated argument arose as to the best way of preventing affrays from happening between Japanese and foreigners. Kido and I had previously agreed that the Japanese government should discuss the procedure with the foreign representatives; foreigners should be informed that to break through a procession is an offence in Japanese eyes, and Japanese on the other hand should be taught that they must not use weapons, but simply arrest offenders and hand them over to their own authorities. And that, when a *daimyō's* train was to pass along a thoroughfare, constables from a mixed force of Westerners and Japanese should be stationed to keep the road clear.

Willis dissented from this view, and maintained that the only way to preserve the peace between foreign rowdies and Japanese bullies was to keep them apart, and to carry the high road round at the back outside Kobe. My argument against this, in which Kido concurred, was that a change of road would give rise to a great deal more ill-will between the opposite nationalities than the murder of a few foreigners, and that from what we had hitherto seen in this country a little fighting would open the eyes of the Japanese and make us all better friends than before. We held it was better to apply caustic at once than to let the disease linger on and attempt to cure each symptom as it presented itself. We did not settle the question, but I noted down what precedes as being a Japanese view.

In the evening I went to call on Ōkubo Toshimichi, a Satsuma *karō*, who was one of the councillors of the Home Department. Last year he and I had sent presents to each other but had never met, so I wished to make his acquaintance. Instead of merely exchanging formalities, we had some interesting conversation. He said that seven thousand infantry were being sent to Hakone, and five thousand to a pass on the Nakasendō. Satsuma and Chōshū were determined to prosecute the war, and perfect unanimity prevailed among the *sanyo* (councillors). Even Echizen and Higo, who at first

317

had been opposed to the use of force, were now working hand-in-hand with the other clans. The *daimyō* of Ogaki, who was a councillor of the Finance Department, until recently an adherent of the Tokugawa, had expressed his hope that the expedition against Edo would soon be sent on its way. Probably the emperor would accompany the army in person, a step which would greatly weaken the rebels. He thought that the return of Roches to France would have the effect of determining the *shōgun* to submit, as he would have no one to rely on for material assistance. If he submitted, his life might be spared, but the lords of Aizu and Kuwana must lose their heads.

At Osaka the discovery had been made of the diary kept by a confidential adviser of Yoshinobu's, in which the false hopes that had given rise to the expedition against Kyoto at the end of last month were plainly expressed. It said the other clans were getting tired of Satsuma, and that even Chōshū was divided into two parties, one for war the other for peace. It said that Gotō Shōjirō was inclined towards making terms with the *shōgun*, and that the court desired to see him back in Kyoto. But, said Ōkubo, Yoshinobu was in too much of a hurry, and now the whole situation had completely changed; those who previously had wavered were now convinced of the Bakufu's weakness, and were eager to be first in striking a blow at the Tokugawa.

At Ōkubo's request I explained to him as well as I could the working of our executive government in combination with the parliamentary system, the existence of political parties and the election of members of the lower house. The Kōbe incident he said was pretty well settled, and his account agreed in the main with what Saigō and Gotō had told me. Next day however there arrived a very peevish letter from the chief, complaining that the Kōbe incident did not appear to be nearing a settlement, that sufficient preparations had not been made at Osaka for the reception of the foreign representatives, that he doubted whether he would ever go there at all, and winding up by ordering Willis and myself to rejoin him by the 24th at the latest. This gave me one day more at Kyoto, but it considerably upset Willis' arrangements, as he had calculated on a fortnight's stay. Ōkubo having called to return my visit, and Yoshii also, I took the opportunity of urging on them the necessity of settling the incident at once. They replied that they did not belong to the department concerned, but undertook to see Gotō and

Higashikuze, and repeat to them what I had said. I had to go, but left Willis to await further orders.

On February 23, Saigō came to say good-bye to me, and gave me two large rolls of red and white crape and two of gold brocade. He said there was no possibility of my carrying back the final decision of the Kōbe incident. When he was gone, Yoshii came in. He told me Sir Harry perfectly well understood the cause of the delay, and had consented to wait a week. A letter had gone from Higashikuze to him, which had probably crossed his to me. The final decision would probably be made on the morrow or the day after. Date Munenari (Uwajima) and Gotō would go down next day to Osaka, and Higashikuze would follow with the sentences of the Bizen men as soon as they were made out. Both Saigō and Yoshii begged that Willis would stay five or six days longer.

The war news was that the town and territory of Kuwana had submitted to the imperial messenger, but the retainers replied that they could not undertake for their lord, who was in Edo, having accompanied Yoshinobu thither. Everyone in Kyoto hoped that the Edo people would resist instead of peaceably submitting, for the western men were all "spoiling for a fight."

At three o'clock in the afternoon I therefore set out alone. It took me a long time to get through the city to the Gojō bridge, as I completed my sight-seeing as I went, and I did not reach Fushimi till dark. There I found Ōyama's elder brother, who was Satsuma agent (*rusui*), and from words dropped by Notsu, the captain of my escort, I learned that the orders to march on Edo were expected to be issued in a day or two. At nine o'clock we embarked for Osaka in a fifty *koku* flat-bottomed boat, long and narrow, with a roofing of coarse straw mats supported by rafters resting on a pole laid from one end of the boat to the other, horribly uncomfortable, and especially so when crowded. We got to our destination at 6.30 next morning, and I crossed to Kobe in the gunboat. Notsu said that in the recent fighting the heads of all the wounded who could not escape had been taken off, a proceeding hardly reconcilable with what we had been told about the resolution to spare the lives of prisoners, unless it was done to put them out of their misery.

The next entry in my journal is of February 29, 1868, when Date came over from Osaka. On arriving he went to the consulate by invitation from the chief to have lunch, and began to talk about the foreign representatives being presented to the emperor, who was to be brought down to Osaka, perhaps by March 13. We had to stop this interesting communication in order that he might go to call on the other ministers. In the evening I went to see him, when he told me Roches had asked to see Saigō, Ōkubo, Komatsu and Gotō, as he understood they were the leaders of the Kyoto movement; this had greatly annoyed the dear old man, who resented being ignored in that fashion, and said he hated Roches and his interpreter. Roches had sent word to say he would call next morning, and it was with difficulty that I persuaded him to receive the visit, instead of going on board HMS *Ocean* on Sir Harry's invitation. Inoue Bunda, whom I saw that day, told me the French consul at Nagasaki had refused to pay duties to the provisional government and had threatened war, especially against Satsuma and Chōshū. We had a good laugh over this exhibition of impotent wrath.

Harakiri

Next day, March 1, 1868, Date introduced to the foreign representatives Sawa Nobuyoshi, one of the five fugitive court nobles of 1864, who was proceeding to Nagasaki as governor, together with Ōmura Sumihoro, the *daimyō* of Ōmura, who was to furnish his guard. Sawa wore rather a forbidding expression of countenance, not to say slightly villainous, but for all that had the look of a good companion, and a year or two later, when he was minister for foreign affairs, we liked him greatly. Omura Tango no Kami, to give him his full title, was a weak, sickly looking man, who did not utter a word during the interview, and seemed even afraid of speaking to a foreigner. Sawa's son, a dissipated-looking young man, with the white complexion of a woman, was also present.

After the compliments were over, these three were turned out of the room, and we learned that the Kōbe incident would be wound up by the decapitation of the responsible officer. Early that morning the chief had been asking my opinion about the advisability of granting a reprieve, or rather a mitigation of the penalty. Mitford learned from von Brandt that the colleagues knew him to have leanings that way, and that he was believed to have put forward Dirk de Graeff Polsbroek, the Dutch political agent, to advocate clemency. Mitford and I had however agreed previously that lenience would be a mistake, and that was the view I maintained in reply to Sir Harry.

Date and Sawa came to dinner that evening with the chief, an arrangement which he fancied he had kept secret from his colleagues, but they knew of it as soon as the invitation was accepted. Afterwards there was a long conversation that lasted until midnight, a principal topic being the proposed

visit of the emperor to Osaka. Date said the object of the excursion was
to open the mind of the young sovereign by showing him something of the
outer world, and also a big English man-of-war. Of course, he added, if the
foreign diplomats were there at the time, they might be presented. Parkes
said the emperor might receive the diplomatic body as a whole, but not
each minister separately, his object being to secure priority of presentation
for himself, as he had already written home for new credentials. Date
suggested that the capital might possibly be moved from its present position
to Osaka, as it was situated at a spot hemmed in by mountains, to which
all supplies had to be transported by water. My own belief was that Satsuma
and Chōshū wanted to get the person of the emperor into their own hands
in order to make him march with the army, and secondly to have him on
the seacoast in order to be able to cut and run whenever it might become
necessary. This was confirmed by the fact that the emperor had issued an
order announcing that he was taking the field in person. In reply to a
question as to the fate of the ex-*shōgun*, Date said it would depend on circumstances, which no one could foretell. The people of Osaka, aware of
the anti-foreign policy of the late emperor and the former political opinions
of Chōshū, supposed that since the court and Chōshū had come into power,
foreigners would be generally obnoxious, not any longer having the
Tokugawa power to defend them. It was the reason of the populace having
wrecked the various legations. Perhaps the Bizen people had been driven
by the same notions. This last suggestion furnished an additional ground
for our refusing to reduce the capital sentence.

By this time Roches had come back to Kobe. This to the great annoyance
of his colleagues, who believed he had played a trick on them in leaving his
secretary here as chargé d'affaires in order that he might not be
unrepresented while he played the part of French minister in Edo.

It did not cause us, that is Mitford and myself, much surprise when in
the afternoon of the next day Godai and Itō came to ask for the life of Taki
Zenzaburō, the retainer of Hiki Kiyokado, who had been condemned to
perform *harakiri* as the penalty for ordering his soldiers to fire on foreigners.
A long discussion took place between the foreign ministers that lasted for
nearly three hours, in which Sir Harry voted for clemency, but the majority
were for the sentence being carried out.

It was half-past eight o'clock in the evening when Godai and Itō were called back into the room and told in a few words that there was no way but to let the law take its course. So we started at nine o'clock, Mitford and myself, with a single representative of each of the other legations. We were guided to the Buddhist temple of Seifuku-*ji* at Kobe, arriving there at a quarter to ten. Strong guards were posted in the courtyard and in the ante-chambers. We were shown into a room, where we had to squat on the matted floor for about three-quarters of an hour. During this interval we were asked whether we had any questions to put to the condemned man, and also for a list of our names. At half-past ten we were conducted into the principal hall of the temple, and asked to sit down on the right hand side of the dais in front of the altar. Then the seven Japanese witnesses, Itō, Nakashima Sakutarō, two Satsuma captains of infantry, two Chōshū captains, and a Bizen *ōmetsuke* took their places.

After we had sat quietly thus for about ten minutes footsteps were heard approaching along the verandah. The condemned man, a tall Japanese of gentleman-like bearing and aspect, entered on the left side, accompanied by his *kaishaku* or best man, and followed by two others, apparently holding the same office. Taki was dressed in blue *kamishimo* of hempen cloth; the *kaishaku* wore war surcoats (*jinbaori*). Coming before the Japanese witnesses they prostrated themselves, the bow being returned, and then the same ceremony was exchanged with us.

Then the condemned man was led to a red sheet of felt-cloth laid on the dais before the altar. On this he squatted, after performing two bows, one at a distance, the other close to the altar. With the calmest deliberation he took his seat on the red felt, choosing a position that would afford him the greatest convenience for falling forward. A man dressed in black with a light grey hempen mantle then brought in the dirk wrapped in paper on a small unpainted wooden stand, and with a bow placed it in front of him. He took it up in both hands, raised it to his forehead and laid it down again with a bow. This is the ordinary Japanese gesture of thankful reception of a gift.

Then in a distinct voice, very much broken, not by fear or emotion, but as it seemed reluctance to acknowledge an act of which he was ashamed— declared that he alone was the person who on the fourth of February had outrageously at Kobe ordered fire to be opened on foreigners as they were trying to escape, that for having committed this offence he was going to rip up his bowels, and requested all present to be witnesses.

He next divested himself of his upper garments by withdrawing his arms from the sleeves, the long ends of which he tucked under his legs to prevent his body from falling backward. The body was thus quite naked to below the navel. He then took the dirk in his right hand, grasping it just close to the point, and after stroking down the front of his chest and belly inserted the point as far down as possible and drew it across to the right side, the position of his clothes still fastened by the girth preventing our seeing the wound. Having done this he with great deliberation bent his body forward, throwing the head back so as to render the neck a fair object for the sword.

The one *kaishaku* who had accompanied him round the two rows of witnesses to make his bows to them, had been crouching on his left hand a little behind him with drawn sword poised in the air from the moment the operation commenced. He now sprang up suddenly and delivered a blow the sound of which was like thunder. The head dropped down on to the matted floor, and the body lurching forward fell prostrate over it, the blood from the arteries pouring out and forming a pool.

When the blood vessels had spent themselves all was over. The little wooden stand and the dirk were removed. Itō came forward with a bow, asking had we been witnesses. We replied that we had. He was followed by Nakashima, who also made a bow. A few minutes elapsed, and we were asked were we ready to leave. We rose and went out, passing in front of the corpse and through the Japanese witnesses. It was twelve o'clock when we got back to the consulate, where we found Sir Harry waiting up to receive our report.

The newspaper reports which reached England of this execution, and of the subsequent execution by *harakiri* of eleven Tosa men at Sakai gave a very distorted view of the facts. Charles Rickerby, the owner and editor of the *Japan Times* of Yokohama, was responsible for the attempts to mislead public opinion in both instances. He invented an account of the proceedings witnessed by Mitford and myself that was entirely false, and wound up by saying it was disgraceful for Christians to have attended the execution, and that he hoped the Japanese, if they took revenge for this "judicial murder" would assassinate gentlemen of the foreign legations rather than anyone else.

As for being ashamed of having been present at a *harakiri* on the ground that it was a disgusting exhibition, I was proud to feel that I had not shrunk from witnessing a punishment which I did my best to bring about. It was no disgusting exhibition, but a most decent and decorous ceremony, and far more respectable than what our own countrymen were in the habit of producing for the entertainment of the public in the front of Newgate prison. The countrymen of this Bizen man told us that they considered the sentence a just and beneficial one. As regards the case of the Tosa men at Sakai, no punishment was ever more righteously inflicted. These Japanese massacred a boat's crew of inoffensive and unarmed men, who were never alleged to have given the slightest provocation. Twenty were condemned to death, and one could only regret that Captain Abel-Nicolas Bergasse Dupetit Thouars judged it necessary to stop the execution when eleven had suffered, for the twenty were all equally guilty, and requiring a life for life of the eleven Frenchmen looked more like revenge than justice.

A few days afterwards all the ministers returned to Osaka. We went over on board HMS *Ocean*, Captain Stanhope. She was an iron-clad, of 4000 tons, carrying twenty-six muzzle-loading rifled guns of the Woolwich pattern, enough to blow any vessel on the station into tiny fragments. With us went Date and Polsbroek, and the transport *Adventure* conveyed our baggage. Our former temporary residence having been destroyed by fire, we were accommodated at temples in Nakadera-machi, and were fortunate enough to light upon some of the furniture stolen by the mob after we decamped in January. The townspeople recognized us as "the foreigners who ran away the other day," but they were very civil, and did not shout after us as they rudely did in the last days of the ex-*shōgun*'s occupation of the city. From Edo we heard reports that the feeling among Tokugawa people was that he should be compelled to perform *harakiri* and that his principal advisers should be beheaded, in order to appease the imperialists. It was difficult not to feel a certain degree of sympathy for him, mingled with resentment, for he had let us believe he would fight at Osaka, while he had made up his mind to beat a retreat. If he had told us the truth we could have remained there tranquilly, for we were well assured of the friendliness of Satsuma and Chōshū.

The *Ocean's* steam launch landed us at the foreign settlement, and we marched through the city with our guard to our new quarters. There had been a great deal of talk about the emperor being brought down to Osaka to see some steamers and to meet the foreign ministers, but I hoped this would not happen. If we were to have an audience of His Majesty, we ought to have it at Kyoto, otherwise the ceremony would lose half its significance.

In the afternoon Date Munenari and Komatsu Kiyokado paid friendly visits to Sir Harry. It was evident that we were in a fair way to regain the diplomatic ascendancy of which we had been deprived by the recall of Sir Rutherford Alcock in 1864. When Date and Higashikuze called next day on the foreign representatives they came to us last of all, which was convenient. Sir Harry spoke to them about the proposed audience of the emperor. They acknowledged the advantages that would result from its taking place at Kyoto instead of at Osaka, but were evidently not prepared to promise that immediately. The American, Prussian and Italian representatives had told Date that they wished to leave in three days' time. This caused some consternation in the minds of the Japanese, who desired to keep them for the audience, while they fully appreciated what the chief told them, namely that the three representatives who wanted to get away would not stop for an audience that was to be merely incidental to the emperor's visit to some Japanese steamers. It would be unsuitable to the dignity of the representatives to be presented to His Majesty while at Osaka on a visit made ostensibly for a different purpose. I myself greatly hoped that the way in which the chief had put the matter would induce the Japanese to invite the ministers at once to Kyoto. That would be the consummation of the imperialist theory and scheme. Von Brandt had said privately that he would not accept even if asked, but publicly had said he would, while the American minister was apparently of the same mind. Sir Harry had proposed that the emperor should receive the whole diplomatic body together, on one day, and not accord separate audiences until they could present credentials, and this suggestion had been readily adopted.

On March 7, 1868, an important conference was held between the foreign representatives and high Japanese functionaries, Date, Higashikuze, Daigo Dainagon a court noble appointed governor of Osaka, and *karō* of Owari,

Echizen, Satsuma, Chōshū, Tosa, Geishū, Hizen, Higo and Inshū, practically all the great territorial nobles of the west. It is a remarkable fact that the lords of Echizen, Bizen and Inshū, now ranged among the enemies of the Tokugawa, were descended from the founder of that house. The conference took place in the vast hall of the Buddhist temple of the Nishi Hongan-*ji*.

The Japanese ministers expressed their good wishes for the extension of friendly intercourse between Japan and foreign countries, and declared that the *daimyō* there represented heartily supported the foreign policy of the emperor. Then discussions arose about the ministers going up to Kyoto for an audience of the emperor, about exchange of foreign coin for Japanese and the sale of land in the foreign settlements at Osaka and Kobe. We were told that letters were expected from Kyoto in a day or two fixing a date for the audience, so that the ministers could go up one day, see the emperor on the next, and come down again, thus being absent only three days from Osaka. Roches was of course deadly opposed to accepting any such arrangement. Van Valkenburg the American, von Brandt and de la Tour the Italian seemed unwilling to commit themselves too deeply with the imperialists. The chief tried hard to conceal his determination to accept the invitation in any case, while Polsbroek put on an appearance of indifference. Roches attempted to get an unconditional refusal conveyed to the Japanese ministers, but was unsuccessful thanks to the watch I kept over his interpreter Shioda, and finally the decision was left to depend on the contents of the letters expected from Kyoto. Yamauchi Yōdō, the older lord of Tosa, was reported to be very ill at Kyoto, and the services of Willis were asked for on his behalf. This request was readily acceded to by the chief, and Willis started the same evening accompanied by Mitford.

My personal relations with the Awa clan had long been of an intimate character, and it was therefore no surprise when Hayamizu Sukeyomon, formerly Awa agent at Edo and now at Osaka, came to call on me on March 8, bringing a present of silk for Major Crossman in return for the treatises on artillery the latter had sent to Kaishū. It was with great regret that I learned from him of the death of that friendly and hospitable old gentleman on January 30. His son and successor, who had been kept at home till the period of mourning expired, was now expected at Osaka on his way to Kyoto. Hayamizu brought a budget of Edo news that proved afterwards to be little better than mere gossip, such as that Itakura was reported to have committed suicide by *harakiri* because the other ministers of state differed from him in opinion; that the *fudai daimyō* and *hatamoto* talked of compelling Yoshinobu to disembowel himself; of cutting off the heads of Aizu and Kuwana in order that those two families might escape destruction. He had not heard of Yoshinobu being allowed to retire into private life (*inkyo*), and thought it absurd to suggest such a step under existing circumstances. His conduct had been too shabby for him to become entitled to such consideration.

On February 10, 1868, Hori Naotora, one of the Second Council, had performed *harakiri*, after having vainly endeavoured to persuade Yoshinobu to take that step, and offering to accompany him in the act. All Edo applauded Naotora and said Yoshinobu ought to follow his example. The Bakufu, said my friend, had no desire to fight. The Awa clan was now supporting the emperor and was taking part in the expedition to subjugate the Tokugawa, and would like to make a declaration to the foreign representatives such as was made by the other clans on the previous day.

In the afternoon I went to Date to inquire whether he had any news from Kyoto about the invitation of the ministers. He said they would be asked to start on the 11th, but the date of the audience not having been fixed, the invitations could not be sent out. I advised him to go at once to invite each of the ministers and to say that the day after their arrival in Kyoto would be appointed for the audience. He and Higashikuze, after all, had written asking for that arrangement to be made, and therefore no doubt existed that it would eventually be done. So off he started, beginning with the French minister, who kept him to dinner, but declined going to Kyoto until he could perceive actual evidence of the emperor's supremacy. He was answered that even were the Bakufu restored with all its original powers, the emperor being undoubtedly the sovereign of Japan, and the *shōgun* only his vicegerent, no offence could possibly be given by being received in audience by the former. From him Date went to the Italian, Prussian, American and Dutch representatives. The first three refused on the ground of pressing business at Yokohama, but the last said he would act in the same way as the British minister. And when Munenari came to our chief, he accepted the invitation.

Massacre of French Sailors at Sakai

Unfortunately, just at this moment news was received that a boatload of Frenchmen had been massacred by the Tosa troops at Sakai. This put an end to the conversation and to all hope of going to Kyoto for an audience. Two men were reported killed on the spot, seven missing, seven wounded, while five escaped unhurt. The account received by Date just as he left the French legation was that only one had been killed. It was evident to everybody that the execution of the Bizen officer had not had the effect of a warning. Confusion, despair; hopes dashed to the ground just on the point of fulfilment. No better accounts being given by Date and Higashikuze on the following morning, and the missing sailors not having been given up, the foreign ministers resolved to withdraw their flags. When the two Japanese ministers called on the French minister to express their deep regret, he refused to see them, and addressed a letter to the Japanese authorities demanding the surrender of the missing men by eight o'clock the following morning. The French, Italian, Prussian and American representatives embarked. We and the Dutch political agent remained on shore.

But on the morning of March 10, the British flag was formally lowered, and Sir Harry went on board the *Ocean*, leaving Russell Robertson and myself at the vice-consulate, with Lieutenant Bradshaw and six men of the 2/ix. The dead bodies of the seven missing French sailors having been found, Date and Higashikuze went on board the French flagship *Vénus* to inform Roches. But by some curious blunder the boxes containing the corpses were sent first to the British transport *Adventure*, where they were mistaken for cases of curios belonging to our legation, and how the discovery was made of the real nature of the contents I never heard, but they did not arrive at the French flagship till late in the afternoon. I saw Date on his way back, who said he was greatly pleased with the moderation with which the French minister was treating the affair.

Next day Sir Harry landed, and carried off Bradshaw and his men. He instructed me to call on Date and tell him that the representatives would consult together after the funeral as to the reparation to be demanded from the emperor's government, and that if they were unanimous the Japanese might feel assured that the demands were just. In that case the best thing they could do would be to accept them without delay. On the other hand, if the requirements of Roches exceeded the bounds of justice, the other ministers would refuse to join him, and the Japanese government could then appeal to the French government and those of the other foreign powers. In Sir Harry's own opinion a large number of the Tosa men ought to suffer death, but he did not approve of pecuniary indemnities. Having given me these instructions he went off to Kobe to attend the funeral of the murdered Frenchmen, eleven in all. Robertson and I called on Date to deliver the chief's message, and after having executed our commission, we went with Komatsu and Nakai to a Japanese restaurant and had a feast in the usual style.

We got home about seven o'clock, and as the day was still young we took it into our heads to give ourselves an entertainment, and with a guide carrying a lantern went to the quarter of the town where such amusements are provided, to a house to which I knew that a foreigner had been introduced, and that by Tosa people. The master said he was afraid of his trade being injured if he received foreigners, but suggested our applying to the local authority for permission.

While we were still in the shop a Tosa man came down from a room upstairs, and on seeing us asked for his sword, but the people of the house refused to give it, and led him away. It never entered my head that the master of the house wished to get rid of us on account of his Tosa guests. So we went to the municipal office, and came back with the desired permission, but the landlord was still not satisfied. We were conversing with him when the same Tosa man came down sword in hand, and squatting down before us with a threatening air, demanded to know who we were and what we were doing there. I replied we were English officers and was about to explain what we wanted, when he interrupted by fiercely questioning our right to be there. One of his companions, roused by the disturbance, came downstairs and carried him up again, the women taking his sword and hiding it. The peaceful man then came to us and was offering an apology, when the madcap descended again with a naked weapon in his hand, at least that was Robertson's impression. His friend rushed to stop him. A struggle took place on the stairs, and we bolted through the door into the street. The master of the house came out after us with our lantern, saying our guide had disappeared, and as he was not to be found, the old man had to escort us home.

Mitford and Willis arrived back from Kyoto on the 12th, Sir Harry's letter giving permission for the latter to remain having crossed him on the way. Having made arrangements for his going back again, we went on board the *Adventure* to see the chief, and while we were there Date and Komatsu arrived to tell him what the French minister's demands were:

> 1st, the execution of all the men concerned in the massacre (about twenty Tosa men and twenty townspeople armed with fire-hooks, they told us);
> 2nd, $150,000 for the families of the murdered men;
> 3rd, apology of the principal minister for foreign affairs at Osaka (this was Prince Yamashina Akira, a lord of the Blood);
> 4th, apology of the Tosa *daimyō* Yamauchi Yōdō on board a French man-of-war at Susaki (the port of Tosa);
> 5th, the exclusion of all Tosa armed men from treaty ports and cities.

These had all been agreed to. We then returned ashore and started Willis on his way back to Kyoto.

Next day we moved over to Kobe on board HMS. *Adventure*. All the foreign representatives had addressed notes to the Japanese government counselling them to comply with the French demands. Hase Sanmi, a court noble, arrived as an envoy from the emperor to the French minister bearing a message of condolence. He afterwards saw Sir Harry and arranged with him that he should go to Kyoto for an audience of the emperor, as soon as this affair was disposed of. Roches had not fixed any date, but it was expected by the Japanese authorities that everything would be finished by the 16th. Roches seemed to be harping on one string, that it would be regrettable if any single representative went to Kyoto by himself, and Komatsu, who told us that he had expressed himself to Hase in that sense, thought that this was intended as a hit at Sir Harry. However, Polsbroek had also promised the Japanese that he too would go up to Kyoto as soon as satisfaction for the Tosa outrage were afforded.

Next day Date arrived at six o'clock with Komatsu and went on board the French flagship to deliver to Roches the note accepting his demands. The 5th demand was understood to mean not merely that no Tosa troops should garrison treaty ports and cities, but that no Tosa samurai of any class should be allowed at the treaty ports. This appeared to be too severe, and we held that it would have to be modified. After he had finished with Roches, Date came over to see Sir Harry and to tell him what had been arranged. Two officers and eighteen rank and file were to perform *harakiri* at Sakai at two p.m. the next day, and Yamashina Akira was simultaneously to call on Roches to deliver the apology, and also invite him to Kyoto. On the day after that the lord was to call on Sir Harry, at the same hour, on board HMS *Ocean* at Kobe. We were to leave Kobe for Osaka on the 19th, pass the night of the 20th at Fushimi, and enter Kyoto the next day. On the 22nd we were to receive visits, and have audience of the emperor on the 23rd. This was only a private and confidential arrangement with Date, and would only become official after Yamashina Akira delivered the formal invitation.

In accordance with this programme the lord, who was a first cousin once removed of the emperor, and principal minister for foreign affairs, came to Kobe on the 18th to call on Sir Harry and Polsbroek. We learned from him that Roches had begged off nine out of the twenty condemned men, taking only one life for each of the murdered Frenchmen, and that he had decided to go to Kyoto having heard from Date that Sir Harry would accept the invitation. The head priest was dressed in the same costume as the other court nobles we had seen, a purple silk robe (*kariginu*) and a small black-lacquered wrinkled hat perched on the top of the head. His age might be about fifty, and he wore a short beard and moustache. His teeth bore marked signs of having been once dyed black. He was accompanied by Higashikuze, a son of the latter, and by Mōri Motoisa, son of Mōri Motomitsu. This young man was to go to England with the son of Sanjō Sanetomi and young

Nakamikado. It was expected, they said, that the emperor would move down to Osaka about the end of the month, and remain there until Edo was finished with. Yoshinobu had sent an apology through his relative, the lord of Echizen, but it was not considered satisfactory, and military operations would be continued.

It was only later that we learned that it had been Captain Dupetit Thouars, commanding officer of the *Dupleix* to which ship the murdered sailors belonged, had been deputed by the French senior naval officer to witness the execution with a party of his men. Finding that the completion of the proceedings would involve the detention of his men on shore after dark, he had raised his hand after the eleventh man had suffered. The nine whose lives were spared were grievously hurt, we were afterwards told, and no wonder, considering what the spirit of the Japanese samurai was. Patriotic death poems by the men who suffered the extreme penalty were afterwards circulated among the people.

The following are prose translations of some of these:

Though I regret not my body which becomes as dew scattered by the wind, my country's fate weighs down my heart with anxiety. As I also am of the seed of the country of the gods, I create for myself today a glorious subject for reflection in the next world. The sacrifice of my life for the sake of my country gives me a pure heart in my hour of death.

Unworthy as I am I have not wandered from the straight path of the duty which a Japanese owes to his lord. Though reproaches may be cast upon me, those who can fathom the depths of a warrior's heart will appreciate my motives. In this age, when the minds of men are darkened, I would show the way to purity of heart. In throwing away this life, so insignificant a possession, I would desire to leave behind me an unsullied name. The cherry flowers too have their seasons of blossoming and fading. What is there for the Japanese soul to regret in death?

Audience with the Emperor at Kyoto

On March 19, 1868, the whole legation crossed to Osaka in HMS *Adventure*. I left my Japanese escort behind, as they would have been in the way at Kyoto, and probably, being Tokugawa retainers, in fear of their lives the whole time. Our party slept at the vice-consulate, and next day we rode up to Fushimi, escorted by Komatsu Kiyokado and a couple of Hizen officers, one of whom named Nakamuta was the commander of the *Eugénie*, a steamer recently acquired by Nabeshima. The party on horseback consisted of Sir Harry, Lieutenant Bradshaw and myself, with the legation mounted escort. We went nearly the whole way at a foot's pace, the road being in fairly good condition, but the bridges at Yodo having been burnt during the recent fighting we had some difficulty in getting across the Kizu River, which falls into the river there.

We got to Fushimi about six o'clock, and found comfortable quarters prepared for us in the guest rooms of a Buddhist monastery, where we were well looked after by some Hizen officers. The rest of our party, together with the infantry guard of the 2/ix, were to come up in boats, starting at three o'clock in the afternoon, and travelling through the night. They gradually reached Fushimi next morning, and we managed to make a start about ten o'clock. The first half of the way we were escorted by Hizen men, who were then joined by Owari troops, and here we were met by Gotō and our cheery little friend Nakai. The streets were crowded with spectators, who observed perfect order. Chion-*in*, a very fine Buddhist monastery at the foot of Higashi-yama, had been prepared for our accommodation, and guards were posted consisting of Higo, Awa and Owari troops. We found the Owari officials who were in charge to attend to our comforts very dilatory people, and as yet quite unacquainted with foreigners and their requirements. The apartments assigned to us were magnificently decorated, altogether in the style of a feudal noble's palace, such as we had seen at Tokushima the previous year. Shimazu Hisamitsu (father of the lord of Satsuma) had occupied them for some time when he first visited Kyoto. As soon as we settled in, a grand feast of many dishes in Japanese style was served up to us, but of course we had brought our own cooks and utensils with us, for most of us were unaccustomed to Japanese food. Old Yōdō of Tosa, whom Willis had been attending, was reported to be out of danger and in a fair way of recovery.

The 22nd March was spent by the chief in making a round of visits. It took the Owari folk three hours to get us the necessary palanquins and bearers. We called first on Yamashina Akira, who was very affable and jolly, his dirty beard shaved off, and his teeth dyed black in correct style. He was dressed in the costume called *nōshi*, and wore the tiny black lacquered hat as before. The conversation turned upon the delightfulness of the occasion which had brought the British minister to Kyoto. Just after leaving the lord's residence we were stopped in the road to let Prince Komatsu Akihito pass. He was on horseback, a stoutish, swarthy, thick-lipped young man. His hair was just beginning to sprout, for until recently he had been in the Buddhist priesthood. Our next visit was to Sanjō Sanetomi, who had had his title of Dainagon just restored to him, a pale effeminate-looking undersized man of thirty-three years of age. He discoursed very formally on the happiness it gave to all the court people to see foreign ministers in Kyoto.

From there we went through the enclosure known as the Nine Gates, past the Imperial Palace. It was surrounded by a finely stuccoed wall four feet thick at the base, with gates like those of a Buddhist temple, very neatly thatched with small shingles. Iwakura Tomomi, whom we called on next, had his temporary residence just inside and opposite the Kuge-*mon*, the gate on the west of the palace. He was a severe-looking oldish man, but frank in speech. He told the chief it was true that the emperor and court nobles had hated foreigners hitherto, and talked of "barbarian-expelling" (*jōi*), while the Bakufu was all for "opening the country." But now that was completely changed. They had especially to thank the English for having

335

been the first to recognize the truth that the emperor was the sovereign. Itō told me that after we had left the house Iwakura expressed to him a fear that he might have given offence by speaking too frankly about the former attitude of the court towards foreigners.

We then went to the Hizen *yashiki*, and saw the lord, a young good-looking man of about twenty-four years of age; he had been appointed to the department of foreign affairs, but we would not discover that he had any great aptitude for official work. Date and Higashikuze luckily were not in when we called. We also visited the younger Chōshū lord, Mōri Motonori, whom we easily recognized by his likeness to the photograph taken when Admiral King was in Chōshū. At the other houses we had been accommodated with chairs, but here we had to squat on the floor in Japanese fashion, and when we rose to leave it was with difficulty that we could straighten our knee joints. We exchanged with him hearty expressions of goodwill and congratulations on our ancient friendship.

On returning to the Chion-in we found Date and Gotō who had come to discuss the details of the audience that was to take place on the morrow. They expressed much anxiety lest the emperor should find some difficulty in making his speech to the minister, as he had not up to the present ever spoken to anyone but inmates of the palace, and it was only ten days since he had first shown his face to a *daimyō*. So we finally arranged that His Majesty's speech should be written down, that he should try to repeat it, hand the copy to Yamashina Akira, who would read it out, and then hand it to Itō for translation. The document was finally to remain in Sir Harry's possession. Then the latter would reply directly to the emperor through Itō acting as interpreter. The only member of the legation staff to be admitted to the audience was Mitford, as he alone had been presented at court in England. He was to be introduced by Yamashina Akira, and the emperor would salute him with the word *kurō*, which might be freely rendered by "Glad to see you." The Shishinden where the audience was to take place was, they told us, a large hall twenty-eight yards deep by thirty-six in length, with a floor of planking, with a dais and a canopy for the emperor, and another dais, rather lower, specially arranged for the ministers. *daimyō* who were received in audience had, we were assured, to kneel on the bare planks. The three foreign representatives, Roches, Sir Harry and

Polsbroek were to assemble in one room, and be thence conducted into the presence of the emperor.

It was now our turn to suffer an assault at the hands of the fanatics of patriotism, from which our constant advocacy of the rights of the sovereign afforded us no protection.

It was arranged that we should start from the Chion-*in* for the palace at one o'clock on March 23. The procession was to be headed by the mounted escort, led by Inspector Peacock and Nakai, then Sir Harry and Gotō, myself and Lieutenant Bradshaw, the detachment of the 2/ix, followed by Willis, J. J. Enslie, Mitford in a palanquin (being unable to ride) and five naval officers who had come up with us.

We descended the whole length of the street called Nawaté opposite to the main gate of the Chion-*in*, but just as the last file of the mounted escort turned the corner to the right, a couple of men sprang out from opposite sides of the street, drew their swords, and attacked the men and horses, running down the line and hacking wildly. Nakai observing what was passing jumped down from his pony and engaged the fellow on the right, with whom he had a pretty tough fight. In the struggle his feet got entangled in his long loose trousers, and he fell on his back. His enemy tried to cut off his head, but Nakai parried the blow, receiving only a scalp wound, and pierced the man's breast with the point of his sword at the same time. This weakened him, and as he was turning his back on Nakai he received a blow on the shoulder from Gotō's sword, which prostrated him on the ground, and Nakai jumping up hacked off his head.

In the meanwhile the troopers on the left had turned, and some of them pursued the other villain, who rushed down the street from which Sir Harry and I had not yet emerged. I had only just realized what was taking place. My presence of mind had deserted me, and as he passed, my sole idea of defence was to turn my pony's head round to ward off the blow aimed at me. It was a narrow escape, as I afterwards found, for the animal received a slight cut on the nose, and was also wounded on the shoulder an inch or two in front of my knee. As soon as I recovered my equanimity I moved up to the head of the procession. There I saw Sir Harry Parkes, in his brilliant uniform of an envoy and minister calmly sitting on his horse in the middle of the cross-roads, with Inspector Peacock close by, also on horseback, and a crowd of Japanese spectators. The Japanese infantry, three hundred men of Higo, who had led our procession had disappeared, as had also those who had originally brought up the rear. But our Japanese grooms stuck to us with the greatest cool pluck. Behind me was the infantry guard of the 2/ix, facing to the left. Upon them he hurled himself, cutting one man over the head and inflicting a severe wound, but here his career came to an end, for one of the soldiers put out his foot and tripped him up, and others drove their bayonets into him. Nevertheless he managed to get to the end of the line, where being stopped by Mitford's palanquin, he fled into the courtyard of a house, dropping his sword outside. Here he was found by Bradshaw, who discharged a pistol at his head, but the bullet struck the joint of the lower jaw, and did not penetrate the bone. On this he fell down in the yard, and became nearly insensible.

Our wounded were too numerous to admit of our proceeding to court. Nine of our escort were wounded, and one of the 2/ix guard, besides Nakai and Sir Harry's Japanese groom. We therefore procured bearers for the palanquins which had been abandoned by their frightened porters, and returned to our quarters without any further mishap. When the wounds were examined it was found that none were in a vital part, though there had been much loss of blood. A cut into the knee of one man, and the almost complete severance of the wrist of another were the worst cases. It was a great piece of good fortune that we had such an experienced surgeon as Willis with us. The captured assailant appeared to be a Buddhist priest, at least his head was shaven. Assisted by a retainer of Sanjō's we examined him. He expressed great penitence, and asked that his head might be cut off and exposed publicly to inform the Japanese nation of his crime. His wounds were attended to by Willis, and he was carefully deposited in the guard-room. Nakai brought the head of the other man back with him, and kept it by his side in a bucket as a trophy. It was a ghastly sight. On the left side of the skull a terrible triangular wound exposed the brain, and there was a cut on the right jaw which apparently had been dealt by the sword of one of the escort.

My diary contains no further entry until the middle of May, and letters I wrote to my parents narrating the incidents which befel us at Kyoto have not been preserved. A very full account of this affair, written by Mitford to his father, was communicated to the *Times*, and the despatch of March 25 in which the chief reported the whole affair was included in a volume of "confidential print" and has not been published. As long as we remained at Kyoto I was so busy with interpreting between the chief and Japanese high functionaries and in translating documents that my journal had to be neglected, and my memory of what occurred over fifty years ago, left unrecorded at the time, is scarcely full enough to afford material for completing this chapter unaided.

It will readily be comprehended that this fanatical attack on the British minister, who had proved himself a cordial friend of the imperialist party, caused a feeling of utmost consternation at the court as soon as the news was received there about four o'clock in the afternoon. The French minister and the Dutch political agent had punctually reached the Palace, where they were kept waiting for the arrival of their colleague. As he failed to make his appearance their reception was hurried through, and on leaving the audience chamber they received the notes Sir Harry had sent off informing them of what had happened.

About six o'clock in the evening there came to him straight from the court Tokudaiji Sanetsune, Echizen Saishō, Higashikuze, Date and the lord of Hizen to express the deep regret of the emperor. The minister replied that he would leave the matter in the hands of the emperor's government. He considered that a graver outrage had been committed upon the emperor than upon himself, and he felt assured that the government would know how to vindicate the honour of their sovereign. They manifested a degree of feeling and concern which showed that remonstrance from him was not needed to make them sensible of the gravity of the offence. They reproached themselves for not having taken better precautions for his safety, and deplored the disgrace attaching to themselves for an outrage committed on a foreign representative especially invited by the emperor to Kyoto. He added that of course their apologies would take a written form, but he recurred to arguments he had previously addressed to various members of the government as to the necessity of an enactment that should attach the penalty of an ignominious death to all samurai who committed murderous attacks on foreigners instead of allowing them to die with credit by their own hand; as in the case of the eleven men who were executed for the murder of the French seamen at Sakai. He urged also that the emperor's government should make known by public proclamation that His Majesty really desired to cultivate friendly relations with foreign powers. It was their duty to eradicate the spirit of hostility towards foreigners to which so many had fallen victims, and which was fostered by the erroneous idea entertained by a certain class that in attacking foreigners they were doing the emperor good service. Accordingly the written apology was delivered next day, together with a copy of the sentence depriving the prisoner of his rank as samurai, and passing a sentence of decapitation on him. Sanjō, Iwakura, Tokudaiji, Higashikuze and other ministers called to offer their regrets, and promised that the proclamation should be posted on the public notice-boards which were a feature in every town and village. They offered also in case any of our wounded should die, or be deprived of their livelihood by inability to perform their duties, to provide suitable compensation.

This affair having been satisfactorily disposed of, the chief agreed to have an audience with the emperor, which took place on March 26. Of course we were not able to make such a show as on the 23rd, since most of the mounted escort were incapacitated by the severity of their wounds. On the other hand extraordinary precautions were taken for the security of the party in passing along the streets. As had previously been arranged, of the legation staff only Mitford was presented. The minister and he ascended the Shishinden by steps at the north end, entered by the door on the south, and issuing from it after the audience descended by steps at the south end. Those of us, like Willis and myself, and the other members of our party walked through the courtyard past the hall of audience, and rejoined them as they came down again. The emperor was the first to speak, and his speech ran as follows:

I hope your sovereign enjoys good health. I trust that the intercourse between our respective countries will become more and more friendly, and be permanently established. I regret deeply that an unfortunate affair that took place as you were proceeding to the palace on the 23rd instant has delayed this ceremony. It gives me great pleasure therefore to see you here today.

To this the minister made the following reply:

Sire,

Her Majesty the Queen is in the enjoyment of good health. I shall have great pleasure in reporting to my government Your Majesty's inquiries and assurances of friendship. The condition of the foreign relations of a state must ever be dependent upon its internal stability and progress, and Your Majesty is taking the best measures to place the foreign relations of Japan upon a permanent footing by establishing a strong general government throughout Your Majesty's dominions, and by adopting the system of international law universally recognized by other states. I am deeply sensible of the manner in which Your Majesty has been pleased to notice the attack made upon me on the 23rd instant, and I appreciate the exertions of Your Majesty's ministers on that unfortunate occasion. The memory of it will be effaced by the gracious reception which Your Majesty has given me this day.

The foreign representatives left Kyoto the following day. Saegusa Shigeru, the captive of our bow and spear on the 23rd, was executed that morning. Three supposed accomplices before the fact were sentenced to perpetual exile, but we were never convinced of their guilt. If it had been proved against them they ought to have suffered the same penalty, but the chief did not care to press the point.

It was Sir Harry's wish that I should remain at Osaka to keep up communication with the court, but I persuaded him to leave Mitford there for the purpose. Two motives actuated me. I wished to get back to my newly acquired house at Edo, and Mitford knew much more than I did about English parliamentary institutions, which was a subject in which the leaders of the samurai class at Kyoto, and especially Gotō Shōjirō, were greatly interested. For their hope was to base the new government of Japan on a representative system.

New Credentials at Osaka

On March 31, 1868, I arrived back at Yokohama with the chief, and went up to Edo on April 1 to find out the state of things there. I took Noguchi and my six Japanese escort men with me. The latter were lodged in a building by the gate of my house. My chief source of information was Katsu Kaishū who had been the head of the Bakufu navy. To avoid exciting attention I used to visit him after dark. The van of the imperialist army had already arrived in the neighbourhood of Edo, the advanced posts being at Shinagawa, Shinjiku and Itabashi. Slight skirmishes with detached bodies of disbanded Edo troops had taken place on the Kōshiū and Kisō roads, which had delayed the arrival of the imperial forces for a day or two. Small parties of Satsuma and Chōshū men wandered about the streets of the city unmolested, and a smaller Satsuma *yashiki*, near our legation, was re-occupied on March 7 by a few soldiers of that clan. Arisugawa no Miya, the commander-in-chief, was reported to be still at Numazu, half a day's journey west of the top of the Hakone Pass. Yoshinobu was residing in retirement at the Tokugawa mausoleum of Ueno, straining every effort to keep his retainers in a submissive temper towards the emperor, by means of notifications to the people and a body of armed police.

Already as early as March 4 a proclamation had been issued declaring that the ex-*shōgun* was determined to submit to any orders which might be given to him by the emperor, and that no opposition was to be offered to the imperial troops. The lord of Aizu and his clansmen had retired to their home at Wakamatsu in Ōshū, after dismantling all the clan establishments in Edo. Nearly all the other *daimyō* who had been residing in Edo until recently had either returned to their territories or gone to Kyoto to give in their allegiance to the emperor. The *hatamoto*, or retainers of Tokugawa below the rank of *daimyō* were daily following their example.

The people of the city, ignorant of the demands about to be made on Yoshinobu, and mindful of the misfortunes some of them had experienced when the Satsuma *yashiki* were attacked in the previous December, were apprehensive of a general conflagration. Some had removed their household property, but the shops were still open, and the panic was by no means general. The forts in the bay of Edo were handed over to the imperialists on April 4, after the guns bearing on the city had been dismounted. This was the news on the 8th. On the 12th I went up again for a three days' stay, and found the city much quieter, owing to a feeling that the terms offered to Yoshinobu would be such as he could accept.

Katsu, who was now commander-in-chief of the Tokugawa forces, told me that he and Ōkubo Ichiō had charge of the negotiations. On the other side Saigō represented Prince Arisugawa Taruhito, the imperialist commander-in-chief who was still at Sumpu. The demands made on Yoshinobu were that he should surrender all arms and munitions of war, all vessels of war and other steamers, evacuate Edo castle, and execute those of his officers who had been foremost in prompting and conducting the attack on Fushimi. When these demands were complied with the emperor would show clemency towards the ex-*shōgun*. The nature of the further conditions covered by the word "clemency" was the subject of negotiations between Katsu and Saigō, which took place at a house in Shinagawa. Katsu was willing to agree to any arrangement that would save the life of his chief and secure sufficient revenue to support his large body of retainers. He had hinted to Saigō that less favourable terms would be met by armed resistance. Yoshinobu also desired to retain possession of his steamers and munitions of war, and had addressed a petition to the emperor on this subject. Saigō, carrying this petition and Katsu's verbal proposals, had returned to Sumpu to lay them before Arisugawa. From there he had journeyed to Kyoto, but was expected back on the 18th. Katsu said he was ready to fight in defence of Yoshinobu's life, and expressed his confidence in Saigō's ability to prevent a demand being made which might not only be a disgrace to the emperor, but prolong the civil war. He begged that Sir Harry Parkes would use his

influence with the emperor's government to obviate such a disaster. This
the chief did repeatedly, and in particular when Saigō called on him at
Yokohama on April 28, he urged on him that severity towards Yoshinobu
or his supporters, especially in the way of personal punishment, would
injure the reputation of the new government in the opinion of European
powers. Saigō said the life of the ex-*shōgun* would not be demanded, and
he hoped that similar leniency would be extended to those who had
instigated him to march against Kyoto. Yoshinobu was still at the monastery
at Ueno, but some of his late advisers, whom he had ordered into strict
seclusion (*kinshin*) had secretly fled. Amongst these Katsu mentioned
Ogasawara, late chief minister for foreign affairs, Hirayama, whom we used
to call "the old fox," Tsukahara, an official whom we greatly liked, and Oguri
Tadamasa, a finance minister. The most remarkable statement Katsu made
to me was that at a conference between the ex-*shōgun*'s ministers and Roches
in February the latter strongly urged resistance, and that the officers of the
French military mission were persistent in advising the fortification of the
Hakone Pass and other measures of a warlike nature. On the whole Katsu
was of opinion that he and Ōkubo Ichiō would be able to arrange satisfactory
terms, if they could manage to escape the hot-heads of their own party who
were threatening their lives.

By this time the first division of the imperialist naval force had arrived
to co-operate with the army which had advanced by land. There seemed to
be little likelihood of fighting, but even a peaceable settlement would be
disadvantageous to the prosperity of the city. Now that the *daimyō* whose
wants had been supplied by the merchants and shopkeepers had left for
their country homes, the population would naturally decrease. It was a sad
thing that Edo should decline, for it was one of the handsomest cities in
the Far East. Though it contained no fine public buildings, its position on
the seashore, fringed with the pleasure gardens of the *daimyō*, and the
remarkable huge moats surrounding the castle, crowned with cyclopean
walls and shaded by picturesque lines of pine trees, the numerous rural
spots in the city itself, all contributed to produce an impression of greatness.
It covered a huge extent of ground, owing to the size of the castle, and the
large number of official residences, intersected by fine broad well-gravelled
streets. The commercial quarter was actually smaller than the city of Osaka.

Newspapers, to a large extent in the nature of gazettes, had lately been started in Kyoto and Edo, and contained a great number of interesting political documents, which I had to translate for the information of my chief. Previously we had been obliged to rely on such manuscript copies as we could obtain from our friends in *daimyōs' yashiki*, and the supply was limited. Nor were the papers that came into our hands altogether trustworthy. There was as much forgery of memorials, manifestoes and correspondence as in any other part of the world in a time of political excitement. There were rumours about this time that the capital would be transferred from Kyoto to Osaka. It was an arrangement we welcomed, for it would have been very inconvenient to establish the foreign legations at Kyoto, so far inland and away from our sources of supply, subject to great cold in winter and excessive heat in summer. Even at Osaka, close to the sea, the climate was almost unbearable in July and August. But as everyone knows, Edo was after all was the centre of government, and its name changed to Tokyo.

During this period my time was passed half at Edo gathering information and half at Yokohama making translations and drawing up reports. Bread and beef were unprocurable at Edo, and I could not afford to set up a cuisine in European fashion, so while there I used to have my food brought in from a well-reputed Japanese restaurant close by, and came to like it quite as well as what I had been accustomed to all my life.

As early as the end of November 1867 Sir Harry had applied to Lord Stanley for letters of credence to the emperor. No time was wasted in their preparation and despatch, and they reached him at the end of March 1868. But it was not till the middle of May that things had quieted down at Yokohama sufficiently to allow of his leaving that part of the country. By that time Sidney Locock and his family had left for home, and his successor Francis Ottiwell Adams had arrived. We started from Yokohama in the admiral's yacht *Salamis* on May 15, Sir Harry, Adams, the senior student interpreter John James Quin, and myself. Next afternoon we anchored in the harbour of Oshima, between the island of that name and the southernmost point of the province of Kii. On a neck of land there was a small village, very dirty, stinking and labyrinthine, surrounded by prettily wooded hills, where we started several pheasants in the course of a walk.

At dusk we weighed anchor, and reached Kobe at nine o'clock the next morning, where we found HMS *Ocean* and *Zebra* already in harbour. We had passed HMS *Rodney*, the flagship of Admiral Sir Harry Keppel, on the way up the Kii Channel. These ships were assembled off Osaka to give *éclat* to the presentation of the first letter of an European sovereign to the rightful sovereign of Japan. We got to the Osaka bar about noon, and afterwards Adams, Quin and I went ashore with the baggage.

The chief did not land until the 18th, when a salute was fired from the fort in his honour. We then became busily occupied with the arrangements for the presentation of the minister's credentials, of his staff and a large number of naval officers. We took up our quarters at the vice-consulate for the sake of convenience in communicating with the squadron outside the bar. The 22nd was fixed on as the day for the ceremony. Then the credentials had to be translated into Japanese, and the number of officers to be presented agreed upon. I had to be present, much to my annoyance, for I possessed no diplomatic uniform. The chief offered me the loan of a sort of staff jacket of blue serge fastened in front with frogs, and an old pair of trousers with gold lace down the sides, but I put them away in a cupboard and went to court in plain evening dress.

As soon as Sir Harry landed he was visited by Gotō, one of the two samurai who had fought in our defence at Kyoto on March 23, and by Date. With the latter we had a discussion about the recently published edict against Christianity that revived the ancient prohibition, but in less stringent terms. Date admitted that the wording was objectionable, and said that he had caused it not to be exhibited on the public notice-boards at Osaka and Kobe. He had tried to get the expression (translated "evil" or "pernicious" sect) altered, but said it would be impossible to suppress the proscription of Christianity altogether. Sir Harry responded that religious toleration was a mark of civilization, and to us he said privately that the presentation of the Queen's letter was a good opportunity which we ought to turn to account. Afterwards I had a long talk with Nakai on this subject, and suggested that instead of specifically mentioning Christianity the decree should merely forbid pernicious sects in general.

It was clear that the Japanese government would not be induced to revoke the law completely, for that would be to give a free hand to the Roman

Catholic missionaries at Nagasaki, who had already made themselves obnoxious by the active manner in which they had carried on their proselytism. It was, however, agreed that Sir Harry should meet Sanjō, Date, Gotō and Kido on the following day to dispose, if possible, of this question, but Nakai warned me that not even the heads of the government (*sōsai*) could make a definite promise; they were not absolute, as he said. So on the 19th we had a palaver at the Nishi Hongan-*ji*, at which Yamashina Akira, the president of the Foreign Board, was present, besides those already mentioned, and several more. They defended what had been done on the ground that the hostility to Christianity was still intense, and that in popular opinion it was allied to magic or sorcery. This I knew myself to be a fact. I had once been asked by a Japanese to teach him "Kiristan," which he believed would enable him to discover what his wife was doing in his absence from the house. They admitted that an error had been committed in describing Christianity as a pernicious sect, and said that this wording would be altered. To have published nothing would have been tantamount to toleration, "silent approval" as the Japanese expression goes, and upon this they could not venture.

On the 24th Sir Harry recurred to the subject with the same set of ministers, with whom Iwakura was joined. Perhaps it was on this occasion that a young samurai of Hizen, Ōkuma Shigenobu, whom we had not met before, assured us that he knew all about the subject, for he had read the Bible and the "Prairie-book." It appeared that he had been a pupil of Dr Guido Herman Verbeck, an American missionary at Nagasaki. Sir Harry gave them a copy and a Japanese version of a despatch on this subject, which had been received from Lord Stanley. The other foreign diplomats took the same line, but their united remonstrances produced little effect, and the measure of exiling to other parts of the country some four thousand Japanese of all ages and both sexes mostly from the village of Urakami near Nagasaki, was unflinchingly carried out.

The presentation of the minister's letters of credence took place on the 22nd. Admiral Keppel landed in the morning accompanied by his flag-Captain Heneage, and Captain Stanhope of the *Ocean*; Commander Pollard and Lieutenant Kerr in command of a gunboat; Pusey, commander of the

Salamis; his secretary William Risk, and Garnier, flag-lieutenant, and joined us at the vice-consulate. The legation party included the chief, Adams, Mitford, who had just been gazetted second secretary, and myself. Our procession consisted of a hundred marines from HMS *Rodney* and the same number from HMS *Ocean*, twelve palanquins in which such of us rode as had legs flexible enough, four of the legation escort on foot, and two bodies of Japanese troops who preceded and followed us.

We arrived punctually at one o'clock at the Nishi Hongan-*ji*, assigned for the performance of the ceremony. The theory of the emperor's presence at Osaka was that he was at the head of the army operating from Kyoto against the rebellious Tokugawa chief at Edo. He was therefore obliged to put up with such accommodation as he could find in the Buddhist monasteries, which were not very imperial in their appointments. We were ushered into an ante-chamber which was merely a part of the hall of audience divided off by screens. Down the middle ran a long table covered with cloth of gold, about the only piece of splendour in the place. On one side of this we took our seats, the Japanese ministers for foreign affairs on the other. Tea and sweetmeats piled on wooden trays were brought in for our refection, and we had to wait about half-an-hour before the chief of the ministry entered the room and made the polite speeches necessary on such an occasion.

In a few minutes more we were informed that everything was ready, whereupon the second and third ministers proceeded to usher us into the throne room. This was an apartment of considerable size down each side of which there ran a row of wooden pillars supporting the roof. On a dais at the extreme end sat the emperor, under a canopy supported by black-lacquered poles, and with the blinds rolled up as high as was possible. We advanced up the middle of the room in double column, the one on the right headed by the admiral and composed of naval officers, the other headed by the minister, and consisting of the legation staff. Everyone made three bows, first on advancing into the middle of the room, the second at the foot of the dais, the third on mounting the dais, which was large enough to afford place for us all. The emperor rose and stood under the canopy from the moment that we began to bow. The principal minister for foreign affairs and one other great personage knelt, one on each side of the throne.

In front of the throne, on each side, stood a small wooden image of a lion. These are of great antiquity and are much revered by the Japanese people. Behind the throne a crowd of courtiers were ranged in a double row, wearing little black paper caps and gorgeous brocade robes of various hues. As the emperor stood up, the upper part of his face, including the eyes, became hidden from view, but I saw the whole of it whenever he moved. His complexion was white, perhaps artificially so rendered, his mouth badly formed, what a doctor would call prognathous, but the general contour was good. His eyebrows were shaven off, and painted in an inch higher up. His costume consisted of a long black loose cape hanging backwards, a white upper garment or mantle and voluminous purple trousers.

The proceedings were as follows: the minister stood in front of the emperor's right, with the legation behind him in order of seniority, the admiral with his personal staff and the other naval officers on the imperial left. Sir Harry then recited his address, which he had got by heart. It seemed truly absurd when one at last stood face to face with the recipient. Then Itō, who discharged the functions of interpreter on the occasion, read the translation, and we all bowed. Sir Harry stepping forward put the Queen's letter into the hand of the emperor, who evidently felt bashful or timid, and had to be assisted by Yamashina Akira, whose part was to receive it from the emperor. Then His Majesty forgot his speech, but catching a word from the personage on his left managed to get out the first sentence, whereupon Itō read out the translation of the whole that had been prepared beforehand. Sir Harry then introduced each of us in turn, and next the admiral, who presented his officers. The emperor expressed the hope that all was well with the squadron under his command, and we retired backwards out of the presence into the ante-chamber, bowing as we went, and congratulating ourselves that everything had passed off without a hitch.

In the evening we went to dine with Date, who gave us a banquet cooked as nearly in European fashion as he could manage.

Next day we celebrated the Queen's birthday in advance by firing salutes, and a large party of Japanese nobles went on board the *Rodney* to lunch with the admiral. Yamashina Akira proposed the Queen's health, which was responded to enthusiastically by everyone present. Many of the guests were intelligent and well behaved, but the lord of Chōshū, who insisted on my sitting next to him, behaved like a great baby, and drank more champagne than was good for him. One felt however that Japanese lords could not be blamed if they were weak-minded, their education being planned so as to produce that result. The son of the emperor's maternal uncle was possessed with a huge desire to see a European cat, while another great man wanted to get sight of a negro, and we had great difficulty in satisfying their wishes. The principal minister for foreign affairs, who had of course to be saluted, desired that as little powder as possible should be used, because the sound of a violent explosion hurt his ears. One of the great attractions was the *Rodney*'s band, which played a great deal of noisy music for the benefit of the admiral's guests, and the bandmaster of the *Ocean* gained great applause by composing a march and a Japanese national anthem, which he dedicated to the emperor.

The conference held at Osaka on the following day (a Sunday), at which among other things the Christian question was discussed, lasted for six hours, and that meant six hours for me of interpreting from English into Japanese and from Japanese into English. So it was a certain amount of relief to me when on the 25th we reembarked on board the *Salamis* to return to Yokohama. The emperor left Osaka on the 28th and returned to Kyoto, the submission of the ex-*shōgun* being held to justify this step.

Mito Politics

Adams and I set up housekeeping together in the first secretary's house at Yokohama, but I still kept on the Japanese *yashiki* I had rented at Edo, and spent a great deal of time there watching the course of events. From time to time I returned to Yokohama to report to my chief, or else reported to him by letter. I was very busy in making translations from the official gazette that was now being published at Kyoto and the popular newspapers that had sprung into existence at Edo. One of these contained documents of the highest interest, the terms communicated to Yoshinobu on April 27, the acceptance of which by him involved his retirement to Mito on May 8, and the provisional recognition of Tokugawa Iesato as the head of the Tokugawa clan. Edo castle was occupied by the imperialist forces, and the troops of Satsuma, Chōshū and other clans moved freely about the city.

On June 23, 1868, I went up to Edo for a three days' stay with Adams. In the local papers I read interesting communications that were probably fictitious. One was said to be written by a retainer of the head priest of the Chion-in, where the British legation had been lodged in March. Though he regarded the expulsion of foreigners difficult to achieve, he recommended that the organization of the army be diligently taken in hand, so that they might be humbled and kept in subjection. He also deprecated audiences being granted by the emperor to foreign representatives. Another such paper professed to represent the views of Chōshū "irregular troops" and protested against audiences being granted, because such friendly treatment of foreigners would prevent the nation from affording hearty support to the emperor when the time should arrive for "expelling the barbarian."

When I mentioned these publications to my friend Katsu, he replied that a council of court and territorial nobles (*kuge* and *daimyō*) was held at Kyoto about the end of May, at which the former expressed the opinion that a favourable occasion for expelling foreigners from the country had now presented itself. Their attempt to introduce Christianity at Nagasaki might be alleged as the justifying ground of the measure. He said the *daimyō* were silent and the emperor, on being referred to, took no notice of the proposal. Katsu was not very accurately informed, but it is a fact that on May 14 the principal members of the government and *daimyō* in attendance on the emperor at Osaka were summoned before His Majesty at the Hongan-*ji*, and were informed that Christianity was on the increase at Urakami, a village near Nagasaki. He asked for their opinion as to the best way of dealing with the matter, and it was understood that their replies would be published in the government gazette. Date denied to Mitford the part of the story that said the meeting was for the purpose of considering whether an anti-foreign policy might not be resorted to. It was difficult for us to obtain accurate information, and probably every Japanese in the position of Katsu or Date experienced similar difficulty. I do not think these documents ever saw the light, and the suggestion is very natural that some of them were of such a character that it was considered advisable to suppress them.

The formal appointment of Tokugawa Iesato, a mere boy of six years of age, took place on June 19, and the leading men of the Tokugawa clan waited on him the following morning to present their felicitations. The situation and extent of the territory to be left to the clan had not then been determined. Katsu told me that Sanjō, who had arrived in Edo on the 13th, was waiting for reinforcements expected from the south and west before announcing a decision on these points. He gave me statistics about the revenue hitherto accruing to the *shōgun*'s government that showed, to his satisfaction at least, that it would not be possible for the emperor to derive any income from forfeiture of that revenue, and that here was danger of his government falling to pieces for want of funds. Higashikuze, who was then in Edo, said to me that the revenue to be granted to the Tokugawa would not be fixed until that part of the clan still in arms against the emperor was entirely reduced to submission.

The war was being vigorously prosecuted near Niigata in Echigo and in the neighbourhood of Aizu. I myself saw a considerable body of southern troops march into Edo on June 25, which effectually contradicted the hopes of the Tokugawa people that the imperialists were weakening, and that some of the western clans, in particular Higo, were likely to afford them sympathy, if not actual support.

Roches finally left Yokohama on June 23, 1868, having been succeeded by Maxime d'Outrey, with the intention of visiting Osaka and Nagasaki on his way home. His policy had proved a complete failure, as far as supporting the *shōgun* against the emperor was concerned. He had succeeded however in procuring for French engineers the construction of the arsenal at Yokosuka and the engagement of a French military mission, which were continued for several years after the establishment of the new government.

Noguchi had an elder and a younger brother, the latter of whom had joined the followers of the Tokugawa who after the withdrawal of Yoshinobu to Mito had gathered themselves together in the mausoleum enclosure at Ueno. Thence they issued forth at night and assassinated imperialist soldiers from time to time. At last it was decided to attack them in their stronghold, and early in the morning of July 4 an advance was made which led to the destruction by fire of a considerable part of the city lying between the outer moat and the main gate of Ueno, and also of the great temple building that occupied the centre of the enclosure. The burial places of the *shōgun*s were not damaged. Prince Kitashirakawa Yoshihisa, the imperial lord who had always resided there in the character of abbot, and whom the recalcitrant Tokugawa men talked of raising to the throne as emperor, was carried off by the survivors at the end of the day. The fighting began at eight o'clock in the morning and was over by five o'clock in the evening. During this affair I was at Yokohama, having been kept there since my last visit to Edo at the end of June.

At the beginning of that month Willis and I were in Edo together for a few days, while he attended to wounded men of the Satsuma and other clans, such as Toda, Chōshū and Bizen. The latter occupied the Tōzen-*ji*, which had formerly been the British legation. Willis recorded in his report that the Bizen men received and treated him with great courtesy, which showed that they entertained no feelings of hostility against foreigners, and regarded the death of Taki Zenzaburō as a just retribution for the attack on foreigners at Kobe in the previous February. The condition of these wounded men was deplorable, for at that time Japan had no experienced surgeons, and the treatment of gunshot wounds was of a very amateurish character. There were but few cases of sword-cuts. Subsequently some of the more urgent cases were at Willis' suggestion sent down to Yokohama, and towards the end of July there were 176 patients in the building appropriated as a military hospital. Under the previous government it had been a school for instruction in the Chinese classics. Two-thirds of the number were Satsuma men, Chōshū and Tosa soldiers together made up a fourth. About forty had been wounded in the recent fighting at Ueno, the others had received their injuries in the expeditions to the north of Edo against Aizu. Willis' services were so greatly appreciated that the minister was asked in October to lend them again to the troops which had been fighting in Echigo. This arrangement was facilitated by the fact that he was now vice-consul at Edo, a post which he was unable to take up because the opening of the city to foreign residence and trade had to be deferred. He was relieved at Yokohama by Dr Joseph Bower Siddall who had been appointed medical officer to the legation early in January.

On July 29, 1868, I went to Edo with Adams, and spent four days in visiting Ōkuma, Katsu and Komatsu, but though I must have reported to my chief the result of the conversation with these persons of importance, I have no record, except of voluminous translations from the Japanese of anti-Christian pamphlets and political documents of all kinds. I went alone to Edo again on August 17, and next day called on Ōkuma, whom I found in bed looking very ill. From him I learned that fighting had commenced on the 13th at Imaichi, near Nikkō. The imperialists were victorious and were still advancing on Aizu, 75 miles further. A messenger who left Echigo on the 8th reported that Niigata was still held by Aizu men. Subsequently to the capture of Nagaoka by the imperial troops more fighting had taken place, in which both sides lost heavily. The imperialists were holding their ground, and expected further reinforcements that would enable them to advance on Wakamatsu, the capital of Aizu, at the same time as the divisions from Shirakawa and Akita. The lord of Hizen, Ōkuma's own chief, had been urged by his troops in Shimotsuke, where Imaichi is situated, to lead them against the enemy, but his councillors (*karō*) had dissuaded him from taking the field.

Since the beginning of the year several constitutions had been framed and issued one after the other, and about this time I was engaged in translating the newest edition, which bore the date of June. It showed marked traces of American political theories, and I have little doubt that Ōkuma and his fellow-clansman Soyéjima, pupils of Dr Verbeck, had had a considerable part in framing it. "The power and authority of the Daijōkan (*i.e.* government), threefold, legislative, executive and judicial," was the wording of one article. By another it was provided that "All officers shall be changed after four years' service. They shall be appointed by a majority of votes given by ballot. When the first period for changing the officers of government arrives, half of the present staff shall be retained for an additional space of two years, in order that there be no interruption of the public business." In this we seemed to hear an echo of the "spoils system." Ōkuma explained that the "executive" represented the executive department in the United States constitution, "consisting of the president and his advisers," but that in fact it was the head of the Shintō religion, finance, war and foreign departments. It is needless to say that this state paper has long ago been superseded by the existing Itō constitution of 1889.

Then I went on to Katsu. He said that Sumpu (now called Shizuoka) was to have been formally handed over to the Tokugawa family two days previously, but as a matter of fact it had always formed part of their possessions. He took down from a shelf a memorandum in which he had noted down some years before the names of the ablest men in different clans. Many of them were already dead. Satsuma and Chōshū accounted for the largest number; of the Tokugawa clan there were very few. All our friends of Satsuma, Chōshū and Tosa were among the number of those still living. While I was there Tsumagi Nakazukasa, who had given me a dinner a couple of months earlier, came in. He had returned a few days before from Mito, where he had left Yoshinobu, employing his leisure in the composition of Japanese poetry, and not expecting to be invited at present to take a share in the government. This was an absolutely baseless notion on his part, if he in reality entertained it. He had sent an affectionate message to Katsu, which Tsumagi appeared to be afraid of delivering in my presence, but it proved to be nothing more than a warning to care for his personal safety, which was said to have been threatened by the hot-headed younger Tokugawa men. He said that about five hundred Mito men had gone to join Aizu.

The outcome of their conversation was that there was nothing in the existing political situation to cause them anxiety. The Tokugawa people were desirous of getting Katsu to take office under Tokugawa Iesato, but he was unwilling. I asked him whether he had heard of a general feeling of dislike towards the English. That he replied was an old thing, dating from the time when Sir Harry used to advise the *shōgun*'s ministers to refrain from attacking Chōshū. The idea was no doubt fostered by Roches, who told them that unless they asked the British government to lend naval instructors, the English would back up the *daimyōs*' party. The want of confidence in British friendship was the reason why Dutchmen had been engaged to bring out the *Kaiyō-maru*, a ship of war constructed in England for the lord of Higo by Glover & Co. of Nagasaki, which had come into the possession of the emperor's adherents. I had heard from Komatsu and Nakai that imperialist troops landed from the *Kaiyō-maru* at Hirakata, about August 5 or 6, had gained a victory there over a mixed force of Sendai men and Tokugawa *rōnin*, and this was confirmed by Tsumagi.

On August 19, I walked as far as the Nihonbashi, the bridge in the centre of the city from which all distances were measured by road. From there I walked to the huge hotel at the foreign settlement constructed under the supervision of the Tokugawa government for the accommodation of foreigners. The commercial quarter was very lively, the streets were crowded, especially by samurai belonging to the imperialist forces, but the neighbourhood of the *daimyōs*' yashiki below the castle was like a city of the dead. On the 20th I had a visit from Kawakatsu Hiromichi, an ex-com-missioner for foreign affairs. He said that Sumpu castle was little better than a ruin, and that there were no houses that could receive the Tokugawa retainers. He would like to become a retainer of the emperor (*chōshin*). His family was not originally in the service of the Tokugawa family, but was of more ancient descent. He would be satisfied if he was made a minister of public instruction. Mizuno Wakasa, a former governor of Yokohama, and Sugiura Takesaburō, another Tokugawa man, would probably be employed by the imperialist government to make all the arrangements with regard to the foreign settlement at Edo. Akitake, the younger brother of Yoshinobu, then still in France, was to be fetched home to succeed the late lord of Mito, who had died just about the time of Yoshinobu's retreat thither.

About a hundred and thirty *hatamoto* went up to Kyoto in February and by surrendering to the emperor, secured the possession of their lands. He regretted that he had lost everything through not following their example. The Tokugawa family were to retain 700,000 *koku* of lands, which would enable them to keep a good many retainers, but not all the 30,000 who had hitherto belonged to the clan as *go-kenin*. My own Japanese escort, who belonged to the body of *bette-gumi* created several years before to act as guards and escorts for the foreign legations, three hundred of whom were to be kept together for that purpose, all wanted to become emperor's men.

On August 21, Komatsu and Nakai came to call on me. They said the troops sent by way of Hirakata to Tanagura in Ōshū had been completely victorious, and that more would speedily follow. In fact, while we were talking, five hundred Satsuma men marched past the house along the main-road by the seashore in order to embark for the north. Kido, who had gone to Kyoto to report the state of affairs at Edo, was expected back soon. They thought that a good deal of pressure would be necessary to induce the very conservative Kyoto court to bring the emperor there. That afternoon I called on Ōkuma, who was still very unwell, and, like most of the Hizen people, not disposed to be communicative. From him I went to Nakai, who showed me the draft of the state paper by which Gotō overturned the late government in the previous October. It differed slightly from the published copies, in that it contained proposals for the engagement of French and English teachers of language, to get military instructors from England, and to abolish the *shōgun* and reduce the Tokugawa clan to the same level as the others. These were all struck out on reconsideration in order to avoid exciting a suspicion that Gotō and his political allies were too partial to foreigners, and provoking the hostility of the *fudai* and *hatamoto*. He had also the drafts of a letter from Higashikuze to Sanjō, in which, among other things that strengthened the Aizu resistance to the imperial troops, he reported foreign vessels had anchored at Niigata and supplied the rebels with arms and ammunition. Higashikuze said that on his informing the foreign representatives of this, they replied that they would put a stop to the practice. I pointed out to Nakai that this must be a mistake. The ministers having issued proclamations of neutrality had nothing to do with their enforcement. If the Japanese authorities wished to put an end to this traffic, they had merely to notify the foreign representatives of the blockade of the port of Niigata, and that a vessel of war was stationed there to prevent communication with the shore. This must have appeared a very strange doctrine to him, but international law was a complete novelty in Japan in those days. He also showed me the draft of Komatsu's letter to Kyoto about the treatment of the Nagasaki Christians, embodying the arguments recently used to him by Sir Harry, and advocating the adoption of milder measures.

Next day I went again to see Nakai, and found with him a very attractive Satsuma man named Inoue Iwami, who was greatly interested in the development of the resources of the island of Ezo. He was full of schemes for its colonization from Japan, and for the introduction of the European system of farming under the supervision of a German named Reinhold Gaertner. He said that Shimizudani Kinnaru, a young court noble of about 25, was to be governor of Hakodate, and that he intended to make him learn English. We discussed various leading personalities with considerable freedom—I hinted that Higashikuze, in spite of his rank, was not the best representative man to send to Europe as minister. I thought Date or Iwakura or even Matsudaira Kansō of Hizen would do better. He replied that Iwakura could not be spared. The most important and interesting suggestion he made was that the emperor must move to Edo, and make it his Capital, as otherwise it would not be possible to keep in order the rebellious clans of the north. Both he and Komatsu, who joined us later on at a restaurant on the river, approved of what I had suggested about the blockade of Niigata.

On August 23, I dined with Komatsu and Nakai to meet Ōkubo, the Satsuma statesman who had suggested the removal of the capital from Kyoto to Osaka earlier in the year. I have no doubt that the final decision to make Edo the centre of government, and to change its name to Tokyo or Eastern Capital was largely his work. He was very taciturn by disposition, and the only information he vouchsafed was that Date would go to Sendai to endeavour to persuade the *daimyō*, who was the head of the Date family and all its branches, to abandon the cause of Aizu. Komatsu talked a good deal about the English naval instructors who had been engaged by the previous government, whom he evidently wished to get rid of, and I encouraged him to dismiss them, for I felt it would not be fair to insist on their keeping these officers in their service during a period of civil war, when the British neutrality proclamation prevented their making use of them. Komatsu told me that their plan was to retain the services of the commissioned officers, but to send the petty officers and seamen back to England.

About two months before this time some Higo men had called on me, and said they were going north to Tsugaru. They argued that any other system than feudalism was impossible in Japan. Now I heard that the Higo clan had privately sent messengers to Wakamatsu to endeavour to effect a reconciliation between Aizu and the *daimyō* of the west and south, but Aizu replied that matters had gone too far, and the questions at issue must be decided by the sword. I thought it likely that these envoys from Higo were the men who had been to see me, as the ideas they entertained seemed to be similar.

The translation of the June constitution, which superseded one that had been promulgated in March, had given me a great deal of trouble. I was unable to decide upon the best name in English for the second department. It might be Imperial Council, Privy Council, or Cabinet. It appeared that the officials of this department were merely secretaries to the two prime ministers, and had no real executive authority. The administration, furthermore, was divided into this nameless department and the other four which followed it. This was Ōkubo's explanation. Yet it was pretty evident that this constitution would not be the final one, and it seemed to me to contain in itself the elements of change. There were so many appointments held by dummies of high birth, while the real work was done by their underlings. The ancient ranks and precedence had been practically done away with, and I could not help thinking that the court and territorial nobles (the *kuge* and the *daimyō*) would have to be struck out of the list of officials. There was hardly one of them fit to occupy the head of a department, and yet these appointments were confined to them, no commoner being eligible.

August 25 was chiefly occupied with arrangements made with Nakai for the opening of Edo on October 1, by instructions from the chief, the abolition of the absurd existing rules about passports for foreigners proceeding to Edo, and for ordering one of the naval instructors there to buoy the channel. The ex-*shōgun*'s government had arranged to have a huge hotel built for the accommodation of foreign visitors, and the owners would have liked to let it, but it seemed unlikely that any foreigner would undertake to run such an establishment on his own account. I advised that they should engage a man from Yokohama to act as steward for the proprietors, make out the visitors' bills, and purchase the necessary wines and provisions.

It was evident that the imperialists were gathering their forces for a combined attack on Aizu. As Nakai said, if they could not crush them with their troops they now had in the field, they never would succeed. An American sailing barque named the *Despatch* was hired for $3000 to carry men to Hirakata. On August 25 I saw two hundred men march through Shinagawa to embark for the north; on the 22nd a large body of Chōshū men arrived, and were billetted in Sengaku-*ji*, the temple on whose grounds the 47 Faithful *Rōnin* were buried. And Nakahara Naosuke, a Satsuma man, usually believed to be their admiral, but in reality an artillery officer, had been sent to Echigo with four companies of artillery, and great things were expected of him.

On August 26 I went to see Katsu, and found him greatly relieved in his mind as the result of a visit paid to him on the previous day by Komatsu. He said that Sumpu castle had been handed over to the head of the Tokugawa clan on the 18th, but that the territories assigned to him had not yet been vacated by their previous possessors, who were very difficult to move, so that the lands at present available did not exceed 80,000 *koku* in extent. He hoped Tokugawa Iesato, by which, of course, he meant the guardians of the six-year-old child, would not go to any great expense in building or in engaging crowds of retainers. He said that the *Kaiyō-maru*, the flagship of Enomoto Izumi, who commanded the Tokugawa fleet, was supplied with provisions by that clan. Enomoto, otherwise known as E. Kamajirō, was a naval officer who had been trained in Holland.

I asked him whether the son of the late lord of Mito was dead, or whether he was to be set aside in favour of Tokugawa Akitake. On this he gave me the following account of Mito politics, which had been a puzzle for many years to foreign observers.

Tokugawa Nariaki, commonly called "the old lord of Mito," was the younger son of Tokugawa Harutoshi, and his childhood's name (*zokumyō*) was Keisaburō. His elder brother Narinobu was the heir, and his portion as a younger brother was only 200 *koku*. Being averse to society on account of his deafness, he spent his time in wandering about the country and acquainting himself with its actual condition, and no doubt then formed the habits of simplicity and frugality that distinguished him in after life. On the death of Harutoshi, Nariaki's elder brother succeeded him, but dying shortly afterwards, left the fiefdom vacant. By that time two parties had gradually formed themselves in the Mito clan, one supporting the ancient Kyoto policy of the author of the Dainihonshi, the other, fearing Nariaki, forming an alliance with the court of Edo, at that time ably directed by Mizuno Tadakiyo, father of Tadahiro until lately a member of the *go-rōjū* (Council of State). The latter party schemed to set aside the claims of Nariaki in favour of an adopted heir from the then *shōgun*'s family. A will of the late lord was however discovered, in which he declared his desire that the claims of blood should be respected, and his brother Nariaki be appointed as his successor. The will was backed up by a strong party known as the Tenguren, and Nariaki became lord of Mito. This was in 1834 when he was about thirty years of age.

The new lord was bent on carrying out certain reforms that the luxurious habits of the age appeared to him to render necessary. With this object he obtained a relaxation of the ancient rule that required the head of the house of Mito to be a resident in Edo. It was all the more easily obtained because he had rendered himself obnoxious to the *go-rōjū* by the ostentatious manner in which he seemed to reprove their pomp and luxury by the simplicity of his own dress and manner of life. Retiring to his province on the pretext that it was necessary for him to superintend personally the government of the clan, he devoted his time to drilling troops in the only fashion then known in Japan. Openly advocating the supremacy of the emperor and non-intercourse with the Western world (*sonnō jōi*), he secretly introduced into the province every Dutch scholar he could find and made himself acquainted as far as was then possible with the resources of European science. With incredible labour he constructed from drawings contained in old Dutch books a frigate, which long lay at Yokohama for the protection of foreigners, but had he believed been since broken up. The report of his doings having been brought to Edo, it was represented to the *go-rōjū* that the drilling of men and building of warships were merely preparations for carrying out the traditional Mito policy, and that the lord was plotting rebellion. In 1844 he was compelled to retire into seclusion, and he was succeeded by his son, the late lord, then a mere boy.

In 1851 a Dutch man-of-war made its appearance at Nagasaki and caused no slight consternation at Edo. It was said that the Nagasaki Dutchmen were becoming restive, and that the ship was merely a precursor of the English, who at that time bore the detestable reputation of being a nation of pirates ready for any violence. Succeeding events proved to the *shōgun*'s government that Japan was in danger of being forced into relations with European powers; the advent of Commodore Matthew Calbraith Perry and his squadron heightened their alarm to such a degree that they yielded to the voice of public opinion, and inviting the old lord of Mito to Edo admitted him again into their councils.

In 1858 *shōgun* Iesada died, and the old lord of Mito wished to secure the succession to his seventh son, who having been adopted as heir to the house of Tokugawa Yoshinobu was in a legitimate position to become the *shōgun*'s heir. It was at this moment that Ii Naosuke came to power, and though it is uncertain whether he had a previous understanding with the Kishū family that they should furnish an heir, it is certain that he found them ready to comply. Hhis influence was strong enough to force old Mito to retire a second time into private life, and to order Echizen, Tosa and Uwajima, who had supported the Mito claims, to resign their fiefdoms to their sons. The assassination of Ii Naosuke a couple of years later by Mito men was the consequence.

Other influences were then at work in the west. The Kyoto policy and the expulsion of foreigners had been warmly espoused by Satsuma and Chōshū. Hence the bond of union between them and the Tenguren section of the Mito men, who on hearing that civil war had broken out at Kyoto, made their appearance before the castle of the lord, and demanded that he should carry out the clan policy. This action proving unsuccessful they raised the standard of rebellion on Mount Tsukuba in Hitachi, from where they were expelled by the forces of the *shōgun* after some hard fighting. Their fate among the mountains of Kaga was a well-known tale. Takeda Kōunsai, who had been driven by the force of circumstances to join them, and several hundred of his comrades were beheaded at Tsuruga. The remainder of the Tenguren fled to Kyoto, where the ex-*shōgun*, at that time still bearing the name of Tokugawa Yoshinobu, took them into his pay. Now that the revolution of the previous January had so completely changed the face of affairs, these men had returned to their native province. They were headed by Takeda Kinjirō, a grandson of Kōunsai. Their political opponents, whom they styled *kantō* (traitors), finding themselves on the losing side, and likely to be in a perilous minority (since the Tenguren were backed up by the imperialists), had gone off to Echigo to the number of some five hundred. The Tenguren, out of gratitude to their former protector, had determined to set aside the heir in favour of Akitake, Tokugawa Yoshinobu's younger brother, and had despatched agents to bring the latter back from Paris.

That day Nagaoka Moriyoshi, younger brother of Hosokawa Morihisa, arrived by sea with a large number of retainers, and on the 29th the lord of Awa marched in in great pomp with about six hundred men. On the 28th I had a great feast with Komatsu, Inoue Iwami and young Matsune of Uwajima. One of the party drank so much *sake* that he lay down on the floor and went to sleep. In half an hour's time he woke up quite sober, and was able to repeat the process.

From September 8 to October 17 Adams and I were absent on a wild-goose chase after the Russians who were reported to be occupying the northern coast of Ezo, in the course of which HMS *Rattler*, in which we had embarked, was wrecked in Sōya Bay. But as this was not concerned with the progress of political events in Japan, it seems unnecessary to occupy space in narrating our experiences. We were rescued by the French corvette *Dupleix*, captained by Dupetit Thouars.

Capture of Wakamatsu

November 6, 1868, was celebrated with much pomp and ceremony as being the emperor's birthday. A review of the regiment was held at Yokohama to which Sir Harry invited Sanjō, now promoted to the rank of Udaijin. The foreign men-of-war joined with the Kanagawa fort in firing a royal salute, which the party viewed from my upstairs verandah overlooking the bay. Besides Sanjō we had Nagaoka Moriyoshi, Higashikuze Michitomi and Madenokōji Michifusa. A luncheon at the minister's residence followed, and the swords of honour sent out from England for presentation to Gotō and Nakai in recognition of their gallant conduct on March 23, were handed over. Nakai at once girt his on, and strutted about with a gold-laced cap on his head, to his own great delight and the intense amusement of the rest of the company. As it happened to be the second day of the Yokohama races it was proposed that the whole party should adjourn to the race-course. Sanjō and Higashikuze, who had on white *maedare* and black-lacquered paper caps, declined. I rode down with Madenokōji and Nagaoka, who enjoyed themselves immensely. On returning home I took Nakai in with me and gave him tea. In exchange for this he informed me that news had been received of the capture of the outer castle of Wakamatsu, and that only the inner ring and citadel remained in possession of the defenders. He also said the emperor would arrive at Edo about November 27.

Next day I went up to Edo on board a Japanese steamer belonging to the Yokosuka arsenal with Sanjō, Higashikuze, Nagaoka and Nakai. By a mistake of Nakai's about the hour of leaving I kept the party waiting for me at the custom house and a mounted messenger had to be sent to fetch me. I hurried down and found them sitting quietly smoking. They protested against my apologising. How different from some Europeans!

On the 8th Mitford and I went to call on Katsu. His wife had gone off to Sumpu, but he remained to do the "head muck-and-bottle-washing" (*miso-zuri*) of the clan. He hoped to obtain the Shimizu lands, amounting to 110,000 *koku*, for feeding the retainers who had lost their lands and pay. Instead of the lands promised in Ōshū, part of Mikawa and the whole of Enshiū had been conceded, but the *daimyō* hitherto entitled had not yet given up possession. Yoshinobu had preceded Tokugawa Iesato to Sumpu. Katsu also had a story that Brunet, one of the French military instructors, went off in the *Kayō-maru*, when the Tokugawa naval squadron left the Edo anchorage on the night of October 4. We doubted this, as we knew that he had just received promotion in the French army. Nevertheless it turned out to be a fact. He was accompanied by another officer named Caseneuve, and several other Frenchmen.

We also visited Nakai, who gave us a first-rate dinner from the hotel. He said that the citadel of Wakamatsu was captured on October 29. He had also received a letter from Kido placing the question of the emperor's coming to Edo beyond a doubt. And as we returned to my house we found that great preparations were already being made in anticipation of His Majesty's arrival, roads being re-made, bridges rebuilt, and ward-gates being constructed in side streets where they had never existed before.

One of my *bette*, Sano Ikunosuke, called to present his thanks for having been selected by the court to remain one of the Edo guard for foreigners; all my sixteen men had been engaged for this service. He said that the Shimizu domain had been granted provisionally to the Tokugawa family for the purpose mentioned by Katsu. Today (November 9) was the last day on which men of the Tokugawa clan could send in their names for service under the emperor. In some cases they would receive about half their former revenue, but others would be better off than before, because their allowances, though nominally diminished, would be issued in rice instead of money at a low fixed rate.

That evening Mitford and I dined with Nagaoka at the Higo *yashiki* in Shirokane, close by our legation, Higashikuze and Nakai being the other guests. It was a dinner in European style served from the hotel in a picturesque two-storeyed house, built in the garden so as to command a view over the *nagaya* in the direction of the bay. In the garden there were some splendid trees and pretty shaded nooks. Hosokawa himself was there, very fat and amiable, very small eyes and a tendency to "fly catching." On the 10th I went back to Yokohama.

At an interview on November 16 between all the foreign representatives, Higashikuze and Terashima, the Japanese ministers stated that Wakamatsu castle had surrendered on November 6 to the imperial forces. The two lords, father and son, in robes of ceremony and preceded by a retainer carrying a large banner inscribed with the word "surrender" (*kōfuku*), and followed by the garrison, likewise in robes of ceremony and with their heads shaven, came to the camp of the besiegers and gave themselves up. The castle and all the arms it contained were handed over, and the two lords retired into strict seclusion (*kinshin*) at a Buddhist monastery in the town. Nakamura Hanjirō, the chief of staff (*gunkan*) wept when he went to take delivery of the castle and its contents. It was a pleasure to us to see how the countenances of some of those who had to listen to the story fell, for they had counted on a desperate resistance on the part of Aizu to defeat the imperialist party and frustrate the policy of the British legation. Now that this exciting episode was at an end, the speedy submission of the other northern clans could be counted on with confidence.

The detailed report made by the Hizen clan, dated November 16, published in the *Kyoto Gazette*, shows that the garrison included samurai soldiers 764, troops of a lower class 1609, wounded 570, outlaws from other territories (*rōnin*) 462; women and children 639, officials 199, civilians 646, personal attendants of the lords 42, and porters 42. There was no record of the number of men killed in the defence.

On November 19, I went to Edo with Captain Stanhope, Charles Wirgman the artist, and Dr. Siddall, after breakfasting with Dupetit Thouars on board the *Dupleix*. Adams and William Marshall went up by road. On our arrival possession was at once taken of Siddall, by a Japanese doctor named Takeda Shingen, and he was carried off to the military hospital established at the Tōdō *yashiki* in the Shitaya quarter.

On the 21st Adams, Mitford, Marshall and Wirgman went to the Yoshiwara and had a feast in fine style at the Kimpeirō, part of which was furnished in Western style for such Japanese guests as liked it. The admission of Europeans into that quarter of the town, from which they had until then been jealously shut out, was hailed as the dawn of a day of friendly intercourse of the frankest character. Next evening I gave a great entertainment at my own house. There were three *geisha* from Shinmei-mae and two *taikomochi* (jesters). We kept it up boisterously till midnight. The jesters performed a foreigner and his escort arriving at the Kawasaki ferry on the way to Edo, and meeting with the usual obstruction at the hands of the men placed there to guard the crossing. My escort men also exhibited some comic scenes, much to their own satisfaction and to the delight of the household, who were admitted to a room at the top of the stairs.

Letters arrived from the chief to say that he wanted a stand erected for himself opposite to the gate of our former legation buildings, in front of Sengaku-*ji*, for him to see the emperor pass in (he was expected to reach Edo on the 27th), and that Higashikuze and I must go down to Yokohama on the 24th to see himself. We wrote in reply to say that a stand was altogether an impossibility, seeing what Japanese etiquette was in such matters, and that I could not leave Siddall alone in Edo without someone to interpret for him. So next day Wirgman and I went over to see Siddall, and found that the Tōdō *yashiki* had now been turned into a general hospital. Here we fell in with old Ishigami, the Satsuma doctor who married a daughter of old Freiherr von Siebold by a Japanese mother, a very cheery person. After lunch we went with him and a crowd of other Japanese doctors to Ueno, intending to get in and examine the scene of the fighting that took place on July 4, but the gate was shut in our face, and though we waited and argued patiently for a whole hour with the sentries, we could not convince them that we might safely be admitted. I think our Japanese companions felt even more annoyance than we did. The gateway was riddled with bullets, and it was evident that a pretty stiff fight had taken place there in July.

We stayed the night at the hospital, and spent a jolly evening with Ishigami and another doctor named Yamashita. Next morning, in spite of the bitter cold, we went round the wards with the doctors. All the state apartments of the *daimyō's* mansion (*goten*) had been converted into wards, and provided with iron bedsteads and hair mattresses. There was a very plucky little Tosa boy, probably a drummer, who had had his foot amputated. Then our attention was attracted to an aristocratic-looking little surgeon from Chōshū, with his sleeves turned up like ruffles over a pair of delicate little wrists.

At noon there came the two brothers Notsu, Shichizayemon and Shichiji, who persuaded Wirgman and myself to go to the Yoshiwara with them, instead of keeping an engagement with Nakai. Siddall compounded *mistura vini gallici*, and after partaking of this we started on a journey of exploration. It was a terribly cold day, with a gale from the north-west coming straight down the plain from the snowy peak of Asama-*yama* and other mountains of Shinshū. The Yoshiwara lay right out in the middle of the rice fields, occupying a considerable extent of ground. It was entered through a narrow gate at the end of a long causeway. After passing this gate, we were introduced into the upstairs rooms of a rather shabby house, evidently much frequented by the Satsuma clan. *Geisha* were of course sent for, and the *sake*-cup circulated merrily.

Towards nightfall it was proposed that we should visit the Kimpeirō, a hideous house furnished in what was regarded as European style; but we stayed there only a few minutes, and then returned to the house where we had first been entertained. Here we had more drinking, dancing and playing at *nanko*. In this game a wooden chopstick is broken up into six pieces, of which each player receives three. He puts in one palm as many as he thinks fit, and guesses at the total of what his hand and the hand of the other player contain. If he guesses right, the loser has to drink, and his turn comes to give the challenge. Evidently this is the way to get speedily drunk. We stopped there till a message came from Ishigami to say that he was awaiting us at another house to drink sober again. We went in search of him to a restaurant on the river bank, the Yumeirō, where much singing, dancing, drinking and *nanko* followed, till we had had enough of it, and came home by boat to the hospital, accompanied by three of the *geisha*.

Next afternoon the artist and I said good-bye to Siddall, and walked over to Nakai's, but not finding him at home, we went to the hotel for refreshment, where we sat down in the garden and found ourselves over-whelmed with melancholy at the ugliness of the building. For five cups of tea and a bundle of Manila cheroots the manager charged us a dollar, to the surprise and horror of the Japanese boy who waited on us. To him it appeared an exorbitant demand. The cheroots were perhaps worth 20 cents, which left 16 cents for a cup of tea. On getting home to Takanawa we found that Rickerby, the proprietor and editor of the *Japan Times*, had just arrived in a boat from Yokohama to witness the ceremony of the following day.

November 26, 1868. About ten o'clock in the morning the emperor passed into Edo, having slept at Shinagawa. Mitford, the artist, Rickerby and I saw the procession from the open space recently created in front of the new gate of what had previously been Sir Harry Parkes' diplomatic residence, now transformed into a sort of foreign office. The display could not be described as splendid, for the effect of what was oriental in the courtiers' costumes was marred by the horribly untidy soldiers with unkempt hair and clothing vilely imitated from the west. The emperor's black-lacquered palanquin (*hōren*) was to us a curious novelty. As it passed along the silence which fell upon the crowd was very striking. Old Date, who rode between it and the closed chair in which the emperor was really seated, nodded to us in a friendly manner. Rickerby wrote and published an excellent newspaper account of the whole show a few days afterwards in the *Japan Times*.

In the afternoon he and I walked to Kaian-*ji*, a Buddhist religious house at Shinagawa, celebrated for its very pretty plantations of maple. From there we proceeded to a house of entertainment, the Kawasakiya, close by, to drink *sake* and crack jokes with the girls about the lord of Bizen, who had passed the night there. The house was full of troops from the west, but they scarcely took any notice of us, and in fact all those we met on the road ignored us completely. It must be said that whenever I went out into the streets of Edo I was always accompanied by my Aizu samurai Noguchi and from four to six of my personal escort of the *bette-gumi*.

On the 28th Sir Harry and Dr. Charles Richard Alford, the bishop of Victoria, Hongkong, came up to Edo, and were entertained in European style at the new foreign office by Date and Higashikuze. Machida and Mōri, young Satsuma men, were also of the party. Both had been in England and spoke English, the latter, who was only about wenty-one, particularly well.

Next day Mitford and I went to call on Nakai. We met there Machida, and Yamaguchi Hanzō, a Hizen samurai, who brought with him a man who had just returned from Sakai Tadazumi. He reported that Tadazumi had submitted on the 4th instant, and that two foreigners, one an American, the other an

Englishman, both from Hakodate, were present as spectators. Nakai, who was a member of the local government of the city, had given in his resignation because he found that the governor-general instead of placing confidence in himself and the other officials, was in the habit of upsetting their arrangements on the complaint of a few wretched tradespeople.

Wirgman and I went down to Yokohama on the 30th, walking as far as Namamugi-*mura* (where Richardson was murdered in 1862), from where we took boat across to the foreign settlement. At Kawasakiya in Shinagawa we fell in with Notsu Shichizaemon and Ijiū-in, with two Kurohane men and one from Utsunomiya, companions on the occasion of our visit to the Yoshiwara, of whom the Satsuma men were on their way home. There was a large consumption of *sake* and Japanese dishes, and much incomprehensible Japanese spoken. Further on, at Ume-*yashiki* or Bairin, as it had now become the fashion to call this very pleasant halfway house between Edo and the ferry at Kawasaki, we found Ōyama, who was like the others returning to Kagoshima as the civil war was practically at an end. We drank many parting cups together, and then walked with him to his hotel at Kawasaki.

The road was full of homeward bound Satsuma men and Tokugawa people going to Sumpu. A report had got about that difficulties had arisen between Satsuma and Higo, and that the latter in conjunction with Arima and Chikuzen were going to fall upon the great clan. It said that in consequence of this the troops were rushing off as fast as possible to forestal the attack. Another rumour, much credited by the French legation, was that Aizu surrendered only on condition that the Satsuma troops should be withdrawn from the east and north of the country, and the emperor come to Edo. But as others besides the Satsuma fighting men were also going home, these stories were easily discredited.

On December 3, I went back to Edo, halfway in a *kago* (common palanquin) from Kanagawa, and on foot from Kawasaki. At the Ume-*yashiki* I met Mizuno Chinami, hurrying back from Shimoda where he had been put ashore from HMS *Manila*. Here was the late governor of Yokohama, who last year used to ride in a state palanquin (*nagabō*), with a large cortége and preceded by running footmen crying *shitaniro*, "down on your knees," now travelling in a wretched cheap hackney *kago*, without a single retainer. For all that he seemed cheerful enough. A good deal of my time in those days was passed in the compilation of an English-Japanese dictionary of the spoken language and in reading Japanese novels.

On the 4th I went over to the hospital, where I found Siddall with his hands full, wounded men from Echigo having begun to arrive. Willis had gone on from Echigo to Wakamatsu to look after the Aizu wounded, of whom there were nearly six hundred men in the castle when it was surrendered. My new pony Fushimi, a present from Katsu before he left Edo, carried me splendidly. The imperialists who crowded the streets appeared to admire with envy a black chimney-pot hat I was wearing. On the 5th I went there again to pass the night, with Ishigami and Yamashita. They complained bitterly of one Maeda Kyōsai, who had been appointed chief of the hospital, and said that the patients had threatened to cut off his head because he spent his time in driving about the city in a carriage and pair instead of attending to his duties. The reflection came naturally that you cannot make a silk purse out of a sow's ear, or give the standing of an European physician to a Japanese half-educated apothecary.

On December 9, I went to the hotel to dine with Machida. The indispensable Nakai was there, also Ōkubo Toshimichi and Yoshii Kōsuke. The latter had left Wakamatsu on December 1. Willis was there looking after the wounded, of whom he said there were at least two thousand on the Aizu side alone. Snow was lying deep both in Echigo and Aizu. Shōnai was pacified, and the whole country might now be said to be at peace, a state of things that of course was displeasing to anti-imperialists, whether among diplomatists or merchants. Information had arrived that the murderers of the two sailors of HMS *Icarus* in August 1867 had been discovered. They were from Chikuzen and the party to which they belonged was said to number nine in all. This of course would be welcome news to the Tosa people. It was strange that retainers of Chikuzen, who entertained Admiral King so hospitably in January should have been guilty of such a wanton crime.

The newly issued paper money, known as *kinsatsu*, was much discussed, and it was evidently creating a great ferment among the people. Uchida, the mayor (*nanushi*) of Kanasugi, who had been to see me a few days earlier, said that a refusal to receive these notes in the payment of taxes was the only obstacle to their free circulation. Nakai denied the correctness of the statement that taxes might not be paid with them, but he thought that in the end it would be necessary to establish a proper banking system by giving authority to the great firm of Mitsui to issue notes against a reserve of coin or bullion. It was a matter of vital importance to the imperial government, which had not found any money in the Tokugawa treasury, and the emperor had always been kept very poorly supplied by the *shōgun*'s ministers.

Enomoto Seizes Ezo

On December 11,1868, Machida came to me with a report from Hakodate that the Tokugawa pirates, as they were styled after their refusal to surrender and their exodus from Edo Bay on October 4, had landed at that port from the *Kaiyō-maru* and her consorts. The rebels were led by a member of the French military mission sent out in 1866 who had gone off with them when they left the bay. It was very annoying for the French legation that this officer should have violated the neutrality proclaimed by the minister and have joined rebels against the authority of a sovereign with whom France maintained friendly relations. A fight had ensued near Hakodate, in which a large number of imperialists were killed or wounded. The Yokohama foreign press reported that the emperor's men had won the victory at a place about 15 miles from the port. According to despatches received from the consul the rebels had had by far the best of it.

The foreign residents were in a great state of alarm. The consul wrote thus: "As the enemy approach we shall retire towards the hill. If he comes nearer, we shall go up the hill, and should it come to the last extremity we shall have no resource but to put our trust in an over-ruling power."

Nakai came on the 13th to talk about the new paper money, and the difficulties with foreigners to which it would give rise. Tom Glover's opinion was quoted in favour of a paper circulation, but he did not himself agree that a merchant, who was naturally an interested party, should be regarded as an authority on currency. This paper money had been issued to the troops, who forced the shopkeepers and the hucksters on the high roads to accept it in payment. But this could not go on long, for the paper did not pass current amongst the civilian population.

We spoke about the state of foreign relations. He admitted that the old distrust of foreigners still existed; the foreign representatives were regarded as a necessary evil, to be endured, but not to be embraced. Nothing pleased the emperor's government so much as to see the diplomatists living at Yokohama, and the idea of asking their advice upon any matter was never entertained for a moment. In fact the representatives were looked upon much in the same light as the agents (*rusui*) of the *daimyō*, *i.e.* persons sent to Japan by their respective governments to receive the emperor's orders, whenever occasion might arise. The representatives were themselves partly to blame for this state of things. Fine houses, comfortable living and whole skins at Yokohama were doubtless preferable to makeshifts and dangers at Edo, but for all they knew or could learn of pending international questions they might just as well be resident at Hongkong.

Another day was spent with the mayor of Kanasugi and three or four retainers at the classical Kongō Daiyu theatre in Iigura-chō, to see *nō* and *kyōgen*. Minami Torajirō was also among the audience. This was a young Aizu samurai, who had come to see me with his countryman Hirozawa the previous April, when I had a great argument with the latter about Japanese politics and especially about the part our legation had played. It was the first time a foreigner had been present at this kind of theatrical performance. *nō* is a sort of tragedy or historical play, *kyōgen* is low comedy. There is no scenery and the costumes are all in an ancient style. The stage is about twenty-four feet square, and a long passage on the left connects it with the greenroom from which the actors make their appearance. There are two hundred *nō* plays, and printed books of the text, known as *utai*, could be bought for a trifling cost. They are delivered in slow recitative to the accompaniment of music, or rather dissonance, of the fife and small drum. The orchestra, likewise dressed in antique fashion, were seated on campstools at the back of the stage.

The *kyōgen*, which pleased me most, were *Suehirogari*, in which a sort of Moses Primrose is sent to Kyoto to buy a fan, and is cheated by the merchant into paying five hundred *ryō* for an umbrella, and *Obagasake*, in which a fellow having tried in vain to persuade his aunt, a rich old curmudgeon, to give him some *sake*, puts on a devil's mask and frightens her into submission, while he goes to get drunk at the store room where the liquor is kept. He threatens to eat her if she looks his way. Her cries,"Oh fearful to behold; spare your retainer's life"; her anger on discovering in the drunken and sleepy demon her rascally nephew, were infinitely diverting.

The *nō* I could not understand until I borrowed the book from a Japanese lady in the next box, and was able to follow the text. This was *Hachi no ki*. Sano Genzaemon, who has been deprived of his feudal estate, entertains a Buddhist priest at night. Having no food to offer him nor fuel to warm the room, he cuts down his own favourite dwarf plum, cherry and pine trees, and makes a fire of the branches. In return for this the holy man persuades the lord of Kamakura to restore to him his forfeited lands. There were at that time three other companies of *nōyakusha*; Kanze Daiyu, Kōshō Daiyu and Kompara Daiyu. The audience consisted entirely of the samurai class.

The two Aizu lords were brought to the suburb of Senji on December 15. Matsudaira Katamori (now, like all other rebels, shorn of his title) was placed in the charge of Inshū, and Wakasa in that of Chikuzen. Prince Komatsu Akihito, the commander-in-chief of the imperialist forces engaged in Echigo and Oshū, was expected to arrive in Edo on the 17th. And on or about the 16th the foreign representatives were officially notified of the restoration of peace. The guns and stores of HMS *Rattler*, which had perforce to be left behind at Sōya when the *Dupleix* brought us away, had been offered to the emperor's government and accepted. This was the news heard from Ōkubo and Yoshii, whom I met at Nakai's on the 16th.

To protect the British and French subjects at Hakodate, the *Satellite* and *Vénus* were despatched there on the 14th, the former conveying our secretary of legation Adams. Up to December 5 however that place had not been threatened with an attack from the fugitive Tokugawa navy.

My old writing master Tezuka, who came to call, gave me the following statistics about his clan. The chief's name was Sengoku Hisatoshi, and he ruled over territories assessed at 30,000 *koku*. The actual yield to the *daimyō* was 16,000 *koku* of rice; of this 8000 *koku* were accounted for by fiefs held by retainers; 4000 *koku* were required for the maintenance of the *daimyō's* personal establishment, and an equal quantity went in expenses of administration. The latter included official salaries, cost of journeys to court at Edo, of soldiers in the field, arms, etc. The clan numbered no more than 60 samurai families. Its constitution as regards the offices of *karō* and *yōnin* was the same as in the case of other clans. In accordance with orders promulgated in No. 5 of the *Kyoto Gazette* the old practice of hereditary office-holding had been abolished, and a system of promotion by merit established in its stead. In order to carry out these new arrangements, he thought the hereditary fiefs of the retainers ought to be equalized.

When I went back to Yokohama on the 18th I found that news had been received of the capture, which I had anticipated, of Hakodate by the runaway Tokugawa ships, and the flight of Shimizudani Kinnaru with all his staff. The consul was, as one would expect, very seriously alarmed. And from the *Satellite*'s expedition to the spot one could not look for any results of importance.

On December 21, a great conference was held at the legation in Yokohama of the chief with Date, Higashikuze, Komatsu, Kido, Machida and Ikebe Goi (of Yanagawa in Kyushu). The first thing they wanted was that Sir Harry would arrange to give Yamaguchi Hanzō a passage on board an English man-of-war to Hakodate, in order that he might open negotiations with the rebel leaders. The chief seemed to fear that this would involve him too much in the opinion of the public as a partizan of the imperial government, and he advised them instead to despatch a common messenger across the strait from Aomori bearing written offers to treat. Seeing that they could not induce him to accede to their request, they acquiesced in his suggestion, but in such a half-hearted manner as to make one doubt whether they would follow his advice. A great discussion took place on the Christian question, in which the Japanese spoke very reasonably, and Sir Harry likewise, until he unfortunately lost his temper over the arguments used by Kido and made use of very violent language such as I do not care to repeat. The result was that they promised to write notes to the foreign representatives announcing the emperor's intention of showing clemency to the converts.

Next day Ikebe came to me to explain the theory of the imperial paper currency, but I did not understand much of what he said, and we wandered off into other subjects, especially Christianity. The old fellow professed to be not only an admirer of its doctrines, but also a believer.

In the afternoon the chief and I went to return Date's call at what had formerly been the governor's official residence at Tobe, a suburb of Yokohama. They had a long conversation, especially about the Christian question and the representative system, and Sir Harry tried to pump him about the future capital. Would it be at Kyoto, Osaka or Edo? We had of course read what Ōkubo Toshimichi had written on the subject early in the year. The old lord gave him some very polite "digs in the ribs" about his violent language of the previous day, saying that when people became animated in conversation, spectators were apt to think that a dispute was going on, whereas instead of that being the case, it was merely that the speakers were in earnest; and naturally every man desired to express his own views. The chief replied that his animation was caused by the extreme regret he felt at seeing the Japanese do things that were prejudicial to themselves. On this Date observed that it did them good now and then, to be got angry with (*hara wo tatte morau*). This set the chief "a-thynkynge," and as we were driving home he suddenly said: "I think they would never have spoken to the other representatives about Christianity, had it not been for the little piece of excitement I got up yesterday." I replied: "Well, it may be so but I think you hurt Kido's feelings; he shut up at once and preserved a marked silence." "Did you think so?" he said, "I am sorry to think he was offended." I then said: "If you will excuse my speaking freely, I believe that although that sort of thing may have a good effect in a particular case, it makes the Japanese dread interviews with you." Upon this the chief declared that he would have Kido to breakfast the next morning, and begged me to write him as polite a note of invitation as possible.

Audience with the Emperor at Edo

On January 2, 1879, I went back to Edo (as we long continued to call Tokyo). The city had been opened to foreign trade and residence on the 1st, and dear old William Willis was installed as H.M. vice-consul. He and Adams had returned on December 29, the one from caring for the wounded in Echigo and Aizu, the other from Hakodate.

On January 5 we had an audience with the emperor. On this occasion Sir Harry asked a large number of naval and military officers, besides Captain Stanhope, R.N., of the *Ocean*, and Colonel Norman, in command of the 2/ix. So the list of persons to be presented, fixed originally at twelve, was increased to double that figure. As usual the chief had mismanaged the business, because he insisted on doing it all himself instead of leaving details to his subordinates, and he did not even know the names of those who were to be presented. The squadron furnished a guard of a hundred marines. The costumes worn were very various, especially those of the legation and consulate men. It was a terribly cold day, snow falling, which changed into sleet, and then into rain by the time we reached the castle. What made things worse was that we had to ride on horseback instead of driving in carriages.

The audience took place in the palace of the Nishi-no-Maru, just inside the Sakurada Gate. We were allowed to ride over the first bridge, past the usual *geba*, or notice to alight, right up to the abutments of the second bridge, where we got down. Here we were met by Machida, who conducted us into the courtyard, from which we ascended at once into the ante-chamber. The lord of Awa, Sanjō, Higashikuze, Nakayama Dainagon and Ōkubo came in and exchanged the usual compliments. Then we were

378

ushered into a very dark room, where the emperor was sitting under a canopy rather larger than that used at Osaka. It was so dark that we could hardly distinguish his dress, but his face, which was whitened artificially, shone out brightly from the surrounding obscurity. The prime minister stood below on the right and after the emperor had uttered a few words of inquiry about the Queen's health, and congratulated the chief on continuing at Edo as minister, read the emperor's speech. To this Sir Harry replied very neatly. After the audience, which took up no more than five minutes, was over we cantered back to the old legation building in Takanawa, now converted into a branch of the Japanese Foreign Office, where we had great feasting beginning by an entertainment in Japanese style, very good of its kind, followed by a late luncheon supplied from the hotel. Awa and Higashikuze presided in our room. The American minister and the North German chargé d'affaires were also present. Higashikuze proposed the health of the Queen, the President and the king of Prussia *en bloc*, after which we drank to the health of the emperor.

Katsu had come back to Edo, and early in January was to start again for Sumpu, to lay a foundation for negotiation with the Tokugawa runaway ships at Hakodate. On the 8th a review of the English troops in garrison at Yokohama was held for the entertainment of the lord of Awa, as our particular friend, and a party of young court nobles. These were not men of political importance, and I do not think we ever heard of them again. The rapidity of the fire from the Snider rifles was a surprise to all the spectators.

On the 9th the chief and I having ridden up to Edo in the morning, he had an important interview at the Hama-*goten*, the sea-side palace of the *shōguns*, with Iwakura. Kido, Higashikuze and Machida were also present. Many compliments were offered to Sir Harry, and assurances of the gratitude which the emperor's government felt for the hearty recognition they had received from Great Britain. To this succeeded some confidential conversation. It was intended that the emperor should return to Kyoto to be married, and also for the performance of certain funeral rites in honour of his late father. When these ceremonies were completed he would come again to his Eastern Capital to hold a great council of the empire. The date of this was not yet fixed; it might be in the first month of the Japanese calendar, perhaps in the third. Sir Harry advised Iwakura to notify this to all the foreign representatives.

The question of foreign neutrality and the situation at Hakodate were then discussed. Iwakura denounced very eloquently those of the ministers who, while recognising the emperor as sovereign, granted the status of belligerents to the Hakodate pirates. Sir Harry declared for himself and the French minister, Maxime d'Outrey, that no neutrality existed, and that they did not recognize Enomoto and his associates as belligerents; nor did van Polsbroek. To this Iwakura responded, "Why does the American minister still allege a declaration of neutrality as the ground of his refusal to hand over the *Stonewall Jackson* to the lawful government?" Sir Harry replied that the declaration in question had been of very great service to the emperor's government, that but for its existence Enomoto would now be in possession of the iron-clad ram, and that he himself had been mainly instrumental in procuring the signature of that document. This was quite true. An excellent lunch was served from the hotel, and we parted from our hosts just at sundown, both parties well satisfied with each other.

I went on January 10 to visit Siddall at his hospital on the other side of the city. There I found Willis, who on the way there from Tsukiji, the foreign settlement, had been threatened by a swash-buckler. We discussed together the means by which the Japanese government might be induced to apply for the services of Willis for a year in order to assist them in establishing their general hospital. So we told Ishigami that Siddall was to be recalled to the legation, and that Higashikuze must ask for Willis. The emperor had presented Willis with seven rolls of beautiful gold brocade, and Higashikuze wrote a nice letter thanking the dear old fellow for his services to the Japanese wounded warriors.

On January 12 we heard that the *Kaiyō-maru* had sailed from Hakodate, with her rudder lashed to her stern. Her destination was supposed to be Esashi, where fighting was going on. It was believed that the pirates were running short of money and rice. The Ainu were reported to have joined the people of Matsumae in resisting the pirates.

I had some interesting conversation with Ikebe Goi, whom I went to see on the 13th. At his lodgings I met a young man named Yoshida Magoichirō, a councillor of the Yanagawa clan. We talked about Christianity, and Ikebe cited the Sermon on the Mount as a composition that pleased him more than anything written by Buddhist or Confucian sages. I remarked that the Christian religion reversed the Chinese saying: "Do not unto others as ye would not that others should do unto you"; upon which he quoted the command to turn the other cheek to be smitten. After a little he began to talk about my chief's violence in conference, and said: "Now in his case, when he gets in a rage, so far from offering the other cheek, I feel inclined to kick him out of the room." Ikebe said that the emperor would leave for Kyoto about January 17 or 18, and that a notification had been issued announcing his departure during the first decade of the 12th month, to return again in the spring.

On the morning of the 15th I was summoned by the chief to Yokohama in a great hurry to attend a conference between Iwakura and the foreign colleagues. I rode the twenty miles on my pony Fushimi, in two hours and a half without drawing bridle, and arrived at the legation to find the conference just assembling. Iwakura addressed to the colleagues pretty much the same arguments as he had made use of at the Hama-*goten* on the 9th. They put a number of questions to him by way of reply, and at last said they could not give answer to so important a matter as he had laid before them without mature consideration. Iwakura then said that he would take the opportunity of saying a few words about the causes of the existing political situation. The present emperor was the descendant of sovereigns who ruled the country more than two thousand years back. The Bakufu was an institution not more than seven hundred years old. Still, the power had been in its hands, and it was during the continuance of its authority that the Americans came to the country in 1853. The *shōgun*'s people were sharp enough to see the necessity and advantage of entering into relations with foreign countries, while the emperor's court, followed by the greater part of the nation, professed the anti-foreign policy. The country thus became disturbed, and the authority of the *shōgun* could no longer be maintained. Then both the emperor and the *shōgun* died, and the latter's successor, a man of ability, was able to see the absolute indispensability of a government directed by the emperor. Sincerely convinced of this, he surrendered the power into the hands of the emperor, not as a mere gift, but because it was the only way of solving the political difficulties that existed. Thereupon the emperor's government changed its policy with regard to foreigners and did what never could have been done under the late sovereign, that is, entered into relations with the treaty powers. Hitherto our relations had been merely commercial, but the government hoped that they would improve and become something like those which existed among European and other civilized nations. The foreign ministers replied that they would consult together, and send him a reply without delay.

Sir Harry came up on the 19th from Yokohama to tell Iwakura the result of yesterday's conference of colleagues on the subject of neutrality. We were to have met him at Hama-*goten*, but when we got there we found the gates shut, and since no orders had been received to admit us, we came away. As we were returning to the legation Mori Arinori came after us in a great hurry, and begged the chief to turn back, but he refused, and said Iwakura might come to see him. This message was misunderstood by Mori, and there was more delay, but at last everything was arranged, and Iwakura came at half-past seven to the legation, accompanied by Higashikuze. Iwakura had sent through Mori to ask me to come to Edo, in order that he might speak to me personally, but I took no notice of this request, treating it merely as an invitation to the chief, or rather as a request to me to be present on the 19th in order to interpret. He asked Sir Harry what had been the result of the conference of foreign ministers, and all he could say was that it had been adjourned. It appeared that the colleagues were willing to make a declaration that the war was over, but were not willing to give up the *Stonewall Jackson*. To justify her retention they would not withdraw their notifications of neutrality. To us this appeared highly illogical. After Iwakura had repeated all his arguments and had added that so far from desiring to get hold of the *Stonewall Jackson* in order to attack Enomoto, the emperor's government were determined to offer him lenient terms, the chief declared that in his own opinion the war had ceased, and that the neutrality lapsed with it, and that he was ready to state this in writing. Iwakura said that the emperor was very desirous of knowing the answers of the ministers, and had therefore ordered him to stop behind for five days in order to try to settle this question and to rejoin him at Shimizu, a port on the Tōkaidō. He said he would like to get Sir Harry's answer confidentially, so that the emperor might have a pleasant souvenir to carry away with him.

Iwakura also said that the emperor's government had made a sufficient display of power by reducing the provinces of Ōshū and Dewa in six months, whereas in former wars twelve years had been nothing. He said their intention was to adopt a humane line of conduct, and had therefore ordered the two Tokugawas of Sumpu and Mito to proceed against the remaining rebels, and if they succeeded in arranging matters Yoshinobu would be pardoned and restored to favour. He had himself seen Katsu, who believed the offer of lenient terms would induce submission. The emperor's government would not however consider any capitulation satisfactory that was not accompanied by a complete surrender of arms and ships of war. If the rebels proved obstinate they must be reduced by force. This frank statement drew out a favourable reply from Sir Harry. Iwakura also appeared to be alarmed about the attitude of Russia, and asked whether she might not possibly enter into an alliance with Enomoto. The chief thought this unlikely.

The interview lasted three hours, and ended with many thanks from Iwakura and apologies for having kept Sir Harry waiting at the gate of Hama-*goten*. The chief on his side undertook to do everything possible to bring his colleagues round to his view and to induce them to send in their answer by the 25th, and he engaged to publish his own reply in the *Japan Herald* of the same day—that would be as decisive a manifestation of his policy as he could possibly give. I was greatly pleased myself to find that he had now made up his mind to "go the whole hog."

The emperor passed through Takanawa about eight o'clock the following morning, on his way back to Kyoto. His train appeared to be smaller than on the occasion of his entry. News arrived from Hakodate on January 21 that the *Kaiyō-maru* had got on the rocks near Esashi and was expected to stick there. Her guns had been thrown overboard and buoyed.

The sentences on Aizu and Sendai were promulgated on the 21st, with the penalties inflicted on other *daimyō* of the northern provinces, and a few more who had held out to the last. The Aizu lords were let off with their lives, but the whole of their territories were confiscated. Sendai was reduced from 625,000 to 280,000 *koku*. The reigning lord was made to retire, and was succeeded by a son of our old friend, Date of Uwajima.

On the 22nd a further conference of the ministers was held with reference to the question of withdrawing the declarations of neutrality, and the little Italian minister, who came up to Edo on the 23rd, assured us that only Sir Harry and Polsbroek were willing to consent, the others having refused. Letters however arrived from Sir Harry showing that all the colleagues had agreed to write a *note identique* acknowledging that the war was over, but demanding a short delay in order to concert measures for the simultaneous withdrawal of their notifications. Also a note from him instructing me to arrange an interview with Iwakura for Adams and Louis Gustave Lannes de Montebello (secretary of the French legation) in order that they might hand to him the petition which the Tokugawa rebels at Hakodate had asked Maxime d'Outrey and Sir Harry to forward to the emperor. The translation of this document was made and sent off at once. Then, after learning from Higashikuze that 2 o'clock was fixed for the interview, Mitford and I went off to Kido, to whom I gave a copy of the *note identique* about neutrality. He at once pitched on the 'short delay' clause as unsatisfactory, but I could only give him my opinion that this was inserted as a sort of compromise; it was better, I said, for the emperor's government that all the ministers should agree to recognise that the war was over, even with this slight drawback, than that only two of them should have recognised the fact and the other four have continued to declare themselves neutral. A memorandum reached us from Adams stating the nature of the final arrangement, and suggesting that the government should make it generally known by publishing the correspondence in their official Gazette.

Then I went off to Higashikuze's place, to meet Adams, Montebello and Dubousquet (an officer of the French military mission who ultimately became interpreter to the French legation), who arrived there about a quarter past two. Proceedings began by Montebello handing in d'Outrey's copy of the *note identique*. Iwakura at once pointed out the sentence in the letters of the English and French ministers that spoke of 'a short delay,' and asked what was its meaning. Both Adams and Montebello replied that they had no authority to say anything on this point, but they undertook at his request to write to their chiefs, and obtain if possible a definite date. I also whispered to Yamaguchi Hanzō to tell Iwakura afterwards that Kido already knew all about the compromise. The business of handing over the petition of the Tokugawa rebels was then proceeded with. Iwakura was told that in delivering this document the ministers did not offer any opinion on its contents, and they renounced for themselves any idea of acting as mediators. However, as the Japanese foreign minister had expressed to both of them his desire to learn if possible the feelings and intentions of the fugitives, they were very glad to have this opportunity of complying with his request.

Iwakura replied that these men had now been declared rebels, and the two clans of Mito and Sumpu had been ordered out against them. He said the proper course to adopt in presenting the petition he had just read was to send it through the chiefs of those two clans. From the hasty glance he had cast over the document he could not profess to judge of its merits, but he was glad to see that the petitioners had some desire, however slight, of returning to their allegiance. (But if he had been aware of the extreme bumptiousness of the letter to Parkes and d'Outrey in which the petitions were forwarded, he would hardly have thought so.) Still, while thanking the ministers, and appreciating the disinterestedness of their motives, he could not consent to receive the petition through such a channel. Would the ministers mind forwarding it through the Tokugawa clan?

Adams and Montebello declined to have any business relations with the clan, and after some urging from the French side, Iwakura said he would accept the petition temporarily and give his answer tomorrow. We then returned home and Adams despatched a report to the chief.

Next day (the 25th) in the afternoon came fresh instructions. Adams was to go to Iwakura, inform him of the surprise felt by both ministers at the refusal to accept the petition, and state that the expression 'a short delay' in the *note identique* respecting neutrality meant what it said. After consultation with Montebello, it was decided to ask for an interview with Iwakura at ten o'clock on the morning of the 26th, and a letter to that effect was sent off to Higashikuze. Before an answer could be received at the legations there came a letter from Yamaguchi Hanzō written by Iwakura's order, refusing to accept the petition, and saying that as he was going down to Yokohama next day to see the representatives on the subject of neutrality, he would take the opportunity of speaking to the two ministers about the other matter as well. However, Higashikuze's reply to our letter soon arrived to say that Iwakura's departure was postponed for a day, and that he would see the two secretaries as proposed by them.

On the 26th, as I was unwell, Mitford went in my stead to interpret for Adams. Iwakura receded from his previous attitude and declared himself ready to receive the petition from the two ministers, but said he intended to return it to the Tokugawa fugitives without taking any notice of its contents. Further, that he was determined to demand from the ministers the meaning of the words 'a short delay.' He also addressed a letter to the two ministers thanking them for the trouble they had taken about the petition, which he characterized as impertinent. It would therefore have to be returned directly. This was a slap in the face for our two chiefs, who ought never to have presented the petition, considering the covering letters received by them, which threatened to throw down the gauntlet to the emperor's government if it did not leave them in quiet possession of Ezo. But Sir Harry was drawn on by the fear that d'Outrey would manage to get the petition accepted, and thereby win prestige. If so, d'Outrey's little game was frustrated by Iwakura's good luck or perspicacity.

The following day I had to rush down to Yokohama for Iwakura's meeting with the foreign representatives. He asked what they meant by 'a short time.' They appeared to him to have had time enough already. When issuing their original notifications of neutrality they had acted immediately on receiving the communication of the emperor's government. Why hesitate now? The colleagues fenced a little with the question and then retired into another room to consider their answer. When they emerged they announced their readiness to issue proclamations in fourteen days' time at the furthest. With this Iwakura was forced to be content. But our chief had gained the battle, and was correspondingly rejoiced. Iwakura left the same afternoon in the *Keangsoo* for the port of Toba in Shima. Higashikuze informed the ministers that Edo was to be the capital of the country, after the emperor's return there next Japanese New Year, but this decision was not at present to be made public. He displayed a map of the city and offered them the whole waterside from the Kanasugi Bridge to the Hotel for sites on which to build legations, except the Owari *yashiki*, where the Foreign Office was to be. All but Sir Harry declared their unwillingness to accept sites. I remarked to myself that he was gradually getting out of the bad habit of believing all the Japanese told him to be lies.

Last Days in Edo

Iwakura had sent me a present of a beautiful lacquered cabinet by way of thanks for the trouble I had taken in interpreting for him on various occasions. And on January 28, 1869, when I returned to Edo I found a letter from Sameshima Seizō with presents from the lord of Satsuma, Ōkubo, Yoshii and himself. The letter said:

> The lord of Satsuma wishes me to give you his thanks for your kindness and the trouble you have hitherto taken for his sake. He presents you the two boxes, and the rest, though a little, Ōkubo, Ioxy and myself present you merely to thank you for your kindness. We hope you will always keep them as our memorial.

The lord's present consisted of a silver boat in the form of a peacock (called Takarabune, or Ship of Treasures) and the lacquered stand, besides two rolls of white silk. Yoshii sent two pieces of Kiyomizu porcelain, and each of the others two pieces of white satin brocade. The spelling Ioxy, which is in accordance with ancient Portuguese orthography of Japanese names, shows that this letter came in English.

My translation of the sentences of the northern *daimyō* was published in the *Japan Herald* of January 30. This state paper completed the discomfiture of the *sonbakka* diplomats, the term invented by the Japanese for foreign ministers who supported the cause of the Bakufu as far as was possible.

February 11 was the Japanese New Year's Day, which I passed at Edo. Rice cakes (*mochi*) had been prepared and decorated in proper fashion with a Seville orange and fern, and dried fronds had been hung up in the alcove (*tokonoma*) of my study. Silk cushions had been provided for a guest and myself to sit on as we ate our *zōni*. This is a soup in which pieces of fried *mochi* are soaked. On the first day of the year one is eaten, on the second two, on the third three. A New Year's drink called *toso* was also provided. This is a sweet *sake* mingled with spices. It is drunk from porcelain cups of gradually decreasing size, placed on a stand. Every member of the household came in turn to wish me a happy new year, and to thank me for the *o-seibo*, or presents given to them at the end of the year, proportioned to the respective merits of the different servants.

Next evening I gave an entertainment to my Japanese escort, to which the legation writer Ono Seigorō, Mitford's teacher Nagazawa and my household were also invited. Mitford and I sat on white brocade cushions at the head of the room, with a big lacquered brazier between us. The Japanese guests were ranged along both sides of the room and at the end. I had to apologize by way of form for sitting on a cushion, which as host I ought not to have done, under the pretence that it made my knees sore to squat on the mats. There was a great deal of stiff conversation at first, until the *sake* was brought, and the waiting women from the restaurant that supplied the dinner, the *geisha*, Noguchi's wife and a very clever girl from Yokohama made their appearance. We had comic dances, charades, songs and the Manzai new year's dance. An immense quantity of *sake* was drunk, and everyone departed well pleased by twelve o'clock.

Alexander Siebold, who had been in France with Tokugawa Akitake, had at last arrived back in Japan, releasing me from the duties that had kept me two years longer than provided by the existing rules about leave of absence. On February 14 he and I went to call on Katsu, who had been such a valuable source of political information ever since the downfall of the Bakufu. Katsu thought the Tokugawa rebels at Hakodate would give in their submission. At parting he gave me his *wakizashi* (short sword), and we separated with many mutual expressions of regret. He was quartered in an outhouse at the Kishū *yashiki*, where old Takenouchi, a Kishū retainer who had been our purveyor of news and papers current among the *daimyō yashiki*, was also living. We had to go into his rooms and drink a cup of tea. There I found the secretary of Date Gorō, a distinguished Kishū official, to whom I sent my farewell compliments.

We got back to my house just in time to rush off again, to a dinner at the hotel, given by Higashikuze in honour of my departure. Besides Mitford, Siebold and myself, the other guests were the the lord of Bizen Ikeda Akimasa, the court noble Ohara Jijū, Kido, Machida, Mori Arinori, Kanda Kōhei, professor at the School of Languages and editor of one of the recently established Edo newspapers, and Tsuzuki Shōzō of Uwajima. It was a very pleasant party. Little Akimasa greeted me very politely, said he had heard a great deal about me, but had not had a previous opportunity of meeting me, so had taken advantage of this farewell entertainment to make my acquaintance. I had the post of honour at the left of Higashikuze. After dinner they drank my health in bumpers of champagne and wished me a pleasant voyage.

Everyone had some commission to give me. The Japanese government wanted six expensive gold watches and chains. Tsuzuki Shōzō, who presented me with a farewell letter written in the name of old Date, asked for a copy of Hertslet's treaties. Besides parting gifts from the lord of Satsuma, Ōkubo, Yoshii and Sameshima, I received presents from Machida, my Japanese escort men, and a host of other people, including Kido.

The latter spoke to me confidentially after dinner about the advantages which would result to Japan from opening a port in Korea, not so much material as moral, by teaching the Koreans to look abroad outside their own country. Both he and Mori talked about the native Christians and asked my advice. I counselled moderate measures, and long notes to the foreign ministers now and then to keep them quiet. I acknowledged the difficulty of instilling the idea of toleration into the minds of the whole Japanese people by act of parliament, and told them of the disabilities under which Protestants had lain in Spain until recently, but I did not see the advantage of Mori's suggestion of allotting lands in Ezo to the Christians with the free exercise of their religion. Tsuzuki confided to me as a great secret the intended visit to England of a young Bizen *karō* named Tokura. Altogether we spent a very satisfactory evening, in spite of the long distance we had to go for our dinner.

Next day I left Edo for good. As I passed the entrance to the barracks of the legation mounted escort of London policemen, Inspector Peacock and the men came out to wish me a pleasant journey. Noguchi, Mitford's teacher Nagazawa and four of my Japanese guard came down the road as far as Ume-*yashiki*, where we had a parting cup. Higashikuze sent me a complimentary letter, regretting my departure, and presenting me with a big lacquered cabinet as a mark of the emperor's appreciation of all I had done to smooth diplomatic relations. Kido also wrote, asking me to communicate to him any information about Japanese affairs that I might pick up in Europe, promising to answer any letters I might send him, wishing me a fine voyage and a happy arrival in England.

On February 24, 1869, I sailed from Yokohama in the P. and O. steamer *Ottawa*, 814 tons, master Edmond. Lady Parkes also was on board on her way to England, and the English community paid her the compliment of sending out a band, which played *Home, Sweet Home* as the anchor was weighed. I felt the tears come into my eyes. It would be hard to say whether they were caused by the emotion that a much-loved piece of music always produces, or by regret at leaving a country where I had lived so happily for six years and a half. With me I had my faithful Aizu samurai, Noguchi Tomizō.

Glossary

akeni:	Wicker trunk for luggage.
anata:	You.
ashigaru	Foorsoldier.
awabi:	Rocksucker, haliotis japonicus.
baishin:	Under vassal.
bette:	a member of the corps of guards.
bette-gumi:	The corps of guards enrolled for the protection of the foreign legations.
bugyō:	Commissioner.
chadai:	Tip made to an innkeeper.
cha-no-yu:	Tea ceremony.
chōteki:	Rebel against the imperial court.
daimyō:	Feudal lord.
denka:	Highness.
doma:	The pit in a theatre.
dōshin:	Constable.
fudai daimyō:	Vassal *daimyō*.
gaikoku bugyō:	Commissioners for foreign affairs.
gaimushō:	Ministry of foreign affairs.
geba:	Notice to alight from horseback.
geisha:	Female musician, employed at dinner-parties.
gijō:	Head of an administrative department.
gisō:	Councillor acting as intermediary between the emperor and the *shōgun*.

go-kenin:	Retainer of the Tokugawa family.
go-kurō:	Trouble, used in the sense of 'thank you.'
go-rōjū:	The shōgun's council.
goten:	The palace of a *daimyō*.
gunkan:	Army inspector.
hakama:	Trousered skirt.
haori:	Lightweight silk jacket originally meant to be worn by men as a component of the *hakama*.
harakiri:	Self-immolation by disembowelment.
hatago:	Charge for entertainment at an inn.
hatamoto:	Direct retainer, or "bannerman," of the *shōgun*.
heika:	Majesty.
hikido kago:	Palanquin with sliding doors.
hiraketa:	Civilized.
honmaru:	Keep of a castle.
honjin:	Oofficial inn for the use of *daimyō* at a posting town.
hōren	Phoenix-chariot, name given to the emperor's palanquin.
ichibu:	Silver coin weighing 8.66 g, with an alloy of 0.21% gold and 98.86% silver.
inkyo:	The retired head of a family.
jinbaori:	War-surcoat.
jingasa:	war hat.
jinketsu:	Cleverest person.
jinrikisha:	Rickshaw.
jinshin fuoriai:	Unsettlement of the popular mind.
jōdan:	Elevated floor.
jōi:	Expulsion of barbarians.
jōyaku:	Chief clerk.
jūbako:	Stack of open boxes for holding food, the top one of which alone has a cover.
kago	Palanquin.
kaiseijo:	government school for teaching European languages.
kaishaku:	"Best man" of one who is performing *harakiri*.
kakke:	Beriberi.
kakurō:	Unceremonious appellation of the *shōgun*'s Council.

392

kami:	Title corresponding to earl, baron, when following the name of a province, but after the name of a government department equivalent to minister.
kamishimo:	Official samurai costume, consisting of a stiff sleeveless jacket pointed at the shoulder, and a long pleated shirt.
kamon:	Family crest.
kantō:	rebel, traitor.
karayō:	Chinese style of running-hand script.
kariginu:	Gala dress of a noble.
karō:	Chief retainer of a daimyō.
katakana:	Japanese syllabary.
kenshi:	Official inspector.
kerai:	Retainer of a *daimyō*.
kikiyaku:	Agent for the sale of a *daimyō* 's produce.
kinsatu:	Gold-note, paper-money.
kinshin:	Voluntary self-confinement in expiation of an offence.
kyōgen:	Comical play performed during the interlude of a Nō play.
kiribō kago:	Palanquin suspended from a sinlge pole.
kōfuku:	Surrender.
koku:	Measure, equal to about 5 bushels, used also as a measure of land assessment.
kokushi:	*Daimyō* whose fief comprised one or more provinces.
kōtei:	Emperor, the same as the Chinese term 'hwang-ti.'
kōtō:	Way of greeting in which one touches the floor with one's forehead.
kubō-sama:	Title applied by the people to the *shōgun*.
kumi-gashira:	Vice-governor.
kanpaku:	Chief advisor to the emperor.
kanrei:	Administrator for the *shōgun*.
machi-kata:	Municipal officer.
maedare:	Apron.
metsuke:	Inspector whose duty was to report on the proceedings of others.
mikoshi:	Litter carried in religious pageants.
mirin:	Condiment used in cooking and brewed from rice.

miso:	Paste made from fermented soy beans and used chiefly in the preparation of soup.
mochi:	Rice cake.
mokusa-nuri:	Lacquered articles showing a seaweed pattern.
nagabō:	"Long pole," used to denote a palanquin with an extra long pole.
nanko	Name of a game.
nanushi:	Mayor.
nōshi:	Noble's court dress.
nōyakusha:	Nō actor.
ōbiroma:	Hall of audience.
ohaguro:	Dye used for staining the teeth.
o-hiruyasumi:	Midday rest.
o-koyasumi:	Slight rest.
oku go-yūhitsu:	Official private secretary.
ō-metsuke:	Chief metsuke.
onna-gochisō:	Entertainment at which women were employed to amuse the guests.
one-ryū:	Japanese style of running-hand script.
o-shiro jō-in:	Hall in the *shōgun*'s palace inside the castle.
o-yasumi nasai:	"Good-night," literally "be pleased to repose."
peggi:	Corruption of a Malay word, used in Japanese to mean "go away."
rambō rōzeki:	Disturbance and violence.
reiheishi:	Envoy sent by the emperor to worship at the tomb of Ieyasu at Nikkō.
ryō:	Japanese coin of account, formerly equivalent to about 1-1/3 Mexican dollar.
ryōgake:	Pair of wicker-trunks for luggage, suspended from the opposite ends of a pole carried on the shoulder.
rōjū:	Councillors of the *shōgun*.
rōnin:	Masterless samurai.
rusui:	Person left in charge of an establishment during the absence of the owner or master.
sake:	Light liquor brewed from rice, mostly drunk mulled.

sakuron:	Political discussion.
samurai:	Member of the military class, entitled to wear a pair of swords, a longer and a shorter one.
sanyo:	Councillor.
sarampan:	Corruption of a Malay word used in Japanese to mean "broken."
sazai:	Shell-fish named *Turbo cornutus*; which also furnishes mother-of-pearl.
seiitai shōgun:	Generalissimo for the subjugation of barbarians.
seishi:	Herald.
segare:	Familiar word meaning son, and used only by the father in speaking of him.
sessha:	Self-depreciatory word used for the pronoun of the first person.
shibori:	Crape resembling the Indian *bandhanna*.
shibukami:	Thick paper rendered tough by being soaked in the juice of the unripe persimmon fruit.
shinsen-gumi:	Body of armed samurai or two-sworded men.
shirabe-yaku:	Director in an administrative department.
shishinden:	Name of the emperor's hall of audience.
shiro-in:	Private drawing-room.
shisetsu:	Literally "purple snow," a patent medicine.
shitaniro:	Down!
shōgun:	Hereditary military ruler during Japan's fuedal era.
sōkaisho:	Municipal office.
sōsai:	Chief minister.
shugo-shoku:	Office of the guardian of the emperor's person.
shuku-yakunin:	Alderman of a posting-station.
shussei:	Administrator, minister.
tabakobon:	Tray with charcoal-holder and ash-pot.
tai:	*Serranus marginalis*, sometimes called sea-bream.
taikomochi:	Professional jester.
tateba:	Halfway teahouse between two posting-stations.
tenshi:	Central tower rising from the keep of a castle.
tensō:	Officials who report the *shōgun*'s decessions o the emperor.

tobae:	Caricature.
tokonoma:	Alcove in which scrolls and ikebana are put on display.
toso:	New-year's drink.
tozama daimyō:	Outside *daimyō*.
wakizashi:	Literally, "side inserted sword," is an auxiliary sword with a blade between 12 and 24 inches in length used for fighting at close quarters.
wasabi:	*Eutrema wasabi*, root of a plant belonging to the same order as horse-radish.
yakatabune:	House-boat.
yakubyō:	Official indisposition.
yakunin:	Official.
Yamato-nishiki:	Cotton brocade.
yashiki:	Mansion of a *daimyō* or lesser noble (also at trading centres the depōt for the sale of a *daimyō*'s produce received as payment of rent or taxes in kind).
yogi:	Large stuffed bed-gown, used as a coverlet.
yōnin:	Hereditary councillor of a *daimyō*, of lower rank than *karō*.
yūgekitai:	Literally "brave fighting-men."
yukata:	Informal light cotton *kimono*.
zokumyō:	Name borne by a male child until adolescence.
zōni:	Soup eaten at New Year.

Index

A

Abe Junjirō 212
Abe Masato 124–25, 128, 130
Adams, Francis Otiwell 13, 45, 345, 348,
  351, 366, 384, 386
Alcock, Rutherford 13, 76–78, 81, 83, 111,
  132, 142, 182
Alford, Charles Richard 369
Amagasaki 165, 263
Arigawa Yakurō 127
Arisugawa Taruhito 343
Aston, William George 211, 238
Atami 172
Atsugi 43

B

Baldwin, George Waler 113, 116–17, 120
Bellecourt, Gustave du Chesne de 36
Bird, Robert 113–14, 116–17, 120
Brandt, Max August Scripio von 151, 274,
  299, 303, 306
Bright, John 73
Brin, Leon Jules 311
Brown, Samual Robbins 34, 39, 41, 43
Bruce, Frederick 3–4, 298
Buller, Alexander 148

C

Cachon, Mermet de 123–24, 130, 132

Camus, Henri 74, 81
Capital of the Tycoon, The 182
Cato Maior de Senectute 42
Chion monastery 334, 336–37, 351
Chōhō temple 175
Chūshingura 35
Clarendon, George William Frederick
  Villiers of 136
Clarke, Woodthorpe Charles 35–36, 56, 68
Colloquial Japanese 41
Council of State 23, 261, 263, 361

D

Daichū temple 134
Dannoura 89, 109
Date Gorō 389
Date Munenari 146, 247, 265, 308–309,
  319, 326, 328–31, 336, 339, 346, 352,
  369, 376–77, 383
Dupetit Thouars, Abel-Nicolas Bergasse
  325, 333, 363, 366

E

Echizen Saishō 339
Edo Bay 4
Elgin, James Bruce 1
Endo Kinsuke 77, 255, 293–94
Enoshima 11
Enslie, James Joseph 78

Eusden, Richard 43, 143, 272
Evans, George de Lacy 13

F
Fletcher, Lachlan 117
Flowers, Marcus Octavius 116, 249, 251, 257
Foster, Tom 143, 145
Fuji River 202–203
Fuji, Mount 202
Fukumoto Shima 270
Fukuzaka Kōzō 301
Fushimi 180–81, 185–86, 225, 228, 233, 268, 273–74, 288–89, 300, 312–14, 319, 332, 334, 343, 371, 381

G
Gaertner, Reinhold 358
Girard, Prudence Séraphin Barthélemy 95
Glover, Tom 373
Godai Tomoatsu 70, 158, 162, 295, 308–309, 313, 322–23
Gotō Kyūjirō. See Nakai Kōzō
Gotō Shōjirō 243–44, 247–48, 262, 265, 268, 271, 301, 305, 316, 318–19, 334, 336–37, 341, 346

H
Hachiōji 11, 138
Hakodate 6, 27–28, 42, 129, 143, 146, 148, 209, 272, 358, 370, 373, 375–76, 378–79, 380, 383–84, 388
Hakone 11, 172, 185, 202–203, 300, 306, 317, 342, 344
Hama-goten 379, 381–83
Hamana Bay 194
Harata Junji 98
Harris, Townsend 12
Hase Sanmi 331
Hayamizu Sukeyomon 327
Hayashi Bokuan 83, 105, 145
Hayashi Kenzō 154, 158, 162, 270

Hegt, Henri Alexander Noordhoek 124
Hepburn, James Curtis 34, 36
Hewett, William 209, 237, 242
Higashikuze Michitomi 74, 278, 301–302, 304, 306, 308–309, 329, 332, 336, 339–40, 352, 364–69, 376, 378–79, 384–85, 389
Hiki Tatewaki 298, 305, 315, 322
Hikushima 94, 96–97, 102
Himeshima 78–79, 83–84, 96, 100
Hirakata 185, 289, 314, 356, 357, 360
Hirayama Seisai 225, 254, 279, 282, 293
Hirozawa Hyōsuke 98, 103
History of Japan, The 182
Hodges, George 287
Hodogaya 37, 58
Hoffmann, Johann Joseph 39
Hongaku monastery 165
Hongan temple 223, 271, 327, 347–48, 352
Hori Naotora 328
Hosokawa Morihisa 257, 363, 366

I
Ibara Kazue 103, 105–106
Ii Naosuke 307, 362
Ijichi Shōji 311
Ikebe Goi 376, 380
Ikeda Akimasa 389
Ikeda Ise 298
Ikuta River 297
Inaba Masami 261, 263
Inoue Bunda 77, 86, 168, 249, 255, 320
Inoue Iwami 363
Inoue Kaoru 55
Inoue Masanao 195
Inoue Masaru 77
Inoue Shinzaemon 158
Iseki Sayemon 146
Ishikawa Toshimasa 260, 269, 274, 286, 287, 290
Ishiyama temple 227
Isota Kenzō 98

Itakura Katsukiyo 160, 177, 227, 229, 263, 270–71, 274, 282, 289
Itō Hirobumi 77, 95–96, 103, 108, 110, 249, 250, 254–55, 269, 270, 281, 301, 303–305, 322–24, 336, 349, 355
Iwakura Tomomi 230, 335, 340, 358, 380–87
Iwashita Sajiemon 255, 268, 278, 301, 304–305
Iwōjima 4

J

Japan Times 132, 137, 175, 278, 324, 369
Japanese Grammar 39
Jenkins, Griffith Richard 36, 114
Joseph Heco 250

K

Kagoshima 56–57, 68, 87, 128, 145, 148–49, 152, 158, 168, 250, 262–63, 316, 370
Kaian temple 369
Kaientai 250
Kaiseijo 181, 260, 392
Kajiwara Heima 169
Kamakura 11, 22, 113, 115, 375
Kambara 202
Kanagawa 7, 8, 13, 29–30, 34, 36, 38, 41–42, 45, 46, 53, 58, 62, 84, 113, 129, 137, 173, 190, 364, 370
Kanazawa 11, 213, 217, 220, 222
Kanda Kōhei 389
Kanda Shrine 50
Kaneko Taisuke 261
Kasuya Yoshiaki 270
Katsu Kaishū 239, 240–41, 261, 342–44, 352, 354–55, 360, 365, 379, 383, 388
Katsu Koroku 239, 240
Katsura Kogorō. See Kido Takayoshi
Kawakatsu Hirokazu 263
Kawakatsu Hiromichi 181, 356
Kawara Zenzayemon 169

Kawasaki 11, 36, 46, 54, 367, 370
Kawasakiya 369, 370
Kawazu Sukekuni 309
Keppel, Harry 237, 257, 346
Kerr, Walter 163
Kido Takayoshi 150, 249, 254, 257, 270, 304, 317, 376–77, 379, 384, 389, 390
Kikkawa Kenmotsu 270
Kikuchi Takayoshi 63
Kimpeirō 366, 368
Kitashirakawa Yoshihisa 353
Kizu River 186, 289, 334
Koba Dennai 271, 279, 281, 283–84, 311
Kobayashi Kotarō 55
Kōchi 243–44, 246, 249, 252
Koide Hozumi 209
Kokura
Komatsu Akihito 300, 306, 309, 313, 335, 375, 376
Komatsu Kiyokado (Tatewaki) 158, 166, 167–68, 256, 262, 270, 314, 320, 326, 330–34, 354, 356–60, 363
Komeda Keijirō 225, 243
Kubota Sentarō 136, 277
Kumamoto castle 257
Küper, Augustus Leopold 63, 83, 98
Kurazawa Uhei 169
Kushi, Cape 87, 97
Kuwana 191, 192, 277, 319
Kyoto Gazette 366

L

Lake Biwa 187, 225
Liggins, John 39
Locock, Sidney 143, 175, 275, 279, 281, 290–91, 307
Long, George 42
Lowder, Fred 92
Lowder, George 92, 95

M

Madenokōji Michifusa 364

Maeda Kyōsai 371
Maedamura 86–90, 92, 94, 109
Makino Tadayuki 282
Mamiya Hajime 120
Mansei 174, 260
Mariko 50
Markham, Albert 40
Marshall, William 35, 36, 56, 68, 366
Matsudaira Kansō 230, 307, 358
Matsudaira Katamori 375
Matsudaira Munehide 131–32, 186, 261
Matsudaira Nobuyoshi 277, 282, 289
Matsudaira Norikata 261, 263
Matsugata Masayoshi 230
Matsugi Kōwan 70
Matsuki Kōwan. See Terashima Munenori
Matsumai Takahiro 130
Matsune Kura 153, 156, 158, 178–79, 233, 363
Matsune Zusho 247
Matsuoka Jūdayū 148, 151
Medhurst, William 39
Meiji, Emperor (Prince Mutsuhito) 302
Milne, John 44
Minami Torajirō 374
Mishima 203
Mitajiri 163
Mitarai 271
Mitford, Algernon Bertram Freeman- 141, 166–67, 169, 175, 178, 210, 227, 237–38, 248, 263, 267, 275, 277, 294, 297, 321, 323, 336–37, 340–41, 348, 365, 369, 384, 388–90
Mitsuke 196
Mizoguchi 139
Mizuno Tadahiro 122, 361
Mizuno Tadakiyo 361
Mizuno Wakasa 356
Moji 97, 102, 109
Monryō monastery 174
Montebello, Louis Gustave Lannes de 384, 385

Moore, Lewis 68
Mori Arinori 237, 382, 389
Mōri Izumo 98–99, 103
Mōri Motoisa 270, 332
Mōri Motomitsu 332
Mōri Motonori 336
Mōri Takumi 270, 274
Moriyama Takichirō 53, 276
Morrison, George Staunton 12
Mukōyama Kōson 307
Mutsu Yōnosuke 285
Myburgh, Francis Gerhard 120, 138

N

Nabehama 102
Nagahama 224
Nagai Naokoto 263
Nagai Naoyuki 270, 289
Nagai Uta 255
Nagamatsu Bunsuke 271
Nagaoka Moriyoshi 257, 363–65
Nagata Chūhei 256, 257
Nagoya 192
Nakahara Naosuke 360
Nakai Kōzō 262, 265, 306, 330, 334, 337–38, 346–47, 356–60, 364–65, 368, 369, 371, 373, 375
Nakajiku 225
Nakasendō 317
Nakashima Sakutarō 323
Nakayama Dainagon 378
Nakazawa Kensaku 78, 83
Namamugi 36
Nanao 180, 212–16, 219–20
Nanbu Yahachirō 174, 307
Naozaki Yahichirō
Nashimoto 289
Neale, Edward 12–13, 31–32, 36–39, 45, 54, 56–57, 60–66, 68–69, 72–76
Niigata 80, 180, 208, 209–14, 219, 273, 353–54, 357,–58
Niiro Gyōbu 149,–51, 251, 253, 255–56

Nijō castle 289, 315
Nikkō 177, 196, 354, 394
Nishinomiya 270–74, 283, 286, 298, 301, 305, 315
Noel, Gerard 264
Noguchi Tomizō 148, 154, 173, 178, 193, 197, 205, 226, 228, 244, 258, 293, 311, 353, 369, 390
Nokogiri, Mount 4
Notsu Shichizaemon 370
Numata Torasaburō 137, 238

O
Ō Island 146
Oda Nobunaga 19, 192
Odawara 172, 204
Ogasawara Nagamichi 63–64, 74, 124, 130, 261, 272, 306
Oguri Tadamasa 344
Ohara Jijū 389
Oi River 200
Ōkubo Ichiō 343, 344
Ōkubo Toshimichi 230, 278, 317–18, 358–59, 371, 375, 377–78, 387
Ōkuma Shigenobu 347, 354–55, 357
Oliphant, Lawrence 1
Ōmura Sumihoro 253, 301, 321
Ono Seigorō 388
Osaka castle 269, 311–12
Oshima, Cape 287
Ōtsu 187, 226, 227
Outrey, Maxime d' 353, 380, 384–85, 386
Ōyama Iwao 310–11

P
Pagès, Léon 39
Parkes, Harry 119–21, 135, 146, 156, 159, 162–63, 167–69, 175–78, 180, 185–86, 204, 210–13, 215, 218, 224–26, 228, 234, 236–39, 241, 243, 247, 250, 270–71, 279, 282, 286, 290, 292, 297, 305–307, 310, 315–16, 319, 320, 322, 324, 329–32, 334, 336–41, 343, 345–47, 349, 356, 369, 376, 379–80, 382–85, 390
Perry, Mathew Calbraith 1, 362
Polsbroek, Dirk de Graeff 151, 321, 332, 337
Portman, Anton 132
Pruyn, Robert Hewson 111

Q
Quin, John James 287, 345

R
Reed, Eugene van 190
Renkō temple 139
Richardson, Charles Lennox 35, 56, 68
Rickerby, Charles 132, 137, 369
Risk, William 348
Robertson, Russell 2, 45, 256, 293, 331
Roches, Léon 128, 132, 174, 279, 303, 304, 320, 322, 330, 331, 332, 336
Rodriguez, João 39
Rokugō River 139
Rosny, Leon de 39
Russell, John 82
Ryūsen temple 50

S
Saedani Umetarō 264
Saegusa Shigeru 341
Saigō Takamori 128, 158, 159, 160, 161, 162, 166, 178, 230, 232, 233, 245, 256, 262, 263, 268, 269, 270, 271, 273, 278, 314, 315, 316, 318, 319, 320, 343, 344
Saionji Yukie 265, 310, 316
Sakai 179, 293, 324–25, 329, 332, 340
Sakai Tadaaki 283
Sakai Tadaka 122, 261
Sakai Tadazumi 286, 369
Sakura Island 70
Sameshima Seizō 387

Sanjō Sanetomi 74, 278, 308–309, 332, 335, 338, 340, 378
Sano Ikunosuke 365
Sara-Yashiki 35
Satano. Cape 77
Sawa Nobuyoshi 74, 321
Second Council 113, 122, 128, 225, 263, 328
Seifuku temple 323
Seismological Society 44
Sekido 139
Sengaku temple 134, 360, 367
Sengoku Hisatoshi 375
Sensō temple 50
Seta 187, 225
Shiba 50
Shibata Sadatarō 61, 63
Shibata Takenaka 168, 264, 295
Shibayama Ryōsuke 174, 307
Shiji Bunda 97, 98
Shimazu Hisaharu 149, 256
Shimazu Hisamitsu 36–38, 75, 149–50, 153, 190, 255–56, 262, 264, 335
Shimazu Ise 149–50
Shimazu Nariakira 256
Shimazu Sachū 128, 159
Shimazu Tadahiro 286
Shimazu Tadayoshi 256, 262, 264, 314
Shimizu Seiji 115–17, 120
Shimizudani Kinnaru 358, 376
Shimoda 27–29, 129, 370
Shimonoseki 76–79, 81, 85, 89, 92–93, 97, 98–108, 111–13, 121–23, 129, 147, 150, 168, 249, 258, 304
Shinagawa 49
Shinano River 211
Shinmei-mae 367
Shinosaki Hikojirō 262
Shinosaki Yatarō 270
Shinsengumi 300
Shioda Saburō 279, 281
Shiraishi Chiwaki 209–10
Shishido Bizen 96, 98, 103, 255

Shishido Gyōma 96, 98, 103
Shōfuku temple 299
Shōōtei 267
Siddall, Joseph Bower 354, 366–68, 380
Siebold, Alexander von 45, 54, 69, 124, 126, 128, 131–32, 136, 141, 388, 389
Siebold, Philipp Franz Balthasar von 18, 43, 367
Sōkoku temple 314
Sugi Tokusuke 96, 98, 110
Sugiura Takesaburō 356
Suidomura 185
Sutō Tajima 265

T
Tachibana Taneyuki 128
Takabatake Gorō 225–27
Takajimaya 187
Takaoka Kaname 41, 55, 57, 60
Takasai Tanzan 42
Takayashiki 259
Takeda Kaidō 289
Takeda Kinjirō 363
Takeda Kōunsai 363
Takeda Shingen 366
Takemoto Hayato no Shō 58
Takemoto Masatsune 58, 61
Takenaka Shigetaka 289, 292
Taki Zenzaburō 322, 354
Tamagawa 138, 250
Tanaka Konoye 256
Tateyama 212
Tempōzan 273, 291–93
Tempōzan, Cape 126
Tenguren 361–63
Tenryū River 195
Terashima Munenori 70, 167, 284, 299, 301, 304, 308, 366
Tochinoki Pass 224
Tōdō Takayuki 186, 292, 300, 314
Tōkaidō 7, 11, 43–46, 57, 174, 182–83, 187, 307, 382

Index

Tokaku 266–67
Tokudaiji Sanetsune 339, 340
Tokugawa Akitake 357–60, 363, 388
Tokugawa Harutoshi 361
Tokugawa Iemochi 145
Tokugawa Iesato 351–52, 356, 360, 365
Tokugawa Ieyasu 177, 224
Tokugawa Nariaki 361
Tokugawa Narinobu 361
Tokugawa Yoshinobu 145–46, 151–53, 156, 159, 164, 250, 261, 263, 269, 276–284, 288–88, 291–96, 302, 306–307, 318–19, 328, 333, 342–44, 351, 353, 355, 357, 362–63, 365, 383
Tokushima 229, 235, 238, 241, 335
Tonomi 78
Tour, Vittorio de la 151, 303
Toyotomi Hideyoshi 156
Tōzen temple 12, 47, 54, 134, 353
Tracey, Richard 208
Tsugaru 20, 359
Tsukahara Kanjirō 224, 226, 282
Tsukahara Masayoshi 224
Tsumagi Nakazukasa 282, 355
Tsuruga 180, 186, 208, 225, 363
Tsurugaoka Hachiman shrine 113
Tsuzuki Shōzō 389

U
Ueno 50
Uji 187, 226–28
Ume-yashiki 46, 370
Umenoki 189
Urado 243, 244, 246, 249
Uraga 4
Urakami 253, 254, 347, 352
Utsunomiya 370

V
Verbeck, Guido Herman 347

Vidal, Owen Alexander 172
Von Brandt, Max 51
Vyse, Howard 36, 37

W
Wade, Thomas Francis 4
Wakamatsu 342, 354, 359, 364–66, 371
Watanabe Kurata 96, 98
Watanabe Noboru 301
Wilkinson, Hiram Shaw 143, 291
Willis, William 36, 55, 59, 76, 138, 275, 288, 291–92, 297–98, 309, 311, 313, 317, 335, 337, 340, 354, 371, 378, 380
Winchester, Charles Alexander 113, 135
Wirgman, Charles 138–39, 175, 191–93, 197, 313, 366

Y
Yahagi River 194
Yahiko, Mount 209
Yamada Teisuke 169
Yamada Uemon 98
Yamagata Keizō 110, 255
Yamagata Taiga 255
Yamaguchi 79, 101, 105
Yamaguchi Hanzō 369, 376, 384–85
Yamamoto Jinsuke 255
Yamao Yōzo 77
Yamashina Akira 331–32, 335–47, 349
Yamauchi Yōdō 246–48, 253, 266, 273, 327, 331
Yamazaki 292, 314
Yodo River 123, 273
Yokosuka 151, 353, 364
Yoshida Torajirō 255
Yoshii Kōsuke 159, 166–67, 262–65, 299, 301, 314, 316, 318–19, 371, 375, 387
Yoshiwara 9, 366, 368, 370
Yu-meirō 368
Yura 123, 131, 235

TOYO PRess: Explore Dream Discover

Editorial supervision: William de Lange. Book and cover design: Chōkei Studios. Printing and binding: IngramSpark. The typefaces used are Perpetua, Prescript, and Herculanum.

www.ingramcontent.com/pod-product-compliance
Lightning Source LLC
Chambersburg PA
CBHW032047020426
42335CB00011B/227